NARRATIVE THEOLOGY AND MORAL THEOLOGY

Moral thinking today finds itself stranded between the particular and the universal. Alasdair MacIntyre's work on narrative, discussed here along with that of Stanley Hauerwas and H.T. Engelhardt, aims to undo the perceived damage done by the Enlightenment by returning to narrative and abandoning the illusion of a disembodied reason that claims to be able to give a coherent explanation for everything. It is precisely this – a theory that holds good for all cases – that John Rawls proposed, drawing on the heritage of Emmanuel Kant. Who is right? Must universality be abandoned? Must we only think about morality in terms that are relative, bound by space and time?

Alexander Lucie-Smith attempts to answer these questions by examining the nature of narrative itself as well as the particular narratives of Rawls and St Augustine. Bound and rooted as they are in history and personal experience, narratives nevertheless strain at the limits imposed on them. It is Lucie-Smith's contention that each narrative that points to a lived morality exists against the background of an infinite horizon, and thus it is that the particular and the rooted can also make us aware of the universal and unchanging.

ASHGATE NEW CRITICAL THINKING IN RELIGION, THEOLOGY AND BIBLICAL STUDIES

The *Ashgate New Critical Thinking in Religion, Theology and Biblical Studies* series brings high quality research monograph publishing back into focus for authors, international libraries, and student, academic and research readers. Headed by an international editorial advisory board of acclaimed scholars spanning the breadth of religious studies, theology and biblical studies, this open-ended monograph series presents cutting-edge research from both established and new authors in the field. With specialist focus yet clear contextual presentation of contemporary research, books in the series take research into important new directions and open the field to new critical debate within the discipline, in areas of related study, and in key areas for contemporary society.

Series Editorial Board:

Jeff Astley, North of England Institute for Christian Education, Durham, UK
David Jasper, University of Glasgow, UK
James Beckford, University of Warwick, UK
Raymond Williams, Wabash College, Crawfordsville, USA
Geoffrey Samuel, University of Newcastle, Australia
Richard Hutch, University of Queensland, Australia
Paul Fiddes, Regent's Park College, University of Oxford, UK
Anthony Thiselton, University of Nottingham, UK
Tim Gorringe, University of Exeter, UK
Adrian Thatcher, College of St Mark and St John, UK
Alan Torrance, University of St Andrews, UK
Judith Lieu, Kings College London, UK
Terrance Tilley, University of Dayton, USA
Miroslav Volf, Yale Divinity School, USA
Stanley Grenz, Baylor University and Truett Seminary, USA
Vincent Brummer, University of Utrecht, The Netherlands
Gerhard Sauter, University of Bonn, Germany

Other Titles in the Series:

The Politics of Praise
Naming God and Friendship in Aquinas and Derrida
William W. Young III

Nietzsche and Theology
Nietzschean Thought in Christological Anthropology
David Deane

Narrative Theology and Moral Theology

The Infinite Horizon

ALEXANDER LUCIE-SMITH
Tangaza College, Nairobi, Kenya

ASHGATE

© Alexander Lucie-Smith 2007

All rights reserved. No part of this publication may be reproduced, stored in a retrieval system or transmitted in any form or by any means, electronic, mechanical, photocopying, recording or otherwise without the prior permission of the publisher.

Alexander Lucie-Smith has asserted his moral right under the Copyright, Designs and Patents Act, 1988, to be identified as the author of this work.

Published by
Ashgate Publishing Limited
Wey Court East
Union Road
Farnham
Surrey, GU9 7PT
England

Ashgate Publishing Company
110 Cherry Street
Suite 3-1
Burlington
VT 05401-3818
USA

Ashgate website: http://www.ashgate.com

British Library Cataloguing in Publication Data

Lucie-Smith, Alexander
  Narrative theology and moral theology : the infinite
  horizon. – (Ashgate new critical thinking in religion,
  theology and biblical studies)
  1. Narrative theology 2. Christian ethics
  I. Title
  230'.046

Library of Congress Cataloging-in-Publication Data

Lucie-Smith, Alexander, 1963–
  Narrative theology and moral theology : the infinite horizon / Alexander Lucie-Smith.
    p. cm. – (Ashgate new critical thinking in religion, theology and biblical studies)
  Includes bibliographical references and index.
  ISBN-13: 978-0-7546-5680-7 (hardcover: alk. paper)
  1. Christian ethics–Catholic authors. 2. Narrative theology. 3. MacIntyre, Alasdair C. 4. Hauerwas, Stanley, 1940– 5. Engelhardt, H. Tristram (Hugo Tristram), 1941– I. Title.

BJ1249.L83 2007
241'.042–dc22

2006018846

ISBN 978-0-7546-5680-7

Printed and bound in Great Britain by Printondemand-worldwide.com

Contents

Acknowledgements		*vii*
1	Narrative Theology as a New Approach to Theology	1
2	Alasdair MacIntyre	13
3	Stanley Hauerwas	33
4	H.T. Engelhardt	47
5	The Rawlsian Alternative	73
6	Beyond Rawls	109
7	The Augustinian Approach	123
8	Three Models of Narrative Theology	165
9	A Narrative Moral Theology in Practice	199
Bibliography		221
Index		231

Acknowledgements

This book began life as a thesis written for the doctoral examination in theology at the Gregorian University, Rome, under the rather ponderous title of 'Narrative as a means of establishing moral method and creating ethical language: contrasting approaches to narrative, community and tradition.' The thesis tried to examine how narrative can provide the basis for moral reasoning and ethical language, and at the same time, the implications and presuppositions of the question, namely: how does narrative relate to the allied ideas of community and tradition? The thesis was supervised by Fr Philipp Schmitz SJ, to whose patience and kindness I am greatly indebted. The second reader for the examination was Fr Michael Paul Gallagher SJ. To him my thanks.

Three people read the thesis in its final stages and made useful suggestions: Mgr Charles Drennan, Brendan Walsh and Salley Vickers. For their help and encouragement I am most grateful. Finally, in revising the text and preparing it for publication, I had the invaluable assistance of Fr Tim Redmond, Principal of Tangaza College, who with the greatest dedication looked at the entire text in detail, bringing to bear his expertise as a theologian, a scriptural scholar, an expert in computer formatting, and, perhaps most importantly of all, a lover of good English expression. For all his hard work I am deeply grateful. Naturally, all the remaining mistakes are mine alone.

In addition, I must thank all those kind and dear friends whose support was so valuable during the long, sometimes overlong, period that this book took to write. They know who they are.

My thanks go to the New City Press, New York, for their kind permission to reproduce passages from their translation of the works of St Augustine.

Finally, this book is dedicated to the memory of three wise women: Dorothy Bednarowska, who taught me as an undergraduate to love English literature; Anna Haycraft (Alice Thomas Ellis), my one time editor, who taught me how to write, in so far as I am able; and Elizabeth Heskett, my mother, who taught me my first and best lessons in morality.

Alexander Lucie-Smith,
Ngong Hills,
Kenya

Chapter 1

Narrative Theology as a New Approach to Theology

What do we mean by the words 'narrative theology'? It will be useful, right at the beginning, to attempt an answer. A narrative theology is one that starts not with abstract first principles, but with a particular story; it is inductive rather than deductive. The story it examines is found, or 'embodied', in a community's tradition, and is usually taken to sum up or encapsulate the community's beliefs about itself, the world and God. Moreover, the story is rooted in the community's particular experience of itself, the world and God. This is in contrast to the approach that begins with abstract first principles that are assumed to hold good for all times and places. Such first principles, taken to be self-evident, either divinely revealed, such as the precepts of the decalogue, or philosophically based, such as Kant's categorical imperative, will tend towards universal truths and exceptionless norms; however, narrative theology, anchored in a particular community and its tradition, may be more modest in scope and may well imply that universalism is a mirage.

Neither of these approaches is new: in fact the deductive and inductive approaches are as old as theology itself, and St Thomas Aquinas was aware of this when he wrote his manual for beginners, the *Summa Theologiae*, which provides a useful illustration of the distinction between the two paradigms outlined above. In the first question of the *Summa*, he asks if Christian theology be a science.[1] Indeed it is not, he tells us, because it deals with individual persons and events such as Abraham, Isaac and Jacob, whereas a science does not deal with individual cases but with general and universal principles.[2] However, this view is advanced only to be disproved by the rest of the *quaestio*. Sacred doctrine, Thomas concludes, is not principally concerned with individual cases, but rather bases itself on divine revelation. Individual cases have value only as illustrations.[3]

From this it seems clear that at the start of the *Summa* Thomas chooses a deductive course and not an inductive one. Yet we can but notice the two contrasting approaches: on the one hand, theology is about Abraham, Isaac and Jacob, a history lived out by individuals, recorded in a story that is considered normative by future generations; but on the other hand, theology is based on a timeless divine revelation; this latter is the foundation that Thomas chooses. But there is a third possibility that Thomas does not consider, and which might be considered the nub of narrative theology: it can be argued that divine revelation, rather than being seen as a set of abstract

---

[1] St Thomas Aquinas, *Summa Theologiae*, Prima Pars, quaestio 1, art. 2.
[2] *Summa Theologiae*, I, 1, 2, ad 2.
[3] *Summa Theologiae*, I, 1, resp 2.

principles, ought to be seen as an event and understood as a narrative: in other words, the story of Exodus, the subsequent story of the Chosen People, the story of Jesus, his death and resurrection, these are the substance of divine revelation. Furthermore, it is precisely through narrative that God reveals himself to us, and narrative is his chosen means of communication. This would mean moving individual stories from the category of useful illustrative examples to the very heart of theology itself.

In discussing the question of theological language, Thomas is aware that once we posit that God speaks to us in revelation, this raises a problem as to how we speak of him.[4] All language is our own, and thus even theological language is human language. But must the content of that language then be exclusively human, not divine? Can God be comprehended within human language if he is to remain God? This conundrum has also troubled narrative theologians. Can God be a story, or be in a story? If all is story, then is God himself and theology too just another story among many? One encounters a contradiction: once God becomes a character in the drama, then he ceases to be the creator of the drama. It is important then to remember that if God is an actor in the drama, then it is not in the way other characters are, for he must remain distinct from the drama and somehow above it. This implies that narrative theology, if it is to remain theology, must not collapse into some sort of religious literary theory; but nevertheless it can, with due caution, draw on what is termed literary theory.

In his consideration of theological language, Thomas asks whether we should use metaphor and symbol as part of theological language. Narrative theology would certainly suggest that we should. But Thomas's answer is different. He thinks not. Symbol is appropriate to poetry, 'the most modest of all teaching methods'.[5] Again he says that symbol and metaphor obstruct our understanding of the divine in that they are human.[6]

On the questions of metaphor and symbol, narrative theology takes the opposite view. Poetry, symbol and metaphor are indeed human constructs, but they represent our deepest appropriation of reality, the way we make it our own. Poetry about God may represent our most profound understanding of God and at the same time his most enlightening revelation of himself. We should remember that the Psalter is a collection of poems, written by human beings, and that at the same time it reveals God to us. What emerges here is another basic claim made by narrative theology – that symbol and metaphor, the stuff of story, are not barriers to revelation but rather the language of revelation itself. Thomas will merely admit that symbol and metaphor are useful in giving bodily likeness to spiritual things, which may help the ignorant, though in passing he does admit too the surely important point that people of their very nature like 'representation'.[7] But a narrative theology insists that these things are not merely useful, but intrinsic to theology.

---

[4] See *Summa Theologiae*, I, 1, 9, and also I, 13, 9 and I, 33, 3 for a discussion of theological language.
[5] *Summa Theologiae*, I, 1, 9, 1.
[6] *Summa Theologiae*, I, 1, 9, 2.
[7] *Summa Theologiae*, 1a, 1, 9. resp. 1.

In short, narrative theology relies on a different paradigm: the human story is the meeting place between men and women and divine revelation, and not something that can be considered the opposite pole to revelation. A narrative theologian would never talk of 'figurative disguising';[8] though they would agree with Thomas that we speak of eternity only after the manner of temporal things[9] – though the narrative theologian would justify this in a different way.

So narrative theology presents a contrasting approach to the more deductive theology of the *Summa*. But just how will narrative theology be a different sort of theology? If we adopt a narrative approach, instead of an arguing from self-evident or divinely revealed first principles, will it mean that we will never arrive at conclusions that are exceptionless? Instead of a universally valid moral theology must we content ourselves with merely a set of rival theologies based on competing narratives nourished in particular communities and traditions and which are unintelligible outside the contexts of those communities and traditions?

An example may illuminate this point: H.T. Engelhardt, whose work will be discussed in Chapter 4, claims that Catholic opposition to abortion in all cases is not truly based on a universalist and abstract approach as it claims (such as human rights theory or the Kantian categorical imperative) but on the theological belief that life starts with conception, which, he claims, of its nature is not a belief that can be shared with unbelievers. This theological belief is incarnated in liturgy, as illustrated by the feasts of the conceptions of Christ and the Virgin being celebrated nine months before their respective birthdays. In other words, belief about the sacredness of life is based on a narrative (the stories of Jesus and Mary), nurtured in a tradition (the liturgy) and a community (the Church).[10]

There are three points worth making here. First, if Engelhardt is right, it means that the abstract and universalist argument which is so often presented as the argument against abortion is in fact an illusion, an attempt to disguise the 'real' reason for the belief, which is a narrative reason: in other words our moral reasoning is narrative by nature, deny it if we can. Secondly, this narrative reasoning may seem arbitrary: what has the nine month gestation of Jesus and the Virgin got to do with the licitness or otherwise of abortion? Why should that particular detail in that particular story be taken as normative? Thirdly, this argument would only register in the consciousness of a person who frequents the liturgy of the Church, in other words, who lives the life of the Catholic Church in its fullness: thus, morality is not simply a matter of belief, it is a matter of praxis, of lived tradition. This explains why, according to Engelhardt, Catholic opposition to abortion makes little sense to those outside the Catholic tradition, even though it is couched in supposedly secular and philosophical (that is to say, non-theological) terms, claimed to be accessible to all people of good will.

These three points may give us an insight into what is meant by tradition, and the nexus between community, tradition and narrative. Tradition can be understood

---

[8] *Summa Theologiae*, 1a, 1, 9, resp 2.
[9] *Summa Theologiae*, 1a, 13, 1.
[10] Hugo Tristan Engelhardt, Junior, *Foundations of Bioethics* (second edition, Oxford: Oxford University Press, 1996 p. 277, note 1.

as the furniture of the mind that is shared by a community and which makes their conversation possible. That is to say, tradition is the shared language that makes communication possible, or more accurately, it is the shared understanding of language that makes communication possible. Because words take their meaning from context and from the way they are used historically, a particular tradition can be understood then as the shared cultural understanding that binds a community together. To give an example: the simple word 'law' means something very particular in the Jewish tradition, as do the words 'covenant', 'promise' and 'election'. The meaning of each of these words is embedded in the story of the Exodus. Someone outside the tradition, and outside the story of the Exodus, may well use the word 'law' in a rather different sense, for not only our use of language, but also our understanding of it, is moulded by tradition, the community in which we live, and the story of which we are a part. Thus our very thought processes, our way of reasoning, and our way of expressing ourselves, are moulded by tradition. We write and think in the shadow of what has gone before us, and what we have received from our forebears. Saint Augustine, as we shall see, writes as one who has imbibed the very language of the Bible as well as the language of various Latin writers, especially Virgil. He conceives his life in the *Confessions* as a Biblical drama and also at times as a Virgilian drama, for both the Bible and Virgil have provided him with the means of expressing himself; and at least some understanding of both is necessary if we are to understand him. In this sense, tradition can be best understood by the English word 'mindset' – all those inherited presuppositions that go together to inform our thinking and our self-expression, and which lie deep within us all.

But tradition can be understood in a wider sense as well. Augustine, thanks to his classical education, can engage with both Porphyry and Cicero: they are very different to him, but they live in his world. But at the same time Augustine goes beyond both these authors, using them and developing their ideas. Tradition should, therefore, be understood not just as the shared presuppositions that bind together people like Porphyry, Cicero and Augustine (all of whom can be grouped together in a certain sense, as sharing a culture) but as something more, an approach that is always open to development and restatement in ever greater degrees of clarity or otherwise (for traditions can become moribund), which make rational conversation possible even across the generations. A shared tradition implies dialogue with the authorities of the past, and the possibility of progress, a continuing rational conversation; by contrast, encountering an alien tradition means that one is faced with the opposite of dialogue, sheer bafflement, unless one is able to enter that alien tradition, in which case, it becomes no longer entirely alien.

Mention of 'the authorities of the past' suggests that the person within the tradition regards certain aspects of the tradition as authoritative. This aspect of tradition may make traditional thinking, or better, thinking in a traditional context, antipathetic to many. While many authorities may be engaged with in a critical manner (Augustine attacks but also respects Porphyry) others may be beyond criticism (Augustine does not put Paul in the same bracket with Cicero.) This of course raises the important point of how we justify our choice of authorities: the answer may well lie in the symbiosis we find between authority and tradition, and the fecundity of the tradition that flows from a certain author (or authority). But what must be avoided is the idea that the invocation of authority somehow renders rational discourse redundant.

The idea of a continuing tradition implies that the authorities of the past are not fossilized but are sources of continuing understanding. We return to Shakespeare or the Bible because these are sources whose meaning can never be comprehensively exhausted by a single reading. They transcend simple categorization. The narrative is always open to further explication and exploration and is constantly being enriched by a return to the sources of authority. Thus even these authorities are not beyond criticism in the sense of being beyond fruitful discussion.

In contrast to the idea of a living tradition that engages us at every level, the deductive morality that is presented as a set of disembodied rules, or as a purely intellectual pursuit, is an impoverished morality. Any serious morality, even if it is a set of conclusions from first principles, however intellectually rigorously they may be reached, asks for an assent that can be confused with obedience to the authority that has reached these conclusions. By contrast the morality that comes to us as narrative is asking for a different and more broadly conceived mode of reception. Those who hear the story, as opposed to abstract principles and precepts, are asked to understand the story in a fuller way, using not just their reason but also their imagination. Narrative theology is to be understood by the whole person, as members of the community and tradition in which they find themselves, and above all to be grasped through the liturgy, in which the community comes together as such. In other words, narrative theology starts with a different and indeed more broadly based form of epistemology. However, one must be wary too: does this mean that those who stand outside the community in which the narrative has its home can have no real understanding of the beliefs of the community? Are such beliefs incommunicable, a narrative that makes no sense outside its particular setting?

So, narrative theology may well involve a gain – a turn to a more incarnational, existential and lived morality; but at the same time it may involve a loss: the loss of the idea of universally valid moral truths.

What emerges here are two problems for narrative theology. First, if all moral beliefs are rooted in narrative, tradition and community, which provide their justification, this means that right and wrong are relative terms; what may be right for Catholics in Italy may not be right for nomadic tribes in the Maasai Mara, as both groups live by totally different narratives that reflect their utterly different social and cultural settings. And secondly, there emerges the even more important question, that of justification: to what extent and how exactly does a narrative work when we claim that a certain narrative is our reason for acting in such a way? To what extent does a narrative provide a form of rationality? Or are we saying that morality is not really rational at all, but rests upon some other basis?

These are the questions we will be tackling in the following pages. If we turn to narrative theology, must we abandon all claim to universal truths? And to what extent is narrative the basis for ethical language? Let us now examine these questions in greater depth.

Narrative Moral Theology: Particular or Universal?

Ever since the time of Kant, there has been a strong presupposition that what is morally binding is also universal; and conversely, what cannot be universalized cannot be considered morally binding. This is the nub of Kant's categorical imperative. We see this reasoning reflected in the history of moral theology in the Catholic Church, even when the Kantian method is left behind: scholastic moral theology aims to establish, as a Kantian might put it, moral norms that are exceptionless and eternally valid, which do not rely on either consequences or circumstances for their validity, but are valid whatever the consequences or the circumstances. The evil of certain prohibited acts is seen as intrinsic to the act itself and not dependent on the circumstances surrounding the act. By contrast, what is immersed in historical circumstance is not seen as having universal significance. The universal and the particular are seen as being at opposite ends of the spectrum.

From this point of view, narrative can be of little interest or value. Indeed, it may be thought of as very dangerous, threatening the universal claims of morality. St Thomas Aquinas identifies the decalogue given on Mount Sinai with the universally valid natural moral law,[11] accessible to all through the unaided use of human reason. But a narrative theologian would see the decalogue, and all the accompanying laws in Leviticus, as the crystallization of a lived history, a tradition, nurtured in a particular community (the Chosen People) at a particular time. In stressing the particularity of the Sinai covenant, the narrative theologian could rightly point out that the covenant applies to the Chosen People alone, though its import is clearly of wider significance. One would also want to put the decalogue in its proper context: the fruit of a personal encounter between the Chosen People and God. But does this mean that the decalogue is only of interest to those who are firmly within the tradition of the Jewish people? Surely it is of wider significance.

Let us now tease out the idea that we wish to pursue, keeping this example in view to help us. Without necessarily denying the universal claim of moral theology, one can nevertheless add the following proviso: morality is best understood, perhaps is only to be understood, not as naked and abstract principles, but as part of a story: hence, the Law given on Mount Sinai only makes sense as part of the story of Exodus. The context of the story is essential to the meaning of the moral norms embedded in the story; it is not something added on to the moral norms, not a mere frame, but an essential part of their meaning. Furthermore, the process of abstraction might well kill the true meaning of the moral principles embedded in the story. The story itself is rooted in time and place and in the history of a community, a people. In other words it is impossible to understand the decalogue without understanding as well the history of the Chosen People. Not only our moral theology, but the people itself are constituted by the story: in other words, the Chosen People are chosen and indeed a people because of the Exodus experience. Their identity depends on the frequent and regular remembrance of the story as foundational: hence the annual re-enactment of the Passover, which re-tells the story in liturgical form. The story is thus not just a historical curiosity but a living reality, perpetually full of meaning for them. If the

---

[11] *Summa Theologiae*, I II, 100, 1.

story were to become moribund or disappear, through a moral failure to live up to it, the people would cease to be a people. What emerges here, then, is the unbreakable link between community and story. This applies, we argue, to the Chosen People, but it also applies to Christians, who are constituted as such by the story of the Paschal Mystery, recalled in the Eucharist. There are other communities too who are constituted by other moral stories, celebrated in other forms of remembrance, enshrined in other traditions.

Not only are the people constituted by a story, but so too does their mode of moral reasoning come into existence. In other words, it is through the telling of the story that we discover our ethical power of speech: it gives us the capacity to form, or rather discover, an ethical language. This means that in the narrative of the Eucharistic institution we not only discover the foundations of our community, but also we discover our ethical language as Christians. The words 'Do this in memory of me' may contain the fundamental moral imperative for Christians – and these words cannot be understood outside their narrative context. Thus we see that a moral norm, couched in the language of 'Do this…' comes to us as an integral part of a narrative. The precept of charity cannot be understood outside the context of the Paschal mystery. The conclusion must be then that every moral norm, to make sense, must be presented as part of the narrative of which it forms an integral part. The ethical normative statement cannot be truly conceived outside the narrative: this union between the two is essential and not accidental.

Narrative theology claims that ethical insight is in the story by which a community lives. To the question 'Why are we doing this?' or 'Why ought we to do this?' the answer will be contained in the traditional story that constitutes the heart of the community's identity, rather than simply an argument based on abstract principles. This approach to theology will have considerable ramifications and implications in the way we view human society, the individual members of that society, and indeed the way we see experience and discover meaning. Story or narrative becomes the central paradigm for all of these. Society is that which coalesces around a shared narrative. Experience itself will be seen as having an essentially narrative quality. Human beings as individuals will see themselves as the living embodiments of a particular story, and as tellers of stories, and part of a wider living tradition. And this tradition will be rooted in history, grounded in particularity.

But these assertions raise further questions. How exactly can a community 'own' the story, let us say, of Passover? Perhaps through re-enactment. In which case, how can people re-enact events that took place millennia ago? What is done is done and can never be redone. One cannot simply re-enact something through the sheer force of will alone. What needs to be developed is a careful theory of how people make stories their own, and this will depend on an investigations into the way stories work, and the relationship they have to their hearers or readers.

Leaving this aside, we have said that narrative is grounded in particularity. However, if the particular is the starting place for moral experience, and if moral norms come to us through and in narrative, how do we discover the claims of universal morality in our particular setting? Are the two mutually exclusive? If not, what is the relationship between universal moral truths and the narrative setting in which they are discovered? For if experience is particular and rooted in time and place, and morality is narrative by nature, does this means that moral norms are rooted in time and place too and can perhaps never rise above the particular? If this were the case, then the narrative of each community, though there may be coincidental similarities, is essentially independent of all others, and we could only make particular statements about morality and never general and universal ones. Nothing that could be said could hold good for more than one community, as all moral statements will be confined to a basis of meaning defined by the narrative of which they are part.

If ethical language is seen to be rooted in narrative, community and tradition, this may well mean that it will be unintelligible, or at least only partially intelligible, to those outside that community and tradition, unless of course we can find a way of 'translating' it from one tradition to another. This may be fraught with difficulty: can we really translate the essential norms of Catholic Social Teaching into Marxist terms? And even if we can, ought we to attempt it? Might the attempt be counter-productive? And indeed it does seem that the problem of translation is insurmountable: the laws in the Book of Leviticus do seem unintelligible to us, though to an Orthodox Jew, bred in that community and nourished in that tradition, they make, no doubt, perfect sense. But can this perfect sense be expressed in the language of another tradition? Or is it untranslatable, because the languages of different traditions are radically incommensurable; unless of course one can prove that Christians are able to 'translate' Leviticus into their own tradition without destroying its meaning? But if this attempt at translation proves impossible or self-defeating, are we left with the conclusion that there can be no morality, only moralities in the plural, and moral pronouncements must necessarily be modest in scope and give up their pretensions to universality?

Narrative Theology and Ethical Language

The mood of the postmodern age may well answer these questions that we have raised with a resounding yes. Whilst the Enlightenment presented us with an all-embracing and comforting narrative of an ordered universe, the present age, that of post-modernism, tells us that all is fragmented. In other words, we have come from the world of this narrative:

> Once upon a time there were people who lived on rafts upon the sea. The rafts were constructed of materials from the land whence they had come. On this land was a lighthouse in which there was a lighthouse keeper. No matter where the rafts were, even if the people themselves had no idea where they actually were, the keeper always knew their whereabouts. There was even communication between people and keeper so that in an absolute emergency they could always be guided safely home to land.[12]

---

[12] John Dominic Crossan, *The Dark Interval, Towards a Theology of Story* (second edition, Sonora, California: Eagle Books, 1988), pp. 25–6.

To the world of this narrative:

> There is no lighthouse keeper. There is no lighthouse. There is no dry land. There are only people living on rafts made from their own imaginations. And there is the sea.[13]

This parable raises questions, as it is meant to. Its very neatness alerts us to the fact that we continue to be beguiled by the idea that there is one narrative and a common ethical language to which all can subscribe. We wish for a lighthouse, we long for a lighthouse keeper, though it has to be admitted that these desires do not necessarily prove that such things exist. They may be illusions, objects of wishful thinking. However, the first story makes sense, while we can seriously question whether the second narrative is indeed a narrative at all, for it raises questions about the nature of narrative: is there such a thing as a nihilist narrative, or an absurdist narrative? Or does the very existence of narrative prove that the world is not an absurd place? What does our ability to construct narratives tell us not only about ourselves but also about the objective world in which we live? If we are able to make stories (and stories are human creations after all, but not, importantly, human creations *ex nihilo*) does this not tell us something about the world, namely that it is capable of being shaped, formed, made intelligible? But this leaves us with a further question: how do we judge which narratives make sense and which do not? What is the criterion of sense that we use?

If there is a criterion of meaning that is common to all narratives and undergirds all narratives that make sense, then there is more to narrative theology than accepting fragmentation and mutually incomprehensible narratives. If there were no common core of rationality, and no common tongue, then each particular community could do no more than retire into its tradition and give up all attempts at dialogue with others, quite abandoning any conception of truth as universal and accessible to all. We would each be condemned to stick with our imaginary raft. However, few communities in practice wish to do this; Judaism, though grounded in particularity, sees itself as a light to the nations. And the fact that the story of Judaism somehow makes sense – to those within the tradition, but also to those outside it (though clearly in different ways) – should alert us to the fact that narrative is *per se* rational and not purely arbitrary. We may be in doubt as to how we are to judge the rationality or otherwise of a narrative, but we can be sure that some standard of rationality, which is nevertheless historical, exists. The argument about whether some story makes sense or not is not a senseless argument. We cannot maintain that all stories are *per se* nonsense: the very fact that we tell stories and on the whole listen to them willingly points to the opposite. They do make sense. Stories, narratives, point to the fact that the world itself is an intelligible place. In other words, the existence of narrative points to the existence of a common rationality in so far as all narratives share certain features, and thus to the possibility at the very least of a common language for ethics that makes sense and is not absurd. The fact that narrative is not absurd means there is a presumption too that ethics is not absurd. But this non-

---

[13] Crossan, p. 28.

absurdity of narrative is something that has to be proved through detailed argument and examination of the way stories work.

That there is a common language and rationality to all narratives is expressed, though not in these exact words, by Stephen Crites in an important article that may be considered foundational for the study of narrative theology.[14] Crites sees experience in itself as having a narrative quality: in other words, just as stories connect events through the causality of plot, in life too we find that events are connected as opposed to being merely arbitrary. There is a basic intelligibility to experience. More than this, Crites maintains that the phenomenon of narrative is pre-cultural, in that it is common to all cultures and all language groups, while maintaining too that this is a very hard thesis to prove. But the fact remains that all people tell stories, and that stories can transcend time, place and historical setting.

What Crites points to is the suspicion (which has to be proved, if proof be possible) that narrative language, and thus ethical language too, contains a transcendent element to it: in other words the narrative of a particular community, grounded in tradition and lived history, does at the same time have universal implications for all, and there is therefore a means of expressing universal truths, or perhaps truths that tend to universality, through particular narratives. If narrative is a universal phenomenon – and its does seem that there never was a time when people did not tell stories in order to express meaning and moral meaning too, and that there are stories that transcend culture and history – then it must be capable of expressing universal truths. This contention will be at the heart of the final chapters of this book.

Thus what this book aims to show is that narrative theology, or a theology that uses narrative to find its ethical language, does not necessarily condemn us to the ghetto of sectarianism. Though narrative starts in a community with a shared history, embodied in a tradition, it goes beyond history and tradition to something of universal significance. Furthermore, though we may agree that abstract language that claims to be the language of pure deductive reasoning has its limitations, and that the universalist conclusions it reaches may be more apparent than real, it does not follow that to embrace narrative as the paradigm in theology is to turn one's back on reason and take refuge in an arbitrary choice. It is true that I choose a narrative (or possibly a narrative chooses me), but there are usually grounds for this choice beyond the accidents of culture and birth, and there are usually ways of justifying this choice both to myself and others. It would be very odd if this were not so, for it would be exceedingly difficult to hold some beliefs to be foundational without also being able to give reasons for these beliefs. Narrative fundamentalism is a tiring and trying paradigm which does violence to the capacity of human beings to think. It is inherently unstable, being always prone to the assaults of reasonable doubt. But narrative itself is a form of reasoning rather than an alternative to reasoning.

However, one needs to devise an explanation of how narratives can transcend time, place and culture and rise from the particular towards the universal. Because certain narratives have a universal appeal, the search for universal moral truths may not be as fruitless as the search for the Holy Grail or the unicorn. But this will

---

[14] Stephen Crites, 'The Narrative Quality of Experience', *The Journal of the American Academy of Religion*, 39, 3 (1971): 291–311.

depend on an analysis of how narrative works and what is its connexion is to the world. It will also have to rely on a trustworthy philosophy of the transcendence of language.

Here is the crux: how does a narrative relate to the real world? Is the raft on which we are floating an imaginary construct? Does the word imaginary mean the same thing as having no corresponding reality in the world, as being not the case? If narratives are fictions, does this mean that they are not true, or does the word fiction (from the Latin *fingere*, to make) point to a different type of truth, perhaps a deeper truth than the objective truth, so called, of science? Narrative theology may be leading us to different models of epistemology; and it is certainly asking us to recognize that all stories are true, in that all stories contain truth. Stories are human creations, of course, but human creations can be effected with reference to the Creation: indeed they can only be effected thus. The world of the author (Latin *auctor*, maker) be it ever so fantastical, always bears some relation to our own world, from which the raw materials of authorship and fiction are taken. No one ever creates from nothing.

Summing Up

Let us now try to sum up the main thrust of the argument. Moral theology is best understood as a narrative enterprise, because the language of narrative and the language of morality have much in common. A narrative presents us with a coherent and accessible story, through which we as a community and as individuals come to understand truths about ourselves and our communities and the rules through which we live. It constitutes our identity to a greater or lesser degree and enshrines that which we believe about the world. Narrative sees life as a continuum, lived over a lifetime, and that the part is not to be understood except as in the context of a wider whole. Likewise all moral norms are embedded in the same assumptions: that decisions are made by acting people, taking account, indeed formed by, their pasts, and looking to their futures; moral norms cannot be properly understood as a series of punctiliar or atomic acts, unconnected to character, and the environment that forms character, but like all experience it is narrative by nature. However, it must not be overlooked that narrative, which is a human thing, and which starts rooted in lived experience, tends towards eternal and universal truths. It is rooted, but it is not confined. For narrative language itself often has a transcendent import to it, as does narrative human experience. Thus it is a mistake to assume too stark a polarity between the particularity of narrative and the universal import of abstract rationality. However, narrative is always where we will begin, though it is not necessarily always where we will end, for under certain conditions it may be able to reach universal truths.

In examining narrative further, it will be useful to look at it from four particular points of view. First of all, we will examine the view that narrative is indispensable: that is to say that every position is a narrative position, and that even statements that seem to rely on abstract reasoning are in fact disguised narratives. Furthermore, to make sense of any statement, we have to see it in its narrative setting, we have to examine the narrative of which it is a part. The point of view from which we do this will not of course be one of the purest impartiality, for we find ourselves to be part of a narrative: so in order to understand a statement, not only do we have to recognize that it forms part of a narrative, but we also have to recognize that we ourselves form part of a narrative. This recognition is a necessary precondition of our being able to take any argument further.

Our second point of examination shall be the question of the narrative quality of experience, to borrow the phrase first used by Stephen Crites. Human experience is narrative by nature: that is to say that it has a connected quality to it; our actions and our intentionality suppose pasts and suppose futures. Life is a continuum, as opposed to a collection of individual moments that have no connexion with each other. Narrative enables us to join the dots. Arguments are carried on as narratives, sometimes as traditions over many generations. Such arguments are developed in communities of thinkers, never in isolation.

Thus we can speak of tradition as a socially embodied narrative – our third point. Every tradition, that is every argument that proceeds over the generations, takes place in a community in which the narrative has its home; the narrative sustains the community (be it church or city state or any human association), and the community sustains the narrative. There is a symbiotic relationship between the two. No narrative exists in a vacuum, and no community can be sustained without a narrative that holds it together. A society that has no common core of shared values will not prosper, but be riven by continual strife.

Finally, we need to examine in what way narrative is a rationality, a form of reasoning, as opposed to an alternative to reasoning. Do we adopt a narrative because reason has failed, or do we adopt a narrative because it represents for us the summit of reason? If the Enlightenment project has failed, does this mean that we are forced to take refuge in some sort of decisionism or fideism? What we will need to examine is the way narrative encapsulates a form of reasoning rather than substitutes itself for any reasoning at all. And if this is so, we should be able to see some way for rival narratives to communicate between themselves.

These four points for examination will form the substance of our next three chapters where we will look at the phenomenon of narrative through the eyes of Alasdair MacIntyre, Stanley Hauerwas, and H.T. Engelhardt, Junior.

Chapter 2

Alasdair MacIntyre

At the end of the last chapter we encountered four questions that were raised by a narrative approach to theology, and moral theology in particular. This chapter will look at these four questions in greater depth, by examining the way they have been treated in the work of Alasdair MacIntyre for whom the question of narrative is a central theme. In subsequent chapters we shall look at how similar themes have been treated by Stanley Hauerwas and H.T. Engelhardt, two other writers who take a strong interest in narrative. A strong family resemblance between all three of these authors will perhaps emerge, for all take similar views of the concept of narrative; both Hauerwas and Engelhardt acknowledge a debt to MacIntyre and we shall perhaps be able to detect a progression in their thought. However, though there are similarities, these may prove deceptive in that they mask important differences of approach, and also some startlingly different conclusions.

These chapters do not aim to provide a panorama of the thought of these three authors, but rather to use their work to examine the questions mentioned at the end of the last chapter in the hope of discovering pointers towards the narrative method that all three claim to use. This will then bring about a greater understanding of the implications of narrative theology for moral theology.

We shall consider MacIntyre first, as he is more purely a philosopher than a theologian, though his work has important implications for theology. We shall approach Hauerwas next, and see how he builds on the MacIntyrean approach. We shall leave Engelhardt to the last: he works primarily in the field of bioethics, but his work draws strongly on the concept of narrative, and his most recent book takes a narrative line and is explicitly theological.

Between them these three writers represent three important streams of thought, or traditions, in our world. MacIntyre is a convert to Catholicism (and a former Marxist); Hauerwas can be broadly characterized as Protestant (though with strong Catholic influences); and Engelhardt is a convert to Orthodoxy, whose latest book is specifically in that tradition. Without writing the intellectual biography of all three of our authors, it is nevertheless interesting and perhaps important to see how their approaches to narrative are conditioned by their respective backgrounds – just as one would expect them to be, for each makes the claim, as we shall see, that the tradition from which one springs is of cardinal importance.

The Inescapability of Narrative Thinking

Writing in 1981, Alasdair MacIntyre suggests in 'A Disquieting Suggestion' that forms the first chapter of *After Virtue*[1] that the all embracing narrative of the Enlightenment has imploded, though certain fragments of it survive. However, these fragments no longer make sense as they lack the overall context of the Enlightenment narrative, which was the only setting in which they made sense. What we are left with, as we survey the ruins, are rival and discordant narratives that cannot be reconciled with each other, being incommensurable, and which never arrive at any meaningful conclusion, but are, rather, interminable.[2]

MacIntyre gives two reasons why the Enlightenment Project failed – indeed why the Enlightenment Project had to fail.[3] First, the concept of *telos* was lost, thanks to the idea, theological in origin, that reason can supply no genuine comprehension of man's true end;[4] secondly, 'the distinctively modern self' emerged which 'decisively separates itself from inherited modes both of thought and practice'.[5] The abandonment of history and tradition and above all the concept of the narrative unity of a single life,[6] make moral thinking and moral language impossible, representing as they do the adoption of a type of abstract thought that deliberately prescinds from seeing things in their context and as bearers of histories and traditions.

In place of the failed Project, and its mission to explain everything in one coherent and overarching system, there have emerged a series of rival systems, each, despite claims to be impartial, grounded in a particular tradition, and each mutually exclusive of the other. The solution is to start thinking in a narrative way again; indeed some people – for example liberals and Marxists – are thinking in a narrative fashion, though they deny this. But one needs to make one's narrative thought explicit: one needs to admit and recognize that one's supposedly abstract thoughts are in fact the manifestation of a tradition, bearers of a history, nurtured in a particular community, and told by and to story-telling people. However, few may choose to admit this:[7] for if we do agree that it is so, we also agree that our narrative is just one among many; that my Catholicism or your Marxism are both somehow 'equal' – manifestations of time and place, tradition and culture, and neither capable of making a claim that can be considered universal, valid for all times, places, histories, traditions and cultures. And here we meet the fundamental challenge posed by the analysis of MacIntyre:

---

[1] Alasdair MacIntyre, *After Virtue, A Study in Moral Theory* (London: Duckworth, 1981; second edition, with postscript, 1985).

[2] MacIntyre, *After Virtue*, pp. 1–5.

[3] See MacIntyre, *After Virtue*, Chapter 5, 'Why the Enlightenment Project had to fail', pp. 51–61.

[4] MacIntyre, *After Virtue*, pp. 52, 53.

[5] MacIntyre, *After Virtue*, p. 61.

[6] One of MacIntyre's characteristic and recurring phrases. See, for example, *After Virtue*, p. 204 et seq.

[7] 'Liberals have, for reasons that are obvious in the light of the history of their doctrines, been reluctant to recognise that their appeal is not to some tradition-independent rationality as such.' Alasdair MacIntyre, *Whose Justice? Which Rationality?* (London: Duckworth, 1988), p. 346.

the idea of some universal truth based on universally valid impartial and abstract reasoning is, it seems, a mirage.

These, then, are the important points that MacIntyre brings to our attention: first, meaning is dependant on context. One cannot approach a concept without also studying its origin and the tradition and narrative of which it forms part: hence *After Virtue*, examining the seeming collapse of moral theory, takes the form of an historical enquiry.[8] And secondly, there is no such thing as naked truth. Every truth is historically rooted. The Enlightenment claim to reveal truth in all its nudity and abstraction is a delusion.[9]

These points are developed in *Three Rival Versions of Moral Enquiry*, where MacIntyre talks of the Encyclopaedia as the project that aims to give an answer to every possible question, revealing to its audience a comprehensive doctrine that is coherent in all its parts and which is delivered from a point of view that is universal, utterly abstract and impartial.[10] It is this claim to absolute impartiality that, in his analysis, perhaps best represents the Enlightenment claim: that 'pure' knowledge is possible; the counter-claim, that destroyed the Enlightenment, is of course that there is no perfectly impartial standpoint, only various points of view, each one tainted by presuppositions and partisan choices. It is this idea that MacIntyre characterizes as 'genealogy' and associates particularly with Nietzsche.[11] MacIntyre proposes a new synthesis that may help rebuild something in the ruins of the Enlightenment; and he advances a new method for this, namely a rediscovered appreciation of narrative, community and tradition.

MacIntyre's contention about the existence of a plurality of narratives is not itself a new idea. Long before the postmodern age, as early as A.D. 410, in the twilight of the Roman Empire which MacIntyre evokes in *After Virtue*,[12] Saint Augustine writes in the *City of God* about the interminable philosophical debate that seems to people to get nowhere; about the sickness of the human understanding which makes some impervious to truth;[13] he mocks the pretensions of the philosophical chatterers lost in the fog of their own fallacies;[14] and in his *Confessions*, he makes numerous references to what he calls the empty chatter of the Manicheans, who, though *loquaces* [talkative], indeed *delirantes* [feverishly talkative], have hearts empty of truth;[15] and

---

[8] MacIntyre, *After Virtue*, p. 3.

[9] MacIntyre characterizes the Enlightenment claim as an 'appeal to impersonal, timeless standards'. See Alasdair MacIntyre, *Three Rival Versions of Moral Enquiry* (London: Duckworth, 1990), p. 45.

[10] MacIntyre, *Three Rival Versions of Moral Enquiry*, pp. 18–19.

[11] MacIntyre, *Three Rival Versions of Moral Enquiry*, pp. 49, 59–60.

[12] MacIntyre, *After Virtue*, p. 263.

[13] Augustine, *City of God*, Book II, chapter 1. All quotations are taken from the English translation by D. Zema and G. Walsh, 3 volumes (Washington: Catholic University Press of America, 1977–81). References to the Latin original follow the edition in *Corpus Christianorum, Series Latina*, volumes XLVII and XLVIII.

[14] Augustine, *City of God*, Book XVIII, chapter 41.

[15] Augustine, *Confessions*, III, 6, 10. Also V, 3,3 and 6,10. Of the numerous translations of the *Confessions*, I have chosen to follow that of Maria Boulding, volume one of *The Works of St Augustine, a Translation for the Twenty-First Century* (New York: New City Press,

he makes no secret of the vacuity of his own former profession of *rhetor*.[16] However, though Augustine is concerned with the perversion of language and the way some of his contemporaries have divorced language and meaning, he also firmly believes that only truth convinces and invites his opponents to a genuine debate;[17] this seems to suggest that some sort of worthwhile communication is still possible. Why else would Augustine write in the *City of God* which is addressed in part to unbelievers, unless he believed that some sort of common platform[18] were possible?

MacIntyre's analysis, however, goes much further than that of Augustine: he does not mean, like Augustine, that philosophers disagree and find shared conclusions difficult to reach, but that some sort of consensus is possible. MacIntyre implies, rather, that reason itself has failed us.

> The most striking feature of contemporary moral utterance is that so much of it is used to express disagreements; and the most striking feature of the debates in which these disagreements are expressed is their interminable character. I do not mean by this that these debates go on and on – although they do – but also that they apparently can find no terminus. There seems to be no rational way of securing moral agreement in our culture.[19]

Failure to agree cannot simply be ascribed to malice or ignorance, as Augustine hints; the fragmentation that MacIntyre describes is far more profound: there is (or rather seems to be) no rational way out.[20] However, when MacIntyre says this, it is important to remember that he intends reason in a particular way – the disembodied and attenuated reason that prescinds from narrative thinking; and the employment of differing models of rationality that may pass for the same model but which are emphatically different, which is the major theme of *Whose Justice? Which Rationality?* He detects rival discourses and rival rationalities[21] that cannot be expressed in terms of each other, which are 'untranslatable'. There is no longer any common language, but rather a language that seems outwardly the same but which is intended in profoundly different ways. And hermeneutics cannot sort the differences out[22] – they are too deep for that, as each is anchored in its own tradition. For each rival method of enquiry works within the framework of a differing rationality; there is not one rationality, but many. MacIntyre writes of:

1997). I have chosen to follow the original Latin text *Confessiones*, in the edition of James J. O'Donnell (Oxford: Clarendon Press, 1992).

[16] Augustine, *Confessions*, IV, 2, 2.
[17] Augustine, *City of God*, Book V, chapter 26.
[18] Augustine, *City of God*, Book XIX, chapter 17.
[19] MacIntyre, *After Virtue*, p. 6.
[20] Augustine would never agree with this. He constantly stresses the importance of revelation, but also the usefulness of reason in talking to the pagans who do not share the faith – see for example *City of God*, Book XIX, chapter 1. At the same time Augustine never lets theology collapse into some sort of purely natural reasoning. The things of earth are good, he writes, but they are not the only goods (*City of God*, Book XV, chapter 4.) His is not an earthbound vision.
[21] MacIntyre, *Whose Justice? Which Rationality?*, pp. 1–2.
[22] MacIntyre, *Whose Justice? Which Rationality?* p. 3.

...the conceptual incommensurability of the rival arguments... Every one of the arguments is logically valid or can be easily expanded so as to be made so; the conclusions do indeed follow from the premises. But the rival premises are such that we possess no rational way of weighing the claims of one as against another. For each premise employs some quite different normative or evaluative concept from the others, so that the claims made upon us are of quite different kinds.[23]

MacIntyre warns us:

We all too often still treat the moral philosophers of the past as contributors to a single debate with a relatively unvarying subject matter, treating Plato and Hume and Mill as contemporaries both of ourselves and each other. This leads to an abstraction of these writers from the cultural and social milieus in which they lived and thought and so the history of their thought acquires a false independence from the rest of the culture.[24]

This means that at the very least our starting point must be historical and particular, rather than disembodied and universal; in other words that if we are to be able to make intelligible statements in moral philosophy, we will have to adopt a narrative standpoint and argue in a narrative fashion, as part of a tradition. But perhaps this will entail that our conclusions too will be particular rather than universal. Perhaps we will have to settle for an ethics that is always to be culturally qualified.

However, in *Three Rival Versions*, MacIntyre's characterization of the situation seems to have developed notably since the days of *After Virtue*. Here the dichotomy of either particular and culturally qualified or universal and timeless is presented as being somewhat misleading. The genealogists, led by Nietzsche, and the children of the Enlightenment, led by Descartes, frame

... what they take to be both exclusive and exhaustive alternatives: *Either* reason is thus impersonal, universal, and disinterested *or* it is the unwitting representative of particular interests, masking their drive to power by its false pretensions to neutrality and disinterestedness.

What this alternative conceals from view is a third possibility, the possibility that reason can only move towards being genuinely universal and impersonal insofar as it is neither neutral nor disinterested, that membership of a type of moral community, one from which fundamental dissent has to be excluded, is a condition for genuinely rational enquiry.[25]

In other words, here MacIntyre hints at a third way which starts as an embedded narrative, but which ends by finding truths that are universal and timeless; or put differently, membership of a community and a tradition, that is having a prior allegiance, is the necessary precondition of being able to arrive at universal conclusions. Indeed, this confirms what we have already discovered: as far as MacIntyre is concerned, there is no other way of doing philosophy, except as part of a community, and in a tradition of enquiry; but what is interesting to note here is that

---

[23] MacIntyre, *After Virtue*, p. 8.
[24] MacIntyre, *After Virtue*, p. 11.
[25] MacIntyre, *Three Rival Versions of Moral Enquiry*, pp. 59–60.

such an enquiry can eventually transcend the bounds of the particular. Thus in his later work, as we shall see again, MacIntyre qualifies what seems to be the position taken up in *After Virtue*.

The Narrative Quality of Experience

Two fundamental points have emerged in our examination of MacIntyre so far. First, moral philosophy cannot be understood outside the context of the narrative, community and tradition of which it is part. Secondly, as a result of this, there are no purely abstract ideas: all ideas have a history to them and form part of a tradition of thought, nurtured in some community of thinkers. With these goes a theory of human action.

MacIntyre argues that human action *per se* only makes sense when we see it in its context: the simple act of digging in the garden can mean several things depending on intention, and intention is further understood through the *mis-en-scène* of the character involved.[26] His conclusion is:

> Hence the behaviour [of a man digging in the garden] is only characterised adequately when we know what the longer and longest term intentions invoked are and how the shorter term intentions are related to the longer. Once again we are involved in writing a narrative history.
> Intentions thus need to be ordered both causally and temporally and both orderings will make reference to settings... Moreover the correct identification of the agent's beliefs will be an essential constituent of this task... There is no such thing as 'behaviour' to be identified as prior to and independently of intentions, beliefs, and settings.[27]

In other words, if we are to make sense of human action, then we must make use of the categories of intention, time, causation and setting. These categories are narrative categories (similar to those usually called 'character' and 'plot') and are essential if we are to be able to understand what is happening. In other words, human experience naturally takes the form of a narrative.[28] However, at this point we must be cautious in jumping to any conclusion that MacIntyre believes that human behaviour is thus fully subject to analysis, and that examination of beliefs, intentions and settings will give us a complete picture of the agent's behaviour, at least in theory. This is not so, as MacIntyre is swift to point out a few pages later. For life is at some level subject to uncertainty, and the narrative unity of a life is in some senses not complete.

> Like characters in a fictional narrative, we do not know what will happen next, but nonetheless our lives have a certain form which projects itself towards our future. Thus the narratives which we live out have both an unpredictable and a partially teleological character. If the narrative of our individual and our social lives is to continue intelligibly

---

[26] MacIntyre, *After Virtue*, p. 206.
[27] MacIntyre, *After Virtue*, p. 208.
[28] His conclusion is identical to that of Stephen Crites in his article 'The Narrative Quality of Experience', *The Journal of the American Academy of Religion*, 39, 3 (1971): 291–311. However, MacIntyre makes no reference to Crites in *After Virtue*.

– and either type of narrative may lapse into unintelligibility – it is always both the case that there are constraints on how the story can continue and that within those constraints there are indefinitely many ways that it can continue.[29]

In other words, every narrative is to some extent an unfinished story, and a story that may finish in an infinite variety of ways, though this unpredictability does not make the story inherently meaningless. MacIntyre is careful to strike the balance between unpredictability and teleological constraint; the later saves narrative from nihilism, which is the narrative that claims that there simply is no narrative. At the same time it is interesting to note that some narratives can slip into unintelligibility.[30] In other words, not all human experiences are amenable to narrative exposition, and there are things that make no sense no matter how much we try to reduce them to narrative form.

Furthermore, because no statement is to be interpreted or made except as part of a historical series, the history of thought is a process of evolution, a succession of narratives that are in a constant state of development. This means that while the narrative we hold represents our deepest beliefs about our society and ourselves, at the same time these beliefs are not to be taken as final: there will be more to say. The dialectic goes on, perhaps forever. 'The later is not necessarily superior to the earlier; as tradition may cease to progress or may degenerate,' we are warned.[31] It seems clear that narrative is an art form that like all others is constantly refining itself and its expression of truth and reaches natural limits. It is also an art form that continues over many generations, as we constantly explore the truth of the narrative more deeply. And this truth of dialectic and narrative seems to be a more modest truth than that of Encyclopaedia.

Thus we can see that the central thesis of MacIntyre has to be hedged round with certain reservations. He says very clearly:

> A central thesis then begins to emerge: man in his actions and practices, as well as in his fictions, is essentially a story-telling animal. He is not essentially, but becomes through his history, a teller of stories that aspire to truth. But the key question for men is not about their own authorship; I can only answer the question 'What am I to do?' if I can answer the prior question 'Of what story or stories do I find myself a part?'[32]

One notes that stories 'aspire to truth', rather than encapsulate it or enshrine it in letters graven in stone. For a start, these stories of which I find myself a part may be hard to interpret. Again these stories may in their expression fall short of the story of which we feel we are a part. Again, we can only note that 'stories' appear in the plural: we may feel ourselves to be part of two stories that are somehow in

---

[29] MacIntyre, *After Virtue*, p. 216.
[30] 'Someone may discover (or not discover) that he or she is a character in a number of narratives at the same time, some of them embedded in others. Or again, what seemed to be an intelligible narrative in which one was playing a part may be transformed wholly or partly into a story of unintelligible episodes.' MacIntyre, *After Virtue*, p. 213.
[31] MacIntyre, *After Virtue*, p. 146.
[32] MacIntyre, *After Virtue*, p. 216.

opposition to each other.[33] What then? Because we are story-telling animals, it does not necessarily follow that the answer to the question 'What am I to do?' is an easy one.

What then emerges so far? We have just seen his central thesis: that man is a story-telling animal, not only in his fictions, but in his actions and his practices. Human actions then are narrative realities: they are extended over time, and they cannot be divorced from place and setting. Likewise, we learn through stories, and our concept of selfhood is a narrative concept.[34] We understand ourselves as people who live lives that are essentially connected, who have histories: identity is not simply an illusion, our lives form narrative unities. In fact, narrative is the essential category for all human activity. Thus emerges an essentially benign picture of the world, for MacIntyre seems to be suggesting that narrative not only enables us to understand ourselves, and that lives have meaning and coherence, but it also enables us to make sense of the world in which we live. The horror of the opening chapter of *After Virtue*, reminiscent of science fiction, can find resolution. His final comments in that book speak of the coming of a new Saint Benedict as opposed to Godot, surely a hopeful and hope-filled contrast.[35]

Tradition as a Socially Embodied Narrative

We now need to take this concept of people as story-telling animals further and examine its implications. Alasdair MacIntyre has written eloquently about the relationship between Homer, the society of Homer's day, and the moral character that is embedded both in that society and in the poetry of Homer. Homeric society had a particular idea of the Good, a particular idea of rationality, and a particular idea of practical reason, and all were socially embodied, and summed up in the Homeric epics.[36] We detect the triad of narrative/tradition/community and the unbreakable links between all three. In other words, the Homeric idea of the Good cannot make sense divorced from the community in which the tradition is nurtured. Achilles only makes sense in the setting of the Homeric poems and those poems only make perfect sense in the communities in which they were recited.

Furthermore, for a Homeric man (and it was a man) there was no place outside the story from which this narrative might be judged: the Homeric tradition was 'the structure of normality'.[37] The Homeric tradition was monolithic: the recitation of the poems at the feast of the Panatheneia underlined the identification of the Athena of the poems with the Athena who was patroness of Athens; the poems were a standard school text for boys; the poems embodied a code of behaviour which relieved citizens

---

[33] As MacIntyre acknowledges, *After Virtue*, p. 213.
[34] MacIntyre, *After Virtue*, pp. 216–17.
[35] MacIntyre, *After Virtue*, p. 263. Godot, the off-stage character in Samuel Becket's play *Waiting for Godot*, never turns up.
[36] See MacIntyre, *Whose Justice? Which Rationality?*, Chapter 2, 'Justice and Action in the Homeric Imagination', pp. 12–29.
[37] MacIntyre, *Whose Justice? Which Rationality?*, p. 25.

of the burden of having to justify each and every action they undertook.[38] Ancient Athens breathed Homer.

This picture raises interesting questions about choice. In a Homeric society, how does one think in non-Homeric terms? If we are inside a narrative, how can we ever think in terms that may not be provided by that narrative? How would a Homeric man ever argue, for example, against slavery or for votes for women? Both ideas are not only alien to the Homeric mindset, but seemingly inexpressible in terms of such a mindset. (As we shall see, MacIntyre advances an answer to these questions, but for the moment let us be content to raise the questions and no more.) For if we are narrative creatures and socially and culturally embodied selves, this may well curtail out freedom to choose: how can a Homeric man be anything other than a Homeric man, if Homer is all he knows?

However, MacIntyre does not envisage narrative as a straitjacket. He does state that there is no coign of vantage outside the tradition from which the tradition (any tradition?) can be evaluated. The only way to evaluate one's tradition is from within it. Our point of view of the narrative is that of persons in the narrative. This means that choices are made *within* the tradition, and that it is absolutely futile, then, to imagine a situation in which people come to decisions in a way that may be characterized as 'individualistic', or as a 'collection of strangers, each pursuing their own interests under minimal constraints'.[39] This is simply impossible, because we are not individuals in a purely individualistic sense, but people who form part of a community; we are not strangers, but subject to social ties. We live and breathe a narrative and all our thinking is of its nature narratively formed. We come into contact with other ideas and other narratives through the perspective of our own narrative.

This concept – that the deciding person is not some bare individual but someone who is a product of tradition, lived history and a community that has a narrative – has implications for the concept of justice. Indeed, justice is not simply a 'concept', but rather a lived, embodied tradition, a narrative with content, as opposed to something purely procedural.

In contrast to the idea of justice as procedural and neutral, MacIntyre sees justice as desert as central to the Aristotelian vision of justice, and indeed as the only sort of justice that makes sense in that context. As he says:

> Distributive justice then consists of the application of a principle of desert to a variety of types of situation. But concepts of desert have application only in contexts in which two conditions are satisfied. There must be some common enterprise to the achievement of whose goals those who are taken to be more deserving have contributed more than those who are taken to be less deserving; and there must be a shared view both of how such contributions are to be measured and of how rewards are to be ranked.[40]

The concept of desert, as MacIntyre shows though his examination of Aristotelian justice, is inextricably linked to that of community (common goals or enterprise)

---

[38] As above.
[39] MacIntyre, *After Virtue*, pp. 250–51.
[40] MacIntyre, *Whose Justice? Which Rationality?*, pp. 106–7.

and a specific comprehensive doctrine or narrative (shared view) that forms the basis of that community. Justice depends on having a common enterprise and a common rationality for measuring desert. This was certainly true of Aristotle's day. According to MacIntyre, Aristotle sees 'the highest good to be achieved, that which in an individual life is that for the sake of which all other activity is undertaken, is *theoria*, a certain kind of contemplative understanding';[41] again, the only place in which a person can flourish and achieve this good is the *polis*, indeed the best type of *polis*.[42] Here there emerges an important pointer towards the narrative nature of MacIntyre's thinking. Justice is not simply a bare concept, still less something that can be worked out in a vacuum, or in laboratory conditions of absolute impartiality. Rather justice reflects the socially embodied good of a particular community and that community's common goals and common rationality. The justice of Aristotle's day (at least as portrayed in the *Nichomachean Ethics*) aimed to reward the practitioners of *theoria* and punish those whose behaviour did not accord with it. It did this within the context of the city state. Take away one element, and it is hard to envision the others. Presumably, now that the city state is no more and *theoria* can no longer be considered the highest pursuit of mankind (and vice versa), some other form (or forms) of justice has superseded justice as desert, which more closely reflects the highest aspirations of society and the structure of the society in which it is practised. But the central point remains. Justice is not a matter of abstract thinking, but reflects the social embodiment of the society in which it is practised. This explains, too, why we find different forms of justice in the world: it is one thing in Britain, another in Singapore, another again in Iran – depending on the narrative by which these societies live. But nowhere is it purely theoretical and merely procedural, if MacIntyre is right.

With justice goes a particular idea of virtue, or as MacIntyre prefers, the virtues. Indeed justice, which is informed by a narrative, has the function of promoting the virtues inherent in that narrative, just as Aristotelian justice aimed to produce a certain ideal type, that of the '*enkratic* person... who has learned how to control his desires'.[43]

Because a narrative such as Aristotle's tends to be all-embracing – it gives us a picture of the sort of person we ought to be, the ideal state in which this sort of person can flourish, and the rationality of such a state and people – it presents a vision of the virtues as interconnected. Justice is not merely a matter of correct procedure. For example, an Athenian judge might not simply enquire as to whether a particular citizen were a horse thief, by a procedural investigation, but whether he were a good citizen, which is a much wider question, presupposing a moral judgement made against the backdrop of the narrative that informs Athenian justice, the narrative that tells us what the ideal citizen, the ideal member of the *polis*, should be like. For this is the tendency of narrative thinking – not to see single events in isolation, atomically, as it were, but to see each life as a narrative unity, lived out in community, and to make judgements about that life.

---

[41] MacIntyre, *Whose Justice? Which Rationality?*, p. 107.
[42] MacIntyre, *Whose Justice? Which Rationality?*, p. 104.
[43] MacIntyre, *Whose Justice? Which Rationality?*, p. 112.

Let us, with MacIntyre, consider the case of Brunetto Latini:[44] this unfortunate gentleman ends up in Dante's hell because, though he had many virtues, these virtues were vitiated by one vice. We moderns, as MacIntyre points out, find this conclusion problematic. The point of this is not one to do with sexual ethics as is the particular case of Brunetto, but rather with a much wider case: why should we make any judgement about human character? For a non-narrative thinker, Brunetto's private life is just that, completely private. Besides, the non-narrative thinker cannot presume to judge because no such public standard of judgement, no such narrative, would ever be agreed on in the public forum. A strict Catholic might condemn Bruno, but why should that have the force of law? What we see here then is the way narrative thinking approaches the subject of justice and indeed every subject. Narrative thinking makes connexions, where modern non-narrative thinking refuses to see linkage between, for example, the public and the private. For a narrative thinker, these two concepts interpenetrate.

But narrative thinking is inescapable, according to MacIntyre: our judgements and our justice will reflect our ideas about society and good citizenship which are in turn embodied in a narrative that informs our community. Some liberal thinkers may claim to be able to make impartial judgements and to practice a neutral form of justice that is purely procedural and not dependant on any narrative, but this is an illusion, as liberalism is itself a narrative, and such justice carries within it the promotion of a particular idea of the good and good citizenship, a particular narrative. There is no such thing as a view from nowhere, as we have seen. This vision of MacIntyre's also implies the unity of the political with the moral, another central plank of the Aristotelian vision: after all, Aristotle sees ethics and politics as closely allied activities. For him the *polis* is the locus of ethics, and both subjects form a continuum.[45] In other words justice is not just narratively-based, but also socially embodied, and as such it can never be 'value-free'.

Along with the Aristotelian vision, Alasdair MacIntyre identifies several competing versions of justice:

> Some conceptions of justice make the concept of desert central, while others deny it any relevance at all. Some conceptions appeal to inalienable human rights, others to some notion of social contract, and others again to a standard of utility.[46]

As we have seen, his version is the first, the justice that is inextricably linked with a narrative that points to a particular form of desert, embodied in a particular social setting. With these divergent views on justice we find a similar divergence in views on the nature of rationality:

> To be practically rational, so one contending party holds, is to act on the basis of costs and benefits to oneself of each possible course of action and its consequences. To be practically

---

[44] MacIntyre, *Three Rival Versions of Moral Enquiry*, p. 144. Dante, *Inferno* XV, 30 et seq.

[45] Aristotle, *Ethics*, translated by J.A.K. Thomson (Harmondsworth: Penguin,1953), pp. 26–7.

[46] MacIntyre, *Whose Justice? Which Rationality?*, p. 1.

rational, affirms a rival party, is to act under those constraints which any rational person, capable of an impartiality which accords no particular privileges to one's own interests, would agree should be imposed. To be practically rational, so a third party contends, is to act in such a way as to achieve the ultimate and true good of human beings.[47]

Again, MacIntyre's is the third form of practical rationality, that which is dependant on 'the ultimate and true good' as a standard of rationality. The real cleavage between this sort of justice and any other lies in what he calls 'the radical difference between a justice defined in terms of the goods of excellence, that is, a justice of desert, and a justice defined in terms of the goods of effectiveness'.[48] This latter 'will always be *as if* justice was the outcome of a contract, an episode of explicit negotiation'.[49] Furthermore, justice as desert 'is a disposition to give to each person, including oneself, what that person deserves and to treat no one in a way incompatible with their deserts'.[50] This means that justice as desert has at its heart a vision of the Good. However, contractarian justice sees the virtue of justice as 'nothing other than a disposition to obey those rules [agreed on by contract]. So the virtue of justice is... secondary to and definable only in terms of the rules of justice'.[51] An example is given to illustrate the difference in practical terms:

> And so, from the standpoint of the goods of co-operative effectiveness friendship is a virtue precisely insofar as it is the source of pleasure and utility. From the standpoint of the goods of excellence, however, friendship is a matter of more than pleasure and utility, although it may involve both of these. It is a type of relationship of mutual regard which arises from a shared allegiance to one and the same good or to one and the same set of goods.[52]

And here, in a nutshell, we see the fundamental point about narrative thinking: a narrative proposes a shared set of goods. Indeed the practical reasoning done within a community that shares a narrative and is constituted by it will depend on having a common good.[53] For practical reasoning is about means, not ends and presupposes agreement about ends; it involves reasoning together with others within a determinate set of social relations.[54] Again, we see the link between practical reasoning and community in the assertion that self-knowledge is necessary for practical reasoning, and that this self-knowledge is socially achieved.[55] By contrast, contractarian thinking proposes rules which are the fruit of negotiation, and procedures that seemingly carry with them no allegiance to a shared set of goods.

---

[47] MacIntyre, *Whose Justice? Which Rationality?*, p. 2.
[48] MacIntyre, *Whose Justice? Which Rationality?*, p. 36.
[49] MacIntyre, *Whose Justice? Which Rationality?*, p. 37.
[50] MacIntyre, *Whose Justice? Which Rationality?*, p. 39.
[51] MacIntyre, *Whose Justice? Which Rationality?*, p. 39.
[52] MacIntyre, *Whose Justice? Which Rationality?*, p. 42.
[53] A point made in MacIntyre's most recent book, *Dependent Rational Animals, Why Human Beings need the Virtues* (Chicago and La Salle, Illinois: Open Court, 1999), p. 108.
[54] MacIntyre, *Dependent Rational Animals*, p. 107.
[55] MacIntyre, *Dependent Rational Animals*, pp. 94–5. Also p. 74 for the same point.

But how would this shared set of goods beloved of narrative thinking be possible in the pluralistic society that has emerged from the ruins envisaged in the first chapter of *After Virtue*? For if we agree on very little, how could we possibly agree on a shared set of goods and a shared narrative? This is the challenge with which MacIntyre leaves us; or, as some might prefer to put it, this is the one difficulty that none of his writings is ever able to surmount;[56] it seems we live in a pluralistic world, and no comprehensive doctrine or narrative of the sort he is proposing is ever going to win general acceptance, even if it is Aristotelian justice. Indeed MacIntyre admits as much in the conclusions to all three of his major recent works; all we can do, he hazards, is be conscious of our predicament.[57] This is not to say that MacIntyre has not done moral philosophy and theology a huge service, by drawing our attention to the idea of the inescapability of narrative thinking, the idea of virtue, or more properly, the virtues, the importance of character and tradition, the inadequacy of a merely rule based morality, and the importance of a rationality that is based on the Good. MacIntyre emphasizes too the idea of the community as the school of morality, and morality always having a social context; this is true enough, but whose community, which morality? We must now tackle the question of the criteria of choice between one narrative and another.

The Rationality of Tradition

If narratives and traditions are all we have, then which story is the right one? How do we set about proving the superiority of one tradition over another?[58] Confronted with the rival traditions we encounter, MacIntyre proposes a dialogue between traditions. He does not see this as futile, unlike Nietzsche.[59]

From what we have already said, it may seem that if we are to accept narrative as the fundamental category in ethics, and by extension the idea that narrative is only nurtured in specific communities and traditions, then we are abandoning any idea of morality as being universally valid, as the Enlightenment claimed. If the

---

[56] But he does seem aware of the problem. In *Dependent Rational Animals*, he makes a point of distancing himself from the more radical communitarians, speaking of the 'communitarian mistake, to attempt to infuse the politics of the state with the values and modes of participation in local community', p. 142. Likewise, he is scathing about the doctrine of *Volkism* which sees political society as being co-terminous with community, p. 132. What MacIntyre seems to be advocating implicitly, then, is a position not dissimilar to that of John Rawls, which we shall discuss below – another sign of the development of his thought. Some of the things he says in this latest book about dialogue and intelligibility, and assuming the other's point of view (pp. 148, 150) also seem suspiciously Rawlsian.

[57] MacIntyre, *After Virtue*, p. 263. The endings of *Whose Justice? Which Rationality?* and *Three Rival Versions of Moral Enquiry* are similar in outlook, talking not of agreement but rather of systematizing and recognizing the depth of our disagreement.

[58] 'From this it may well appear to follow that no tradition can claim rational superiority to any other', MacIntyre, *Whose Justice? Which Rationality?*, p. 348, being part of the conclusion to the chapter entitled 'Liberalism Transformed into a Tradition'.

[59] MacIntyre, *Three Rival Versions of Moral Enquiry*, p. 49: 'Nietzsche did not advance a new theory against older theories; he proposed an abandonment of theory.'

Enlightenment Project has failed (and it may well have done so) are we forced to admit the uselessness of discursive rational argument as the solution to all problems, or as at least capable of reaching solid conclusions? This is what a superficial reading of the first chapter of *After Virtue* might suggest.

It seems not, however, if we take seriously what MacIntyre has to say about Aristotelian dialectic in his books. Narrative and the tradition in which that narrative is nurtured, remains an intellectual pursuit, a rational one, rather than an anti-rational and anti-intellectual one. MacIntyre is not proposing the death of philosophy and theology, but rather their renewal. There is nothing in his writings to suggest that MacIntyre is some sort of anarchist who claims that everything has failed, religion and rationality included, and that faced with moral anarchy, we choose our morality with an act of the will, and it is that choice, the force of our will, that makes what we have chosen moral. MacIntyre characterizes such a position thus:

> In five swift, witty and cogent paragraphs he [Nietzsche] disposes of both what I have called the Enlightenment project to discover rational foundations for an objective morality and of the confidence of the everyday moral agent in post-Enlightenment culture that his moral practice and utterance are in good order. But Nietzsche then goes on to confront the problem that this act of destruction has created. The underlying structure of his argument is as follows: if there is nothing to morality but expressions of will, my morality can only be what my will creates. There can be no place for such fictions as natural rights, utility, the greatest happiness of the greatest number. I myself must bring into existence 'new tables of what is good'... Let will replace reason and let us make ourselves into autonomous moral subjects by some gigantic and heroic act of the will...[60]

For MacIntyre this position is the unacceptable alternative to Aristotelian rationality;[61] instead of the heroic act of the will which divorces human moral choice from any thinking process he advocates the altogether gentler tradition of rational dialectic. The tradition, which is to be learned through a long apprenticeship,[62] cannot be understood except within the bounds of that tradition,[63] into which the apprentice is initiated. This is a key concept in the work of MacIntyre,[64] whose idea of tradition, however, has to be understood properly. It does not consist in the blind repetition of what previous generations have said. He writes:

---

[60] MacIntyre, *After Virtue*, pp. 113–14.
[61] MacIntyre, *After Virtue*, p. 256.
[62] MacIntyre, *Whose Justice? Which Rationality?* p. 115.
[63] MacIntyre, *Whose Justice? Which Rationality?* p. 101.
[64] Just to take one example: 'The hostility to the imposition of religious tests which Adam Gifford shared with so many of his contemporaries prevented any recognition even of the possibility that commitment to some particular theoretical or doctrinal standpoint may be a pre-requisite for – rather than a barrier to – an ability to characterise data in a way which will enable enquiry to proceed', MacIntyre, *Three Rival Versions of Moral Enquiry*, p. 17. In other words, if you have no particular standpoint, you cannot think; if you have no tradition, you have no way of absorbing new data; if you are *tabula rasa*, you are destined to remain that way forever.

For it is central to the conception of such a tradition that the past is never something to be merely discarded, but rather that the present is intelligible only as a commentary upon and response to the past in which the past, if necessary and if possible, is corrected and transcended, yet corrected and transcended in a way that leaves the present open to being in its turn corrected and transcended by some yet more adequate point of view. Thus the notion of tradition embodies a very unAristotelian theory of knowledge according to which each particular theory or set of moral or scientific beliefs is intelligible and justifiable – insofar as it is justifiable – only as a member of a historical series.[65]

Thus tradition is more than just raiding the store cupboard of history for useful opinions and a notching up of gobbets from approved authors.[66] Tradition is a sort of conversation or dialogue over time: it is 'an historically extended, socially embodied argument'.[67] In MacIntyre's sense, tradition is always open to development;[68] it represents an argument, rather than the denial of argument. Because this vision is rather nuanced and subtle, it is open to misinterpretation. One can see the invocation of tradition as an attempt to shut off argument, but this is the exact opposite to what MacIntyre is arguing.

That this is so may be seen more clearly from the 'sequel' to *After Virtue*, *Whose Justice? Which Rationality?* which acts as a corrective to some of the positions outlined in the earlier book.[69] While the earlier book seemed to posit a genuine incommensurability between traditions, this is more apparent than real.[70] In the later book, MacIntyre writes:

> From this [the lack of any tradition-independent standards of judgement] it may well appear that no tradition can claim rational superiority to any other. For each tradition has internal to itself its own view of what rational superiority consists in in respect of such topics as practical rationality and justice, and the adherents of each will judge accordingly. And if this is the case two further conclusions will follow. The first is that at any fundamental level no rational debate between, rather than within, traditions can

---

[65] MacIntyre, *After Virtue*, p. 146.

[66] See for example Bernard Hoose, *Received Wisdom? Reviewing the Role of Tradition in Christian Ethics* (London: Geoffrey Chapman, 1994), who alerts us to the pitfalls inherent in the recourse to tradition.

[67] MacIntyre, *After Virtue*, p. 222.

[68] MacIntyre himself is always keen to correct his own earlier conclusions. See *Whose Justice? Which Rationality?* pp. ix–x, and especially his most recent work, *Dependent Rational Animals*, pp. x–xi, in which he says that the present volume aims to correct previous mistakes, and thanks his critics for pointing these mistakes out to him. Thus one can see that MacIntyre's work represents a dialogue, an extended argument over time, and that none of his works must be taken in isolation, but must be seen in the light of further developments. One should read MacIntyre using his own criteria about tradition. Note also in the latter the reference to 'unfinished business in these pages', p. xiii. MacIntyre always maintains that every position is capable of development.

[69] MacIntyre describes the book as the sequel to the earlier work, as well as a corrective to 'more than one error'. *Whose Justice? Which Rationality?*, pp. ix–x.

[70] A point made by C.J. Thompson, 'The Character of MacIntyre's Narrative', *The Thomist*, 59 (1995): 379–405. He writes: 'For the later MacIntyre, however, genuine incommensurability is a fiction' (p. 402).

occur. The adherents of conflicting tendencies within a tradition may still share enough in the way of fundamental belief to conduct such a debate, but the protagonists of rival traditions will be precluded at any fundamental level, not only from justifying their views to the members of any rival tradition, but even from learning from them how to modify their own tradition in any radical way.

Yet if this is so, a second conclusion seems to be in order. Given that each tradition will frame its own standpoint in terms of its own idiosyncratic concepts, and given that no fundamental correction of its conceptual scheme from some external standpoint is possible, it may appear that each tradition must develop its own scheme in a way which is liable to preclude even translation from one tradition to another... Each tradition... [will be] unable to justify its claims over and against those of its rivals except to those who already accept them.[71]

However, this (reminiscent of the scene sketched in the first chapter of *After Virtue*) is largely a matter of seeming and appearance, in other words an illusion. MacIntyre then goes on to give a thoughtful account of just how insights of one tradition can be made comprehensible to people in an other tradition, in a chapter tellingly entitled 'The Rationality of Traditions'.[72] This provides an answer of a kind. But an answer has already been sketched earlier in the book, in the tenth chapter 'Overcoming a Conflict of Traditions'.[73]

For a start, Aquinas leaves each particular argument 'open to be taken further' which provides an important clue to his method of enquiry.[74] No narrative or argument is closed, but can always be developed further – there is always more to be said. In other words, narrative invites argument and engagement, and does not shut them off; it is a form of argument, rather than the denial of argument.

How does the argument – and each position is but a staging post in a continuing argument – proceed when it encounters a rival tradition? The first thing to do is 'to characterize the contention of its rival in its own terms' and then to 'ask whether the alternative and rival tradition may not be able to provide resources to characterize and to explain the failings and defects of their own tradition'. This requires 'a rare gift of empathy as well as of intellectual insight' so that one can see one's own tradition 'from the alien perspective of another tradition'.[75]

This is important, for it tells us how one narrative can engage with others and justify itself in confrontation with others. If rival methods of enquiry had indeed no criteria or methods for resolving the conflict of choosing among them, then we would be left with implicit relativism. But this is not the case with MacIntyre.[76] In a later book he goes further still saying:

Hence in judging of truth and falsity there is always some uneliminable reference beyond the scheme within which those judgements are made and beyond the criteria which

---

[71] MacIntyre, *Whose Justice? Which Rationality?*, p. 348.
[72] MacIntyre, *Whose Justice? Which Rationality?*, pp. 349–69.
[73] MacIntyre, *Whose Justice? Which Rationality?*, pp. 164–82.
[74] MacIntyre, *Whose Justice? Which Rationality?*, p. 164.
[75] MacIntyre, *Whose Justice? Which Rationality?*, pp. 166–7. See also MacIntyre, *Dependent Rational Animals*, p. 150, for another statement of the same point.
[76] Thompson, p. 402.

provide the warrants for assertibility within that scheme. Truth cannot be identified with, or collapsed into warranted assertibility. And a conception of *what is* which is more and other than a conception of *what appears to be the case in the light of the most fundamental criteria governing assertibility within any particular scheme* is correspondingly required, that is, a metaphysics of being, of *esse*, over and above whatever can be said about particular *entia* in the light of particular concepts.[77]

What is important here is not whether we accept MacIntyre's metaphysics or not, but his rejection of the idea that one can only judge the story or narrative by the standards of that story or narrative, and the corresponding relativism that this entails. While narrative, then, is the inescapable grammar of expression, narratives can be weighed up and found wanting in accordance with criteria that lie beyond that particular narrative. So there is a way of judging one narrative against another.

But interestingly, most people who refer to the work of MacIntyre in their own theology make little reference to these points in his work and in fact draw heavily on the first chapter of *After Virtue*, rather than seeing it in the light of these later developments. MacIntyre focuses on incommensurability and untranslatability as apparent states of affairs; but he also points out how these states of affairs can be overcome. As C.J. Thompson points out:

In both *Whose Justice? Which Rationality?* and *Three Rival Versions of Moral Enquiry*, MacIntyre continues his critique of the Enlightenment and post-Enlightenment versions of moral enquiry, but the isolationist theme [in the closing pages of *After Virtue*] is not present in these later works. The persistent interminability of moral debate and the apparent incommensurability of rival traditions of enquiry no longer present an impasse, but an invitation to confrontation with alternative modes of enquiry. The function of narrative in these later contexts is more inclusive than its earlier version. It takes on a more systemic quality of entire traditions of rationality (as opposed to single individuals)...[78]

One cannot emphasize this neglected and overlooked point enough: narrative in MacIntyre, or at least in the later MacIntyre, is not a straitjacket but a means of expression and communication, a means of resolving disputes rather than engraving them in stone. This leads Thompson to remark in passing on MacIntyre's 'optimism',[79] which he is surely right to do.

A cursory examination of MacIntyre's most recent book, *Dependent Rational Animals*, will alert us to further developments in this field. Though the book deals with a topic that does not interest us here, MacIntyre has much to say in passing on the way rationality works that is of great interest to us. For a start he recognizes that human judgement may well be impeded by the habits of the mind.

In philosophy where one begins generally makes a difference to the outcome of one's enquiries. One possible starting point is to acknowledge that the habits of the mind... are genuinely difficult to discard. They are after all our habits, part of a mindset that many of us have acquired, not only from our engagement in the enquiries of moral philosophy, but

---

[77] MacIntyre, *Three Rival Versions*, p. 122.
[78] Thompson, p. 382.
[79] Thompson, p. 383.

from the wider culture which provides the background of those enquiries. So we might do well to begin with a certain suspicion of ourselves. For whatever the philosophical idiom in which we frame our initial enquiries, whatever the philosophical resources upon which we find ourselves able to draw, we will be liable to think in terms that may prevent us from understanding just how much of a change in standpoint is needed.[80]

In other words, while MacIntyre has acknowledged that all enquiry starts within a tradition, and indeed cannot start anywhere else but within a tradition, our background culture, which is essential to the ability to think, may also restrict our thoughts. Because he is aware of the danger that this may involve, this leads him, later in the same book, to stress the need for a certain detachment from our desires if we are to be able to make a judgement about them. He says:

To have learned how to stand back in some measure from our present desires, so as to be able to evaluate them, is a necessary condition for engaging in sound reasoning about our reasons for action. Here one danger is that those who have failed to become sufficiently detached from their own immediate desires, for whom desire for their and the good has not become to a sufficient degree overriding, are unlikely to recognise this fact about themselves. And so what they present to themselves as a desire for their good or for *the* good may in fact be and often enough is some unacknowledged form of infantile desire, a type of desire that has been protected from evaluative criticism. Hence in deliberating they both reason from unsound premises and act from badly flawed motivation. Sound practical reasoning and good motivation are related in sometimes complex ways, but an incapacity to distance oneself from one's desires is a danger to both.[81]

This recalls much of what MacIntyre has said previously about the Aristotelian idea of the *enkratic* person as one capable of controlling their appetites and thus capable of rational discourse;[82] but even though he is talking specifically about desire here, his words can be easily applied to the matter of tradition. One is in a tradition, but at the same time one needs to have a certain mental distance from one's tradition in order to be able to evaluate it critically; if not, one's use of tradition may be fundamentally unsound, and lead to flawed reasoning. As we shall see in later chapters of this book, this theme will emerge as one of great importance. It is important to stress for now that it is not absent in the work of MacIntyre. Once again we see how nuanced his view of tradition is.

To conclude this chapter, then: MacIntyre claims that abstract thought is an illusion, and that all (even seemingly impartial) views come to us as an integral part of a narrative history. The activity of thinking is *per se* narrative and historical. The interminability of modern debates is largely the result of the fact that people have failed to recognize the inescapably narrative nature of their arguments. The solution to this seeming deadlock is then to rediscover the category of narrative and to confront rival traditions with each other, so that they may engage in dialogue.

From this conclusion we can see that we have come some distance from a simple reading of the first chapter of *After Virtue*. While the analysis of the opening chapter

---

[80] MacIntyre, *Dependent Rational Animals*, p. 4.
[81] MacIntyre, *Dependent Rational Animals*, pp. 72–3.
[82] MacIntyre, *Whose Justice? Which Rationality?*, p. 112.

of *After Virtue* represents an eloquent, even dramatic, rendition of the problems facing contemporary moral discourse, MacIntyre does not see the situation as beyond solution. It is thus right to see MacIntyre as a constructive thinker with an optimistic vision of the progress that is possible in the field of moral philosophy, and one who has made an important contribution to our way of thinking.

Chapter 3

Stanley Hauerwas

The same themes that we have examined in the writings of MacIntyre are to be found in the work of Stanley Hauerwas. Hauerwas is, however, more closely concerned with theology, and his writings show the impact of the idea of narrative on theology, thus bringing the questions we have already examined in previous chapters into sharper focus.

Hauerwas frequently writes about narrative, and is a self-declared narrative theologian,[1] the living embodiment of a narrative. Hauerwas calls himself an 'embedded' theologian, acknowledging a debt to MacIntyre[2] and his provenance from a particular faith community.[3] His ethics, as we shall see, are the view from somewhere, time and place bound, determined by a community's history and convictions – indeed, this is the case of all ethics, he says. As a result one cannot talk of 'ethics' as such as if it transcended history, but it must always be qualified by some adjective to show its social and historical character. The Evangelical Methodist professor in Notre Dame cannot, by an act of the will, or by any other means, slough off his own history and adopt an impartial standpoint or perspective, the so-called view from nowhere. He holds that one does theology through the perspective of one's own history, in a community and inside the tradition in which one lives.

This, as we shall see, has profound implications for the shape of the theology that Hauerwas practices. For a start, such theology is always going to shy away from the universalist tendencies of its rivals from within the Kantian tradition, or traditions

---

[1] Hauerwas is a particular champion of narrative theology: see his *Why Narrative? Readings in Narrative Theology*, edited by Stanley Hauerwas and L. Gregory Jones (Grand Rapids: William B. Eerdmans Publishing Company, 1989) which provides the background to his position.

[2] Stanley Hauerwas, *The Peaceable Kingdom* (Notre Dame: University of Notre Dame Press, 1983), p. xiii. This book was published two years after the first edition of *After Virtue*, and, as will emerge, the later book suggests that Hauerwas read *After Virtue* closely. However, Hauerwas's writings on the virtues date back to at least his *Vision and Virtue* (Notre Dame: Notre Dame University Press, 1974). MacIntyre makes no reference to this work in *After Virtue*, so it is hard to posit an influence in the opposite direction, though one may suspect as much.

[3] Or perhaps communities in the plural, for his religious allegiance is hazy. Hauerwas is unable to make up his mind at one point whether he writes as a Catholic or a Protestant; but he acknowledges that his background is of great importance. See *Peaceable Kingdom*, p. xxvi. For more on Hauerwas's particular background, see William Cavanaugh, 'Stan the Man: A Thoroughly Biased Account of a Completely Unobjective Person' in *The Hauerwas Reader*, edited by John Berkman and Michael Cartwright (Durham and London: Duke University Press, 2001), pp. 17–32.

influenced by Kant. Secondly, such a theology is going to advance a particular vision of human beings as story-telling animals, and of theology as best, indeed, only, expressed in story form. It will see the Christian community as a place where stories are told and, in a sense (which may prove problematic) lived out. And finally, such a theology will have difficulty in providing criteria for its justification: for if story is all that we have, how do we pick and choose between narratives? On this last question, already raised by MacIntyre, we shall see that Hauerwas presents us with a different answer.

The Narrative Quality of Religious Experience

Having looked at the territory that Hauerwas has staked out for himself in theology, it is time to examine the way he sees stories working in the field of theology. One example he provides is not entirely satisfactory. He points out that the Ten Commandments only make sense in the context of the Covenant and the history of God's dealings with Israel. In other words the Law, expressed as rules couched in terms of 'Thou shalt not', is not prior in any way to the actual story of the Exodus. It is the story that comes first, the story that contains, indeed is, the ethics. This is an in many ways welcome antidote to the frequently criticized rules-based morality. Hence we see the importance of the text Deuteronomy 6:21–25:[4]

> Once we were Pharaoh's slaves in Egypt, and God brought us out of Egypt by his mighty hand. Before our eyes the Lord worked great and terrible signs against Egypt, against Pharaoh and all his House. And he brought us out from there to lead us into the land he swore to our fathers he would give us. And the Lord commanded us to observe all these laws and to fear the Lord our God, so as to be happy forever and to live, as he has granted us to do until now. For right living will mean this: to keep and observe all these commandments before the Lord our God as he has directed us.

One sees here the nexus between narrative, the account of what God has done, and morality, the keeping of the Law; one also detects the idea of tradition, a continuing narrative over generations, which constitutes an identity: this is what your are to tell your son when he asks you (Dt. 6:20, 21). This tradition is still alive and the story is re-enacted every Passover. But is this to be taken as the paradigm for all moral theology? Yes, says Hauerwas. Christian convictions are narrative by nature and not by chance. Narrative is the fundamental way of talking about God, 'the primary grammar of Christian belief'.[5] Moreover, the self is not a freestanding 'I' but a narrative reality.[6] Above all: 'We know who we are only when we can place ourselves – locate our stories – within God's story'.[7] This last is perhaps the crucial point – but how does one place oneself in a story, let alone in someone else's story?

Hauerwas's insight about narrative leads him to emphasize the Bible as a narrative: the form of the Gospel, says Hauerwas, is the stories of a life, the life of

---

[4] Hauerwas, *The Peaceable Kingdom*, pp. 23–4.
[5] Hauerwas, *The Peaceable Kingdom*, p. 25.
[6] Hauerwas, *The Peaceable Kingdom*, p. 26.
[7] Hauerwas, *The Peaceable Kingdom*, p. 27.

Jesus.[8] In addition, one may note that the Creed is a narrative, and the first part of the Gospels to be written are the strongly narrative parts, the passion narratives. One becomes a Christian at baptism by assenting in faith to the Creed, and one lives as a Christian a narrative that has been informed by the narrative of Jesus, especially the narrative of his passion. 'Faith is, in effect, finding our true life within the life of Christ,' he says.[9] But Hauerwas's point about the narrative of the Gospels masks a question – in what sense are the Gospels stories of the life of Jesus? What is the form or shape of these stories? Again, when he says we are to 'locate our lives in relation to his',[10] this raises very serious questions. Is Hauerwas advancing an ethic of *imitatio Christi*? It might seem so.[11] But this is fraught with difficulty.[12] Indeed Hauerwas seems aware of this, for he writes:

> The theme of 'imitation' is subject to much misunderstanding. In particular it carries with it individualist presuppositions that are antithetical to the social nature of the Christian life. For there is no way to learn to 'imitate' God by trying to copy in an external manner the actions of Jesus. No one can become virtuous by copying what virtuous people do. We can only be virtuous by doing what virtuous people do in the manner that they do it. Therefore one can only learn to be virtuous, to be like Jesus, by learning from others how that is done. To be like Jesus requires that I become part of a community that practices virtues, not that I copy his life point by point.
>
> There is a deeper reason that I cannot and should not mimic Jesus. We are not called upon to be initiators of the kingdom, we are not called upon to be God's anointed. We are called upon to be *like* Jesus, not to *be* Jesus.[13]

This passage reveals the weakness of Hauerwas's thinking. We are called to place our personal narrative within the narrative of Christ – which boils down in the end to some sort of an ethic of renunciation,[14] reminiscent of the work of Thomas à Kempis. Having established the essentially narrative quality of religious experience, Hauerwas seems unable to take us into new paths. For the path of Thomas à Kempis is a very old path indeed and raises insuperable objections. It conjures up what Gustafson calls the 'grim determination to achieve peace and happiness through self-mortification' which is 'egocentric and of dubious moral value'.[15] These are objections to which Hauerwas as a Protestant ought to be very sensitive.

But even Catholics should be disappointed with this conclusion. Surely there is more to a narrative theology than the *imitatio Christi* model criticized by Gustafson? How does or can my narrative interlock with that of Jesus? It is worth noting too that the word 'imitation' has an added nuance in English: it means false. No one could

---

[8] Hauerwas, *The Peaceable Kingdom*, p. 74.
[9] Hauerwas, *The Peaceable Kingdom*, p. 93.
[10] Hauerwas, *The Peaceable Kingdom*, p. 74.
[11] See the section 'Jesus, Israel, and the Imitation of God', Hauerwas, *The Peaceable Kingdom*, pp. 76–81.
[12] James M. Gustafson points out the manifold difficulties of this position. See his *Christ and the Moral Life* (New York: Harper and Row, 1968), pp. 180–87.
[13] Hauerwas, *The Peaceable Kingdom*, p. 76.
[14] Hauerwas, *The Peaceable Kingdom*, p. 95.
[15] Gustafson, *Christ and the Moral Life*, p. 180.

seriously want to be an imitation Christ when they could have the real thing – but how? Why settle for *being like* Jesus instead of *being* Jesus? There is a serious lacuna in Hauerwas's thought here. Hauerwas speaks of 'the vocation to imitate God'[16] but does not lead us to a better understanding of the idea of *imitatio Christi*.

Religious Tradition as an Ecclesially Embodied Narrative

In Hauerwas's writing we meet a strong emphasis on the communitarian aspect of life and on the Church. He writes that community is a necessary condition for truthfulness, and truthfulness is equally necessary for building a non-coercive community. He underlines then the necessary relation between a community and the narrative that sets its topography: the freedom of the gospel is not to be equated with the freedom of the (solitary) individual. To be free then, is to be part of a community.[17]

These points require explication. Hauerwas posits a necessary and reciprocal relationship between community and truthfulness: on the one hand truth is arrived at in a social and historical as opposed to a solitary manner, that is to say in a community; on the other hand no community is truly such unless it is a place where truth is embodied: lies and manipulation deform community; thus a totalitarian state is not a community but a place of coercion, lies being of their nature coercive; but truth sets one free.

Following John Howard Yoder, Hauerwas writes that the Church best serves society by being herself.[18] In another place this is expressed as the Church's challenge as being called to be a 'contrast model' for society.[19] The Church is democratic in that all its members count; but it is not democratic in the sense that no one knows the truth and all opinions are equal, as in a liberal democracy. Its first task is to show a type of community based on the rule of trust and not fear.[20] Because we are a storied people with a storied God who we know through the formation of our characters, our knowledge of God is not an isolated event, but requires the existence of a storied society; it is through such a society, the Church, that the world is given its history.[21] Thus the Church is a community of discourse and interpretation that tells the stories of Israel and Jesus and forms its life in accordance with them. It does not live by one rigid paradigm, but is a living and dynamic tradition.[22] In this way Hauerwas tries to show how the Church is the embodiment of the truthful community discussed above.

---

[16] Hauerwas, *The Peaceable Kingdom*, p. 78.
[17] Stanley Hauerwas, *Truthfulness and Tragedy* (Notre Dame: Notre Dame University Press, 1977), p. 10.
[18] Hauerwas, *Truthfulness and Tragedy*, p. 11.
[19] Stanley Hauerwas, *A Community of Character* (Notre Dame: Notre Dame University Press, 1981), p. 84.
[20] Hauerwas, *A Community of Character*, p. 85.
[21] Hauerwas, *A Community of Character*, p. 91.
[22] Hauerwas, *A Community of Character*, p. 92.

What emerges from Hauerwas's writing on the Church is the vision of the place where the stories of Jesus and Israel are told and interpreted and lived out; but this is not to say that the Church is merely the locus of convenience for such story-telling: rather the existence of the Church is a necessary precondition of the story being told. For without the community, there can be no story, as stories are communitarian by nature, and without a story there can be no community, as communities are story-based by nature: hence the necessary and reciprocal relationship between the two. Likewise the existence of the community depends on its truthfulness; without that, it would become a place of coercion and thus not a community at all.

We see here a strong parallel with what MacIntyre has written about Athenian society; once again we meet the triad of community, narrative and tradition, and the essential mutual interdependence between the three: remove one and the other two become impossible. All are necessary.

Hauerwas's point is further brought out by consideration of what he has to say about modern American political society, to which the Church offers a contrast model. Again the focus is on the question of justice, where Hauerwas stands with MacIntyre. Unlike the Church, modern American political society lives without a story, and thus is not a community at all, for it sees justice as neutral and purely procedural, the result of contract or negotiation in sterile laboratory conditions. However, because people by their very nature have narratives and are formed as narrative beings in communities with narrative histories, such an ahistorical approach to justice is futile. Contractarian justice, such as that of John Rawls, is singled out as:

> ... a stark metaphor for the ahistorical approach of liberal theory, as the self is alienated from its history and simply left with its individual preferences and prejudices. The 'justice' that results from the bargaining game is but the guarantee that my liberty to consume will be fairly limited within the overall distributive shares.[23]

Hauerwas argues that one simply cannot deny the essential nature of tradition and history by adopting a *tabula rasa* in some hypothetical choice situation: history and tradition are essential, inescapable, and cannot ever be put aside: it is an illusion to imagine otherwise. Likewise he criticizes the 'liberal myth' which replaces a shared history with the idea that rules and procedures can solve every problem. Justice cannot be based on self-interest and the principle of consent.[24] Indeed Hauerwas goes so far as to claim that what he calls 'the standard account' of morality makes alienation from self and others the central moral virtue.[25]

Hauerwas also stands closely with MacIntyre in seeing modern (in this case, American) society as subject to endless and interminable debates about questions that will never be settled, and the failure of true moral discourse leading to constant recourse to the courts and a sort of degenerate legalism.[26]

---

[23] Hauerwas, *A Community of Character*, pp. 82–3. The particular reference is to John Rawls's Original Position which we will examine in a subsequent chapter.
[24] Hauerwas, *A Community of Character*, pp. 77–83.
[25] Hauerwas, *Truthfulness and Tragedy*, p. 23.
[26] Hauerwas, *A Community of Character*, pp. 75–6.

These are the criticisms of a narrative theologian faced with what he sees as a liberal consensus, if liberalism is understood as the desire to make decisions unfettered by reference to tradition and community, but with reference to procedure alone; or more particularly, these are the objections that the narrative theologian makes when faced with what has been called the 'disembodied self' of liberal theory.

> Thus we assume... it is more important to be an 'autonomous' person than to be a 'Hauerwas' or a 'Pulaski' or a 'Smith'... Shorn of particularistic commitments essential to public life, we exist as individuals, but now 'individuals' is but a name for a particular unit of arbitrary desires.[27]

For Hauerwas, decisions are not to be made by vainly trying to put one's character, history and social self to one side. To do so, to put particularistic commitments aside, is indeed to make any social life impossible. Human beings are narrative realities and their decisions will reflect, or be made in the light of, their histories. This means that a Mennonite community (for example) will practice a particularly Mennonite form of justice, based on Mennonite values and the Mennonite vision of what people are called to be. Their contribution to society will be as Mennonites. And as with the Mennonites, so with every other type of community. At the heart of justice and the practice of justice will be an ideal of human excellence. By contrast, liberal society, he says, sees politics as concerned with the distribution of desires, irrespective of the content of those desires; it supposes that a just polity is possible without the formation of just people; in fact it refuses to promote or develop virtue on the grounds that this would be an intrusion into the personal realm.[28]

This brings us to another point made by Hauerwas: the American Constitution can only work, as John Adams claimed, given virtuous people, but liberal theory makes no provision for their formation.[29] Once again, this seems to be futile and doomed to failure. Hauerwas believes that there can be no true community without a shared set of beliefs about the good. 'The form and substance of community is narrative dependent and therefore what counts as 'social ethics' is a correlative of the content of that narrative,' he writes.[30] One notices a broad agreement with MacIntyre on this point.

Hauerwas sees action as essentially historical, and as such fitting into a narrative.[31] In this he follows MacIntyre explicitly. He also criticizes the idea of a liberal and explicitly neutral state: the state, to command loyalty and to be able to function properly, must be underpinned, he suggests, by some sort of narrative to which people can subscribe. And political reasoning must be done in a narrative manner, abandoning the myth that decisions can be made in an ahistorical vacuum. It is this myth, and over reliance on procedure, that has brought America to interminable litigation. By taking up this position we can see that Hauerwas is being true to what

---

[27] Hauerwas, *A Community of Character*, pp. 80–81.
[28] Hauerwas, *A Community of Character*, p. 73.
[29] Hauerwas, *A Community of Character*, p. 79.
[30] Hauerwas, *A Community of Character*, p. 10.
[31] Hauerwas, *The Hauerwas Reader*, p. 81, drawing on MacIntyre, *After Virtue*, pp. 211–12.

he sees as his vocation as a theologian – counter-cultural in some ways, but also bearing witness to the society in which he lives.

Hauerwas and the Rationality of a Religious Tradition

How are we to prove the preceding assertions, and above all the underlying assumption that we are all people who are constituted by our stories? As to the objection about how we are to distinguish between competing narratives, Hauerwas has this to say: 'There is no place outside history where we can secure a place to anchor our convictions. We must begin in the middle, that is, we must begin within a narrative.'[32]

This may seem a way of enabling him to sidestep all questions about how we are to justify our narrative: we cannot do so, because all we have are narratives. Thus there is no non-narrative starting-point, methodologically speaking. The narrative is its own justification, it seems. But this seems hardly satisfactory. How are we to distinguish between good and bad narratives? Is one narrative, in absolute terms, as good as another?

An attempt is made to tackle these questions in *Truthfulness and Tragedy*, particularly the section entitled 'Rationality and the Christian Story'.[33] Hauerwas makes clear that he wishes to show that narrative functions as a form of rationality.[34] The meaning and use of notions depends on their narrative context, contrary to what the 'standard account' maintains.[35] Narrative is rational because it has structure, 'the connected unfolding that we call plot', but its intentionality though purposive is not necessary. Indeed, narrative depends on human intentionality, and 'offers just the intelligibility we need for acting properly'.[36] So what Hauerwas maintains here, surely plausibly, is the simple fact that narratives make sense, and thus are not purely arbitrary, though they are not necessary: we can see in a narrative why things are as they are, but we can still imagine them being otherwise.

Hauerwas continues that narratives have plausibility because they succeed in displaying a believable character.[37] But how are we to specify the grounds for preferring one story to another, something we often find quite difficult to do?[38] Hauerwas then approaches this question through a discussion of the story of Saint Augustine as told in the *Confessions*, showing how Augustine moves step by step from one story to another until he arrives at the true story, which is not explanation but narrative.[39] It is this story that gives coherence to a person's life, and which can be judged by certain criteria. Hauerwas writes:

---

[32] Hauerwas, *The Peaceable Kingdom*, p. 62.
[33] Hauerwas, *Truthfulness and Tragedy*, pp. 15 et seq.
[34] Hauerwas, *Truthfulness and Tragedy*, p. 15.
[35] Hauerwas, *Truthfulness and Tragedy*, p. 22.
[36] Hauerwas, *Truthfulness and Tragedy*, pp. 28–9.
[37] Hauerwas, *Truthfulness and Tragedy*, p. 30.
[38] Hauerwas, *Truthfulness and Tragedy*, p. 31.
[39] Hauerwas, *Truthfulness and Tragedy*, pp. 31–4.

Any story which we adopt, or allow to adopt us, will have to display:
(1) power to release us from destructive alternatives;
(2) ways of seeing through current distortions;
(3) room to keep us from having to resort to violence;
(4) a sense of the tragic: how meaning transcends power.[40]

One may well agree with these criteria, but how are we to determine what is a destructive alternative and what counts as distortion? Why Christianity, and why not the Manichees? It all depends on your point of view, your narrative, and Hauerwas does not provide criteria that transcend narrative. All his criteria are internal to narrative itself: some narratives may glorify violence, though clearly Hauerwas's pacifist narrative does not: but can we say that the *Iliad* is to be rejected for that reason? However, he does provide important hints: an irrational or incoherent narrative is to be rejected, which supposes that there is some independent account of what rationality and coherence are. One also notes his interesting but undeveloped point about us adopting narratives, but some narratives adopting us. This may be of importance, for it hints that different narratives may be appropriated in different ways. This question will have to be followed up later.

Hauerwas returns to the question of narrative and rational justification in a later section of the book.[41] Here the question of truth is raised again thus:

> The emphasis on story as the grammatical setting for Christian convictions is the attempt to remind us that Christian convictions are not isolatable 'facts', but those 'facts' are part of a story that helps to locate what kind of 'fact' you have at all.
>
> In other words, I am interested in 'story' and theology not because the narrative form may be a way of avoiding how religious convictions may or may not be true. Instead I hold the more positive view that the story quality of the gospels provides the appropriate context to raise the issue of truth at all.[42]

In other words, narrative is the condition for the question of truth, and without narrative, the question of truth does not arise. But what this seems to mean in reality, bearing in mind what has gone before, is that the justification of the story boils down to its practical application: does the story help us to live in the world? Does it involve us in a way of life?[43] Given that the story is 'a necessary way of seeing, transforming and to some extent re-expressing reality true to the form of human action' and a way of making 'intelligible the muddle of things we have done in order to have a self',[44] the justification of a particular story would seem to depend on its finding a suitable fit with reality. But by what criteria do we judge the appositeness or otherwise of such a fit?

So narrative theology in Hauerwas raises as many questions as it answers. One may maintain that human beings are narrative creatures, as Hauerwas would certainly like to do, and there are three possible reactions to this assertion. One can

---
[40] Hauerwas, *Truthfulness and Tragedy*, p. 35.
[41] Hauerwas, *Truthfulness and Tragedy*, pp. 71–81.
[42] Hauerwas, *Truthfulness and Tragedy*, p. 72.
[43] As above.
[44] Hauerwas, *Truthfulness and Tragedy*, p. 76.

say it is true and it is very important. One can say it may well be true, but it is of minor or no importance. Or one can deny that it is true. But how is one to prove each of these conflicting theses? The only way to go forward in narrative theology seems to be the Hauerwas way: namely to maintain that narrative is somehow 'beyond' proof external to itself; in other words to say that narrative is the way we are – it is constitutive of our being as humans – it is a given that does not need to be proved. This is in contrast to what we have seen of MacIntyre's position on the rationality of tradition and the possibility of dialogue between traditions.

Following Hauerwas, one could maintain that narrative by its nature is not susceptible to 'rational' proof, and that to bring to narrative the alien categories of rationalism is to destroy it. If one is listening to a story, it is necessary to enter into the spirit of the story – otherwise the story makes no sense. One cannot enjoy *Cinderella* without first accepting the preconceptions of the genre: to object that the tale is unrealistic is to miss the point. Such an objection would signify that you did not want to listen to this story, but preferred some other story. This brings us, of course, to the point that is made repeatedly in narrative theology: the story is not free-standing, it is part of a tradition, it is embedded in a nest of preconceptions that make up a tradition, and that tradition is grounded in a community, which in its turn is nourished by stories. The only view is the view from within.

Thus we have a circular, and perhaps closed, movement: a community has a tradition which is explicated in stories which nourish the community, reinforce its tradition, and lead to new stories being told.[45] This supposes, as in the Deuteronomy passage, a symbiotic relationship between theology, prayer, Church or community tradition and liturgy, the 'acting out' of that tradition. This is a specifically religious vision, but, as we have seen, it does not have to be exclusive to religion. It reminds us of the place of Homer in Athenian society, as described by MacIntyre. But Hauerwas's position is different to that of MacIntyre, discussed earlier, concerning the way people of differing narratives can communicate with each other, through recourse to a reason common to all.

The difference of approach between Hauerwas and MacIntyre on the justification of narratives is in fact a difference in approach to the role of reason and, by implication, the role of reason in theology. Hauerwas has much to say on the use of reason in theology, which represents the other side of the coin to his position on narrative. His turn to narrative is the result, one feels, of a diffidence about the role of reason in theology.

Hauerwas calls the idea of God-given unchangeable moral principles into doubt.[46] While some may long for the absolute and be tempted into dogmatism, this merely

---

[45] This is the conclusion of Hauerwas's examination of the novel *Watership Down* by Richard Adams; see *A Community of Character*, pp. 12–35. Earlier, in 'Visions, Stories and Character', originally published in 1973, see *Hauerwas Reader*, pp. 165–170, Hauerwas has the following to say: 'Poetry and literature do not just bolster our moral intentions; they affect how we perceive the world and hence what the moral life is about. For poetry does not just describe the known; it reveals dimensions of the unknown that make the known seem unfamiliar.' (p. 167). But this interesting point about the way narrative points to what lies beyond it is not developed.

[46] Hauerwas, *The Peaceable Kingdom*, p. 1.

masks profound doubt: 'We hold certain beliefs as if they are unconditioned, yet [we] are impressed with the knowledge that all beliefs are the result of environment, and thus at least potentially arbitrary.' This means we are unwilling to expose what we think to critical scrutiny, but prefer to retreat to the fortress[47] or moral exclave. Hauerwas, while stressing the historical particularity of belief, is also aware of a danger: a historical and particular belief system may choose to shut itself off from the world.

But Hauerwas is also aware of the opposite danger, that of a rationalized faith. Like MacIntyre, Hauerwas attacks the Enlightenment, here in the form of Kant whose categorical imperative renders history irrelevant. Indeed Hauerwas notes that Kant tries to make the moral point of view the perspective of anyone, but this desire to make morality necessary and universal distorts the nature of morality. In addition, finding such a universal and necessary foundation to ethics makes religious convictions secondary.[48] This is clearly a major concern with Hauerwas, as we shall see: if we can claim with Kant that morality is accessible to all via reason alone without the need for religious faith, then surely we make faith redundant, and theology with it, leaving moral theology to collapse into some sort of secular ethics. Such secular ethics will be flavourless stuff, having no real attachment to history, in other words to lived situations – though of course one can claim with MacIntyre that Kant's universalism is in fact an illusion and he is a typical man of his time.[49] Above all, universalist ethics will raise a question about the relationship between natural knowledge and revelation: is morality purely natural, or is it revealed, or do the two coincide? Does revelation make natural knowledge redundant, or vice versa?[50] Hence we see the attack on the Enlightenment is not purely philosophical but raises important questions for the very nature of theology itself. As we shall see, Hauerwas stands for, in want of a better phrase, a truly theological theology.

---

[47] Hauerwas, *The Peaceable Kingdom*, pp. 2–3.

[48] Hauerwas, *The Peaceable Kingdom*, p. 11.

[49] 'Kant never doubted for a moment that the maxims that he had learned from his own virtuous parents were those that had to be vindicated by rational test... Although Kant's Lutheran childhood in Konigsberg was a hundred years before Kierkegaard's Lutheran childhood in Copenhagen the same inherited morality marked both men', MacIntyre, *After Virtue*, p. 44.

[50] '…. How do morality and religion relate? Is something right because God commands it, or because it is right? If the latter, then why do we need God to command it?', Hauerwas, *The Peaceable Kingdom*, p. 11. This question has also been tackled by Alasdair MacIntyre: 'Nonetheless the law declared to us in revelation is the same law as that which we recognise in the moral requirements imposed by our own human practical understanding and reasoning, when they are in good order. So that when we become able to hear and respond to what Jesus Christ has to say to us, we do not have to leave behind or discard anything that we have genuinely learned concerning the moral law through reasoning. Grace often corrects, as well as completes, what we have so far taken to be the conclusions of reason, but, when grace does correct us, it is always because we have in some way failed as reasoners', MacIntyre, 'How can we learn what *Veritatis Splendor* has to teach us?', *The Thomist*, 58 (1994): 171–95, p. 175. This article represents one of MacIntyre's few excursions into theology as such, and shows him to be, once again, far more confident about the role of reason than Hauerwas, or, as we shall see, Engelhardt.

On top of this, Hauerwas makes a point that is new and interesting: this sort of Kantian universalism invites people to coercion, on the grounds that dissenters can be characterized as unreasonable and thus ought to be forced to be reasonable.[51] One has to acknowledge the justice of this point – a universalist morality gives those in power an extra stick – that of sweet reason – with which to beat the dissenter. One remembers that this particular book of Hauerwas's is concerned with among other things the centrality of non-violence in Christian ethics.[52]

So Hauerwas does two things: he has made the turn from universalism to historicism, and stressed that reason is fragmented and weak and that the Enlightenment Project has failed. But Hauerwas is a very nuanced writer and is aware, not just of the dangers of a Kantian rationalism but also of the perils of fideism which is the refuge of weak faith: 'The less sure we are of our religious convictions, the more we consider them immune from public scrutiny. But in the process we lose what is essential to their being true, namely that we be willing to commend them to others.'[53] In other words, if we feel that reason has failed us and that our narrative convictions can be justified in no other way except through the narrative itself, then we may retreat into fideism, the belief that faith can do without reason altogether. But Hauerwas points out that faith without reason is not strong faith (though it may seem to be) but a weak faith, frightened to show its face, knowing that it has no real support from the reason that is common to all people. To counter this fideistic temptation, he urges 'the necessity of witness [which is] ... at the heart of the Christian life.' Without such witness we would abandon the world to violence.[54] The necessity of witness to the world might mean some sort of common language in which to speak with the world, but 'Christians are distinct from the world.' There are points of contact between Christian ethics and secular ethics but they are not sufficient to provide a basis for a universal ethic grounded in human nature *per se*. Such an ethic would be minimalist and tempt people to violent coercion of 'irrational' dissenters. From a natural moral law standpoint such violence and coercion become conceptually intelligible, for universal presumptions make the acceptance of dissent difficult.[55]

Hauerwas goes on to provide an attack on the moral autonomy advanced by Joseph Fuchs[56] and Catholic natural law ethics,[57] which both serve to sideline the importance of revelation and the particularity of Christianity. But at the same time Hauerwas is nuanced in his approach: he acknowledges that grace and nature are a continuum.[58] In other words, to see revelation and nature as radically separate is a false dichotomy, and thus natural knowledge and the use of reason will have a role to play in religious moral thinking. He does not deny that 'all knowledge of God is

---

[51] Hauerwas, *The Peaceable Kingdom*, p. 12.
[52] Hauerwas, *The Peaceable Kingdom*, p. xvii.
[53] Hauerwas, *The Peaceable Kingdom*, p. 14.
[54] Hauerwas, *The Peaceable Kingdom*, pp. 14–15.
[55] Hauerwas, *The Peaceable Kingdom*, pp. 60–61.
[56] Hauerwas, *The Peaceable Kingdom*, pp. 57–9.
[57] Hauerwas, *The Peaceable Kingdom*, pp. 63–4.
[58] Hauerwas, *The Peaceable Kingdom*, pp. 58.

at once natural and revelatory'.[59] However, the knowledge of what is human alone is not a sufficient basis for Christian ethics:

> To be Christian is surely to fulfil the most profound human desires, but we do not know what such fulfilment means on the basis of those desires themselves. It is certainly right that life in Christ makes us more nearly what we should be, but that is not to say we must start with the human to determine what it means to be a disciple of Christ. While the way of life taught by Christ is meant to be an ethic for all people, it does not follow that we can know what such an ethic involves 'objectively' by looking at the human.[60]

What is needed then is a reliance on the story of Christ as the basis for Christian ethics; the study of what is human is posterior to this essential *a priori*. But this can lead us into the error of arbitrariness, and he is aware of the counter-charge that 'to emphasize the revelation within the Christian community seems to be anti-rational'.[61] He is thus careful to defend himself from the charge of arbitrariness on the model of divine command theory, the idea that something is good and moral simply because God has commanded it thus, with no reference to natural reason.[62] In so doing, he commits himself to a particular model of revelation.

> It has become popular to say that revelation is not concerned with propositions, but is instead the self-disclosure of God. Thus many speak of 'revelatory events' – the 'Exodus event' or the 'Resurrection event'. They often wish to suggest that revelation does not make claims about what happened, but about the meaning of what happened. In contrast, it is my contention that revelation involves propositional claims, none of which can be isolated by themselves, but are intelligible only as they form a coherent narrative.[63]

In other words, we must see God's revelation of himself as God's revelation of the narrative about himself. God's revelatory narrative will, too, contain propositional claims. Once again we see the a priori nature of the Christian narrative, which is both natural and revelatory: the question as to whether something is right because God commands it or because it is right of itself is thus answered by saying that this either/or dichotomy is a false one; the answer should be both/and, for 'I find the traditional distinction between natural knowledge of God and revelation to be misleading.'[64]

Thus we see how Hauerwas's narrative approach involves the danger of falling into fideism through the rejection of natural reasoning; and we see how stoutly Hauerwas defends himself from such a charge, aware of the dangers of fideism as he is. Whether he in fact acquits himself on all charges is another matter. One person who takes the view that he does not is James Gustafson.

---

[59] Hauerwas, *The Peaceable Kingdom*, p. 66.
[60] Hauerwas, *The Peaceable Kingdom*, p. 58.
[61] Hauerwas, *The Peaceable Kingdom*, p. 64.
[62] Hauerwas, *The Peaceable Kingdom*, p. 65.
[63] Hauerwas, *The Peaceable Kingdom*, p. 66.
[64] As above.

In his 1985 address to the Catholic Theological Society of America,[65] Gustafson says that Hauerwas represents 'the sectarian temptation': instead of trying to seek *aggiornamento*, which could lead to a dilution of the tradition, he has instead chosen to retreat into the tradition, where he can retain his certainties. He has chosen to make the narrative normative, but by what criteria is such a narrative chosen? There is a danger of sectarianism here, and a lack of dialogical interaction. This separates the Church from the culture, but historically the Church has never been separated from the culture; it has always been related to other patterns of life. Religious knowing is not distinct from other sorts of knowing; rather there can be correction and revision across discourses.[66]

This rejoinder to Hauerwas, and indeed his reply that Gustafson is overconfident about the use of reason,[67] underline the fundamental divisions that lie at the very roots of ethics, between those who choose the narrative path and those who do not. What we have here is not simply a disagreement about substance, but a disagreement about method and procedure, aim and scope, all founded on different theological approaches. What the controversy between Hauerwas and Gustafson illustrates most profoundly, though, is the charge that by making the narrative normative we are sliding towards sectarianism, that is to say a theology that turns its back on universal moral values, indeed universal values of any kind.

Indeed, by making the narrative normative, Hauerwas can only be understood in terms of his own tradition, from within it, rather than from the outside. His pacifism, for example, is admirable, but it is hard to justify outside the tradition in which he works: it would be impossible to try to use, for example, the just war theory of Augustine, or even the Saint's concept of peace, to draw out the significance of Hauerwas's position. The two worlds are alien to each other. So does this mean that this is the price we must pay if we are to make narrative the key category in theology? Perhaps like Hauerwas we will opt (or have no choice but to opt) for an ethics that is always to be adjectivally qualified. Hauerwas contends that all ethics is time and place bound, that the structure and nature of ethics is determined by a community's history and convictions. Ethics does not transcend history; similarly ethics always needs to be qualified in some way: there is no 'pure' ethics, but only Jewish ethics, Roman Catholic ethics and so on; this adjectival qualification helps us understand the social and historical quality of all ethics. But, if all morality is particular, this means that wide-ranging agreement may never be reached and that each must retreat to the nearest congenial group of 'moral friends' that he can find. This is exactly what Hauerwas has chosen to do, Gustafson argues.

---

[65] For a discussion of his controversy with Hauerwas, and a suggestion about how it might be resolved see the account of Terence P. Reynolds, 'A Conversation Worth Having: Hauerwas and Gustafson on Substance in Theological Ethics', *Journal of Religious Ethics*, 28 (2000: 395–421, which we shall follow here. Reynolds thinks the controversy is resolvable through dialogue (pp. 412–13) though cynics may think this is just another example of the interminability of moral discourse of which MacIntyre talks in *After Virtue*.

[66] Reynolds, pp. 397–9.

[67] Reynolds, p. 399.

Hauerwas is certainly an interesting and challenging theologian. Most of his books are in fact collections of pieces originally published as articles, and rarely does he develop the full implications of the concepts he holds. We may well agree that the Christian faith is best understood as a narrative, and that we are called to imitate Christ; likewise that a community has to have a narrative if it is to be a real community; but the implications of these beliefs may lead us in directions we might rather not take. Above all he raises important questions about the role of reason in theology and in narrative theology in particular. These are questions to be tackled later. Now let us turn to another philosopher theologian who admires both MacIntyre and Hauerwas, and who shows us in what further directions a narrative theology may lead us.

Chapter 4
H.T. Engelhardt

In Hugo Tristan Engelhardt we meet a thinker who often follows explicitly in the footsteps of MacIntyre and Hauerwas, but who, unlike them, seems to have abandoned all faith in rationality and all real interest in dialogue with those who hold different narratives. As such, Engelhardt is of immense interest, as he shows us one direction (perhaps not the right one) in which narrative moral theology can go, should it choose to do so.

Engelhardt takes as his starting point in the introduction to his 1996 book[1] on the foundations of bioethics a point of view that is distinctly more gloomy than that of MacIntyre in the first chapter of *After Virtue*. Indeed, his view is more reminiscent of that of John Dominic Crossan: the darkness is indeed total and the lighthouse utterly gone.[2] He asserts that finding agreement on ethical subjects is impossible, and that the search for the canonical, secular and concrete ethics is doomed to failure; the best we can do is try to reach agreement on procedure and content ourselves with a content-less ethics, abandoning any attempt to try and find a moral account that will appeal across divisions, an overarching moral point of view that all can share: 'This book,' he tells us right at the start, 'recognises the impossibility of discovering the secular, canonical, concrete ethics'.[3]

The desire to find one point of view, he continues, one narrative, to which all can subscribe – which would entail a common rationality, and a common set of conclusions, not just procedures – is a hangover from the Enlightenment that believed that such an account was possible: indeed Engelhardt focuses on the failure of what he calls (borrowing MacIntyre's phrase) the Enlightenment Project.[4] Today we are faced not with one rationality but competing rationalities, all of which are incommensurable. There is an embarrassment of riches which lead to a deafening moral cacophony; many rival accounts, none of which can be right, all of which must be wrong. As with philosophies, so with theologies: each makes a universal claim, none can command universal allegiance in a world that is fragmented and apathetic, presumably as a result of the fragmentation. The search for a content-rich ethics is an elusive quest, like the search for the Holy Grail or the unicorn. The best that can be done is to agree on procedure,[5] and to allow a necessarily permissive ethics, subject of course to agreement. The alternative is an ethics imposed by one

---

[1] H. Tristan Engelhardt, Junior, *The Foundations of Bioethics* (second edition, Oxford: Oxford University Press, 1996). The first edition dates from 1986.
[2] Engelhardt, *Foundations of Bioethics* p. 9 et seq.
[3] Engelhardt, *Foundations of Bioethics*, p. vii.
[4] Engelhardt, *Foundations of Bioethics*, p. viii, p. xii.
[5] Engelhardt, *Foundations of Bioethics*, p. x.

group on the rest by force, which is clearly unacceptable. Meanwhile each group of moral friends can practice 'content-full' ethics in institutions of its own – Catholic hospitals, Jewish nursing homes, and others such – and meet moral strangers on the very narrow common ground marked out by the two principles of beneficence and permission, which do not establish a canonical morality but rather give a few sparse guidelines that can be followed, 'the sparse morality that binds moral strangers'.[6]

Of interest here is the equivalence that is posed between narrative and rationality. A narrative is not simply the story told, but the way a story is told: all the preconceptions that are shared by teller and hearer that make the story intelligible. In other words, the narrative represents a shared world and a shared rationality. But with the collapse of the Enlightenment Project there is now no common world and no common rationality, and no common story. If one wants to put this in narrative terms, the story is that of the Tower of Babel: a common project that united us all has failed, has collapsed into mutually incomprehensible languages, and all of us have gone our separate ways.

If this is true, the consequences are serious indeed. Engelhardt claims that little can be established by unaided reason in the ethical field – certainly much less than modern followers of Aquinas imagine.[7] We cannot appeal to a higher reason as a way out of our impasse. He denies that natural moral law is accessible to reason alone, but these are things that he does not stop to prove. Engelhardt is convinced that the search for agreement, the very idea of moral dialogue, is simply a waste of time, a failure to realize the existence of 'the irremedial plurality of postmodernity'. People who carry on the search for agreement – and all dialogue presupposes that some agreement is possible, surely – have simply not woken up to this basic fact.

> Many of those who work in applied ethics or bioethics seem to disregard these difficulties that lie at the very roots of modern thought. Many proceed with the task of applying ethics as if it were obvious which secular ethic ought to be applied. Many provide bioethics consultations or advice as if there were one content-full bioethics, one canonical content-full bioethical orthodoxy, that should guide all secular moral decisions and justify all health care policy. Such consultations and advice can then lead to imposing a particular moral vision, ideology, or moral orthodoxy as if it were required by reason itself... The only problem is that such does not exist. Moreover there are diverse and profoundly different moral understandings: bioethics is in the plural. This book explores the consequence of this state of affairs: the irremedial plurality of postmodernity.[8]

If Catholics and other Christians, or people of no faith, co-operate, in, for example, the hospice movement in the United Kingdom, they are in fact doing so in denial of moral diversity, masking their deep divisions with a mere show of harmony. Scratch beneath the surface and this is bound to appear. 'Moral diversity is real' according to Engelhardt; those who believe that moral diversity is in fact capable of

---

[6] Engelhardt, *Foundations of Bioethics*, p. xii.
[7] Engelhardt, *Foundations of Bioethics*, p. 16 and particularly note 32 on p. 31. See also his later book, *The Foundations of Christian Bioethics* (Lisse: Swets and Zeitlinger, 2000), p. 73 and accompanying note for a similar point.
[8] Engelhardt, *Foundations of Bioethics*, p. 9.

being remedied through dialogue and reasoned argument, or else that the differences are more apparent and real, and at root agreement is possible, are simply fooling themselves. Why? Because 'there is no content-full morality without a particular moral commitment. There is no content-full bioethics outside of a particular moral perspective'.[9] This is the fundamental point: there can be no moral belief without a particular moral commitment (such as membership of a faith community); and there can be no moral outlook without a particular moral perspective: in other words, one's beliefs on any single issue cannot be understood to be freestanding, but rather they are in continuity with one's beliefs on everything else, one's moral perspective, one's position in space and time, one's narrative.

Thus what often presents itself as a purely philosophical view (one seemingly backed up by abstract argument) is nothing of the sort, but rather the reflection of the person who holds his position as a member of this or that community, this or that tradition, and a product of their particular lived history. In other words belief is something that comes to us as narrative, not as something that can be sustained through seemingly universal rational categories.

One positive thing must emerge from this. If Engelhardt is right, it means that every moral statement made, however freestanding it may claim to be, must be viewed within its context if it is to be properly understood; it must be seen as part of a narrative and rooted in tradition and community. This in turn means that the moral statement made is not ever merely a statement: it carries with it a commitment to a certain way of life, and a certain outlook on other matters as well. Thus the person making what seems to be a freestanding moral statement is in fact making a statement about the whole of their life. They are advancing a vision about the whole of life. The moral statement is the tip of the iceberg, and what lies beneath the surface is the whole story, perhaps a whole raft of views on family life, God, the role of women and Church discipline and authority,[10] in other words, a narrative.

The Narrative Quality of Experience

One of the things that has emerged so far in our discussion of Engelhardt is the idea that is found in both MacIntyre and Hauerwas as well, namely that there is no such thing as a freestanding statement: every assertion, no matter what its claims are about impartiality and abstract reasoning, is a view from somewhere and reflects the narrative unity of the person's life; every view is part of a narrative. This means further that every view must be examined as part of that narrative if it is to be fully understood. If this is the case, though, what is the narrative that inspires Engelhardt? Let us now take him at his word and see how his personal narrative is informing his views, and what that narrative may be. In so doing we shall discover important divergences from the more moderate positions of MacIntyre and Hauerwas.

Professor Engelhardt is a 'Catholic Orthodox' believer from Texas, a member of the Antiochene Church. The footnotes to *The Foundations of Bioethics* and *Bioethics*

---

[9] Engelhardt, *Foundations of Bioethics*, p. 3.
[10] Engelhardt is himself a case in point. See *The Foundations of Christian Bioethics*, p. 14, for his comprehensive views on patriarchy and by implication the role of women.

and Secular Humanism[11] reveal a man well versed in the Greek Fathers; he admits freely that they are of importance to him and to his beliefs.[12] One acknowledges that everyone has to be 'from somewhere' and to be from Texas does not disqualify one as a thinker! Likewise everyone is embedded in some sort of tradition, and to be embedded in the tradition of the Greek Fathers is surely admirable. But there are two presuppositions here: namely that everyone is rooted in a culture and everyone is rooted in a tradition; and that there is no view that is not culturally-formed and historically-expressed. As we shall see, these concepts are not beyond discussion, but for the moment, let us accept them, and in accepting them make it clear that just because Engelhardt is an Orthodox believer from Texas this does not disqualify him from serious consideration. On the contrary – it may mean that he has important insights that non-Texans and non-Orthodox may have missed. However, one thing has to be tackled at this stage: the view from Texas and Antioch cannot be characterized as a universalist view, but is rather a particularist one; Engelhardt himself would not dispute this; but is the choice of Texas and Antioch arbitrary? Why not Rome and California? Why not Wittenberg and Ohio? Or Geneva and Montana?

There are several answers one can give. One could argue that Antioch is intrinsically more interesting a place than Rome, but this might well lead to an interminable dispute between incommensurable traditions, of the type described by MacIntyre. One could simply say that having been born in Texas, and having come to faith in the Orthodox Church, the Engelhardt we have is the only Engelhardt we are likely to get, and we must choose the real over the ideal. Or else we can simply point out the following: if it takes a lifetime's apprenticeship to master a tradition, and given that we have only one life, it is unreasonable to expect a writer to have mastered more than one tradition. Engelhardt, though well versed in theology and ethics generally, has chosen to devote himself to one tradition, the Antiochene: it is unreasonable to hold this as a fault.

In fact Engelhardt is aware that his approach could be characterized as one-sided. In his recent book *The Foundations of Christian Bioethics*, he writes:

> Augustine of Hippo (354–430) plays little role in the tradition framing this book. This may seem odd. From the perspective of the West, Augustine is Christianity's major first millennium figure. He towers over other Latin Fathers in scope, depth and philosophical character of his work. It is impossible to conceive of the subsequent history of Roman Catholicism or of the emergence of Lutheranism and Calvinism in his absence. But for the East, Augustine was a bishop in far northwest Africa, who wrote in a language inaccessible to many of the major Christian thinkers of his time. [He was] on the periphery of Christianity, both geographically and culturally…[13]

Indeed that Augustine was on the periphery depends purely on your perspective. That Engelhardt writes in these terms is a sure sign that he realizes that his choices

---

[11] H.T. Engelhardt, Junior, *Bioethics and Secular Humanism, The Search for a Common Morality* (London: SCM, 1991) is in many ways the companion volume to *Foundations of Bioethics*.

[12] Engelhardt, *Bioethics and Secular Humanism*, p. 11, note.

[13] Engelhardt, *Foundations of Christian Bioethics*, p. 161.

are open to the charge of arbitrariness. But as we have said, it seems unreasonable to expect the Professor's approach to be that of the Encyclopaedia;[14] but that it is not, does of itself tell us a great deal about his presuppositions: theology and ethics are always the view from somewhere, from some tradition, and in the end the choice of tradition may be immune to rational justification.

One of the foundations of the Engelhardtian narrative is that religious belief cannot be the basis of a common bioethics as religious-based ethics cannot be shared. There is no common ground between religions and no common ground between religions and non-believers. This is because that which is known by faith cannot be translated into that which can be known by reason alone: the two discourses are radically different. That reason can establish a 'content-full' ethics without the assistance of faith is one of the mistakes, as he sees it, of Latin Christianity, which 'involved, in particular, a presumption that its morality could to a great extent be known and understood through reason without faith'.[15] Against this idea Engelhardt maintains that the Catholic hegemony of the middle ages was not born of agreement that came through a common reasoning, but imposed by force.[16] (Engelhardt has some hard things to say about the Inquisition and the intolerance of Catholicism, his point being that a universalist claim by religion is illusory – in the end people toe the line not because they are convinced but to avoid coming to the stake!) Unaided reason can establish very little and Aquinas was wrong to make such claims for it.[17] In an aside he makes clear that his is the Orthodox position – natural moral law is something revealed by God and not accessible to the unaided reason.[18] In ruling out any idea of a purely natural law and natural reasoning, Engelhardt is in fact drawing on his own religious tradition that stresses the weakness of reason and the importance of revelation. Ironically, he is doing the one thing he has previously ruled out as inadmissible: advancing a religiously based concept as a secular idea accessible to all. His assertion about the weakness of reason is revealed as a religiously inspired belief. On Engelhardt's own criteria it should be discounted.

The above of course is only true if we accept Engelhardt's narrative that religious belief has no place in the secular arena, and that faith and reason are radically diverse. Indeed, a belief that depends entirely on revealed faith can have no place in the secular arena simply because it will make no sense to someone who has no faith. Some religious believers, such as the Orthodox, may argue that cremation is wrong as it implies disrespect for the Holy Spirit that once inhabited that human body.[19] Non-believers may well see the coherence (or not) of this view, but, not believing in the inhabitation of the Holy Spirit themselves, they can hardly be expected to agree that cremation should be banned. One would have to advance a rational secular reason to support such a view, and while belief in the Holy Spirit's inhabitation may be rational (in the sense that it is coherent) it is not a reasonable reason or a secular

---

[14] As in MacIntyre's *Three Rival Versions of Moral Enquiry*.
[15] Engelhardt, *Foundations of Bioethics*, p. 4.
[16] Engelhardt, *Foundations of Bioethics*, p. 6.
[17] Engelhardt, *Foundations of Bioethics*, p. 16.
[18] Engelhardt, *Foundations of Bioethics*, p. 16 and p. 31, note 33.
[19] Thus, for example, Engelhardt, *Foundations of Christian Bioethics*, p. 335.

one: those who hold it are not irrational, but there is no compelling reason for non-believers to hold it as well.

But what if, contrary to Engelhardt's narrative, a religious belief can be advanced in rational and reasonable secular terms? I may believe in human rights because human beings are created in *imago Dei*, as the book of Genesis[20] says they are; but I may choose to present this belief about human dignity in purely secular terms, using, for example the arguments of Immanuel Kant. Would my Kantian position about no person being treated as a means but only as an end be vitiated by the simple fact that I am a Catholic believer? Cannot my Catholic morality in effect coincide with a secular morality? Does the fact that I am a Catholic give me no right to speak on moral subjects at all? Of course if one views religion as an irrational phenomenon entirely, one might then say that no religious person ought to be trusted to speak on any topic at all, but this is not a position that Engelhardt espouses.

His position is in fact that the Catholic belief in natural law and the power of reason to settle moral arguments and establish a moral point of view that can be shared with those outside the church is an illusion. Catholic arguments against abortion are familiar to all; they are universalist and abstract in approach, and hold that no abortion may ever be permitted, and that this is a logical and reasonable position to be held by all, and accessible to all. But in an aside,[21] Engelhardt asserts that the Christian position on abortion owes nothing to philosophy but is rather based on tradition and liturgical practice, specifically the celebration of the feasts of the conceptions of the Theotokos and Saint John the Baptist. This 'revealed' reason – or better, opposition to abortion as part of the Christian narrative, expressed in liturgy and story – is the basis for opposition to abortion; the philosophical arguments are presumably a sweetening of the pill in an attempt to get non-believers to agree. But opposition to abortion is in fact faith-based and narrative-based.

Engelhardt tells us that the justification of 'content-full' or substantive morality and its motivation can only be found in God. Morality is rational because God is the ground of all reason. God provides sanctions against misconduct. No secular account can do these things. A turn to moral proceduralism can save a 'shred' of morality, but this will be much less than what we would have wished for. One cannot answer questions about virtue outside a 'content-full' morality or vision of human flourishing,[22] or what we have termed a narrative.

One may well agree with this last statement, but not with the conclusions he draws from it. Certain actions are surely to be condemned irrespective of the narrative we hold. Once again we are faced with an internal contradiction in his position. He believes as a good Orthodox that God punishes sinners. For example, suicide is wrong in the context of a moral community; even though all ought to believe this, there are no secular arguments to communicate the wrongness of suicide.[23] Likewise, he maintains, anyone who has an abortion stands in danger of burning in hell, but the wrongness of abortion is not apparent to the mind unaided

---

[20] Genesis 1:26–7.
[21] Engelhardt, *Foundations of Bioethics*, p. 277, note 1.
[22] Engelhardt, *Foundations of Bioethics*, pp. 12–13.
[23] Engelhardt, *Foundations of Bioethics*, p. 76.

by revelation.[24] This implies that God will punish those who sin in ignorance; and when morality is described as 'rational', 'rational' is not to be taken as open to all, but rather in opposition to 'reasonable', that is coherent, but not compelling. One must therefore question Engelhardt's picture of God. His God is rational but at the same time beyond the grasp of unaided human reason. This would seem to indicate an utterly transcendent idea of God and a refusal to countenance any sort of natural theology.

This diffidence about natural theology – his Greek background – clearly colours Engelhardt's lack of faith about the Enlightenment project as well. Indeed he is consistently hostile to the Enlightenment project in his writing. His sense of God's transcendence can be contrasted with what he sees as the failure of Western Christianity which, by marrying theology to philosophy produced a philosophy that was no longer truly philosophical and a theology that was no longer theological.[25] The two disciplines in his view have to be kept separate if they are not to ruin each other: thus Catholicism has impoverished philosophy, emasculated it by taking away its independence, and also watered down its idea of God. This is a serious accusation and its gravity points to the fact that Engelhardt is just as much a theologian as an ethicist, perhaps more so than he recognizes.

What are we left with? There seems to be a mistake in Engelhardt's reasoning, particularly in the distinction he makes between the terms reasonable and rational. Let us take an example. A Catholic may well oppose abortion because they have celebrated the Feast of the Annunciation nine months before Christmas, meditated on the Gospel of the Visitation, and celebrated the Immaculate Conception nine months before the Nativity of Our Lady. Given that John the Baptist, the Virgin and Jesus himself were individual persons in the womb and from conception, the Catholic will regard abortion with horror. Abortion, in the context of the narrative, is to be condemned. But this does not mean that it is the narrative alone that makes abortion repellent. There are intrinsic qualities to the act of abortion that enable it to be fitted into this narrative in such a way. In other words the narrative is not arbitrary. Moreover, the intrinsic qualities that the narrative discovers in abortion are more than just capable of rational expression, they are compellingly so.

Consider a counter-example. In the context of the Exodus narrative, the eating of pork is forbidden. It is the narrative itself that makes the eating of pork wrong. Outside the narrative, there can be nothing wrong with eating pork. Indeed, no Jew would criticize a Gentile for eating pork, for the Gentile is outside the Covenant narrative. It is the narrative that imposes meaning on the act of abstinence.

In seemingly denying the compelling nature of intrinsic rationality or irrationality that some acts have, Engelhardt is in danger of reducing the idea of narrative to senselessness. The compelling conclusion ought to be that faith and reason go together and do not contradict each other, and do not have to be kept radically

---

[24] Engelhardt, *Bioethics and Secular Humanism*, p. xi.
[25] Engelhardt, *Foundations of Bioethics*, p. 16. Also p. 94, note 80: 'Indeed it has been argued that Western Christianity undermined its very own roots by attempting to establish Christianity by reason. By vainly attempting through reason to prove what faith should show, Western Christianity invited atheism.' See also pp. 20–23, note 7 for more of the same.

separated, which, as we have seen in previous chapters is the view of both Hauerwas and MacIntyre. A narrative can have many justifications, drawing on both faith and reason. In addition, this means that there is no compelling cause, as there would be in Engelhardt's world, to keep church and state, the religious and the secular, radically apart. The world of the Christian and that of the citizen are the same world. But let us look at this proposition in greater detail.

Tradition as Ecclesially Embodied Narrative

There are two main components to Engelhardt's narrative: first, that the failure of the Enlightenment project means that the only public ethics is one that abandons content in favour of procedure, with sparse results, and secondly, the reverse side of the coin, that content-full ethics is only possible in what he terms a 'moral exclave',[26] a moral community that has a vision of the good that is the basis of the moral choices it makes, a place where moral friends who all subscribe to one narrative may meet. Engelhardt finds his own moral exclave in the Antiochene Church, its traditions, its teaching and its liturgy which is the acting out of these traditions and teachings, and the focus of communitarian life.

The language of the above paragraph is not exclusive to Engelhardt. MacIntyre, as we have already seen, speaks of the failure of the Enlightenment Project, and the importance of narrative, community and tradition. The closing pages of *After Virtue* seems to hint at the idea of new moral communities on the Benedictine model. Hauerwas too emphasizes the communitarian nature of the Church. However, of particular interest is Engelhardt's emphasis on the apartness of the moral exclave which is something foreign to both MacIntyre and Hauerwas. While Hauerwas is eager for dialogue between the Church and the world, MacIntyre, at least in his more recent writings, sees dialogue between narratives as not just desirable but necessary:

> To engage in this dialogue of question and answer, so that we make ourselves accountable to others and treat ourselves as accountable to them, we have to become able to assume the other's point of view, so that the concerns to which we respond in giving our account are the ones that are in fact genuinely theirs. If we are successful in so doing, we become able to speak with the other's voice and, if the conversation between us is sufficiently extended through time and is wide-ranging enough in its subject matter, we will become able to speak with the voice of the other systematically, that is, to assert, to question and to prescribe in the light of the other's conception of the other's individual good and the other's conception of our common good. In achieving accountability we will have learned not only how to speak to, but also how to speak for the other. We will, in the home, or the workplace or in other shared activity, have become – in one sense of that word – friends.[27]

---

[26] Engelhardt, *Foundations of Bioethics*, p. 82.
[27] MacIntyre, *Dependent Rational Animals*, p. 150.

But by contrast Engelhardt has already dismissed the very idea of moral friendship. More important for him is liturgy, which may well be an aspect of moral theology that has been neglected in the West. Indeed he writes:

> It is in this context of worship, hierarchical approbation, and eucharistic transformation that there is fullness. It is through the liturgy that the Christian moral life, including Christian bioethics, gains its orientation. It is here that the Church is *katholike*, that the Church has its wholeness or completeness. The sociology of Christian knowledge, morality, and bioethics, is communal, liturgical, eucharistic, and hierarchical. The importance of the liturgical assembly for acquiring the content of Christian belief and therefore of a Christian bioethics is easily underestimated. The Liturgy is not usually appreciated as the focal point of moral theology... [28]

Engelhardt clearly believes that knowledge is gained in a communitarian fashion and not in isolation. However, this 'knowledge' is something infused by liturgical practice, as opposed to the 'question and answer' dialectic between communities that MacIntyre speaks of. While Engelhardt does not stop to explain how this knowledge is acquired, one can nevertheless conclude his idea of knowledge is very different from MacIntyre's. His as yet undeveloped communitarian epistemology fits well with the doctrine that what the Christian believes is what the Church believes and *vice versa*; in other words that belief is not individual but ecclesial. It is a narrative that is of its nature a shared reality. But how it works in practice remains mysterious, perhaps deliberately so.

Engelhardt goes on to argue that the liturgy embodies the living tradition of the Church, and the Church's living tradition is prior to the Scriptures, 'because the Church makes the Scriptures, not the Scriptures the Church'.[29] So the final arbiter in all matters of faith is not the authority of Scripture but the authority of the Church, that is to say the bishops, guaranteed by the indwelling of the Holy Spirit.[30] Disappointingly, then, Engelhardt's discussion of liturgy trails off into a discussion of authority, and not surprisingly either, as his version of Christian ethics is essentially authoritarian, as we shall see. Engelhardt quotes the Liturgy of St Basil as an argument against abortion,[31] but this is not an argument that could possibly be binding on anyone who has not previously acknowledged the authority of the liturgy in these matters. It is not an argument as such, but an authoritative statement.

Contrasted with the authority that flows from tradition and which permeates the Orthodox Church, we have the stark alternative of a world which has no authority apart from the bare permission principle, and certainly no community. This, as far as Engelhardt is concerned, is the only alternative to a moral exclave. There is no third way. Engelhardt avers that no true content-full public ethics is possible at all – something that may remind us of Nietzsche.[32] While MacIntyre proposes a dialogue

---

[28] Engelhardt, *Foundations of Christian Bioethics*, pp. 191–2.
[29] Engelhardt, *Foundations of Christian Bioethics*, p. 193.
[30] Engelhardt, *Foundations of Christian Bioethics*, p. 202.
[31] Engelhardt, *Foundations of Christian Bioethics*, pp. 192–3.
[32] MacIntyre, *Three Rival Versions of Moral Enquiry*, p. 49: 'Nietzsche did not advance a new theory against older theories; he proposed an abandonment of theory.' Just like Engelhardt!

between traditions, Engelhardt sees such attempts at dialogue as futile. There can be no real communication between those inside the moral exclave and those outside it. Each exclave is a closed fortress.

This point is made with force in a recent collection of essays[33] where Engelhardt asks himself whether Roman Catholic moral theology can offer more than secular morality provides. For a Catholic, he asserts, 'The real goal is eternal life'.[34] This being so, he suggests that we need to ask ourselves whether keeping someone alive at great expense is worth it, and not just from a financial point of view. 'At what point may the use of such resources distract from the struggle toward salvation?'[35] This is a very strange question! Engelhardt is here supposing that an unbeliever who has no belief in the afterlife and a Catholic who does should be treated differently when they are in life threatening situations. In other words like cases should not be treated in a like manner, because for a Catholic the cardinal truth is that 'this life is not the only life' and the Catholic has a radically different appreciation of the meaning of suffering.[36] A Catholic patient in hospital, whether that hospital were Catholic or secular, would, one imagines, be alarmed to be informed that their treatment would take a different course from the person in the next bed who was suffering from the same disease, because they were Catholic and the other not! Catholics understand suffering better than others, perhaps: but does this mean they should be given fewer painkillers? Of course not! Like cases must be treated in like ways, whoever the patient is, whatever their beliefs.[37] And the reason for this is quite simple: there is no difference in content between Catholic bioethics and human bioethics, at least in this case.

Engelhardt asks whether Catholic and secular bioethics are indeed materially equivalent – but also asks whether the Paschal mystery adds something to our view of life and death.[38] He seems to think that the answer to the first question must be no; and that Catholic bioethics (and the same must be true for ethics in general) are caught in a cleft stick, claiming to be universal and thus denying any specific Christian character, for 'we are by faith committed to reason's ability to disclose morality's content'.[39]

Engelhardt sees this is a problem because he is clearly wedded to the idea of a specifically Christian bioethics which is the gift of grace. But if we adhere to the standard Catholic view that the Christian revelation adds nothing to the content of ethics, this difficulty disappears. But it is precisely this view that Engelhardt cannot

---

[33] H. Tristan Engelhardt, Junior, and Mark Cherry (eds), *Allocating Scarce Medical Resources, Roman Catholic Perspectives* (Washington, DC: Georgetown University Press, 2002).
[34] Engelhardt and Cherry (eds), *Allocating Scarce Medical Resources*, p. 4.
[35] Engelhardt and Cherry (eds), *Allocating Scarce Medical Resources*, p. 4.
[36] Engelhardt and Cherry (eds), *Allocating Scarce Medical Resources*, p. 10.
[37] For the absurd contrary position, see Engelhardt, *The Foundations of Christian Bioethics*, pp. 382–3, where he imagines what he calls 'Vaticare' which would be dispensed to patients in a Catholic hospital *proportionem status*, ranging in quality all the way from luxury 'Papalcare' down to the less than basic 'MotherTeresaCare'.
[38] Engelhardt and Cherry (eds), *Allocating Scarce Medical Resources*, p. 12.
[39] Engelhardt and Cherry (eds), *Allocating Scarce Medical Resources*, p. 14.

accept, believing as he does that a rational universal ethics is an impossibility. The only possible view is a view from somewhere which will always remain from somewhere and thus only make sense to the people who share that somewhere's suppositions. One cannot make the leap from the particular to the universal; one cannot escape one's genealogy. For Engelhardt the tension between the particular and the universal 'is at the core of the identity crisis of much of contemporary Western Christianity'.[40] Presumably the Orthodox churches, with their more 'embedded' approach and their diffidence about making universal claims, are less troubled by this tension.

What we are left with then is the private moral world, the closed community, the moral exclave, the cosy environment where one can meet with likeminded 'moral friends', what might be called with greater justice the ghetto. For Engelhardt clearly envisions Catholic hospitals that will carry out policies that will appear in the eyes of the general public to be mad, or at the very least without justification. Is this where a narrative moral theology will end up? Though one appreciates that substantive morality is nourished in communities of like minded people, who support their belief with a shared narrative and tradition, any belief that cannot bear exposure in the public forum, any belief that lacks public plausibility, is doubtfully worthy of belief. This is not something that Engelhardt considers – the necessity of dialogue with the world, so that faith may be tested against experience. If the reason of God is not accessible to ordinary people unassisted by grace, is it worthy of belief? If a narrative is not accessible to ordinary people in some way, is it worthy of belief? Is God, in asking us to believe in him and to believe him, asking us to stop thinking at the same time? Does a particular narrative represent a flight from reality? Is there a radical discontinuity between thought and faith? In Engelhardt's book it would seem so.[41]

Further evidence for the dualism at the heart of Engelhardt's thought is found in his treatment of the concept of the secular. He describes the secular city as the place where saint and sinner meet, a neutral place, and claims that this concept is derived from Augustine, the *saeculum* being the place where the Earthly City and the City of God dwell side by side.[42] Again he says: 'The secular identifies the worldly structure we all share, as opposed to the spiritual structures we can share only by special grace.'[43] One notes here a division between secular and sacred, between grace and nature. Of course, people like George Jacob Holyoake (1817–1906) use the term 'secular' to mean that which 'replaces theology',[44] but this must not be allowed to obscure the fact that 'secular' is in origin a religious term, and Holyoake's use of it is radically different from Augustine's, and that Engelhardt's interpretation of

---

[40] Engelhardt and Cherry (eds), *Allocating Scarce Medical Resources*, p. 6.

[41] In fairness, one must point out that Engelhardt seems aware that he may be charged thus. He defends himself in a footnote, p. 31, note 33 of *Foundations of Christian Bioethics*: 'It us not as if there were ever nature without grace. Grace is not a *donum superadditum*. To appreciate the secular world is not to see the world as it is without grace, without the energies of God. It is rather to use the moral language that must be employed with those who live ignoring grace, ignoring those energies…'

[42] Engelhardt, *Bioethics and Secular Humanism*, p. 21.

[43] Engelhardt, *Bioethics and Secular Humanism*, p. 23.

[44] Engelhardt, *Bioethics and Secular Humanism*, pp. 27–8.

Augustine may not be the correct one. Engelhardt treats us to a long section entitled 'Seven Senses of Secularity'[45] and in talking of secular priests mentions the phrase 'in the world but not of it'[46] and one feels that here is the germ of an important truth that cannot be stressed enough: to be in the world (and thus secular) is not to be cut off from God *per se*. Adam and Eve were in the world in the Garden of Eden, but not cut off from God before the Fall, or indeed utterly cut off from him after it. The world, even after sin, remains a place of encounter with God. To be in the world is not to be entirely lost, and worldly things are not entirely deprived of divine grace or the capacity for it. Grace builds on nature and presupposes it; it does not annihilate nature and replace it by something else.[47] Thus one would like to revise Engelhardt's idea that the secular and the sacred are rigidly divided, radically different realms.

Augustine stresses that the two cities, the earthly and the eternal, are commingled on this earth and sometimes hard to distinguish, as Engelhardt notes. But his position in the *City of God* in fact goes further than that and is worth quoting:

> The heavenly city, meanwhile – or rather that part which is on pilgrimage in mortal life and lives by faith – must use this earthly peace until such time as our mortality which needs such peace has passed away. As a consequence, as long as her life in the earthly city is that of a captive and an alien (although she has the promise of ultimate delivery and the gift of the Spirit as a pledge) she has no hesitation about keeping in step with the civil law which governs matters pertaining to our existence here below. For as mortal life is the same for all, there ought to be common cause between the two cities in what concerns our purely human living.

There is no hint of a moral exclave here! And further on in the same chapter, Augustine makes the same point again:

> Thus the heavenly city, so long as it is wayfaring on earth, not only makes use of earthly peace but fosters and actively pursues along with other human beings a common platform in regard to all that concerns our purely human life and does not interfere with faith and worship.[48]

Here we see the language of engagement, rather than separation; though the Church is in exile and on pilgrimage, even alien (words that echo the language of the eleventh chapter of the letter to the Hebrews) the Church still benefits from being in the world and seeks dialogue with the world and non-believers. Above all we have the idea of a 'common platform [*compositionem*]' and 'keeping in step [*concordia*]':

---

[45] Engelhardt, *Bioethics and Secular Humanism*, pp. 22–31.
[46] Engelhardt, *Bioethics and Secular Humanism*, p. 23.
[47] This is a common theme in the work of Aquinas. For example, *Summa Theologiae*, I, qu. 1, art. 8, ad 2: '*Cum igitur gratia non tollat naturam sed perficiat, oportet quod naturalis ratio subserviat fidei sicut et naturalis inclinatio voluntatis obsequitur charitati*' [So that grace may not take away nature but rather bring it to perfection, it is necessary that natural reason should serve faith just as the inclination of the natural will serves charity]. This is exactly what Engelhardt does not hold, namely that *naturalis ratio* should have any role in the service of faith.
[48] Augustine, *The City of God*, Book XIX, chapter 17.

the assumption is that the world and the Church can find a common language and reach agreements about secular matters with those who do not share the faith. Quite different is Engelhardt's view: 'Traditional Christians in a post-Christian world are cultural deviants. They approach everything out of joint with the society around them. Everything is set within an all-encompassing project: salvation... The sum and the parts of all of this [Christian doctrine] are radically counter-cultural'.[49]

One suspects that Engelhardt sees salvation as salvation from the world, rather than of the world. Not for nothing does he speak of the 'chaos engendered by Vatican II'[50] and liken the work of the Council to that of the Red Guards;[51] he also speaks glowingly of Archbishop Levefre and the Society of Pius X.[52] It is clear that his use of the word 'traditional' is a loaded one.

The *saeculum*, the place created by God, is of its nature good – 'This beautiful world,' Augustine calls it, rejecting Origen's view of the soul as imprisoned in the body[53] – and with a potential to perfection: this insight lies at the root of the social teaching of the Catholic Church.[54] Why else would the Church wish to involve itself in the world unless it thought that the world was a place where such involvement would be useful and would bear fruit? Hence the Catholic hospital, of which Engelhardt shows such a marked lack of understanding,[55] is not some sort of theological laboratory concerned with living out the truth that 'the real good is eternal life' but first and foremost a hospital open to all people of all beliefs. A Catholic hospital that refused in principle to admit those who are not Catholics would not be worthy of the name; such a hospital cannot be an exclave and still less sectarian as it exists to serve all humanity. Certainly it has Catholic principles and will not perform, for example, abortion or female genital mutilation, but it is not a walled structure but an open one. Certainly Catholics will wish to talk to their moral friends in the Church, but they regard the whole world as at least a friend in potential, and certainly worth talking to.

The rigid division between secular and sacred that informs the writings of Engelhardt is an aspect of his opposition to the Enlightenment, a retreat, in religious terms, into the heresy of fideism. Of course, Engelhardt accuses the Catholic Church of the heresy at the other end of the spectrum, namely rationalism. He tells us he is opposed to 'the rationalist excesses (and other errors) of the Roman Patriarchate' and describes himself, tellingly, as 'embedded' in Orthodoxy.[56] Again, 'though faith in reason is largely lost, I have not lost the Faith'[57] – note the capital letter, and the way the two faiths are contrasted. Fideism is of course the natural refuge of many

---

[49] Engelhardt, *Foundations of Christian Bioethics*, p. 391.
[50] Engelhardt, *Foundations of Christian Bioethics*, p. 4.
[51] Engelhardt, *Foundations of Christian Bioethics*, p. 10.
[52] Engelhardt, *Foundations of Christian Bioethics*, p. xv and p. 54.
[53] Augustine, *City of God*, Book XI, chapter 23.
[54] Social justice particularly arouses Engelhardt's scorn: see *Foundations of Christian Bioethics*, p. 383.
[55] See the above discussion in Engelhardt and Cherry (eds), *Allocating Scarce Medical Resources*, p. 4. and also Engelhardt, *Foundations of Christian Bioethics*, p. 282.
[56] Engelhardt, *Bioethics and Secular Humanism*, p. 11, note 48.
[57] Engelhardt, *Bioethics and Secular Humanism*, p. xvii.

religious believers in times of philosophical decadence: Luther, who lived in a time of scholastic decay, springs to mind. But is all lost? Is the situation so very desperate? Must narrative be understood as something standing in opposition to rationality and reason? Is every narrative to be consigned to the ghetto?

What we have identified here is a fundamental weakness in the work of Engelhardt, and a weakness implicit at the very least in the work of MacIntyre, and to a greater extent perhaps, Hauerwas as well. If we are to accept narrative as the fundamental category in ethics and moral theology, and by extension the idea that narrative is only nurtured in specific communities and traditions, then, it seems, we are abandoning any idea of morality as being universally valid. If the Enlightenment Project has failed (and it may well have done so) are we forced to admit the uselessness of discursive rational argument? Engelhardt, perhaps more clearly than MacIntyre and Hauerwas shows us the consequences of so doing.

In both *Foundations of Bioethics* and *Bioethics and Secular Humanism*, Engelhardt does his best to disprove the basis for what he calls 'appeals to the formal character of reason'[58] in order to provide moral content. This may be done, he says, either through hypothetical choice theories or hypothetical contractor theories, but both fail, for similar reasons. In the first instance, the perfectly disinterested observer, who has no preferences, will have no moral sense either. He will be useless; if some sort of code of values is chosen, he will no longer be impartial; and how is such a code to be chosen? That was the very problem the theory set out to solve. Likewise, in the situation of a hypothetical contract, the 'thin theory of the good' with which those who are to choose will make their choice will presuppose the choice made.[59] This last criticism is made by others too: the conditions of the choice to be made are fair and impartial in name only.[60] In the other volume, Engelhardt makes this criticism more specific. John Rawls, he says, whose hypothetical contractor theory is the most widely known, presupposes the legitimacy of a particular moral sense, namely that of Cambridge, Massachusetts: his people in the Original Position are supposed to choose the greatest liberty possible; but why should they opt for political freedom? Might they not opt for economic freedom instead?[61] In other words, might they not prefer the opportunity of making lots of money to the enjoyment of political freedom, and accept some restrictions on freedom of speech for example, if this led to greater economic opportunities? Engelhardt is asking us to imagine an Original Position in which the greatest good is not liberty but prosperity,[62] in other words the values not of Cambridge, Massachusetts, but some other (unnamed) country. It is not our task here to defend Rawls – that will come later – but one can note in passing that Engelhardt presupposes what he is trying to argue here: why should political liberty and economic freedom be taken as mutually antagonistic? Why should anyone be asked to choose one or the other? Can one not choose both? One can imagine a

---

[58] Engelhardt, *Bioethics and Secular Humanism*, p. 104.
[59] Engelhardt, *Bioethics and Secular Humanism*, pp. 105–6.
[60] Thus Michael Walzer, *Spheres of Justice* (New York: Basic Books, 1983), p. 5.
[61] Engelhardt, *Foundations of Bioethics*, p. 51.
[62] Engelhardt, *Foundations of Bioethics*, p. 35.

society, surely, in which the freedom to get rich does not involve restrictions on political freedom.

Engelhardt's main objection to Rawls seems to be this: Rawls has set up a hypothetical theory that attempts to justify what it already presupposes; and a professor from Cambridge, Massachusetts, has discovered what he knew already, that Cambridge, Massachusetts, is the nicest place in the world! In other words the argument is circular: the argument, dressed up in abstract terms, betrays its origins. One mentions this, though, to point out that Engelhardt falls into the same trap: his conclusion about the failure of public reason is something that is stated at the outset of his book;[63] he then sets out to prove what he already believes by marshalling the available evidence. This is not the correct method of philosophical enquiry, which should consider evidence in an impartial manner – but such impartiality is impossible, and so we are back where we started. If all points of view are equally hampered by this particularity that can never be universal, so is Engelhardt's too. His theory is just one amongst many, and falls with them, subject to the same objection to any theory.

However, one could rescue the thought of Engelhardt from this criticism by pointing out, as he would surely want to do, that his is not a substantive theory, it is merely a procedure. Neither of the two principles he lays down which are to ensure peaceful co-existence have much by way of content. As for his Orthodox beliefs, grounded and rooted in the Church, these are beliefs that he openly declares – unlike those who pretend that they are able to place such beliefs to one side and argue as if they came from nowhere. In other words, Engelhardt gets full marks for honesty, whereas those who advance hypothetical contractor theories are deceiving the world and possibly themselves as well.

The Irrationality of Tradition

So does this mean that once we peel away the disguise of rationality what we are left with is irreducibly different narratives? Yes, says Engelhardt: rationality, this idea that things can be settled by reasoned argument, is an illusion:

> ... [T]here are major problems in reaching a rationally justified resolution of bioethical quandaries in secular pluralist societies. When the premises held in common are insufficient to frame a concrete understanding of the moral life, and if rational arguments alone cannot definitively establish such premises, then reasonable men and women can establish a common fabric of morality only through mutual agreement. The concrete fabric of morality must then be based on a will to a moral viewpoint, not on the deliverances of a rational argument.[64]

Thus, thanks to the failure of the Enlightenment Project, the inadmissibility of any religious vision, and the failure of natural law thinking, what may be called our general failure to agree on anything, Engelhardt establishes the very narrow basis for

---

[63] Engelhardt, *Foundations of Bioethics*, p. vii.
[64] Engelhardt, *Foundations of Bioethics*, p. 103.

any moral assertion independent of narrative on the idea of mutual agreement and the will to a moral viewpoint, later explicated in his two principles of procedure, that of permission and that of beneficence.

We now need to look at this idea of procedure and the two principals that it involves in greater detail, for in it Engelhardt is spelling out to us what we are left with once we reject narrative. The alternative is not encouraging. First of all, an objection: why should people who cannot agree on anything else decide to agree on his two principles? Why should these two principles win general agreement, when nothing else seems to be able to do so?[65] Secondly, what do we mean by 'a will to a moral viewpoint' that seemingly does not depend on rational argument? Does, can and should the will operate independently of reason? Thirdly, one can note that this disagreement in the moral sphere is attributed to secular pluralism: might one way of finding agreement be to abolish secularity and pluralism?[66] Is he trying to tell us that because the alternative is so terrible, we had better take refuge in narrative?

For indeed, the alternative does seem grim, and the argument does seem to reduce itself to absurdity. Having established agreement as the criterion of the only morality that can be shared by 'moral strangers', Engelhardt then defines the person as being self-conscious, rational and free to choose: the sort of person who can enter into agreements.[67] Clearly this definition is shaped by the centrality of agreement as the sole criterion of morality. Persons have rights because they are free to withhold their permission:

> Persons stand out as possessing a special importance for moral discussions. It is such entities who have secular moral rights for forbearance, because they can deny permission. Competent moral agents are those who participate in moral controversies and can resolve them by agreement. But they may also disagree. Because the fabric of authoritative cooperation among moral strangers depends on agreement, moral agents may not be used without their permission. This moral concern, it must be stressed, focuses not on human beings but on persons. That an entity belongs to a particular species is not important in general secular moral terms unless that membership results in that entity's being in fact a competent moral agent.[68]

If the principle of permission is one of the two very sparse principles that procedural and content-free morality is able to establish, and we can establish no metaphysical or rational basis for human rights beyond this (to do so would involve a narrative that not all could accept), it follows that people have rights simply because they have the ability to say no. However, not all persons are humans, and not all humans are persons: angels, being rational and self-conscious, are persons, while foetuses, infants, the profoundly mentally retarded and the hopelessly comatose are examples of 'human nonpersons'. These human beings are unable to enter into contracts, they

---

[65] Galston makes this same point about Hobbes's people coming to agreement: if they agree on nothing, why should they agree on peace? William Galston, *Liberal Purposes* (Cambridge: Cambridge University Press, 1991), p. 94.
[66] This last does seem to be the conclusion of his latest book.
[67] Engelhardt, *Foundations of Bioethics*, p. 136.
[68] Engelhardt, *Foundations of Bioethics*, p. 138.

cannot be blamed or praised for their actions; they are unable to enter into moral discourse and are incapable of giving permission.[69] All this is undeniably true, and it is true too, as Engelhardt states, that personhood is not reducible to biology, but the conclusion is frightening: such nonpersonal humans have no rights but are entrusted to the beneficence of persons.[70] It is clear then that there is no absolute break against their being humanely disposed of, if that is the kinder option. Of course, a Catholic hospital, in its island of moral friendship, would forbid euthanasia and abortion, but such a ban would have no foundation, would make no sense, in the world of moral strangers where procedural morality based on the principles of beneficence and permission is the only morality possible.

What this example 'proves' is that concepts such as human rights for the handicapped and the inarticulate depend on a narrative which gives dignity and importance to all human beings whatever their state and status. It seems clear that a world without such a narrative – and Engelhardt is the first to admit this – is not the moral world many would welcome with joy. Certainly he himself would not, as he tells us repeatedly.[71] But short of revelation, thanks to what he calls the silence of God, this is the only moral world that is possible, if we are to accept that universal moral laws can only be advanced on such a basis. It is one step from anarchy, but that is simply unavoidable. And yet he seems aware of the absurdity: in a longish discussion he tackles the vexed question as to whether sleeping persons have any rights.[72] After all, if a person is asleep, they are unable to engage in moral discourse or withhold permission. Do they then have any rights at all? Of course, they can be woken up and asked for permission, but does this mean we lose our status as holders of rights every time we fall asleep and regain it every time we wake up? That would an absurd conclusion. But the question itself is absurd. It is true that a corpse has no rights, but a person asleep is not some sort of temporary corpse; but, as Engelhardt would remind us, any discussion of what a person is is impossible as that presupposes some sort of content-full ethics which is an impossibility. Indeed, he solves what he calls 'this major puzzle' by saying that to kill or otherwise mistreat a sleeping person, taking advantage of their temporary inability to give or withhold permission would be 'acting against the possibility of a peaceable moral community'.

Despite this conclusion that it is in fact safe to fall asleep, one feels that nihilism is what we are left with. Why bother having children? Why bother getting married? Neither of these basic human activities makes any sense outside a content-full moral picture, the professor asserts:

> The traditional Judaeo-Christian appreciation of reproduction as a sacred act and the union of the couple cannot be appreciated within a secular context. A secular context lacks either the values to supply such content or the openness to the grace of God to disclose such

---

[69] Engelhardt, *Foundations of Bioethics*, pp. 138–9. Who decides when a coma is hopeless is not touched upon; neither the question of when an infant becomes a non-infant, or what constitutes profound retardation.

[70] Engelhardt, *Foundations of Bioethics*, p. 150.

[71] Engelhardt, *Foundations of Bioethics*, p. 13 tells us that while procedure can save a shred of ethics this is much less than we would have wanted.

[72] Engelhardt, *Foundations of Bioethics*, pp. 151–4.

values. Anything content-full, anything substantial about the meaning of sexuality or the purpose of reproduction can only be appreciated within a particular, content-full moral context. Outside such a context, no one can even understand why it is important to have children. Indeed outside of such a context it will not be possible in general secular terms (aside from financial and similar concerns, including tax consequences) to say why one should even bother to be married.[73]

Here we see an even more radical departure. Context is all. In other words, while a Catholic or an Orthodox believer might feel that marriage and having children is a good thing, willed by God, and that it has meaning in the context of the believer's life, and the narrative of Christianity, and while even a Marxist might consider them worthwhile from within the Marxist narrative, marriage considered in itself and having children considered in itself are completely meaningless activities. They make no sense, they do not contain of their nature clues to their meaning that can be deciphered by the human mind. The world of these phenomena is opaque: it is a tale of sound and fury, told by an idiot, signifying nothing.[74]

Here it seems that Engelhardt oversteps the mark and exaggerates somewhat. If marriage and having children are intrinsically meaningless activities (if that is indeed what he is saying) how are they capable of being part of a narrative? Can that which is intrinsically meaningless become meaningful through context alone? Surely it must have some intrinsic worth if it is capable of being part of a story? To assert otherwise is in the long run to assert that stories are *per se* arbitrary arrangements of elements that have meaning only because we give them meaning. In other words that the story we choose is the right story because we have chosen it, not because the story makes sense of itself.

Against Engelhardt's assertion that marriage and having children are intrinsically meaningless, we might reply that thousands of people every day marry and have children and find these activities worthwhile without perhaps holding some sort of narrative that teaches them that these are intrinsically good things to do. Common sense and our own experience tell us that there is meaning to life and that there is value in existence independent of one's religious (or other) beliefs and that this is not some illusion. But if this is so, then it would mean that some shared moral point of view might be possible after all, even if Engelhardt, like Ugolino of Pisa, has heard the key turn in the door, turn once and turn no more.[75] If, after all, there is an intrinsic rationality to things, then some sort of conclusion about reality can be reached and shared with others: all is not darkness after all. That narrative is possible proves that rationality exists; true, Engelhardt would say – but such a rationality could not be shared beyond the confines of the tradition and community in which the narrative is nurtured.

---

[73] Engelhardt, *Foundations of Bioethics*, p. 277.
[74] The same is said in his later work, see Engelhardt, *Bioethics and Secular Humanism*, p. 137: 'There is nothing one can say *a priori* about the meaning of well-being, the content of the good life, or the meaning of sickness, illness and death.' This sounds like nihilism pure and simple.
[75] Dante, *Inferno*, Canto XXXIII; and T.S. Eliot, *The Wasteland*, Part V.

The anarchic tendency of his work, his fundamental belief about the irrationality of the created order, can be further understood by examining his two principles of procedure.

Engelhardt states that his aim in *Foundations* is to establish, given the failure of the Enlightenment Project, 'a moral framework' or a 'moral perspective', so that those who share no content-full morality will still be bound by a shared moral fabric, which will save them from nihilism and relativism.[76] It is worth noting at this point that procedural ethics is regarded by our author as a moral enterprise, even if it has 'an unavoidably libertarian character' (not that one can attribute any moral value to freedom of choice).[77] However, this morality that binds moral strangers will be 'sparse'[78] – but it will still be morality. Working in a spirit of peaceable negotiation and with a minimum of moral assumptions,[79] we will come to recognize that the only source of secular moral authority is the authority of permission.[80] It is permission that authorizes action and the lack of it that makes that action illicit. This view is neither good nor rational but simply discloses a condition of possibility of human life generally.[81] And indeed, it does seem to be true that peaceful co-existence depends on people asking permission of others before acting in a way that affects them personally: the principle of permission keeps anarchy at bay. It is a fundamental 'school rule'. But the paramountcy of the permission principle establishes that people have no right to be coerced, and every right to do what is wrong in the eyes of others.[82] The second principle, that of beneficence, cannot use force to impose itself and cannot specify any content. Any specific actions must rest on agreement.[83] The principle of beneficence presupposes a moral vision, but this moral vision can only be supplied by the moral community that the individual belongs to[84] if it is to be of any practical use.[85] In fact it appears from the discussion of the two principles that the first, that of permission, is the more binding, and the second, that of beneficence is much less so: one is obliged to ask for permission, but when is one obliged to be beneficent?[86] The ties that bind us to beneficence seem much weaker. Engelhardt concludes somewhat lamely that beneficence is 'a general concern';[87] to fail to be beneficent cuts us off from other beneficent people, but to fail to ask permission puts us outside the peaceable community.[88] This strongly suggests that the principle of permission is by far the more pressing obligation and that beneficence remains

---

[76] Engelhardt, *Foundations of Bioethics*, p. ix.
[77] Engelhardt, *Foundations of Bioethics*, p. x.
[78] Engelhardt, *Foundations of Bioethics*, p. xii.
[79] Engelhardt, *Foundations of Bioethics*, p. 68.
[80] Engelhardt, *Foundations of Bioethics*, p. 69.
[81] Engelhardt, *Foundations of Bioethics*, p. 70.
[82] Engelhardt, *Foundations of Bioethics*, pp. 78, 103.
[83] Engelhardt, *Foundations of Bioethics*, p. 107.
[84] Engelhardt, *Foundations of Bioethics*, p. 108.
[85] Engelhardt, *Foundations of Bioethics*, p. 109.
[86] Engelhardt, *Foundations of Bioethics*, p. 111.
[87] Engelhardt, *Foundations of Bioethics*, p. 115.
[88] Engelhardt, *Foundations of Bioethics*, p. 109.

something of a pious hope. How in the end can one compel people to be kind to each other without some sort of vision of the good that all can share?

Now to what extent is this a moral framework? Engelhardt's people are motivated by the desire for peaceful coexistence and the desire to avoid one moral vision being imposed on them by coercion – the desire in short to keep the Inquisition at bay. They have 'respect for persons'[89] but only in a very limited sense – the respect that means a refusal to interfere in the freedom of another without permission. They have a desire for peace which comes from a simple act of the will: because shared rationality has failed, they turn to mutual agreement as a basis for morality: the 'concrete fabric of morality must then be based on a will to a moral viewpoint, not on deliverances of a rational argument'.[90] In other words being moral is a choice, an act of will, the result of decision – but a decision in the narrow sense, not of the whole person, certainly not of the heart, nor even of the mind – then of the what? Engelhardt's people decide on the two principles not because they are convinced of them rationally or because they accord with some idea of the good, but because they will them into existence. A similar assertion is made in *Bioethics and Secular Humanism*: here[91] resolution of conflict is envisaged though negotiation. Because God is silent, the key to ethics is mutual respect, the non-use of others without their consent. But this non-use is not value-based but integral to the grammar of controversy resolution. 'Mutual respect is accepted because it is the one way to ground a common moral world for moral strangers without arbitrarily endorsing a particular ranking of values.' It is 'the moral point of view that requires the fewest assumptions' and 'intellectually the least costly way of establishing a common moral world' as it has no content and no particular metaphysical viewpoint. Moreover 'a common morality can come into existence through a common will. It is the will to morality that can set nihilism aside.' Again, this is the only way for moral strangers to co-operate.

The above restates what has been said in the previous book,[92] but perhaps more starkly. Everything has failed, religion and rationality included: faced with moral anarchy, we choose our morality with an act of the will, and it is that choice, the force of our will, that makes what we have chosen moral, which as we have seen in our discussion of MacIntyre, is the position of Nietzsche. In prosaic terms, this position is called decisionism, the belief that something is right because I have chosen it. It is of course a sort of fundamentalism: while fundamentalism might espouse a divine command theory – 'It is right because God wills it' rather than 'It is right because it is good' – decisionism makes the person choosing into a sort of God – 'It is right because I say so, or because I have chosen it'. In both theories change can come about as to what is right or wrong with a change of mind. For example, according

---

[89] Engelhardt, *Foundations of Bioethics*, p. 104.
[90] Engelhardt, *Foundations of Bioethics*, p. 103.
[91] Engelhardt, *Bioethics and Secular Humanism*, pp. 119–20.
[92] Engelhardt, *Foundations of Bioethics*, pp. 68-69: 'This account of ethics and bioethics requires a minimum of prior assumptions. It requires *only a decision* [emphasis added] to resolve moral disputes in a manner other than fundamentally by force.' Still later, in Engelhardt, *Foundations of Christian Bioethics*, we have: 'They must *decide* [emphasis added], not discover, how to rank values' (p. 130).

to divine command theorists, polygamy was right in the Old Testament, but God later changed his mind and made monogamy the rule; likewise, the principle of permission is right because we choose it now, but who knows whether our mind will change later? This contractual agreement might well be superseded by another one in the future. The choice seems arbitrary – and indeed it can be nothing but arbitrary simply because there is no other basis for choice, neither nature, nor reason, nor divine revelation, apart from the force of the will. Once again, Engelhardt falls into the trap that he accuses others of falling into – that of making arbitrary choices.

This then is the fatal weakness of Engelhardt's position: we choose the permission principle by an act of the will, unaided by reason, or God, or a vision of moral goodness. Why then should we choose this principle and not another? The answer advanced here is because the principle of permission is the only one that can guarantee peaceful co-existence. But surely some benign dictatorship might do the same? If we were by agreement to submit all disputes to some august body who would arbitrate on the matter and whose word would be final, would that not ensure peace? If the principle rests on the agreement of the parties, the principle's contents can be subject to change, for what guarantee have we got that the decision will be stable?[93] For as Saint Augustine says, 'Only truth convinces',[94] and how can we be convinced by something as fragile as the principle of permission which makes no strong claim to be true, but rather asks to be accepted on the grounds that there is no alternative, except chaos?

The principle of consent is thus vulnerable to objections of this type, if it is conceived as resting purely on a will to morality. But it is vulnerable to an even deeper probing. A simple act of the will is in itself an inadequate basis for any moral point of view, because the will as conceived in this way by Engelhardt rests on an insufficient moral psychology. We remember of course that Engelhardt talks of a minimum of assumptions in the adoption of the principles and the moral point of view they encapsulate, and he would rule out any recourse to moral psychology as a reliance on a metaphysics or even a thin theory of the good that would not win general acceptance. Engelhardt's act of will may seem arbitrary, but so are any grounds on which an objection may be based. It really does seem, then, that nihilism and relativism cannot be avoided after all. All that is left is the will, in this case patient and doctor consent, which establishes content and authority.[95] People count for nothing, 'for within the sparse morality of moral strangers one cannot talk about persons as being valued or having moral worth'; it is their consent that matters, so 'individuals are salient by default'. One can create content and establish authority, but you cannot discover either.[96]

---

[93] Stability, as we shall see, is a major concern of Rawls.
[94] Augustine, *City of God*, Book IV, chapter 26.
[95] Engelhardt, *Bioethics and Secular Humanism*, p. 136.
[96] Engelhardt, *Bioethics and Secular Humanism*, p. 136. In other words, this seems to be suggesting, there is no intrinsic rationality to reality. In that case, we may ask once again, how is a narrative possible?

But does this view not rest on a set of philosophical assumptions? It was MacIntyre who posed the stark alternative between Aristotle and Nietzsche;[97] Engelhardt has clearly taken him at his word and plumped for Nietzsche. He takes MacIntyrean[98] ideas but takes them to a conclusion that is decidedly not optimistic: Saint Benedict[99] may well be in his monastery, but the sprit of Nietzsche is in the forum.

How is this to be overcome? One way would be to develop some theory of the decision-making process that overcomes the simple will to morality of Engelhardt, despite his strictures on the subject. As we have already pointed out, the permission principle is by no means the only choice that would guarantee peaceful co-existence. Some form of gentle or not so gentle coercion might be preferred, if the matter is seen as a mere question of will. But what do we mean by will? And what part does the will play in a human act?

St Thomas Aquinas sees three elements to a human act properly called such: it is the fruit of reason and will and must be for the sake of an end.[100] Now Engelhardt's people clearly have an end in view in their choosing the principle of permission: they wish to ensure peaceful coexistence. Their will chooses this end. But their reason? Indeed from our reading of Engelhardt, their reason is not involved, for their reason would lead them all astray, in divers directions, and make agreement impossible. So Engelhardt, in Thomistic terms, is proposing a human act that lacks one of the basic components of the human act, namely reason. Indeed, given that Thomas defines the will as the power of rational desire,[101] then this act of the will is not really a human act at all, but more akin to the act of an animal who chooses without reason and from appetite alone.[102] In other words, such a method of choice is an act of violence directed against the self: people ought to choose rationally and are doing violence to their rational natures by suppressing them. This of course assumes that the human being is a rational creature, capable of arrival at a rational outcome, an assumption that Engelhardt refuses to make.[103]

Again, imagine that the principle of permission is to be regarded as a law governing the behaviour of moral strangers. But what do we mean by law? St Thomas defines a law as a function of the reason, and makes it clear that the will of the prince has the force of law only if the will of the prince is reasonable. An unreasonable law, an arbitrary law, is no law at all; it is a mere caprice that could lead to anarchy.[104] While the principle of permission may be for the common good, another characteristic of

---

[97] MacIntyre, *After Virtue*, p. 256.

[98] Engelhardt clearly sees himself as something of a disciple of MacIntyre: in his latest book the position of MacIntyre is taken as a reliable starting point: see Engelhardt, *The Foundations of Christian Bioethics*, p. xi.

[99] MacIntyre, *After Virtue*, p. 263.

[100] *Summa Theologiae*, I II, 1, 1.

[101] *Summa Theologiae*, I II, 8, 2.

[102] *Summa Theologiae*, I II, 13, 2.

[103] Engelhardt does define persons as rational, though he has no confidence in their ability to arrive at rational and thus binding conclusions. Thus their rational nature does them little good, but rather leads them into discord. Curiously, if they had not been rational at all, there would be no question of disagreement, one could argue from an Engelhardtian perspective!

[104] *Summa Theologiae*, I II, 90, 1.

law, and agreed on by the appropriate people,[105] it has not been agreed on by a rational process, but by a mere matter of the will. The principle may well be reasonable in itself, but the process by which it was arrived at is not, and it has not been shown to be reasonable. These are not aspects of law that Thomas mentions explicitly, but one can argue that these aspects are implied by what he says about promulgation[106] and what subsequent writers in the Thomist tradition have said about transparency and the duty of lawmakers to ensure that laws are understood and understandable.

It seems evident that the principle of permission, or any other principle for that matter which is chosen through a will to morality, is of its nature not transparent, for it is not arrived at by a rational process. Engelhardt advocates a turn to moral procedure, but then short circuits the entire process through an act of the unaided will. He replaces the bogey of coercion with the spectre of self-coercion. Which is worse? Neither is reasonable. It is our contention then that if people are capable of reason (and no one denies this, though one may deny that they are capable of reaching reasonable conclusions) then to make a decision to leave reason aside is to require them to do violence to their natures. Morality is not simply a matter of the will. It also involves understanding and reason. A morality without either, like Engelhardt's permission principle, would be heteronomous,[107] that is to say imposed on the conscience from outside, and would do severe violence to any Christian's existential foundation;[108] it would violate a person's personal unity by forcing them to accept a belief that has no connection with their other beliefs.[109]

In Engelhardt's vision, the will only steps in when reason has failed and when God is silent. Once again one notes a certain duality. For him, faith and reason are not a continuum, but distinct entities: where one ends, another begins: they are separate sorts of discourse. Likewise the reason and the will work separately, and the will takes over where reason fails. Again, and perhaps most importantly of all, the community of faith, the Church, is seen as a moral exclave, something standing distinct from what we may term, in want of a better word, the world. Arguments are usually couched in terms of either/or as opposed to both/and. We have characterized this as 'the view from Antioch', in other words pointing out that this is a theologically based position rather than one that owes much to philosophy; in fact it might be fair to say that Engelhardt's philosophical position is that philosophy is of little help in

---

[105] *Summa Theologiae*, I II, 90, 3 and 4.

[106] *Summa Theologiae*, I II, 90, 4.

[107] Donatella Abignente, *Decisione Morale del Credente* (Casale Monferrato: Piemme, 1987), p. 17. This book provides a useful overview of the Thomist picture of how a believer (or anyone else for that matter) makes a moral decision. The essential point is that the particular decision is all of a piece with larger existential decisions and never freestanding. Engelhardt's people, however, are called to make a decision in favour of the principle of permission that violates their other beliefs, whatever they may be. This acceptance of the principle for anyone not a complete believer in *laissez-faire* morality is an symptom of schizophrenia: the interiorization of philosophical and moral fragmentation.

[108] Abignente, pp. 19–21.

[109] Abignente, p. 26.

resolving disputes. The attempt to reach universal agreement has failed and we are left with various bioethics that he calls 'sectarian'[110] – a telling use of the word.

Why does all this matter when the main focus of our investigation is supposed to be narrative? It matters for the following reasons: Engelhardt is proposing that we embrace narrative as an alternative to failed discursive rationality; that our narrative, whatever it might be, need not concern itself with those outside our exclave of moral friends; finally, he seems to be suggesting that our choice of narrative rests not on rational and rationally justifiable choice but on a mere act of the will. This in turn suggests that the narrative is *per se* impermeable to reason, and thus that a narrative theology invites the believer to believe with his will but not with his reason. This sort of narrative seems unsustainable and sectarian. If this is indeed the reality of narrative theology, then perhaps we are best off without it.

Engelhardt's position is not one anyone ought rationally to choose, violating as it does the very structure of rationality in its view of the nature of the will. In addition, Engelhardt's procedurally neutral approach is far from neutral but in fact theologically loaded (as he would admit: after all, he claims that neutrality is a chimera). Furthermore, Engelhardt's position, beyond being internally contradictory, also leads to intolerable and often absurd results.

Finally, while not wishing to deny for a moment the importance of tradition, one must question both Engelhardt's understanding of the term and his use of traditional sources. Can one really aim 'to lead Christian bioethics *back* [emphasis added] to where Christian reflections found themselves in the first millennium'?[111] Is this feasible? In his robust defence of what he sees as traditional Christianity, Engelhardt defends a literal interpretation of St Paul's dictum that 'the head of the woman is the man' (I Corinthians 11:3[112]) without being aware that St Paul's provisions for the churches of the first century of the Christian era cannot be applied to the current situation without some intermediate justification. Thus his attack on the feminist movement misses its mark. The term tradition has to be more differentiated than this; likewise the word 'choice' cannot simply be equated with permissiveness.[113] It is for these reasons, among others, that *The Foundations of Christian Bioethics* is a disappointing book for believer and non-believer alike: it tells the believer what they already know, but provides no real reasoning that might convince the non-believer. As he himself says:

> The content and the substance of theology and morality, including knowledge of the existence of God and of the content of Christian bioethics, are not acquired by rational argument itself. If Christian bioethics is to have any content beyond that which is historically conditioned and possess an authority more than that derived from the consent of a particular community, Christian bioethics must be given content and authority by God. Traditional Christianity must offer an intimate connection with God Who can *set aside*

---

[110] Engelhardt, *Bioethics and Secular Humanism*, p. 12.
[111] Engelhardt, *Foundations of Christian Bioethics*, p. xvii.
[112] Engelhardt, *Foundations of Christian Bioethics*, p. 13.
[113] As above.

[emphasis added] the confines of immanence and the historically conditioned character of Biblical texts... A Christian bioethics is more liturgical than scriptural.[114]

Just as in philosophy, as we have seen, Engelhardt makes a Nietzschean leap from reason into the will, so in theology he makes a leap that attempts to overcome the exigencies of reason and the bounds of immanence. Grace does not perfect nature, it annihilates it. God 'sets aside' his own creation and the laws that govern immanence that he himself established. But as far as Engelhardt is concerned, God can do anything he pleases, even break the moral law or the laws of reason: 'When God truly commands, as with Abraham and [the sacrifice of] Isaac, He is beyond the constraints that usually bind human conduct.' No wonder then that 'it is crucially important to discern between the voice of God and hallucinations due to mental illness'.[115] Indeed, failure to do so might be catastrophic! But we should not be surprised that Engelhardt's Christian bioethics in the end boils down to divine command theory. As he himself tells us: 'This chapter addresses the foundations of Christian bioethics that is fundamentalist in being firmly committed to the unchanging fundamentals of the Christian faith, by invoking a view of rationality not accessible in the public forum...'[116] In the end the only virtue is that of obedience,[117] of submission to God, rather than attempting to understand his ways in conscience.

This espousal of sectarian fundamentalism and retreat into traditionalism of the kind that Engelhardt intends, is not something a Catholic (or anyone else for that matter) can or ought to accept. It obscures much that is praiseworthy in his work which Catholics will admire. But to this Engelhardt will have a response: the failure of the present writer to appreciate his position is only to be expected, as this writer is working in an alien tradition. The only way to appreciate traditional Christian bioethics is to become a traditional Christian, that is a member of an Orthodox Church. But tradition is 'an historically extended, socially embodied argument'.[118] It is doubtful than that Engelhardt truly follows MacIntyre's model: his seems to be a closed tradition,[119] and MacIntyre's seems to be open to development; but Engelhardt's represents the denial of argument, rather than argument.

Writing at the beginning of *The Foundations of Bioethics*, having made his gloomy survey of the impossibility of any canonical and content-full bioethics, any single unified and unifying moral narrative, Engelhardt observes that 'These observations concur with those of Alasdair MacIntyre and others: we live among the shattered remnants of once vibrant and integrated moral visions and understandings that could

---

[114] Engelhardt, *Foundations of Christian Bioethics*, p. 167.
[115] Engelhardt, *Foundations of Christian Bioethics*, note 7, p. 384.
[116] Engelhardt, *Foundations of Christian Bioethics*, p. 158.
[117] Engelhardt, *Foundations of Christian Bioethics*, p. 138 on Man's humble submission to God. See p. 80 for the submission of the second Eve, and p. 13 for the implied submission of women to men.
[118] MacIntyre, *After Virtue*, p. 222.
[119] See Engelhardt, *Foundations of Christian Bioethics*, pp. 202 et seq. for a historical survey of Western Christianity which is a travesty of history. Augustine is dismissed in one sentence!

have sustained content-full accounts of proper contemporary health policy.'[120] His particular reference is to *After Virtue* and, one assumes, 'The Disquieting Suggestion' of its first chapter. Thus, according to Engelhardt (following MacIntyre, and in sympathy with Hauerwas) we must turn to a narrative of some sort.

However, what must give us pause is the model of narrative that is implicit in Engelhardt's work, which is at variance with the model of MacIntyre, and which seems to involve some sort of fundamentalist sectarianism, in so far as it rejects reason and rejects universalism. Narrative is advanced as something in contradistinction to reason, not in harmony with it; narrative is advanced as a replacement to failed reason, not as a help to a still viable reason. To refute Engelhardt further one would have to prove that an irrational narrative is not a narrative in any true sense; that narrative is *per se* rational and reflects the inherent rationality of things. That things can be brought into a narrative proves they are not by nature absurd, for no narrative is absurd.[121] Narrative is a form of discursive reasoning. Furthermore, all narratives may be grounded in time and place and culture, as we have said, but this does not necessarily mean that they do not tend to universality of meaning. The narrative that fails to transcend time and culture and place may not be a very good narrative.

We will look at these two caveats in due time; until then we are left, it seems, with the triad of narrative/tradition/community. All the authors considered so far link the three. A community is the place in which a tradition is nurtured, and this tradition is best explicated in various narrative forms: but this does not have to be a circular, and perhaps closed, movement: a community has a tradition which is explicated in stories which nourish the community, reinforce its tradition, and lead to new stories being told. But Engelhardt typifies a closed circular movement: the Orthodox believing community has a tradition (the Greek Fathers) that is exemplified in a moral narrative which in its turn reinforces the tradition and seems impervious to all others. It is to be noted that Engelhardt, as we have seen, supposes a symbiotic relationship between theology, prayer, Church tradition and liturgy, the 'acting out' of that tradition. But this acting out seems to be for the benefit of the community members alone. Engelhardt's narrative theology is stuck firmly in the ghetto, and as a result represents a less advanced position than that of either Hauerwas or MacIntyre, both of whom talk of engagement or witness to the world. But Engelhardt seems to hold both to be futile.

---

[120] Engelhardt, *Bioethics and Secular Humanism*, p. 13.
[121] True? MacIntyre would agree, but Engelhardt would not. Engelhardt, *Foundations of Christian Bioethics*, p. 137 et seq.

Chapter 5

The Rawlsian Alternative

What then emerges from this tour we have taken in the previous three chapters of three leading exponents of the narrative approach to theology? The first thing that must strike us is that while there is a strong family resemblance between the ideas they espouse, this ought not to mask their quite radically different approaches to certain key questions. All focus on the three key ideas of narrative, community and tradition, but this serves sometimes to highlight just how differently these terms can be used. How indeed are we to understand them?

MacIntyre makes a strong case for the connectedness of narrative and its inherent rationality, while stressing that this rationality is not the same as the rationality of the enlightenment: it is not disencumbered, but embedded in tradition, a tradition which flourishes in a community from which fundamental dissent has been excluded, and also a tradition which recognizes certain ideas as authoritative, indeed normative. In other words, narrative thinking, in MacIntyre, never starts from an entirely blank slate. We come to the slate, so to speak, to find that others have preceded us, and we write on the slate bearing in mind, reacting to even, what has already been written there. The narrative is a story that continues over many generations, seeks no clear break from the past, but rather aims to continue the story into the next generation, and which makes little sense when taken out of its historical context. This being MacIntyre's position, we are not surprised to find that he qualifies himself variously as an Augustinian Christian, an Aristotelian, and a Thomist: reading his works we see his progression from one to the other. The important point is not to do with his particular allegiance but with the fact that he is one who works self-consciously within a tradition, and who makes his allegiances plain. By contrast, Hauerwas's allegiances and sources are far more eclectic in scope, and it is hard to fit him into any one tradition even using the most broad categories. By further contrast, Engelhardt is one who fits himself into a very particular tradition, that of the Antiochene Church. What is clear though is that all of these readings of the idea of tradition work in somewhat different ways, for each one employs a differing idea of rationality, and a different idea of what constitutes authority or justification, as we have aimed to show. We are left with the very obvious point that all have their traditions – Catholic, Protestant or Orthodox – but in each case tradition means something slightly, or even dramatically, different.

One conclusion, however, must be this: all three of our authors point to the inescapability of narrative. They hold that there is no statement in theology or philosophy that can be understood, whatever its claims to the contrary, as a bare statement. Every statement comes to us with a history attached to it, the history from which it has sprung and of which it is a part. Thus every truth is historical, and as such, bears the imprint of the tradition of which it is a part and the community in which it was nurtured.

Furthermore, not only is thought narrative in form, so is experience. We make sense of experience through the stories we tell. Our stories encapsulate our beliefs and our way of looking at the world. But this is only possible because experience come to us in narrative form: we can shape our experiences into narratives because the raw material which we receive is in fact 'shapeable'. The matter is amenable to narrative form, because events are never purely 'raw': like MacIntyre's man digging in the garden, events are never bare, but come inviting interpretation. In other words, because cause and effect are real phenomena in the world and not merely human projections, narrative is a possibility and not merely wishful thinking. This idea, which can be taken as foundational, was first proposed by Stephen Crites, as we have seen. Narrative form is not accidental, but intrinsic to reality. We will have reason to return to Crites, for his thesis invites exploration: he takes the view that language and story are common to all humanity, culturally expressed, but preceding culture.[1] Our authors discussed in the preceding three chapters take the view that people are story-telling animals, but they do not focus on the precultural aspects of this, but rather on the cultural manifestations of story. We perhaps ought to ask that given the universality of the phenomenon of story, what is it that all stories have in common, and what might this common structure, if indeed it exists, tell us about humanity and about the world? If there are indeed common precultural elements that are found in all stories, might this not lead us to see in every cultural expression of the story-telling urge an indication of universal truths? But this is not something that our authors touch upon, and nowhere do they hint that in every story there is buried the germ of a universal truth that precedes all cultural expression. For example, if truths come to us in narratives, does it not also follow that a universal truth comes to us in the plethora of narratives that we may meet, namely that cause and effect are not illusory? But this will depend on one important position we must take up. Does the narrative make sense through an act of human willing, or is it intrinsically intelligible? MacIntyre would seem to take the latter view, but the Nietzschean Engelhardt would seem to incline to the former. Here we see the great bifurcation in narrative theology: is the story the 'right' story because it makes sense of itself, it reflects reality, or is it because I have decided that it makes sense to me? Do I make the tables of the law, or do I discover them? As we shall see this is an important distinction.

These stories, whatever their origin, are told in a community of which we are part, and these communities represent the embodiment of the stories we tell. All our authors hold to this. Where they disagree in emphasis at least is on the relationship of the narrative community to other communities gathered around other narratives. MacIntyre talks of engagement and dialogue, Hauerwas talks of witness, but Engelhardt seems content to retire into his fortress. This in turn gives rise to interesting and diverse theologies of the Church as the place where stories are told. All three however emphasize the living link between the Church and its moral theology, and

---

[1] 'The *forms* of cultural expression are not historical accidents. They are not products of culture... They are the *conditions* of historical existence...' Crites, p. 291.

the existential and incarnational aspects of morality. Morality is embodied in the Church, and the Church is the embodiment of an ethical approach. What they do not say explicitly is that a 'new' moral theology must also entail a new ecclesiology, a new conception of the Church. Certainly we can see that the cold abstract reasoning of the Enlightenment produces a certain type of Church life: one that stresses obedience to the Law and the universality of its application, and which sidelines the liturgy's importance as a locus of moral theology, and the scriptures too. However, a 'narrative' Church would be one that would express and emphasize the inculturated aspects of moral theology, its connection to the liturgy, and the origins of that moral theology in the story-telling Church rather than in the realms of abstract reasoning. Such a Church, at least according to Hauerwas, would leave Kant in the narthex, lest he deform Christian teaching, and would perhaps be more democratic in the sense that it would make the lived experience of the congregation the starting point of its moral theology. Such theology would also be closely allied to praxis, unlike abstract belief. And yet, before we are charmed by this vision, let us remember that narrative theology can also be interpreted in a strongly authoritarian key, as is undoubtedly the case with Engelhardt, who sees the authority of the tradition as paramount, as opposed to the way the tradition is lived out today.

When it comes to the relationship between the Church and those outside it, things become more complicated, for we can perceive that our authors take different views about the intelligibility of stories and their justification. For Engelhardt the stories of 'moral friends' are unintelligible to the wider public and the only way to enter the story is to enter the community that tells the story. Hauerwas seems to be close to this view, but he tempers it with his insistence on witness: our stories have to make an attempt to communicate with the wider world. But MacIntyre sees a way of overcoming the seeming incommensurability and untranslatabilty between stories through rational dialogue. What is at stake here are differing views on the role, indeed the very existence, of discursive reason and rationality. What we have tried to show is that Engelhardt and to a lesser extent Hauerwas, maintains a strongly fideistic, fundamentalist and sectarian attitude to narrative. This is because, unlike MacIntyre, they have a vision of narrative as being distinct from rational discourse, whereas for MacIntyre, narrative is a form of rational discourse. This in turn leads to (or is the result of) a fundamental disagreement about the role of rational discourse in matters of faith: can faith rely on reason, or will this be damaging to both faith and reason?

It is this area that we have identified as the main area for further enquiry: is narrative a form of rational discourse, capable of rational justification by both internal and external criteria, or must narrative rely only on internal criteria of coherence and prescind from a common rationality, which is in itself a snare and a delusion? Parallel to this is another allied question: is each narrative inextricably bound up with a particular community and tradition, opaque to outsiders, or is there some narrative that can command universal allegiance?

So, the focus of our enquiry must now be on the nature of narrative itself. We must ask to what extent is a narrative a sort of rational discourse? We must examine the relationship between narrative and discursive reason, and to what extent a narrative can have a universal appeal. Above all we need to examine the claim that a narrative can make no sense to anyone who stands outside the community and tradition in which it is told. These questions have been touched upon so far, but no firm answers have yet been advanced. Before we do so – before we try to answer the questions that Hauerwas, MacIntyre and Engelhardt have raised – we need to look at the alternative to their claims, namely the claim that there is a narrative, accessible to unaided human reason, that can be accepted by all. And to do that we shall examine the work of John Rawls, who proposes exactly such a narrative.

John Rawls: Introductory Remarks

The introduction of the figure and work of John Rawls into this discussion at this stage requires some justification. Rawls takes a different line from that of Engelhardt, Hauerwas and MacIntyre; indeed one might say that his position is diametrically opposed to theirs. Certainly all three of our previous authors, as we have seen, take time to attack what they perceive as the Rawlsian position, as a position markedly opposed to their own. Indeed Rawls revered the universalist Kantian heritage in philosophy, and his life's work was dedicated to proving that rational agreement is possible between people of deeply held differing beliefs,[2] and that there are common moral positions that all can adhere to, at least in the political field. It is precisely this position that Hauerwas and Engelhardt (and perhaps MacIntyre too) see as completely wrong.

So why turn to Rawls now? In the first place, because Rawls provides a contrast, a different approach, which may be taken to prove or disprove, depending on his success or failure, the claims made by narrative theologians. Secondly, because the claims made by narrative theologians are to some extent confused and contradictory, a look at Rawls may help us to arrive at sound conclusions that narrative theology may hold. And thirdly, and perhaps most surprisingly (though not if we hold that all is by nature narrative, whatever the protestations to the contrary), Rawls himself is a narrative thinker, but a narrative thinker, who, in the Original Position, provides us with a new and arresting form of narrative. Furthermore, examination of this type of narrative may help us solve some of the problems about rationality that were raised in the previous chapter.

John Rawls (1921–2002) was the son of a Supreme Court lawyer and a mother who was an early campaigner for female suffrage. A graduate of Princeton, as a young man he entertained the idea of being ordained as a Congregationalist minister, but was in 1943 called up to fight in the Second World War, seeing action as an infantryman in some of the bloodiest battles in the Pacific; he returned to Princeton, having given up any idea of the ministry, and took his doctorate. In 1958 he published an article, 'Justice as Fairness', which contained the seed of what was to become the Original Position. In 1962, after a year spent at Oxford (where he encountered Sir

---

[2] Rawls claims (in 'Justice as Fairness', *Collected Papers*, pp. 393–5) that we do hold settled convictions in common even though the public culture may be of two minds at a very deep level; philosophy cannot deliver agreement. What is needed is a new way of fitting things together so that we may find common ground; this can be done by the concept of Justice as Fairness which is practical not epistemological or metaphysical.

Isaiah Berlin) and spells at Cornell and the Massachusetts Institute of Technology, he was appointed Professor of Philosophy at Harvard, where he spent the rest of his academic career. He has been described as 'one of the most notable and controversial political theorists of his day'; and as a 'modest and unassuming man revered by his colleagues and pupils for his kindness and generosity as much as for the quality of his intellect'.[3]

These biographical details are interesting of themselves, but, Rawls himself would have insisted, of no relevance whatsoever to his philosophy. As we shall see, a major plank in the Rawlsian approach is the idea that moral decisions are to be made without reference to personal circumstances; this is in direct opposition to the narrative approach which sees every moral decision as part of the continuing narrative of a life and contributing to and informed by that narrative. We have already seen that Engelhardt sees Rawls as a typical product of New England, but Rawls, as an adherent of Kantian universalism, is advancing a position that aims to transcend New England or anywhere else for that matter. So, if we are to take a Rawlsian approach, as opposed to an Engelhardtian one, we must put aside all speculation about the various influences that came to bear on John Rawls and cease to try and unravel their significance. But we may well still find ourselves suspecting that the facts of his life were not without significance; and this may well appear in the course of our investigation.

Rawls's major contribution to political theory and ethics was made in 1971, with the publication of *A Theory of Justice*[4] with its careful exposition of the Original Position, which was further developed in his later book, *Political Liberalism*.[5] Further articles followed, and several further books,[6] along with a vast secondary literature.

Before going any further, it may help the reader to give a brief summary of Rawls's position as expounded in the two books mentioned above. Rawls proposes that the rules of justice are those rules that would be agreed on in a special set of hypothetical circumstances that he dubs 'the Original Position'. We are to imagine a situation in which we are negotiating with others about how the basic institutions of society are to be structured, but under a special constraint – we are not to know our own social positions or personal qualities, which might influence our negotiations and urge us to press for arrangements which would suit us personally. This is the

---

[3] These quotations, as well as the biographical details, are taken from the anonymous obituary published in UK newspaper *The Daily Telegraph*, 27 November, 2002.

[4] John Rawls, *A Theory of Justice* (Cambridge, Mass.: The Belknap Press of Harvard University Press, 1972).

[5] John Rawls, *Political Liberalism* (New York: Columbia University Press, 1993).

[6] These were as follows: John Rawls, *Collected Papers*, edited by Samuel Freeman (Cambridge, Mass.: Harvard University Press, 1999) (a very useful one volume collection of important writings spanning his career); John Rawls, *The Law of Peoples, with The Idea of Public Reason Revisited* (Cambridge, Mass.: Harvard University Press, 1999), in which the philosopher applies the ideas of *A Theory of Justice* to international relations; and finally John Rawls, *Lectures on the History of Moral Philosophy* (Cambridge, Mass.: Harvard University Press, 2000), a volume which reveals Rawls's interest in the history of philosophy and the tradition from which he springs.

'Veil of Ignorance' which ensures we will seek a state of affairs where everyone is as well off as possible. In these circumstances, we will opt for two principles: first, everyone should have the greatest liberty compatible with a similar liberty for others; and second, no inequality is to be permitted unless that inequality is for the benefit of all, including the least advantaged. The concept of Justice that emerges from the Original Position is thus characterized as 'Justice as Fairness'. Furthermore, this idea of Justice will in time produce an Overlapping Consensus; that is to say that various citizens who hold competing and mutually exclusive beliefs (or 'comprehensive doctrines') will all be able to acknowledge the shared good of political liberalism and politically liberal institutions, and this consensus will ensure the stability of such institutions.

Rawls devoted his academic life to the explication of this theory of justice and its defence and refinement in face of criticism. It is of interest to ask ourselves why he thought the theory important. However, true to his principles, this was not a question he tackled in any of his writings: the theory stands (or falls) on its own merits, and not propped up by circumstances. If something is universally true, its genesis is irrelevant. However, in a magazine interview[7] Rawls did reveal what he saw as his primary worries about American society, which his work aimed to address. These were the possible failure of public reason and the spectre of constant disagreement between religious and other groups. Oddly, these concerns are not far removed from those of MacIntyre, Hauerwas and Engelhardt. Though Rawls makes little reference to MacIntyre, it is clear that he is exercised by the same problem that grips the other philosopher. How are we to live with and come to terms with pluralism, or a plurality of narratives in society?

One will immediately notice that the Original Position presents a narrative. At the end of the first chapter a narrative was described as a coherent and accessible story, through which people, as a community and as individuals, come to understand truths about themselves and their communities and the rules by which they live. The narrative constitutes their identity to a greater or lesser degree and enshrines that which they believe about the world. In the context of this loose definition, the Original Position is a narrative: it is a story, coherent and accessible through the imagination; it does not purport to describe an actual situation, but is rather a work of fiction that encapsulates a truth that underpins the way society is to be governed, that is, that justice as fairness is best, and the sort of society that holds this as its central value is the best sort of society.

However, narrative goes further and sees life as a continuum, lived over a lifetime, and that the past is to be understood in the context of a wider whole. This is one point where the Original Position diverges from narrative as others understand it. The people in the Position have no pasts, no characters, no history of decision-making to guide them in their decision for justice as fairness. This is an important divergence to which we shall return in due course.

---

[7] 'Politics, Religion and the Public Good, an Interview with philosopher John Rawls', by Bernard B. Prusak, *Commonweal*, CXXV, 16 (1998): 12–16. Reprinted in *Collected Papers*, pp. 616–22.

Narrative assumes that decisions are made by acting people, taking account, indeed formed by, their pasts, and looking to their futures; and that moral norms cannot be properly understood as a series of punctiliar or atomic acts, unconnected to character, and the environment that forms character. It is immediately apparent that the Original Position suggests a different model of decision-making, which may be enlightening.

Finally, we have also seen an emerging polarity between the particularity of narrative and the universal import of abstract rationality. Rawls's Original Position is a story that claims to have universal application, and by considering it we may edge towards the idea of a narrative which starts as rooted in lived experience, but tends towards eternal and universal truths. For the Original Position is a kind of myth, almost an aetiological tale, which is supposed to hold good in all circumstances. When we ask 'Why are we doing this?' the answer is given: 'Because it is what we would have chosen in the Original Position.' The Original Position is a kind of justifying story, a foundational myth, a tale of the origins that explains what we are doing, or should be doing, here and now. But the Original Position, as we shall see, is not culture and place bound: it can be applied in any society and to any people.[8]

Bearing in mind what we have said, we see that the Original Position is a narrative, but one of a peculiar kind. It may in fact be a narrative that stretches certain categories of narrative to breaking point or beyond it. Those who work within the triad narrative/tradition/community contest the suppositions behind the Original Position and the Veil of Ignorance by stressing the importance of community, and see this, and not the 'atomized' individual of the Position, as the primary reality. Decisions are made not by individuals in isolation, and certainly not hypothetically, but by living historically grounded communities, who draw on tradition, and who live out a socially embodied narrative. These communities have as their foundation and as a foundation of their narrative a shared concept of the Good – without such a concept, which is the basis of shared moral language, dialogue in the community is impossible. Communities are organic and all-embracing, and it makes no sense to speak of any situation that predates, literally or figuratively, a community – the atomic individual of the Original Position is thus an impossibility. A person's identity springs from the community in which they are nurtured and the idea of the good that that community incarnates.[9] Not surprisingly, communitarian thinkers deplore the idea of the person who has 'lost' all sense of community and belonging[10] and who seems to be the type imagined in the Original Position. People without a history and without a community can have no narrative. The Original Position is thus, so the charge goes, an ideal choosing situation in which choice itself becomes

---

[8] Which was the point of Rawls's last book, the *Law of Peoples, with the Idea of Public Reason Revisited* (1999).

[9] This last point is made by Charles Taylor, *Sources of the Self, The Making of Modern Identity* (Cambridge, Mass.: Harvard University Press, 1989), p. 3, p. 27.

[10] See MacIntyre's comments on 'modern individualism', *After Virtue*, pp. 220–22; see also Robert A. Nisbet, *The Quest for Community* (Oxford: Oxford University Press, 1969 (but first published 1953)) and his discussion of alienation, 'moral estrangement and spiritual isolation', pp. 8–9 et seq.

an impossibility, for it deals with phantoms not with people, and expects them to make choices without having any of the criteria of choice usually available to human beings.

These opposing points of view raise interesting questions. If Rawls is right, and the Original Position really is a universal narrative and a universally valid method of reasoning (though he himself does not explicitly describe it in these terms), then this must call into question many of the suppositions and claims of the narrative theologians.

We can consider three questions in particular. First: is it true that there can be no narrative without community, and that thought is necessarily communitarian? Or may some distance from oneself and from others be a precondition of moral thinking? To what extent is an all-embracing community possible or even desirable? Might a narrative exist without the prop of such a community?

Secondly: what should be our attitude to pluralism? Is it possible to find narrative unity amidst narrative diversity? Or is the search for some underlying agreement an illusion? Or is a core-value narrative possible?

Thirdly: does the agreement resulting from the Original Position simply represent a pact of convenience between warring parties, or something deeper? Is Rawls's Original Position merely a mask for the fact that no real agreement about justice is possible without a deeply held shared system of belief, that is, a narrative held in common? Or is the Original Position just such a narrative?

An examination of these questions will help us to appreciate the full implications and ramifications of Rawls's work. Examining Rawls's work bearing in mind the standpoint of such writers as Alasdair MacIntyre, H. T. Engelhardt and Stanley Hauerwas may help us to see its weaknesses, and perhaps its strengths as well. It may lead us to a deeper appreciation of what he is trying to do. We will go on to ask: can Rawls's work be used as a sufficient basis for moral reasoning? And if there are shortcomings in the work of Rawls, can these be supplemented in any way? But our fundamental focus remains on the question of narrative and the exact nature of narrative as a means to establishing moral reasoning.

Narrative and Community, or How Decisions are Made

The writers we have been considering up to now presume an unbreakable link between human character and narrative (the thesis that 'man is a story-telling animal' is one expression of this), and likewise a similar link between narrative and community, as well as human character and community. It is supposed, indeed taken as self-evident, (though how it is to be proved is another matter perhaps) that communities (or societies) are constituted by stories: that is, that the members of a group are those who adhere to the same narrative. Moreover, narratives are nurtured in communities, that is to say the story being told presupposes an audience, a community, and a teller who is formed by that community. So what we have is a two way relationship: the community forms the story, and the story forms the community. The people, the crowd, become a community, a congregation, we might say, through listening to the story. Moreover, it is through this narratively constituted community that people discover their true social character: human beings are community animals by nature, not just be accident.

What emerges here as of particular interest to us, is the fact (or perhaps better claim) that we choose as narrative beings and that we are not capable of choice other than as narrative beings. Of course, there are people who change the societies in which they live through courageous and counter-cultural choices, often in fact discovering a new interpretation of the original story, one that is more faithful to the original, but by and large these are exceptions. We choose as we would be expected to choose, as members of this or that society, as characters formed by this or that narrative.

But it could follow from this that if the parameters of choice are formed by character and formed too by society or community, the making of choices may in practice be so restricted as hardly to be free. For this reason, and to avoid this danger, community or society must be envisioned as an open circle and not a closed one: otherwise we may end up setting out the necessary preconditions for choice, that is membership of some society or community, and then in so doing making any true free choice impossible.

In the work of Rawls, choice is envisioned in radically different circumstances. All allegiances are put under the Veil of Ignorance. The Original Position is, or seems to be, detached from concrete historical reality. Rawls is working in the contractarian tradition, which frequently asks us to imagine a group of people negotiating under ideal conditions about the arrangements they are to adopt in society. Is it asking us to think as people who belong to no society, who are socially disembodied beings about to make a choice of the sort of society they wish to join?

Alasdair MacIntyre has observed[11] that the idea of *telos* distinguishes Aristotle and neo-Aristotelians from those working in the contractarian tradition. One side sees man as a creature with a final end; the other as one who can choose between a range of possible ends. MacIntyre writes that Rawls's people are those for whom individuals are primary and society secondary; who lack any shared understanding of the good for man or the good for the community; they are 'individualistic', a 'collection of strangers, each pursuing their own interests under minimal constraints'.[12] This is not altogether justified, perhaps: after all, the Veil of Ignorance is not a 'minimal constraint'. But MacIntyre's fundamental objection seems sound. The people in the Original Position do not know each other, nor for that matter do they know themselves; without a shared understanding, or indeed self-understanding of some sort, what sort of agreement will they come to? Put another way: the narrative is always an expression of finding oneself in society: without this social embodiment, there can be no narrative. Indeed, one could go so far as to say that without social life

---

[11] MacIntyre, *After Virtue*, pp. 54–5.

[12] MacIntyre, *After Virtue*, pp. 250–51. For Hauerwas's criticisms of Rawls, see *A Community of Character*, pp. 77–83. For Engelhardt's criticisms, while the index to *Foundations of Christian Bioethics* gives several references under the entry 'Rawls, John, as fundamental to theology', these entries do not all mention Rawls by name. But we must assume that Engelhardt wants us to see the failings of modern theology as due to the influence of Rawls. See in particular, *Foundations of Christian Bioethics*, p. xv, p. 18. and p. 45.

there would be no language. Rawls's asocial people who share nothing will not even share a common language, either figuratively or literally. For if language is a cultural and historical phenomenon, must it not be put under the Veil too? And if moral language rests on a shared perception of values, must it not be put under the Veil?

Indeed it is hard to see how the people in the Original Position can make any choices or judgements at all without a personal history to help them do so. To what can they refer if not to past experience? Similarly, if these people are ahistorical, they can have no idea of social bonds and ties – all the things that characterize tradition. Indeed Hauerwas goes so far as to claim that what he calls 'the standard account' of morality makes alienation from self and others the central moral virtue.[13] This point is also emphasized by Michael Sandel,[14] who sees the Veil of Ignorance as effectively cutting the participants in the Original Position off from any sort of understanding of their own identity – and thus making any choice they may make not only meaningless but impossible.

It seems then that Rawls is trying to construct a narrative (not that it is explicitly called such) that relies on characters who have no pasts, in other words who are not characters at all but ciphers, cardboard cut outs, 'representatives' as he calls them, but hardly real people at all. But is this necessarily doomed to failure? How are we to understand the Rawlsian approach to decision-making?

No one could seriously dispute that self-understanding is a necessary precondition of understanding the concepts of the good and justice; and that self-understanding must be historical as well. One needs a pre-existing narrative if one is to come to an understanding of new concepts: a person who knows nothing is not in a position to learn anything either. However, at the same time, moral choice, while involving engagement with an idea of the good, also involves a degree of impartiality and disengagement from one's own selfish desires; the good has to be distinct from 'what I want' or from 'what is good for me'. The idea behind the Veil of Ignorance should not be dismissed as making moral choice impossible; it could be argued that impartiality is essential for moral choice.[15]

Rawls makes it clear that the Original Position is not advanced as some sort of historical event; it is rather a 'device of representation'.[16] There never was, and never will be, according to Rawls, a situation resembling the Original Position in reality: it is rather a mental category that enables us to arrive at the greatest possible level of abstraction.[17] The Original Position is a sort of filter of the mind that can be used to judge existing situations. In other words, the Original Position and the Veil of Ignorance are mental devices of representation that enable us to judge rationally about existing situations and 'purify' them in a historical process towards greater

---

[13] Hauerwas, *Truthfulness and Tragedy*, p. 23.

[14] Michael Sandel, *Liberalism and the Limits of Justice* (Cambridge: Cambridge University Press, 1987). For the specific criticisms of Rawls, see in particular pp. 54–64, 152–4 and 161–5.

[15] MacIntyre says as much in *Dependant Rational Animals*, pp. 72–3, as discussed earlier.

[16] Rawls, *Political Liberalism*, Introduction, p. xxix.

[17] Rawls, *Political Liberalism*, pp. 24–6.

expressions of Justice as Fairness. At the end of *Theory*, he answers the charge, made by Hauerwas, that the Veil of Ignorance elevates alienation to the status of a virtue.

> Without conflating all persons into one, but recognising them as distinct and separate, it [the Original Position] enables us to be impartial, even between persons who are not contemporaries but who belong to many generations. Thus to see our place in society from the perspective of this position is to see it *sub specie aeternitatis*: it is to regard the human situation not only from all social but also from all temporal points of view. The perspective of eternity is not a perspective from a certain place beyond the world, nor the point of view of a transcendent being; rather it is a certain form of thought and feeling that rational persons can adopt within the world. And having done so, they can, whatever their generation, bring together into one scheme all individual perspectives and arrive together at regulative principles that can be affirmed by everyone as he lives by them, each from his own standpoint. Purity of heart, if one could attain it, would be to see clearly and to act with grace and self-command from this point of view.[18]

Is this alienation? Or is it in fact rather a re-presentation of traditional Christian virtues of impartiality, fair mindedness and universal charity? It certainly serves to remind us that Rawls is working in a Kantian perspective, seeing morality not as particular, but universal, valid across time and space, and thus the subject of wide-ranging agreement. As such he is vulnerable to the charge that his morality is based on a human nature that has never existed except in the abstract, but he does his best to refute the idea that the Original Position is anything more than a way of thinking, a way of purifying the thought processes. It does not suppose a disembodied picture of human nature, but sees people as 'distinct and separate'. It is not a view from outer space, but a particular view here and now, 'in the world', universalized through the device of the Original Position. Neither does it involve an abandonment of 'each from his own standpoint'. The Original Position creates a bridge then between the particular and the universal. Rawls says as much himself: 'The Original Position enables us to unite in one scheme our more formal and abstract convictions with our more concrete and particular judgements. It uses the intuitive persuasiveness of one to check the plausibility of the other, and vice versa.'[19]

Furthermore, Rawls specifically denies the charge that he sees society as an object of human choice. He writes: 'We are not to think of the original contract as one to enter a particular society or set up a particular form of government. Rather, the guiding idea is that the principles of justice for the basic structure of society are the object of the original agreement.'[20]

In other words, the agreement is made because we already find ourselves in a society; hence the necessity of justice, the need for which is presumed by the anterior fact of social life. In his later work, he says that political society (an important distinction to which we shall have to return) is 'closed': that is to say that one joins it

---

[18] Rawls, *A Theory of Justice*, p. 587.
[19] Rawls, 'Fairness to Goodness' (1975), in *Collected Papers*, p. 270.
[20] Rawls, *A Theory of Justice*, p. 11.

at birth and leaves it at death;[21] everyone, by being human, is a member; membership is not optional.

Embedded here in Rawls's approach is the nucleus of an important point about narrative. We are in the world, in society ('each from his own standpoint'), yet we are capable of thinking in universal terms ('*sub specie aeternitatis*'). There is after all a bridge between the concrete and particular and the abstract and universal and the Original Position is the narrative that provides that bridge. Here we see a major difference from Hauerwas and Engelhardt, both of whom deny the Kantian heritage of moral universalism and claim that morality, grounded in experience remains rooted in history. Against them Rawls is maintaining that there is 'the perspective of eternity' which people in the here and now can attain, that here is a universal narrative that holds good in all circumstances, and that one can bridge the tension between the particular and the universal.

But at the same time, Rawls specifically distances himself from the ideas of community[22] that are so dear to writers such as Hauerwas, MacIntyre and Engelhardt as well as Sandel. Against those who see the essential basis of society as some form of shared values, tradition or narrative, Rawls points out that political society is not the same as community; the former is constituted on a much narrower basis than the latter. A community shares a common end, a *telos*, based on a commonly held comprehensive doctrine, and political society cannot be founded on such a basis as no single comprehensive doctrine can command general consent. As he writes:

> We say that the hope of political community must be abandoned, if by such a community we mean a political society united in affirming the same comprehensive doctrine. This possibility is excluded by the fact of reasonable pluralism together with the rejection of the oppressive use of the state power to overcome it.[23]

Rather, political society must rest on what he calls the 'thin theory of the good'[24] and a non-metaphysical view of the person[25] which eschews any sort of final end. Here we see a further cleavage between Rawls and our other authors. Rawls is ruling out any single overarching narrative if we understand such a narrative to be constitutive of some monolithic single community. No such narrative could gain general consent; and no one would agree to be coerced. Thus Rawls would rule out an Aristotelian society as well as a Koranic one; but he is not ruling out a society, a political society at least, that is guided by the narrative of the Original Position – this is because the Original Position is a different sort of narrative and does not rest on one particular form of political community but rather on political society.

The state, political society, has no comprehensive doctrine and does not thus constitute a political community, but this does not mean that individuals are not able to join associations that do have such a doctrine. Rawls writes elsewhere:

---

[21] Rawls, *Political Liberalism*, pp. 40–41 and also pp. 135–6.
[22] Rawls, *Political Liberalism*, p. 40.
[23] Rawls, *Political Liberalism*, p. 146.
[24] For a discussion of this, see Rawls, *A Theory of Justice*, pp. 396–407.
[25] For a discussion of this, see Rawls, *Political Liberalism*, pp. 29–33.

> But just institutions and the political virtues expected of citizens would serve no purpose – would have no point – unless those institutions and virtues not only permitted but also sustained ways of life that citizens can affirm as worthy of their full allegiance. A conception of political justice must contain within it sufficient space, as it were, for ways of life that can gain devoted support. In a phrase, justice draws the limit, the good shows the point.[26]

Similarly, it is worth pointing out that a comprehensive state doctrine of the sort that Rawls opposes might make this sort of associationism impossible by intruding into every area of the citizen's life and squeezing out the space mentioned above. This is precisely the danger that is mentioned by Robert A. Nisbet, writing in 1953, but raising concerns that are still valid. He paints a grim picture of what he calls the 'tribalistic togetherness' of 'absolute community'.[27] He too foreshadows Rawls by talking of the necessity of a limit to state power, and how human freedom depends on the preservation of an inner sphere which is immune to state intrusion.[28] It is clear that Nisbet has communism in mind as he writes,[29] but what he says can be applied to any single comprehensive doctrine: it will have a natural tendency to suffocate other doctrines.

In the light of Nisbet's thesis we might look on the thin theory of the good with something like favour. Indeed, there is nothing in the thin theory of the good that provokes immediate disagreement, apart perhaps from the thinness of the theory. Confronted by the theory we feel bound to ask why the theory does not go much further – why stop there?[30] The answer, of course, is that if one takes the theory any further, if one attempts to make it less thin in any way, one will immediately run into disagreement with others. The thin theory thus seems to represent a basic minimum on which all can agree – a fruit of what Rawls calls overlapping consensus. This does not seem very satisfying at first sight. But is the theory indeed so thin? Are his persons in the Original Position in fact asked to make choices without any meaningful idea of the good or the person to guide them? Closer examination reveals that Rawls does have a theory of the person and at least an adequate idea of the good.

The Original Position envisages people as being free and equal, as having a sense of justice, and an ability to recognize the good, which they can formulate into a rational life plan.[31] This in itself supposes a not inconsiderable group of ideas about the nature of the human person. But what Rawls does not do is fill in the background. Why are people free and equal, we want to ask. Rawls's answer would be because to think of them in any other way would not be what we would have chosen in the Original Position. For example, in the Original Position no one would assent to the idea of, on the one hand, slavery, or on the other, a hereditary monarchy, simply

---

[26] 'The Priority of the Right and the Idea of the Good', in Rawls, *Collected Papers*, p. 449.
[27] Nisbet, p. 44.
[28] Nisbet, p. 246.
[29] Nisbet, p. 33.
[30] Nisbet, p. 34, makes clear that there is something in human nature that drives many on to want a thicker theory – a sense of alienation, for example.
[31] For a discussion of this, see Rawls, *A Theory of Justice*, pp. 409–25.

because no one would want to be a slave or subject to a hereditary monarch. We choose freedom and equality because these are goods that we know are good for us, and we recognize their opposites as intolerable. Good is defined as that which it is rational for man to choose. (It is this rationality of the good that is the only yardstick, and not the social or cultural background of those who choose; indeed, the people in the Original Position have no background at all, thanks to the Veil of Ignorance.) Hence Utilitarianism, which may lead to the victimization of a group or individual in the name of the greatest good of the greatest number, could not possibly be chosen in the Original Position.[32] It is not good and not rational. And it is here that we see the philosophical heritage on which Rawls draws most clearly. His is a Kantian autonomism: it is human beings who decide what is good, who make the law for themselves.[33] The good is not rooted in some pre-existent moral order, or in God's law, or in anything that is alien to humanity, but rather in what is termed 'political constructivism'.[34] The right is prior to the good, though the two do in fact converge.

Thus it is not true to say that Rawls is working in a vacuum without a true theory of the good and without a true idea of what constitutes the human person. It would be more true to say that his position, though coherent and well founded and of respectable pedigree, is not one many would have chosen themselves. The Catholic reader of *Theory* will be immensely attracted to what Rawls says about 'Perfectionism', a position he rejects.[35] Perfectionism, which is essentially Aristotelian in origin, sees society as having a goal, that of promoting humanity's final end or its perfection. But Rawls rejects this on many grounds: first of all there can be no general agreement or consensus about what such a final end must be.[36] There can be no agreed criterion of perfection; and the people in the Original Position would never arrive at the idea that we all have a natural duty to seek excellence. It is even unfair, he goes on to say, for society to subsidize art for art's sake![37] Simply put, any vision of political community, as opposed to political society, would be incompatible with human freedom and equality. Mankind has no single *telos* – rather each is free to choose in their rational life plan what their individual *telos* is to be; likewise each is free to choose a comprehensive doctrine (a narrative, if that is the preferred term), but no such doctrine (or narrative) can be imposed on others, however reasonable it may appear.

---

[32] Rawls, *A Theory of Justice*, p. 26.
[33] Rawls's debt to Kant is considerable and beyond our scope here. He claims that he detaches the Kantian conception of Justice from the background of transcendental idealism and gives it a procedural interpretation through the Original Position (see Rawls, *Political Liberalism*, p. 285.) In *A Theory of Justice* (p. 256) he describes the Original Position as a procedural interpretation of Kant's theories of autonomy and the categorical imperative, giving content to these formal concepts.
[34] Discussed in Rawls, *Political Liberalism*, pp. 93–6.
[35] Rawls, *A Theory of Justice*, p. 325.
[36] Rawls, *A Theory of Justice*, p. 327.
[37] Rawls, *A Theory of Justice*, p. 239.

This conclusion would seem to lead to a further conclusion that political society has no common good,[38] and that each lives in some sort of cultural vacuum. Indeed Rawls prefers to uses a different phrase, with a different emphasis, alluding to a shared good which is the fruit of Justice as Fairness, which he calls 'civic friendship': the moral virtues that political liberalism fosters are fairness, civility and tolerance.[39] This is one aspect of his work that can be easily overlooked. In his discussion of stability, an important concept in his work, he stresses how Justice as Fairness creates an ever-increasing awareness of the demands of justice; and how the practice of justice brings people to an ever-increasing appreciation of it.[40] This is close to the Thomistic and Aristotelian idea of virtue as a habit, a practice of doing good which gradually becomes ingrained in a person's character until it becomes almost second nature to them. Civic friendship, the ties that bind society together, is not to be dismissed as mere flim-flam: it is rather an evolving shared good and a path to moral progress and greater moral awareness. By no means does Rawls see the Original Position as an end point – rather it is a starting point in a moral journey towards ever increasing degrees of Justice as Fairness, which is a historical process.

It is thus true to say that Rawls does see his politically liberal society as generating some particular virtues. But this process must be understood as a limited one. He says quite clearly:

> Even though political liberalism seeks common ground and is neutral in aim, it is important to emphasize that it may still affirm the superiority of certain forms of moral character and encourage certain moral virtues. Thus, justice as fairness includes an account of certain political virtues – the virtues of fair social cooperation such as the virtues of civility and tolerance, of reasonableness and a sense of fairness. The crucial point is that admitting these virtues into a political conception does not lead to the perfectionist state of a comprehensive doctrine.[41]

One notes that these virtues are minimalist in their import, though certainly not to be discounted. This does not satisfy certain liberal writers, though. Stephen Macedo wishes to see a much more comprehensive picture. He envisages an ideal liberal personality at home in the liberal state, someone characterized by reflective self-awareness, active self-control, a willingness to engage in self-criticism, an openness to change and critical support for the public morality of liberal justice.[42] Such a

---

[38] Rawls says as much in *Political Liberalism*, p. 201. Justice as Fairness having no basis in a comprehensive doctrine rejects the idea of political community and sees society as made up of distinct individuals and groups pursuing their own ends. They have no final end in common. Political institutions are seen as purely instrumental; political society is not a good, but the means to an individual or associational good.

[39] Rawls, *Political Liberalism*, p. 194.

[40] This process is described in *Political Liberalism*, pp. 86 et seq. Citizens acquire a sense of Justice and are ready and willing to co-operate with just arrangements on a reciprocal basis. This builds trust and confidence in those who participate, which grows over time. The same is true for institutions. What Rawls does not explain, however, is how one can ensure that this process of evolution takes place.

[41] Rawls, *Political Liberalism*, p. 194.

[42] Stephen Macedo, *Liberal Virtues* (Oxford: Clarendon Press, 1990), p. 251.

liberalism he admits would not be neutral and would have positive values.[43] It would in certain ways though be intolerant, being deeply at odds with Augustinian Catholicism,[44] while at the same time letting anti-Semites express their views.[45] Macedo concludes his picture by saying: 'Liberalism holds out the promise, or the threat, of making all the world like California', admitting that such a society would have a degree of superficiality and all such societies would tend to homogeneity.[46] This conclusion is enough to convince us that Rawls must be right in refusing to admit any vision of perfectionism and to keep his virtues to a minimum, for the simple reason that the perfectionist state may be one person's dream, but another's nightmare.

Let us now attempt a provisional conclusion. The idea that we all sit and listen to one story that forms us and forms our society into a single community is clearly, in the Rawlsian view, unsustainable. It is unsustainable in practice because no one would choose to live in such a society which tends to totalitarianism. If one narrative is to be thought of as being all-embracing, to the detriment of all other narratives, then we must reject it. Society must allow a plurality of narratives, in so far as it allows a plurality (within limits, as we shall see) of characters, behaviour and beliefs.

But against this we must acknowledge that if society is to hold together it must have some core values and these values can be, or are best, summed up, in a narrative to which all can adhere. But this idea is not the same as the totalitarian-tending vision of the preceding paragraph. The 'core-value narrative' and the 'all-embracing narrative' are narratives of a different type. The Original Position is being advanced, we shall argue later, as a core-value narrative, and not an all-embracing one, not a comprehensive state doctrine; unlike the all-embracing comprehensive narratives of Stalinism and Nazism, the Rawlsian narrative leaves space for other narratives to co-exist with it. It is, in other words, a qualitatively different type of narrative.

What then emerges is that the word 'narrative' leaves room for interpretation, for narratives command allegiance at different levels, and human beings can hold several narratives simultaneously without experiencing contradiction, if these narratives are held at different levels. Naturally, this idea requires a great deal of refinement, but we can already see the nub of the Rawlsian claim: it is possible to hold the narrative of the Original Position along with a more comprehensive narrative such as Catholicism, and there is no contradiction between the belief in Justice as Fairness and the beliefs and practices of the Catholic Church, at least in theory. Indeed, as we shall see, Rawls goes on to posit a beneficial link between the two, striking another blow against the idea that all narratives must necessarily be at war with each other.

Also of interest to those who are concerned with narrative is what Rawls has had to say about the way we make moral choices: his vision is a useful corrective to the idea of embedded decision-making. At the very least we can say this: if it is true that to make a decision a person must be embedded in community, it may also be true that

---

[43] Macedo, p. 258.
[44] Macedo, p. 74.
[45] Macedo, p. 72.
[46] Macedo, p. 278.

a person making a decision needs to adopt a position of impartiality, at least to some degree, in order to ensure that the decision is the fruit of purity of heart as opposed to self or group interest.

Rawls's position as we have seen it so far is clearly distinct from that of the writers who can be loosely characterized as communitarians, and even a 'liberal communitarian' like Macedo. A further aspect of the question lies in the distinction between political society in the narrow sense and deeper visions of community which he holds to be unsustainable. It is to this question that we must now turn, examining the central question of pluralism.

Pluralism: Narrative Unity in Diversity?

At the start of *Political Liberalism*, Rawls considers the question of pluralism and makes clear that he sees it as the central issue in political philosophy today. How can a stable society exist when there is a plurality of competing and incompatible comprehensive doctrines available?

> Now the serious problem is this. A modern democratic society is characterised not simply by a pluralism of comprehensive religious, philosophical and moral doctrines, but by a pluralism of incompatible yet *reasonable* comprehensive doctrines. No one of these doctrines is affirmed by citizens generally. Nor should one expect that in the foreseeable future that one of them, or some other reasonable doctrine, will ever be affirmed by all, or nearly all, citizens. Political liberalism assumes that, for political purposes, a plurality of reasonable yet incompatible comprehensive doctrines is the normal result of the exercise of human reason within the framework of the free institutions of a constitutional democratic regime. Political liberalism also supposes that a reasonable comprehensive doctrine does not reject the essentials of a democratic regime. Of course, a society may also contain unreasonable and irrational, and even mad, comprehensive doctrines. In their case the problem is to contain them so that they do not undermine the unity and justice of society.[47]

What the above means in practical terms is that in a modern democratic society there exist a number of competing and mutually exclusive narratives which underpin the mutually exclusive and competing comprehensive doctrines. No single narrative is affirmed by citizens generally, and no single narrative seems capable of winning general allegiance. This situation bears some resemblance to that outlined by MacIntyre in the opening chapter of *After Virtue*.

However, it is useful to note that political liberalism does not entail, as some might assume, a free for all in the doctrinal (and thus narrative) field. Liberalism is not to be equated with anarchy. Some comprehensive doctrines and their accompanying narratives will be outlawed or at least restricted. In later writings Rawls makes clear that not all permitted comprehensive doctrines will flourish to an equal extent in a politically liberal society and some will find the soil uncongenial; though a constitutional regime is neutral in its procedures as regards comprehensive

---

[47] Rawls, *Political Liberalism*, Introduction, pp. xvi–xvii.

doctrines, it will not necessarily be neutral in its effects;[48] this is a charge that Engelhardt brings against him with force.[49] But for the moment let it suffice to say that Rawlsian pluralism is bounded by what is reasonable, by what would be chosen in the Original Position. Rawls's people would not countenance the worship of Moloch and child sacrifice, nor presumably the right of parents to refuse blood transfusions on behalf of their children. Likewise the sort of arrangements chosen in the Original Position will provide a more comfortable home for some doctrines as opposed to others. Neutrality of effect is simply not practical. Comprehensive doctrines that contradict justice, those for example that involve slavery, would be banned; likewise a comprehensive doctrine that can only survive by controlling the state will wither away in a politically liberal society; but Rawls also recognizes that a politically liberal society will not allow all forms of the good to flourish; the idea of public education may undermine some religions, for example.[50] But despite these important qualifications a Rawlsian society is a pluralist one.

In his approach to pluralism, Rawls shows a marked difference in emphasis and approach from MacIntyre (though as we have seen the position of the first chapter of *After Virtue* cannot be taken as final), Hauerwas and Engelhardt. For them, pluralism is the problem, and is essentially malign. By contrast, Rawls sees it as 'the normal result of the exercise of human reason within the framework of the free institutions'. But the challenge remains: how are we to live with pluralism, the proliferation of different and incompatible narratives?

This question finds some resonance in Catholic theologians as well: John Courtney Murray, writing some thirty years ago, in *We Hold These Truths*,[51] also views pluralism as harmful and divisive and proposes that some sort of consensus can be found based on Natural Law. This seems a forlorn hope in America today, given the impasse produced by, among other things, *Roe* v. *Wade*.[52] Yet the idea of natural law as a common platform and common ground through which agreement on moral and by extension political issues can be reached is, as we have seen in our discussion of Engelhardt, still with us. Some contemporary Catholic theologians[53] make just this claim, though their more nuanced idea of natural law, namely the workings of *recta ratio* which are open to all people, is, one feels rather different to the more naturalistic view of nature as a 'given' of the previous generation, of which Murray is an exponent. One could argue that the workings of right reason, which exist independently of any religious belief, are enough to ensure a consensus in a pluralistic world, and that pluralism itself is the fruit of the poor use of right reason in the past. Thus clear rethinking and a re-evaluation of our past positions, indeed a re-

---

[48] Rawls, *Collected Papers*, p. 460.
[49] Engelhardt, *Foundations of Christian Bioethics*, pp. 370 et seq.
[50] Rawls, 'The Priority of the Right and Ideas of the Good' in *Collected Papers*, pp. 462–4.
[51] John Courtney Murray, *We Hold These Truths* (New York: Sheed and Ward, 1960).
[52] The case was decided 22 January 1973 by the US Supreme Court, which established a constitutional right to abortion on grounds of privacy.
[53] One such is Klaus Demmer, *Shaping the Moral Life* (Washington, DC: Georgetown University Press, 2000), in particular chapter 6, pp. 36–42.

evaluation of our culture, in the light of *recta ratio*, will solve the perceived problem of pluralism and enable us to reach consensus.[54]

It is at this point that Rawls has much to say that is enlightening. He does not see the use of right reason as the cure for pluralism, but rather as its cause. Pluralism is not a malign phenomenon, but the natural outgrowth of a free society: 'This pluralism is not seen as a disaster but rather as the natural outcome of the activities of human reason under enduring free institutions. To see reasonable pluralism as a disaster is to see the exercise of reason under the conditions of freedom itself as a disaster'.[55]

It is implied very strongly that the free use of reason is a positive phenomenon and that the opposite of pluralism, agreement or uniformity, can in fact only be brought about by coercion. A historical sketch – which takes a different view on the ancient polis from that of MacIntyre, and which has some penetrating things to say about the reformation – outlines for us how and why pluralism was born.[56]

Clearly Rawls's perspective differs greatly from that of MacIntyre and Hauerwas. He sees a non-pluralistic world as essentially a police state, rather different to the visions of harmonious community of MacIntyre and Hauerwas. However at the same time, Rawls makes some important distinctions that must not be ignored, as we have seen. While referring earlier to the horrors of coercion, Rawls then goes on to say again that only reasonable pluralism must be admitted, that is to say that a well-ordered society can and indeed must tolerate reasonable though incompatible comprehensive doctrines, but not doctrines that are unreasonable.[57] Pluralism must not contradict reason itself and must have limits. In addition we must not forget the important role that is to be played by the 'Difference Principle':[58] no social inequality is to be admissible, unless that social inequality is for the benefit of the least advantaged in society. This too must act as a brake on certain doctrines and rule them out. Having drawn these distinctions, the well ordered society allows all reasonable comprehensive doctrines. Clearly no one in the Original Position would have chosen to outlaw any religion or any philosophical position,[59] given these limits. That would not accord with Justice as Fairness. And at the same time, no one would choose to elevate one comprehensive doctrine to a special position above any others, whatever advantages this might bring, as this would violate the rights of the minority, however small. Thus the Original Position brings us to an appreciation of toleration for all reasonable comprehensive doctrines, all of which are to be treated impartially in a well ordered society.

This has a further most important consequence. If all comprehensive doctrines are to be treated impartially, this means that the state itself cannot be underpinned by any one such doctrine and there can never be a state religion or even a state philosophy. Of course the state will have some underpinning ideas, but these will

---

[54] For a discussion of this point, see Jean Porter, *Natural and Divine Law, Reclaiming the Tradition for Christian Ethics* (Grand Rapids: Novalis, 1999), especially pp. 30–31 et seq.
[55] Rawls, *Political Liberalism*, Introduction, pp. xxiv–xxv.
[56] Rawls, *Political Liberalism*, Introduction, pp. xxi–xxvii.
[57] Rawls, *Political Liberalism*, pp. 61–3.
[58] Rawls, *A Theory of Justice*, p. 15.
[59] Rawls, *Political Liberalism*, p. 58.

not form a comprehensive doctrine. Justice as Fairness is not a comprehensive doctrine, rather it is something in which all adherents of the various comprehensive doctrines can believe in and practice: it is the content of the 'overlapping consensus' that excludes no one, whatever reasonable comprehensive doctrine they adhere to. Rawls advances Justice as Fairness as a 'freestanding' idea that depends on no comprehensive doctrine for its justification.[60] It is his aim to separate politics from religion and indeed philosophy. Thus political liberalism can be embraced by various groupings, even though each group may do so for differing reasons.[61] Thus can a well ordered society exist in a pluralistic world.

This idea of a freestanding doctrine is what every narrative thinker would reject, on the grounds that no doctrine or narrative can of its nature be freestanding: every doctrine or narrative is rooted in time, culture, place and history. A freestanding doctrine is an illusion; and indeed, as we have seen, Engelhardt claims that the narrative of the Original Position, good for all times and places, is no such thing, but rather the specific narrative of Cambridge, Massachusetts, and thus not freestanding at all.

But this may be to miss the point. Rawls's narrative is perhaps intended to be qualitatively different to, for example, the narrative of the Orthodox Church, or the poetry of Homer. While Orthodoxy and Homer are comprehensive, all-embracing and exclusive of other narratives, Justice as Fairness aims to present an inclusive narrative, all-embracing in a different sense in that it is designed to find a suitably concordant fit with pre-existing narratives. We will shortly look at the implications of this, but for the moment we must note once again that Rawls is advancing a different type of narrative to that of our other authors. For Justice as Fairness and the Original Position presuppose no wider doctrine;[62] other narratives, if what we have considered so far is true, do presuppose some wider doctrine and act as Trojan horses for such doctrines: in other words, to be Homeric, you have to accept numerous presuppositions about the nature of human beings, gods and the role of women and slaves in society; to practice Justice as Fairness, you do not have to make such wide-ranging presuppositions. This means that if what Rawls is claiming is justly founded, we will have to re-examine our presuppositions about the nature of narrative: is it indeed possible to hold a narrative like that of Justice as Fairness which can coexist with some other narrative of a comprehensive nature? An answer will depend on an examination of how we hold narratives and how narratives work. But first of all we must examine whether a doctrine such as Justice as Fairness can indeed be freestanding, or whether this is in fact merely a dangerous illusion.

---

[60] This is perhaps the central contention of the entire book. As Rawls says, *Political Liberalism*, p. 40, 'Justice as Fairness elaborates a political conception as a free-standing view from the fundamental idea of democratic society, presupposing no wider doctrine.' This central point is repeated in various forms throughout the book.

[61] Again, this is one of the book's central contentions: the conception of justice must be limited, Rawls says, to the 'domain of the political' (p. 38) if it is to gain cross-party support. Thus he aims to separate political concepts from concepts that form part of a much wider vision. Political concepts are, he says (p. 13) 'narrow in scope'.

[62] Rawls, *Political Liberalism*, p. 40.

Rawls's vision of unity in diversity needs to be tested. We need to ask whether the narrative of the Original Position stands up to criticism and whether the overlapping consensus that it produces is a real consensus. Or will we find it wanting as we found Engelhardt's two principles wanting?

For a start, is Rawlsian political liberalism, the belief that there can be no doctrinal monism in the body politic, just another form of scepticism? Is it saying that all beliefs are purely subjective, all positions relative, and that truth is essentially unattainable? Is it making the best out of a bad job, and failing to tackle head on the challenge of pluralism, by making a virtue out of necessity? If this were true it would mean that Justice as Fairness would be illusory, just another relativist position: for why should people who can agree on nothing else, agree on Justice as Fairness? Why should one story make sense when no other story can make sense?[63]

In fact Rawls strongly denies that he is sceptical as regards the truth; rather he takes the view that political liberalism (as distinct from what he calls comprehensive liberalism) not being a comprehensive doctrine, stands back from the question of truth.[64] It makes no judgement between the various reasonable comprehensive doctrines present in a society. Political liberalism can have no position on such questions, for if it did it would no longer be political liberalism – rather it would have entered the fray as a competing comprehensive doctrine. As for the question of truth, truth is attainable, but thanks to what he calls 'the burdens of judgement'[65] the process is a difficult one; and it is these burdens of judgement that explain in the first place why pluralism exists. In examining Rawls' account of the burdens of judgement we see that he is far more modest in the claims he makes for *recta ratio* than some contemporary Catholic writers. Rawls does not deny the importance of hermeneutics – he is merely acutely aware of the difficulties that lie in the way of the human mind when grappling with questions of truth. The very reasonableness of competing doctrines makes uniformity itself unreasonable, he concludes.[66] This is a position which he shares with others such as Hauerwas: the claims of reason to solve every problem and bring all to agreement can no longer be sustained: but this is not because reason itself has failed, but because of the difficulties human beings experience in confronting reasoned argument. Rawls is realistic as opposed to pessimistic about the powers of reason.

MacIntyre, Hauerwas and Engelhardt, confronted by the weakness of reason all advocate a turn to narrative. Narrative is seen as a surer way of reasoning by MacIntyre; but we suspect that Hauerwas and to a greater extent Engelhardt see narrative as a way of sidestepping reason. Rawls, confronted with the burdens of judgement, advocates a strikingly similar path, namely a turn to the 'expository

---

[63] We have already seen that the two principles of Engelhardt are vulnerable to this objection.

[64] Rawls, *Political Liberalism*, p. 63.

[65] Rawls, *Political Liberalism*, p. 55. The burdens of judgement that make consensus 'a practical impossibility, born out by historical experience', though Rawls does not deny 'certainty *per se*' (p. 63), are as follows: the complexity of the evidence to be evaluated; the vagueness of concepts; the weight of cultural conditioning; the differences in normative considerations; and the fact that social institutions impose different criteria of selection.

[66] Rawls, *Political Liberalism*, p. 61.

device'[67] of the Original Position. Hence we need not worry that because the burdens of judgement are so heavy, that we may never arrive at the family of ideas that make up political liberalism. Political liberalism relies on the idea of representation that is the Original Position – a way of thinking that cuts through, bypasses perhaps, the usual difficulties in any thought process that seeks to attain the truth, by leaving the question of truth aside in favour of the right.[68] As for whether this family of ideas that is political liberalism constitutes just another comprehensive doctrine, this time by the back door, Rawls's answer is based on the idea of Kantian autonomy: the rightness of political liberalism does not depend on any pre-existing moral order, but rather on pure procedural justice.

> Taking the original position as a case of pure procedural justice, we describe the parties' deliberations so that they model citizens' rational autonomy. To see this, we say that there are two ways in which the parties are rationally autonomous. The first way is that the appropriate principles of justice for specifying fair terms of social cooperation are those that would be selected as the outcome of a process of rational deliberation, a process visualised as being carried out by the parties. The appropriate weight of reasons for and against the various principles available is given by their weight for the parties, and the weight of all reasons on balance determines the principles that would be agreed to. Pure procedural justice means that in their rational deliberations the parties do not view themselves as required to apply, or as bound by, any antecedent given principles of right and justice. Put another way, they recognise no standpoint external to their own point of view as rational representatives from which they are constrained by prior and independent principles of justice. This models the idea that when citizens are fairly situated with respect to one another, it is up to them to specify the fair terms of social cooperation in the light of what they each regard as to their own advantage, or good.[69]

Simply put, the people in the Original Position are not arguing about positions, or the standard-bearers of traditions; all that baggage is left at the door to the conference chamber and put out of sight behind the Veil of Ignorance. Rawls's people are autonomous, independent, quite unlike MacIntyre's people who are historically and community bound and formed. Thus, procedural justice, one cannot but note, according to Rawls, seems to be less fraught with difficulty than the pursuit of the truth which encounters the burdens of judgement.

What we see here is a crucial difference that separates Rawls from those who claim to be working as champions of narrative. Pure procedural justice for them is an illusion as no one can make a decision that does not somehow reflect the decisions they have already made in their lifetime. There simply never was a decision made in the sterile laboratory conditions envisaged by Rawls when he talks of pure procedural justice. But, as we have already seen, one might argue to the contrary that decisions, though personal, in other words engaging the consent of the whole person who decides, must also be fair and impartial. People need to put aside their own points of view and take in the wider picture.

---

[67] Rawls, *A Theory of Justice*, p. 21.

[68] This is what Rawls terms 'political constructivism' (see *Political Liberalism*, pp. 93–6) based on Kant's distinction of good and right.

[69] Rawls, *Political Liberalism*, p. 73.

What we see here is an emerging divergence between two different types of narrative: a narrative that incarnates our world and our history and our community, on the one hand, and on the other, a narrative that represents an at least partial disengagement from all three. In other words: one that invites us to think about the here and now, and another that invites us to look at the here and now from a critical distance.

Rawls's approach is not to be dismissed out of hand. And if Rawls's approach is right, there ought to be no contradiction between his method of decision-making and that of another narrative – rather the two ought to be complementary, for political liberalism allows for all reasonable comprehensive doctrines. In other words, a Catholic or a Muslim could come to the same position as Rawls – a belief in Justice as Fairness – drawing on the reasonable comprehensive doctrines which are Catholicism and Islam. On the surface, the overlapping consensus, the idea that everyone can come to the same conclusion from a variety of incompatible starting points, seems to work. But if this is so, it means that something else is also true. One cannot be a Catholic and a Muslim at the same time; these narratives are mutually exclusive; however, one can be a Catholic and a Rawlsian, or a Muslim and a Rawlsian, at the same time. In other words Justice as Fairness, unlike comprehensive doctrines/narratives, can co-exist with a variety of other narratives. Thus once again we see that the Rawlsian narrative is a narrative of a different type to that proposed by our other authors, a narrative that is held at a different level.

However, there is more to be said: once Justice as Fairness has been established and proved that it can get along with (almost all) other narratives, what then? What is the final end of this well ordered society?

Once again we come up against the question of *telos*. Political liberalism, refusing to be a comprehensive doctrine denies that either human beings or human society has a final end.[70] Furthermore, is its refusal to be a comprehensive doctrine, and its desire to be free-standing, a source of weakness? Will this mean it will fail to command loyalty and support, fail to be, in Rawls's preferred term, stable?[71] In other words is a free-standing narrative, one that has no roots, a practical impossibility?

Clearly these questions are closely related. Political liberalism, as history has proved, is notoriously unstable. A political constitution that aims to be freestanding and thus not reliant for support on either history or religion or some sort of philosophy, can easily be toppled. While Rawls writes well about civic friendship and the political virtues that Justice as Fairness will breed,[72] the fact remains that a

---

[70] Rawls, *A Theory of Justice*, p. 264. Here Rawls makes a basic point that is re-elaborated in the later volume. The Original Position, he says, accounts for social values with a theory of Justice that has an individualistic basis. It denies the concept of community, or the idea of society as an organic whole greater than the sum of its parts, on the grounds that this concept is too hard to define and too hard to be clear about. The contractual position is more open to precision. However, from an individualist position one can arrive at some explanation of community; otherwise the theory of justice would fail.

[71] Rawls is deeply concerned with the stability of society, and discusses it at several points. For one example, see *A Theory of Justice*, pp. 455–8.

[72] For example, Rawls, *A Theory of Justice*, p. 458; and also Rawls, *Political Liberalism*, p. 86.

society without a firm and rooted foundation of some sort will always be vulnerable to the siren call of someone or some group that offers a comprehensive doctrine, however spurious that doctrine may be. Every political plant needs roots to survive the storms that may shake it; every society seeks some sort of *raison d'etre* for its existence. As Iris Murdoch has pointed out: 'High morality without religion is too abstract, high morality craves for religion... Religion symbolizes high moral ideals which then travel with us and are more intimately and accessibly effective than the unadorned promptings of reason.'[73]

Justice as Fairness on its own may not be enough to command loyalty, especially in difficult times. It may not be sufficiently readily accessible to the general population's understanding, in practical terms. It may be a narrative that is simply too weak to live and survive in this world. Mankind longs for a closer union, a deeper communion. This is surely reflected in the writings of communitarians such as Hauerwas and MacIntyre, and the following they have found. It is also reflected in the writings of those who would try and flesh out Rawls's work and advance liberalism as a comprehensive doctrine, as Stephen Macedo suggests. Certainly his vision is more colourful that Rawls's! We should remember too what Nisbet has to say about the quest for community: some may prefer the 'millennial sense of participation in heavenly power on earth' and 'a moral community of almost religious intensity' that a totalitarian regime may bring with it.[74] On a less exalted note, some may follow William Galston and wish to see a thicker theory of the good undergirding the liberal state.[75]

Leaving aside the accusation that communitarians are essentially nostalgic, as Stephen Holmes[76] has claimed, the denial of a final end or of an underpinning comprehensive doctrine to society does make Rawls's position unsatisfying. His answer – that one can choose one's form of community or one's own doctrine, without making such choices universal or compulsory – fails to answer the basic question: what is society for? But let us return to Rawls's discussion of this problem and see if he can advance a rational answer to it.

In the first place, Rawls wants all constitutional questions, that is to say questions that affect the state, to be settled by recourse to the political alone. Political values override all others. Just as it would be wrong to use political power to enforce Church doctrine on the grounds that such a course is unreasonable (though Church doctrine may be *per se* perfectly reasonable), so it is also wrong to use political power to enforce truth.[77] Rawls has earlier asserted that political power is always coercive[78] and it does seem to be a valid point that no one would want to live in a society where

---

[73] Iris Murdoch, *Metaphysics as a Guide to Morals* (Harmondsworth: Penguin, 1993), p. 484.
[74] Nisbet, p. 33.
[75] William Galston, *Liberal Purposes: Goods, Virtues and Diversity in the Liberal State* (Cambridge: Cambridge University Press, 1991), pp. 174–7.
[76] Stephen Holmes, 'The Permanent Structure of Anti-Liberal Thought', in *Liberalism and the Moral Life*, edited by Nancy Rosenblum (Cambridge, Mass.: Harvard University Press, 1989), pp. 227–53.
[77] Rawls, *Political Liberalism*, p. 138.
[78] Rawls, *Political Liberalism*, p. 136.

the possibility of being coerced to believe a certain comprehensive doctrine existed: in short, none of us would have chosen that arrangement in the Original Position. Thus society must do without an overarching comprehensive doctrine as the basis of its political constitution. However, the overlapping consensus can depend on a plurality of reasonable comprehensive doctrines,[79] so though freestanding, it also has the virtue of being able to adapt itself to a range of beliefs. Thus Justice as Fairness which is the object of the overlapping consensus is a moral object that can be affirmed on moral grounds.[80] However, this 'sufficiently concordant fit' between political and other values[81] still does not entirely free us from the criticism implied by Iris Murdoch's insight: is such naked morality, without the aid of religion, history or patriotism, enough to ensure the stability of the state? Does Rawls, by ruling out any comprehensive doctrine, deprive his political concept of its most potent supports? And at the same time, we can suspect that his overlapping consensus, affirmed on moral grounds, is in fact a comprehensive doctrine by the back door. Indeed, he admits that the broader and deeper the overlapping consensus becomes, the more it becomes a comprehensive doctrine or to rely on one.[82]

Thus we see a nascent self-contradiction in Rawls's work: he wishes to advance a free-standing idea, but at the same time admits that such a free-standing idea may well put down roots. One might point out that this is the result when one tries to do ethics without an anthropological basis: sooner or later, some sort of anthropology will sprout forth from the ethics! Similarly, and this is the real question, can one advance a narrative without that narrative expanding to become the one and only narrative? For narratives have a tendency to fill themselves out, and this is detectable in Rawls too: having been given the bare bones of a story – the Original Position – we soon feel the urge to put flesh on these bones. In other words the idea of a freestanding narrative may well be an illusion – and we may in fact find that starting with Rawls we end up with Galston and Macedo – fully-fledged comprehensive liberals.

This is the first problem, one to which we will have to turn again. Let us now consider the allied question. What is society for? As we have seen a strict Rawlsian will have to answer as follows: 'Society is not for anything. It has no final purpose. It is founded on Justice as Fairness, which is a moral concept, but this supposes an individual good as opposed to a communitarian or common good. The whole is not greater than the sum of the parts. The political is a narrow concept and not to be confused with wider concepts such as community.' It seems undeniable, then, that Rawls's vision rests on an individualistic basis, an 'atomism' that many see as the fundamental flaw in all liberal theories.

That this is so has occurred to several liberal thinkers. Galston speaks of 'liberal community' without any suggestion that this is an oxymoron, and of the positive values that liberals have in common and which bind them together. He rejects Rawlsian neutrality and claims that liberalism is more substantive and purposive than

---
[79] Rawls, *Political Liberalism*, p. 145.
[80] Rawls, *Political Liberalism*, p. 147.
[81] Rawls, *Political Liberalism*, p. 158.
[82] Rawls, *Political Liberalism*, p. 154.

it is usually considered.[83] But the truth of the matter is that Galston, like Macedo, is describing liberalism as such, a comprehensive doctrine, and not political liberalism which can be endorsed by those who do not accept comprehensive liberalism. Galston defeats Rawls's purpose, which is to create a 'Big Tent' and not another California.

However, Galston does have some important insights into the question of the common good. As we have seen, Rawls rejects all ideas of perfectionism, on the grounds that no consensus would be reached in the Original Position over a unitary good for human beings. Expressed like that, one has to agree. We may not all see the point of the arts, we may not all agree that opera is essential to the good life, and so we cannot agree on the question of state subsidies for the arts.[84] But the idea that the good is unitary is challenged by Galston and rightly so: he says that there is no one good for all, though there may be a common core of values that lies at the heart of each individual good.[85] The idea that one size fits all, the idea of a unitary good, he dubs 'moral monism', a clearly dangerous idea.[86] But if there are many goods how do we judge between them? If goods are heterogeneous, how do we rank them? The fact is that we do do so, even though we may not have worked out a formula that explains the process.[87] And indeed, who was the better person, Mother Teresa or Jane Austen? It is an unanswerable question, simply because the good takes many forms. The women mentioned encapsulate splendid lives, though very different ones; they would, though, have agreed on a common core of values. Galston concludes by saying: 'The fundamental argument for a diverse society is not, as some believe, that our reason is incompetent to judge among possible ways of life. It is rather that the human good is not one thing but many things.'[88] MacIntyre would agree with this; not all good people are the same, and there can be a unity in diversity and vice versa. Galston then takes his argument towards the justification of desert and even the heredity principle[89] and an exposition of the virtues for liberals in a liberal society.[90] One practice that Galston approves of is the awarding of medals to soldiers for bravery, for courage is a virtue and should be rewarded, especially when it is exercised in defence of the state. Would this have been admitted in the Original Position? Would Rawls's people agree on this particular good? It is hard to see pacifists admiring the good soldier.

The Galstonian alternative makes us realize just how much we must leave behind the Veil of Ignorance, and just how little can be secured in the Original Position; much may be regained through the Overlapping Consensus, but even Rawls reminds

---

[83] Galston, pp. 3–9.
[84] Rawls, *A Theory of Justice*, p. 332.
[85] Galston, p. 181. Rawls agrees with him, *Theory of Justice*, p. 448: 'Individuals find their good in different ways, and many things may be good for one person that would not be good for another.' For a similar point, see Rawls, *Political Liberalism*, pp. 182–3.
[86] Galston, p. 177.
[87] Galston, p. 181.
[88] Galston, p. 194.
[89] Galston, p. 196.
[90] Galston, p. 221 et seq.

us that here is no society without loss.[91] A constitutional regime may spell disaster for your fervently held comprehensive doctrine – but that is the price one pays.[92]

Certainly Rawls is individualistic. The Original Position posits people who are not bound together by previous ties, but who are, nevertheless, prepared to co-operate with each other in the search for agreement; however, altruism is specifically excluded in order to underline the pure rationality of the choices to be made. But altruism can come into the equation later.[93] Certainly altruism remains a problem for Rawls, and we shall have to turn to this later as well.

What emerges here is a vast abyss between Rawls and such thinkers as MacIntyre and Hauerwas, to mention only two, and even Galston and Macedo. One deals with the highest level of abstraction, the others emphasize the embodied self, the importance of history and tradition, the solidity of narrative. Rawls's narrative, if it can be classed as such, which many would doubtless deny, is of a very different type. There seems to be no common ground between the two opposing camps, and the difference is more than a mere difference of emphasis. But what remains at stake here is what we have characterized as the central claim of Rawls's position, namely that there can be a narrative (that of the Original Position and Justice as Fairness) which is freestanding, this is, not dependant on a comprehensive doctrine: in other words, a narrative that holds good for all times and places, without having necessary roots in one tradition or one particular community.

Rawls's Idea of Justice

Another possible objection to Rawls's Original Position is to say that the overlapping consensus has no content, and that Justice as Fairness is an illusion. In other words, the story of the Original Position may well 'work' as a story, but its fruits are derisory, in that the Position is not really about justice but about securing the largest share for oneself, in other words, it is about selfishness merely dressed up as justice. In other words, the concept of justice can only be arrived at as the result of a fully developed narrative; the Rawlsian narrative will merely produce an idea of justice which is a shadow of true justice in that it will have no real moral content.

Is each party in the Original Position motivated purely by self-interest and concerned with maximizing their own position at the expense of the others? At first sight the answer seems to be yes. Rawls admits that social life is marked by conflict as well as by identity of interests and that this conflict centres on the distribution of benefits. Everyone wants a larger rather than a smaller share. Hence social justice centres around the question of the distribution of rights and duties. As Rawls expresses it:

---

[91] Galston, p. 146. Rawls makes it clear that his state would be neutral in procedure and not in effect; liberal structures will have an effect on some doctrines more than others for good or ill (see Rawls, *Political Liberalism*, p. 193–7.) The point re loss comes from Isaiah Berlin (see note, p. 197, *Political Liberalism*).

[92] Rawls, 'The Idea of Public Reason Revisited', *Collected Papers*, pp. 588–9. Also 'The Priority of Right and Ideas of the Good', same volume, p. 463.

[93] Rawls, *A Theory of Justice*, p. 584.

> Let us assume, to fix ideas, that a society is a more or less self-sufficient association of persons who in their relations to one another recognised certain rules of conduct as binding and who for the most part act in accordance with them. Suppose further that these rules specify a system of cooperation designed to advance the good of those taking part in it. Then, although a society is a cooperative venture for mutual advantage, it is typically marked by a conflict as well as by an identity of interests. There is an identity of interests since social cooperation makes possible a better life for all than any would have if each were to live solely by his own efforts. There is a conflict of interests since persons are not indifferent as to how the greater benefits produced by their collaboration are distributed, for in order to pursue their ends they each prefer a larger to a lesser share. A set of principles is required for choosing among the various social arrangements which determine this division of advantages and for underwriting an agreement on the proper distributive share. These principles are the principles of social justice: they provide a way of assigning rights and duties in the basic institutions of society and they define the appropriate distribution of the benefits and burdens of social cooperation.[94]

One sees at once that he does not envisage some sort of law of the jungle: there is conflict, but there is also identity of interests, or peace. The question of identity of interests and peace is prior to that of conflict: there is only conflict about shares derived from cooperative ventures, because these cooperative ventures have already been undertaken; solitaries do not need to discuss such arrangements. We might ask from where did this realization come, that cooperation is better than solitude? Or, as perhaps it is common sense to say that humankind can achieve more together than alone, how did this intuition arise? Again we note that Rawls's people, who for the most part observe the rules (but not always – they are human, after all), have a conception of moral obligation that precedes the Original Position, in which the rules of cooperation are to be worked out. This assertion is fundamental to the whole structure of Rawls's thought. If there were no sense of moral obligation, this recognition of certain rules of conduct as binding, each person could return to his den and pursue the life of nature, red in tooth and claw. But where does this sense of moral obligation come from? How do we become aware of it? There are clearly assumptions here that need to be examined, and we will turn to them later.

Rawls goes on to say that 'inclination to self-interest makes vigilance against one another necessary' before mentioning the concept of civic friendship that emerges from a shared conception of justice.[95] It thus seems from the above that there may be some justice in Hauerwas's criticism that the Original Position has self-interest at its heart, though Hauerwas does point out that the self-interest is limited by the thought for the disadvantaged that Rawls stresses as well.[96] The people in the Original Position are conceived of not as brothers and sisters but rivals, if indeed they have to be vigilant *against* each other. But does this mean that Rawls's people are in fact merely untrammelled egotists, out to get their own way at the expense of others? Fuller examination of the text reveals the following:

---

[94] Rawls, *A Theory of Justice*, p. 4.
[95] Rawls, *A Theory of Justice*, p. 5.
[96] Hauerwas, *A Community of Character*, p. 83.

...While men may put forth excessive demands on one another, they nevertheless acknowledge a common point of view from which their claims may be adjudicated. If men's inclination to self-interest makes their vigilance against one another necessary, their public sense of justice makes their secure association together possible.[97]

Rawls's people are not *purely* self-interested; they also have a balancing view of what is due to others. This seems to be a more nuanced view than that which Hauerwas allows for.

It is quite true that Rawls talks repeatedly of self-interest, but he is careful to distinguish it from selfishness and the baser instincts in general. Right at the beginning of *A Theory of Justice*, he establishes the inviolability of the person as a sacred principle that can never be violated for a supposed greater good: 'Each person possesses an inviolability founded on justice that even the welfare of society as a whole cannot override.'[98] This establishes an important brake on human self-interest, which must give way when another person's rights are at stake. For the same reason he rejects classical utilitarianism: the principle of utility would never be chosen in the Original Position, because, as each participant wishes to protect their own interests, no one would want to risk enduring loss for themselves in order to maximize the good of others. Rather the Original Position leads to the greatest possible equality in rights and duties and the realization that social and economic inequalities are just only if they result in compensating benefits for everyone, in particular for the least advantaged. This does not mean some are to have less so that others may prosper (the utilitarian argument) but rather that there is no injustice in greater benefits for a few if it leads to improvements for the less fortunate.[99]

The above is a rather sophisticated argument which aims to show how self-interest, when properly followed in the Original Position will in fact lead to greater equity. Simply put, Rawls sees self-interest – or more exactly, self-interest in the participants of the Original Position – as working against oppression and inequality. The Original Position is a device that draws the sting from self-interest by setting up a situation in which all the parties are perceived as equal – a position of symmetricality. Thus one's own self-interest works in favour of others rather than against them.

Further to this we have other arguments advanced more explicitly by Rawls: he says that people in the Original Position want to advance their own ends, which means maximizing their share of primary social goods. They wish to have the highest score possible without scoring off others; the process is not a game, as no one is trying to win.[100] Once again we see an odd mixture of the selfish and the altruistic at work here. As for the specific question of whether the Original Position is egotistic or not, while the people in the Original Position have no interest in others and their desires, yet those who hold to the principle of Justice as Fairness in ordinary life will not necessarily have the same attitude. The principles of justice must lead people to give thought to others. Furthermore, contractarian theory will not produce the results we want, says Rawls, unless the parties are motivated by benevolence – and

---

[97] Rawls, *A Theory of Justice*, p. 5.
[98] Rawls, *A Theory of Justice*, p. 3.
[99] Rawls, *A Theory of Justice*, pp. 14–15.
[100] Rawls, *A Theory of Justice*, pp. 144–5.

mutual indifference and the Veil of Ignorance (in the Original Position) produce the same effects as benevolence, in that they force each person to take the good of others into account. The Original Position will seem egotistic, he concludes, if one looks at only one of its two conditions.[101] Thus Rawls can claim with some justice to have bridged the gap between social values and individualism:[102] the theory of justice has as its starting point the individual and their needs and desires; through the perfect symmetry of the Original Position – which rests on mutual indifference and the Veil of Ignorance – the individual comes to assent to a social arrangement which is for the good of all. Thus we see a passage from self-interest to a wider benevolence. We can also see, in contrast to Hauerwas, that self-interest is not necessarily immoral and not to be considered as simple selfishness. Also what we see emerge here once again is that the idea that the Original Position is a way of thinking, a story that encapsulates a rationality. By 'adopting' the Original Position we can turn our self-interest into interest in the welfare of all. This shows us too the narrative nature of the Position: it is a story which once adopted changes our way of thinking and acting.

As for the question as to whether the Original Position means no more than making the best of a bad job, Rawls returns to this question in his later work *Political Liberalism*, which introduces the idea of the Overlapping Consensus that is the product of the Original Position. This does not rest on epistemological scepsis[103] but admits that epistemological certainty is a practical impossibility. It suspends judgement on moral questions, seeing justice as reasonable as opposed to true, adopting a narrow vision that restricts the question to the realm of the political alone.[104] Thus Rawls defends himself against the charge that the Overlapping Consensus rests on pure cynicism and opportunism. Furthermore, he rejects the charge that the Overlapping Consensus is a mere *modus vivendi*, a mere equilibrium between opponents dependant on circumstances. This is not so, as the Overlapping Consensus has as its object Justice as Fairness which is a moral concept; because it is such, later power shifts will not affect the stability of the consensus, which is deep and broad. Above all the consensus is not indifferent or sceptical as regards truth, which would bring it into fatal conflict with all competing comprehensive doctrines; rather, liberalism puts religion 'off the agenda'.[105]

It is at this point that we may perhaps detect a moment of inconsistency in Rawls's position. The Overlapping Consensus is on the one hand a moral position shared by all the parties – and yet on the other hand the Overlapping Consensus stands back from endorsing any one comprehensive moral doctrine. Indeed, Rawls seems

---

[101] Rawls, *A Theory of Justice*, p. 148.
[102] Rawls, *A Theory of Justice*, p. 264.
[103] Rawls, *Political Liberalism*, p. 63.
[104] Rawls, *Political Liberalism*, Introduction, p. xx.
[105] Rawls, *Political Liberalism*, pp. 147–51. It is precisely this point that Engelhardt cannot accept – see *Foundations of Christian Bioethics*, p. 371. From a totally different perspective, Brian Barry argues that Thomas Aquinas would refuse to enter the Original Position on the grounds that 'he would deny the deliberations of a collection of people artificially denied the possibility of knowing the truth about God could have any bearing on the question of the right institutions for a society to have' (Brian Barry, *Justice as Equality*, (Oxford: Oxford University Press,1995), p. 185).

aware of this contradiction, for he asks a few pages later[106] whether the Overlapping Consensus is not in itself a comprehensive doctrine, and admits that the broader and deeper it becomes the more it becomes a comprehensive doctrine or at least comes to rely on one. But he is able to escape the seemingly inevitable consequences of this position by pointing out that the Overlapping Consensus is a political conception rather than a moral theory as such; the difference between the two being largely a matter of scope and range of application, the political conception of justice being for the main institutions of political and social life, not for all life.[107] This of course would rule out the developments that Galston and Macedo see as desirable, namely liberalism's becoming a comprehensive doctrine. But it raises another question – just where does the boundary lie between the political and social and the other aspects of life? Is it indeed possible to make any meaningful distinction between political and social and, for example, moral? To put it another way, how do we distinguish between the private and the public? This distinction is at the heart of Rawlsian liberal theory, and it is a distinction that communitarian and narrative thinkers are loath to accept at face value. Their contention is that the private and public interpenetrate. Because each individual life has narrative unity, we cannot divide the public self from the private self. How in fact are the two aspects of life related? Can we divide private and public? And if not, can we describe how they interpenetrate?

But these are not questions that Rawls ever confronts. We are left in the dark about just how we are to divide public and private. We have already seen why liberalism cannot be adopted as a comprehensive doctrine in dealing with the arguments of William Galston and Stephen Macedo, but we must now consider Susan Moller Okin's point about the way the family is excluded from most contemporary writing about justice. Rawls, she points out, takes the family unit as already just, and leaves that structure immune from scrutiny in the Original Position.[108] However, there is a need for justice in the family, as it is in the family that we first come to have a sense of ourselves and our relations with others which is at the root of moral development.[109] So it does seem, as Okin suggests,[110] that the private/public dichotomy is a weak one, and that power is distributed just as much in the family as in the public forum – so why should family structure not be open to discussion in the Original Position? Okin backs this argument up with reference to the well-known feminist assertion: 'The personal is political.'[111]

Funnily enough, in direct contrast to the studied moderation of Okin, Engelhardt accuses Rawls of the exact opposite: trying to abolish the concept of privacy, and

---

[106] Rawls, *Political Liberalism*, p. 154.

[107] Rawls, *Political Liberalism*, pp. 174–5.

[108] Susan Moller Okin, *Justice, Gender and the Family* (New York: Basic Books, 1989), p. 9.

[109] Okin, p. 14, pp. 18–19.

[110] Okin, p. 111.

[111] Okin, p. 124. Rawls, however, disagrees: 'We are not required to treat our children in accordance with political principles', he writes ('The Idea of Public Reason Revisited', in *Collected Papers*, p. 598.) The reason is that justice deals with the general structure of society and not structures such as the family and indeed the Church. See his reply to Okin and others in this article, pp. 595–601.

interfere in family life.[112] But the question remains – how do we draw the line between the political and the private? Rawls attempts an answer in 'The Idea of Public Reason Revisited',[113] which introduces the idea of 'The Proviso'. The article lays down what constitutes 'Public Reason': it is part of the idea of democracy itself;[114] it is made up of the basic moral and political values that govern the relations between government and citizens;[115] it is distinct from the background culture;[116] it is reciprocal, in that it is what others may be reasonably disposed to accept, neither aiming to manipulate or bamboozle.[117] The Proviso states simply that citizens may introduce their comprehensive doctrine into the discourse of public reason whenever they wish, provided that their point is consonant with public reason and not couched in terms that are exclusively religious.[118] There is nothing in this idea that contradicts the traditional distinction between revelation and natural reason. Public discourse must rely on the latter not the former. There is much that Rawls says that recalls John Courtney Murray.[119] It is for this reason that Catholic opposition to abortion is always couched in terms of natural law, and hardly ever of Holy Scripture. Galston expresses it thus: the private is what you may legitimately believe but which cannot be made the basis of public policy. For example, a government official may believe the Second Coming to be imminent, but he must continue doing his job, making normal provision for the future.[120] This seems to be an entirely sensible conclusion, quite in accord with traditional Catholic teaching about the autonomy of the secular sphere. But the suspicion remains: has that government official really left his beliefs about the Second Coming at the office door? Is he in fact capable of doing so?

What emerges here is an important difference about the way we view the self. Are we capable of multiple loyalties? Are we capable of being loyal to one narrative for one time and not at others? Are we capable of being loyal to a narrative and also being distant from it when necessary? These are questions we will have to examine in greater detail.

In the meantime, in answer to the question posed at the start of this section of our discussion, we must say that Rawls makes a convincing case that the Overlapping Consensus that is derived from the Original Position is not a mere pact of convenience or *modus vivendi*, but something of real moral value. Nor is the narrow concept of the political unsustainable. At the heart of Rawls's vision lies not just making the best of a bad job, the sort of consensus that comes out of necessity and is no consensus at all, but rather a moral vision, a true narrative, of some importance. But this moral vision, this substantive narrative, at the same time raises important questions: if people are capable of being part of an Overlapping Consensus what does this say about their way of thinking and believing?

---

[112] Engelhardt, *Foundations of Christian Bioethics*, pp. 375–6.
[113] First published in 1997, reprinted in the *Collected Papers*, pp. 573–615.
[114] Rawls, *Collected Papers*, p. 573
[115] Rawls, *Collected Papers*, p. 574.
[116] Rawls, *Collected Papers*, p. 576.
[117] Rawls, *Collected Papers*, p. 578.
[118] Rawls, *Collected Papers*, p. 591.
[119] Murray, especially the discussion on public philosophy, p. 80 et seq.
[120] Galston, p. 178.

Does the Work of John Rawls Represent a Universally Valid Narrative?

We now aim to draw together the observations we have made about the work of John Rawls, concentrated as they have been on the idea of the Original Position, and see if they are sufficient to underpin a general theory of moral reasoning. In other words, is the narrative offered by the Original Position the sort of narrative it claims to be, that is, one that can command general agreement, valid in and of itself, for all times and places?

In the first place, one can point to the strengths of Rawls's work, which are considerable. Rawls has succeeded in elucidating an elegantly conceived and attractively expressed theory that unites questions of fundamentals with questions of praxis. The Original Position establishes Justice as Fairness as the only possible criteria that would be adopted in such a position and provides a yardstick by which all states of affairs can be measured. He gives Kant's purely formal categorical imperative a procedural content, as well as providing us with an instrument of thought. Above all, Rawls's thought is firmly anchored in the Kantian heritage, seeing the individual and his rights as being inviolable, and provides a response to the errors of utilitarianism, which can be used to trample on the dignity of the individual. At the same time, Rawls is never distracted by the sort of metaphysical discussion that hampers so much ethical theory, relying as he does on procedure alone. This of course means that Rawls's approach is highly abstract – but at the same time can thus be used to accommodate a wide variety of circumstances and situations.

Secondly, as we have seen, Rawls provides a coherent account of the social nature of man, and the goods that come from sociality, while at the same time upholding the goods of the individual as opposed to that of the group.

Thirdly, Rawls presents a coherent account of reasonable pluralism, pointing a way to a consensus which is both broad and deep but which at the same time does not force individual consciences but respects their independence and dignity.

Fourthly, Rawls establishes the moral nature of political society while at the same time stressing its limitations, thus once again striking a balance between the public and the private.

Bearing these achievements in mind, it can well be asked whether the Original Position might not indeed be used as a basis for moral thinking generally. Can we approach all moral problems, prescinding from conceptual debate, by asking what would have been adopted in the Original Position? Can we leave discussion of the Good and the True to one side and concentrate on the Right, and happily find, as Rawls has suggested, that the Right will coincide with the Good? May we indeed find that 'human understanding and belief are complementary not contradictory'?[121]

Several Catholic writers have answered in the positive to the above questions. R. Bruce Douglass sees Catholicism and Liberalism as learning from each other. 'There can be successful dialogue among people who find themselves disagreeing in principle even on matters of 'ultimate' importance – dialogue that changes the

---

[121] United States Bishops, 'Economic Justice for All', no. 61, quoted in David Hollenbach, *Justice, Peace and Human Rights* (New York: Crossroad, 1988), p. 75.

way the people involved end up looking at things,' he writes.[122] This dialogue calls to mind the Original Position. Again, such dialogue promotes civility, which in turn leads to an improved chance of shared vision and an improved quality of the vision, in other words a creative development of the American 'proposition'.[123] This calls to mind the way the Overlapping Consensus develops. Clearly, Douglass sees Rawls's thought not as a threat to the integrity of religion, but an opportunity for the diffusion of religious ideas. His optimism is in marked contrast to the pessimism of Engelhardt. David Hollenbach sees a practical convergence between Rawls and the Church in social matters.[124] In another book, Hollenbach takes Rawls' definition of a person as one who participates in society and links this with one of the themes of Catholic social teaching, describing basic justice as the demand for minimum levels of participation in the life of the human community.[125] One swallow does not make a summer, but the Catholic Rawlsian approach would seem to indicate that there is a suitably concordant fit between Catholicism and Rawlsian liberalism.

To some extent, it seems, we can construct a Catholic Rawlsian approach. Many moral problems concern what Rawls calls social justice, or the distribution of rights and duties.[126] In dealing with these the Original Position can help clarify our thinking; in dealing with people from other traditions the idea of restriction to the political and the Overlapping Consensus may help as well. And yet at the same time it has to be acknowledged that not all questions of justice concern distributive justice in this narrow sense. We are also faced with questions of commutative justice; but the central preoccupation of justice – that of giving to each their due – goes far beyond mere distribution of rights and duties. If we are to give each human being what they deserve[127] we are faced with a moral obligation that transcends the Original Position. Indeed, as Rawls points out, the Original Position rejects justice as desert, on the grounds that the criteria that determine who deserves what cannot be defined, and because justice as desert fails to distinguish between moral desert and legitimate expectations. That to which someone is entitled bears no relationship to that person's intrinsic worth. A person's moral worth does not relate to their effectiveness. Endowments are not deserved. Thus no principle of justice exists that aims to reward virtue.[128] Indeed, Rawls writes: 'The principles of justice that regulate the basic structure and specify the duties and obligations of individuals do not mention moral

---

[122] Douglass, 'Introduction', in *Catholicism and Liberalism, Contributions to American Public Philosophy*, ed. R. Bruce Douglass and David Hollenbach (Cambridge: Cambridge University Press, 1994), p. 10.

[123] Douglass, 'Introduction', p. 14.

[124] Hollenbach, in 'A Communitarian Reconstruction of Human Rights', in *Catholicism and Liberalism, Contributions to American Public Philosophy*, ed. R. Bruce Douglass and David Hollenbach (Cambridge: Cambridge University Press, 1994), p. 133.

[125] David Hollenbach, *Justice, Peace and Human Rights* (New York: Crossroad, 1988), pp. 81–2.

[126] Rawls, *A Theory of Justice*, p. 4.

[127] For a discussion of the theory of Justice as desert, see MacIntyre, *Whose Justice? Which Rationality?* pp. 103–9, which takes issue, implicitly, with Rawls on this subject.

[128] Rawls, *A Theory of Justice*, pp. 310–11.

desert, and there is no tendency for distributive shares to correspond to it'.[129] Such an arrangement, we are reminded, would not have been chosen in the Original Position. No fair society, then, would ever have a committee for the reward of virtue and the punishment of vice. By what standards does one judge virtue and vice, after all? And would it be fair to penalize those who fail in virtue? Surely in this matter, Rawls is quite right: 'bad' people and 'good' people ought to be treated equally before the law. The distinction made in the Elizabethan Poor Laws between 'sturdy beggars' and 'the deserving poor' is a discriminatory one. To extirpate such a distinction, though, may be hard: hence we see again the usefulness of the Original Position, corresponding as it does to purity of heart,[130] which makes no distinction between persons. The Good Samaritan, after all, did not stop and ask whether the man fallen among thieves *deserved* to be helped – he simply helped him, quite leaving to one side the question of whether he was a good person or not.

But this brings us to another meaning often attached to the concept of desert: what are we bound to give to people who may not be deserving in the usual sense? In other words, what are we to give to people simply because they are human? This is the sort of justice that goes beyond the questions of reward and punishment to deeper questions of human dignity. It is indeed difficult to argue that people *deserve* health care or decent housing on any other grounds than the fact that they are human. Likewise, the Good Samaritan stopped and helped his fellow human being, simply because he was his fellow human being, rejecting the concepts of Jew and Samaritan, but embracing that of common humanity. Can this particular idea of desert form the basis of justice? Rawls's thin theory of the good and his non-metaphysical view of the person would make this question difficult for him: for how can one consider what a human being deserves *qua* human being without either?

On the question of virtue, another inadequacy becomes noticeable. Rawls does talk at length, as we have seen, about the virtues of justice which the practice of justice engenders, but he speaks of justice as an isolated virtue. Indeed he has no choice but to do so, as he is careful to separate the political virtue of justice from the other 'private' moral virtues which would be inculcated by a comprehensive moral doctrine, which, as we have seen, not be chosen in the Original Position. Justice in Rawls is a freestanding virtue. This means that the Aristotelian vision of the virtues as interconnected is lost.

In conclusion, it seems that though Rawls does have a theory of the good (the 'thin theory of the good' as we have seen) this theory is minimalist in its approach. This should not surprise us, for, as we have seen, Rawls says time and again that he aims to reduce the scope of justice to the realm of the political alone. This of course denies the unity of the political with the moral, another central plank of the Aristotelian vision: after all, Aristotle sees ethics and politics as closely allied activities. For him the polis is the locus of ethics, and both subjects form a continuum.[131] By hiving one off from the other, Rawls is in fact impoverishing both.

---

[129] Rawls, *A Theory of Justice*, p. 311.
[130] Rawls, *A Theory of Justice*, p. 587.
[131] For the intimate relationship between the two, see Aristotle, *Ethics* (London: Penguin, 1953), pp. 26–7.

Chapter 6

Beyond Rawls

Our conclusion in considering the work of John Rawls and the Original Position in particular is that it is a narrative that only goes so far. While it can be held by different people from different communities for different reasons – while it can find a fit with various other narratives – it fails to arrive at universality. This requires further examination, though.

In our discussion in the previous chapter we alluded to a type of desert which aims to give to people what they deserve simply as human beings; but perhaps this idea is best not discussed at all under the concept of desert, but rather under the question of supererogatory acts. It is here that Rawls freely admits that his work fails to arrive. That Rawls discusses it at all shows that it is an important question in ethics. The fact that the Original Position cannot contend with it is a sign of the limitations of the minimalist approach that the work of Rawls is forced to take for some of the reasons outlined in the previous chapter.

A supererogatory act is one that goes beyond the mere call of duty. One who gives up his life so that another may live is not obliged to do so, but such heroic self-sacrifice would be considered worthy of praise, even if the failure to do so would not be considered blameworthy. The person who acts in such a way does so out of pure altruism; this is sometimes characterized as a love of the human race, a love that the human race had not earned or deserved by any particular action, but a love given gratuitously to a human being simply because they are human.[1] But Rawls specifically rules this type of action out of court: the theory of justice, he says, assumes a definite limit on the strength of social and altruistic motivation; it assumes people are not willing to abandon their claims; however, this does not imply selfishness 'in the ordinary sense'. An altruistic society is beyond justice, and has no need to appeal to justice, because it does not see self-sacrifice as being in any way unjust. However, he concludes, even in an altruistic society justice would have a theoretical role to play as an expression of the harmony of society.[2] Earlier he maintained that while the love of mankind may lead to acts of supererogation, justice makes no such demand.[3] Further on, he says that the love of mankind and the desire

---

[1] For an interesting discussion of supererogatory acts, see James O. Urmson, 'Saints and Heroes', *Essays in Moral Philosophy*, ed. I. A. Melden (Seattle: University of Washington Press, 1958), reprinted in *Ethics, History, Theory And Contemporary Issues*, eds Stephen M. Cahn and Peter Markie (Oxford: Oxford University Press, 1998), pp. 699–708. Urmson points out that these acts go beyond the normal classifications of moral acts, thus exposing the weakness of most moral theories that fail to take account of them.

[2] Rawls, *A Theory of Justice*, p. 281.

[3] Rawls, *A Theory of Justice*, p. 192.

to promote the common good are not for ordinary persons; heroic or saintly morality does not contradict justice, but goes beyond it.[4] These are small but significant points and indeed correct ones. Justice does not demand the sort of sacrifice that Rawls or Urmson has in mind. Presumably it was not justice in the Rawlsian sense that made the Good Samaritan stop, but something else: charity, perhaps. But can there ever be justice without charity? Once again we come up against the limits of justice as conceived by Rawls. Thus Rawls is unable to give an account of, or provide any basis for, the acts of supererogation which form an important part of the ethical landscape. This is surely a major omission and one which shows up the work of Rawls as minimalist in its import.[5] His is a story that only goes so far, and no further.

The above assertion requires proof, however. This can best be done by considering some counter-arguments. In an interesting article,[6] Susan Wolf argues that what she terms 'moral sainthood' is not a model of personal well-being towards which it would be particularly rational or good or desirable for a human being to strive. An upper limit has to be set to altruism if the pursuit of moral sainthood is not to damage other non-moral values. She concludes:

> [I] call into question the assumption that it is always better to be morally better. The role morality plays in the development of our characters and the shape of our practical deliberations need be neither that of a universal medium into which all other values must be translated nor that of an ever-present filter through which all other values must pass. This is not to say that moral value should not be an important, even the most important, kind of value we attend to in evaluating and improving ourselves and our world. It is to say that our values cannot be fully comprehended on the model of a hierarchical system with morality at the top .[7]

But this conclusion is not as damning as it might first appear. The person contemplating a supererogatory act – for example the sacrifice of their life – must weigh up the moral goods and non-moral goods at stake and find a just proportion between the moral good upheld (the principle at stake, whatever it might be) and the physical evil incurred (in this case, the loss of life). No one could deny that moral goods are secured at a cost, and that the cost must be a proportionate one. Likewise, not every principle is worth the sacrifice of a life, all would agree. This essential distinction between two types of good, the moral and the physical, largely removes the difficulty under which Susan Wolf labours. Thus we could conclude that a supererogatory act will have value when it finds a proportionate balance with any physical evil incurred. Though how this balance is to be found is another matter.

---

[4] Rawls, *A Theory of Justice*, p. 479. He notes at this point that he follows the account of heroism given by Urmson.
[5] The topic is not mentioned, as far as I can see, in any later works of Rawls.
[6] Susan Wolf, 'Moral Saints', *The Journal of Philosophy*, 79, 8 (August 1982): 419–39; reprinted in *Ethics, History, Theory and Contemporary Issues*, pp. 708–21.
[7] Susan Wolf, *Ethics, History, Theory and Contemporary Issues*, pp. 720–21.

But is this conclusion sound? Another article offers a challenge.[8] Judith Jarvis Thomson, its author, asks us to imagine the following story:

> You wake up in the morning and find yourself back to back with an unconscious violinist. A famous unconscious violinist. He has been found to have a fatal kidney ailment, and the Society of Music Lovers has canvassed all the available medical records and found that you alone have the right blood type to help. They have therefore kidnapped you, and last night the violinist's circulatory system was plugged into yours, so that your kidneys can be used to extract poisons from his blood as well as your own. The director of the hospital now tells you, 'Look, we're sorry that the Society of Music Lovers did this to you – we would never have permitted it if we had known. But still, they did it, and the violinist is now plugged into you. To unplug you would be to kill him. But never mind, it is only for nine months. By then he will have recovered from his ailment, and can be safely unplugged from you.' Is it morally incumbent on you to accede to this situation? No doubt it would be very nice of you if you did, a great kindness. But do you *have* to accede to it?[9]

The question really needs no answer. When considered in a Rawlsian light, it is clear that no one in the Original Position would lay down that the person plugged into the violinist must put up with the arrangement for nine months. It is an intolerable violation of their freedom. It is a situation that no self-interested person would chose for themselves, or, by extension, for anyone else. From the point of view of Justice as Fairness, it seems both unjust and unfair. Even taken from the point of view of the violinist, it seems too much to ask that someone should make such a sacrifice. And indeed the truth is, in the parameters of the situation laid down by Thomson, while it would be very nice of you if you did, you do not in truth have to put up with the unconscious violinist – to do so goes beyond justice. It is a supererogatory act – admirable, but not required as a duty. We might admire someone who did so – but we could not blame someone who did not.

However, once we strip away the analogy and confront an actual case – that of a woman who is left pregnant as a result of rape – this conclusion seems doubtful. There are many reasons why we would reject the morality of abortion in this case, but this is not an essay on abortion, and we can leave that aside: our main purpose is to show that Rawlsian justice cannot provide an answer in this case, for Rawlsian justice sees duty to the other (whether unconscious violinists or unborn persons) as strictly limited and places an upper limit on what one person is called to do for another. However, even as we broach the subject, we encounter a problem. We have spoken of supererogatory acts – and here both Rawls and Urmson would agree – as acts that go beyond the call of duty, acts that transcend simple obligation: but this is not to say that a person who does a supererogatory acts does not feel a call of duty. Urmson gives us the case of a soldier, who, by throwing himself onto a live grenade, saves his comrades' lives. No one could have ordered him to do this as his duty, however:

---

[8] Judith Jarvis Thomson, 'A Defense of Abortion', *Philosophy and Public Affairs*, 1 (1971): 47–66. Reprinted in *Ethics, History, Theory and Contemporary Issues*, pp. 737–48.

[9] Judith Jarvis Thomson, *Ethics, History, Theory and Contemporary Issues*, p. 738.

In so far as the soldier had time to feel or think at all, he presumably felt he ought to do that deed; he considered it the proper thing to do; he, if no one else, might have reproached himself for failing to do his duty if he had shirked the deed. So, it may be argued, if an act presents itself to us in the way this act may be supposed to have presented itself to this soldier, then it is our duty to do it; we have no option... [However,] subjectively, we may say, at the time of the action, the deed presented itself as a duty, but it was not a duty.[10]

This distinction may not be very helpful – objectively supererogatory acts are not a duty but the person who does the deed feels impelled to do so as a duty subjectively – but it does highlight the problem we are confronting. The pregnant woman who bears a child at the cost of her life, the soldier who gives up his life for his friends – and many such there have in fact been – acts in a way that cannot be explained or justified by the theory of justice as expounded by John Rawls. At the same time such a person acts in accordance with a sense of imperative and duty, in a way that is generally admired and that unquestionably achieves a great good. (Clearly we do not agree with Susan Wolf's estimate of moral saints.) Here we find an objection to the theory of Rawls that cannot, it seems, be overridden. Rawls takes no account of acts of supererogation or what may be termed the call to perfection and heroism; he claims, furthermore, that no such account can be made as it lies outside the realm of justice. Does Rawls, in short, set his sights too low?

It is worth returning to Judith Jarvis Thomson for a moment to show how the limits of justice are revealed by her consideration of abortion. Her conclusion is as follows:

> We have in fact to distinguish between two kinds of Samaritan: the Good Samaritan and what we might call the Minimally Decent Samaritan. The Good Samaritan went out of his way, at some considerable cost to himself, to help one in need of it. We are not told what the options were, that is, whether or not the priest or the levite could have helped by doing less than the Good Samaritan did, but assuming they could have, then the fact that they did nothing at all shows they were not even Minimally Decent Samaritans, not because they were not Samaritans, but because they were not even minimally decent.[11]

The conclusion, then, is that we are obliged to be Minimally Decent Samaritans (and the law can compel us to be such), but no law can compel us to be Good Samaritans. Though Thomson does not say so specifically, it is clear that she agrees with Rawls – that supererogatory acts lie beyond the realm of justice as Rawls conceives it.

We can conclude this discussion then by the following: Rawls gives us a useful and enlightening model in matters of distributive justice, but the theory has its shortcomings, as we have tried to show by the examination of this one aspect of supererogatory acts. A Rawlsian world would be full of Minimally Decent Samaritans, but provides no basis for the action of Good Samaritans. As such it would be a morally impoverished world. Thus we need to search for a basis for morality that goes beyond Rawls's rather minimalist vision and which opens up a wider horizon for moral endeavour.

---

[10] Urmson, *Ethics, History, Theory and Contemporary Issues*, p. 702.
[11] Judith Jarvis Thomson, *Ethics, History, Theory and Contemporary Issues*, p. 745.

If we need convincing further, Judith Jarvis Thomson gives us another example, this time not imaginary, as is the case of the Unconscious Violinist, to back up her claim as to the limited nature of moral exigency:

> ... the story of Kitty Genovese, who, as you will remember, was murdered while thirty-eight people watched or listened, and did nothing at all to help her. A Good Samaritan would have rushed out to give direct assistance against the murderer. Or perhaps we had better allow that it would have been a Splendid Samaritan who did this, on the ground that it would have involved a risk of death for himself. But the thirty-eight not only did not do this, they did not even trouble to pick up the phone to call the police. Minimally Decent Samaritans would call for at least doing that, and their not having done it was monstrous.
>
> After telling the story of the Good Samaritan, Jesus said, 'Go, and do thou likewise.' Perhaps he meant that we are morally required to act as the Good Samaritan did. Perhaps he was urging people to do more than was morally required of them. At all events it seems plain that it was not morally required of any of the thirty-eight that he rush out to give direct assistance at the risk of his own life. In no state in this country is any man compelled by law to be even a Minimally Decent Samaritan to any person; there is no law under which charges could be brought against the thirty-eight who stood by while Kitty Genovese died.[12]

This case, or rather our author's treatment of it, raises several interesting questions. Judith Jarvis Thomson fails in the first place to distinguish between law and morality. A law may compel us to shun evil, but it can hardly impel us to seek the good with the same rigour. However, we experience many moral obligations that are not backed up by legal requirement. It may well be true that in America no law exists that forces people to go to the help of those who are being murdered at the risk of their own life, but this is not the same as saying that no one is obliged to do so. To stand by when someone is being murdered, is, on the face of it, indefensible; the fact that it is not illegal in America is irrelevant. But Thomson seems to confuse morality with rules and laws, whereas morality transcends rules and laws; given the operation of chance and history, no amount of rules and laws can foresee every eventuality;[13] certain cases must fall outside the provision made by law, but they do not fall outside the realm of morality. Here Thomson is admitting, perhaps unwittingly, one of the shortcomings of the Rawlsian system, the simple fact that one cannot find a rule to cover every eventuality. Further to this, a rule or law is abstract; a case like the one above is concrete and possibly demands a new rule be formulated if the existing rules fail to cover the eventualities of the case: in fact, what the Kitty Genovese case demands is not a rule but a ruling, as is possible in English common law – an

---

[12] Judith Jarvis Thomson, *Ethics, History, Theory and Contemporary Issues*, p. 746. No reference is given for the Genovese case, but the facts seem clear enough. The case is the subject of the expressively title article 'Thirty-eight Who Saw Murder Didn't Call the Police', by Martin Gansberg, *New York Times*, 27 March 1964.

[13] Saint Thomas Aquinas makes exactly this point in *Summa Theologiae*, I II, 96, 6, where he says that it is permissible to break the letter of the law for the sake of the common good, from whence the law gets its force, for 'nobody is so wise as to be able to forecast every individual case.'

English court would, perhaps, have no trouble finding the thirty-eight guilty on the grounds that they made 'common purpose' with the murderer. But the fact remains that in the Original Position it would be difficult if not impossible to frame a rule that would cover such a case. One might adopt the maxim 'Everyone must go to the aid of his neighbour in need, provided that the cost to himself is not disproportionate' but this might be impossible to implement. Who is to decide whether the cost is proportionate or not? How can the value of Kitty Genovese's life be weighed in the balance against yours or mine?

The thirty-eight bystanders may be able to hide behind legal immunity in the United States, but we cannot admire them. The rules may be on their side – and Thomson thinks that they could not have been compelled to act beyond phoning for the police (an action which may not have saved Kitty Genovese's life) – but their failure to act reveals them to be deficient in several virtues: they have an inadequate sense of justice, no concern for the common good, no charity, no courage. However, as we have seen, Rawls's position is that these virtues lie beyond the concerns of legislation. As Hauerwas points out, liberalism is concerned with establishing a just polity without creating just people, because it sees the task of developing virtue as an intrusion into the personal realm.[14] Thus a liberal society may well have to live with a number of Kitty Genoveses. To this point a Rawlsian would reply that the individual is inviolable, as laid down right at the beginning of *A Theory of Justice*,[15] and that what happened to Kitty Genovese is lamentable and not to be approved of in any way. Quite so. But can Rawls's people prevent a repetition without violating the other principle, that of Justice as Fairness?

In fact some of what Rawls writes of in *Theory* seems to apply rather well to such cases as Kitty Genovese's. His discussion of the natural duty that all have to uphold justice acknowledges that there will be some who will wish to shirk their share of this duty.[16] There will be some then who will wish to sit by when injustice is being done. However the duties of mutual aid and mutual respect are to everyone's advantage. He writes:

> While on particular occasions we are required to do things not in our own interests, we are likely to gain on balance at least over the longer run under normal circumstances. In each single instance the gain to the person who needs help far outweighs the loss of those required to assist him, and assuming that the chances of being the beneficiary are not much smaller than those of being the one who must give aid, the principle is clearly in our interest. But this is not the only argument for the duty of mutual aid, or even the most important one. A sufficient ground for adopting this duty is its pervasive effect on the quality of everyday life.[17]

This is all very well as far as it goes, but what happens when the price to be paid is too great, as in the Genovese case? What if the Good Samaritan had had only two denarii in the whole world? It would seem that one cannot compel people in

---

[14] Hauerwas, *A Community of Character*, p. 72.
[15] Rawls, *A Theory of Justice*, p. 3.
[16] Rawls, *A Theory of Justice*, p. 336.
[17] Rawls, *A Theory of Justice*, pp. 338–9.

these circumstances to act for the good of their neighbour. It would be unfair for them to have to give up their lives or their last two pennies. There seems to be a contradiction then between the two principles: a fair society may not be able to ensure the inviolability of all persons. Kitty Genovese is violated, but the only way to have prevented it would have been to insist on an unfair law which forced people to an act of supererogation that went beyond justice. We are faced with the possibility that rules of themselves cannot ensure that all get their just deserts.[18] And Rawls hints as much in his language, speaking of the natural duty of mutual aid; he tries to make out that this natural duty is one we would choose in the Original Position, but as the above makes clear, we would only be able to do so in a very limited sense.[19]

Thus we have no way of accounting for the morality of supererogatory acts, acts that go beyond the requirements of law, and we are left in the uncomfortable position of maintaining that the people who neglected to help Kitty Genovese were not at fault from the point of view of justice. The solution may lie in examining the two basic principles of justice that would be adopted in the Original Position. These are as follows: first, that everyone should have the most extensive liberty compatible with a similar liberty for others; and secondly, that social or economic equalities should not be permitted unless they work to everyone's advantage (including the worst off) and are attached to positions open to every one.[20] This, as we have said, is what would have been adopted in the Original Position – the imaginary and non-historical locus in which rights and duties are 'distributed'.[21] As we have already seen the failure to provide an arrangement that would have saved Kitty Genovese's life, thanks to the rejection of supererogatory acts by those in the Original Position, violates the second principle. Thus the Genovese case presents a problem to the Rawlsian approach even when seen from an exclusively Rawlsian point of view. It is not what we would have

---

[18] This point is made by MacIntyre in a different context. Knowing how to act virtuously always involves more than rule following, he observes in *Dependent Rational Animals*, p. 93. This is undoubtedly true: rules do not form an exhaustive code for human conduct, as we have established. But it is important to note too that the Original Position is not a rule in the narrow sense, but rather an approach, a state of mind that helps us to arrive at specific rules. MacIntyre's solution to the problem of the famous violinist would be to invoke the virtue of *misericordia* (*Dependent Rational Animals*, pp. 119–28), which in the end turns out to be rather similar to the Original Position: when confronted by a handicapped person, one should think 'I might have been that individual' (p. 128), which of course is the essential mechanism that informs the Position. However, it is also important to note that MacIntyre implicitly criticizes the Position in the same book, claiming that giving is never symmetrical in practice, but in fact often unconditioned, again based on the realization 'this could have been us' (p. 100); thus MacIntyre hints at some sort of recognition of the other that is the source of all acts of supererogation.

[19] Michael Walzer, *Spheres of Justice* (New York: Basic Books, 1983), p. 33, considers the same question of mutual aid and arrives at a similar conclusion: I should stop and help if the risk or cost to myself is reasonable. There is always a limit, and 'my life cannot be shaped by these encounters'.

[20] Rawls, *A Theory of Justice*, pp. 14–15.
[21] Rawls, *A Theory of Justice*, p. 4.

chosen in the Original Position; but the Original Position does not allow us to choose otherwise; ergo, there is a flaw in the Original Position.

This flaw can be pinpointed when we say that rights and duties are not necessarily *distributed*, but perhaps *recognized* or *discovered* in the Original Position. Or if we wish to stick with the Rawlsian terms, we might say the following: rights and duties are recognized, but then imperfectly distributed – that is, the distribution does not perfectly actualize the situation that we recognize. This would explain the fate of Kitty Genovese. We recognize her rights, but we find no way of ensuring that she receives them in the distribution. So the flaw in the Position can be isolated thus: the Position is an as yet imperfect means of ensuring Justice as Fairness, a filter of the mind that does not work perfectly, something that is akin to purity of heart without capturing it fully. Or in another way: the Position is a narrative that fails to tell the story in its entirety. Its lack of completion as a narrative is revealed by placing it side by side with the narrative of the Genovese case; thus we see one narrative being challenged by another. Or in other terms still, despite the Position, we find that the practice of justice does not entirely square with the theory of justice. This alerts us to the fact that a narrative, even if it is the Original Position, can find it difficult to capture the totality of the insight it wishes to express.

Our conclusion must then be this: Rawls's maxim, derived from Kant, about the inviolability of the person,[22] must be taken seriously. It is this concern with the inviolability of the person which leads to the question of justice arising in the first place; it is the inviolability of the person which leads to the Original Position's being advanced as the best means of ensuring that person's rights. The inviolability of the person is prior to all the theory that follows.

However, it is commonly asserted that Rawls's vision is that of Cambridge, Massachusetts. Karen Lebacqz writes that while Rawls attempts to reason out a theory that lacks historical particularity, and advances a theory that is supposed to be universal, valid for all times and places, nevertheless he reveals certain western biases. Rawls emphasizes the individual, not the collective; he approves of capitalism, the market, the status quo.[23] In other words, he is in fact describing his own culture, and his universalist theory is culture bound.[24] Rawls himself, in his later writings, comes close to admitting this. He writes that:

> Justice as fairness... tries to rely solely upon basic intuitive ideas that are embedded in the political institutions of a constitutional democratic regime and the public tradition of their interpretation. Justice as fairness is a political conception in part because it starts from within a certain political tradition.[25]

The use of terms such as 'tradition' and 'embedded' may make us think that the distance between Rawls and MacIntyre is perhaps not so great after all. But this does

---

[22] Rawls, *A Theory of Justice*, p. 3.
[23] K. Lebacqz, *Justice in an Unjust World* (Minneapolis: Augsburg, 1987), p. 54.
[24] A point familiar from Engelhardt, see *Foundations of Bioethics*, pp. 51 et seq.
[25] From 'Justice as Fairness, Political not Metaphysical' (1985), reprinted in *Collected Papers*, p. 390. For a similar idea, see 'The Priority of Right and Ideas of the Good' (1988), same volume, pp. 450 and 459.

not mean that Rawls can or ought to be dismissed as the view from Massachusetts, even if his culture has shaped his outlook – one could hardly expect it to do otherwise. Reading Rawls one is often reminded that he is an American. However, we need also to remember that at the heart of Rawls and at the basis of his theory are 'basic intuitive ideas', chief of which is the inviolability of the person. These are basic – self-evident, not founded on anything else; and intuitive – that is to say fundamental and transcending culture, though naturally coming to us through culture. But the inviolability of the individual is not something that can be reduced to a cultural perception peculiar to Massachusetts; before the culture lies the ethical insight which gives the culture meaning, and this ethical insight is not reducible to anything gleaned from the culture.[26] Rawls's basic foundation, the importance of persons, is something perceived as, dare we say it, *a priori*.[27]

We can clarify the above by making two points. Virtue is not a means to happiness, but an absolute. Ethics is not a means to an end but an end in itself. One meets the individual, not to use her or him for one's own ends, but because, in Kantian language, man is an end in himself, not a means to an end. Ethics involves this coming up against the hard rock face of the person and their rights – that which is not me, and not invented by me, but rather discovered by me. In other words, the human spirit receives the law, but does not make it. As we see in Rawls, there are two types of language in talking of ethics: we can say we *distribute* rights and duties in the Original Position; but he also speaks of people *recognizing* rules as binding.[28] The first suggests that ethics is a human production, the result of negotiation and bargaining and agreement. The second suggests that ethics is something that we discover, something that exists prior to our experience and indeed our existence.

We might be inclined to think that Rawls's Original Position is all about the search for reasonable agreement, but we ought not to forget that it is also the fruit of insight. This depends though on how we see what goes on behind the Veil of Ignorance. As we have hinted above there are two strands to the language Rawls uses.[29] Michael

---

[26] '*Theory* was careful to say that it was not making universalist claims that transcend cultures and history. But the structure of the work implied otherwise', writes David Hollenbach in 'A Communitarian Reconstruction of Human Rights', in *Catholicism and Liberalism*, p. 134.

[27] Quite different is the approach of Michael Walzer. He says: 'The theory of distributive justice begins then with an account of membership rights... For it is only as members somewhere that men and women can hope to share in all the other social goods... that communal life makes possible' (*Spheres of Justice*, p. 63). Rawls, however, writes of what is due not to persons as members of this or that community, but to persons as such.

[28] Rawls, *A Theory of Justice*, p. 4.

[29] See for example, *A Theory of Justice*, pp 113–16: some duties are contractual, but other duties are natural and do not depend on contract at all; they are neither voluntary nor connected to institutions; they are universal and general and apply unconditionally. Also see *Theory of Justice*, p. 263: 'The two principles of Justice are not contingent upon existing desires or present social conditions.' This rather contradicts what he says, quoted earlier, in *Collected Papers*, p. 390, about his work being embedded in tradition.

Sandel detects the same thing. In a lengthy consideration of the language that Rawls uses to describe the Original Position,[30] he comes to the following conclusion:

> But what begins as an ethic of choice and consent ends, however unwittingly, as an ethic of insight and self-understanding. In the final passage of the book [*Theory*], the language of choosing and willing is displaced by the language of seeing and perceiving, as the voluntarist image of Kant gives way to the cognitive image of Spinoza... The secret to the original position – and the key to its justificatory force – lies not in what they *do* there but rather what they *apprehend* there. What matters is not what they choose but what they see, not what they decide, but what they discover. What goes on in the original position is not a contract after all, but the coming to self-awareness of an intersubjective being.[31]

This has been our conclusion as well. Rights and duties are not simply distributed in the Original Position, but recognized; rules and obligations are not decided upon, but acknowledged. For in the Original Position, argument and decision are overtaken by the power of ethical insight.

So what can then be concluded from this discussion, bearing in mind our primary concern with the concept of narrative? It is this: the Original Position is a narrative which aims to do justice to the power of the ethical insight into the primacy of the importance of the person and the inviolability of the person. However, the narrative does not quite fulfil the task it sets out to do, as the cases (or narratives) of Kitty Genovese and the Famous Violinist show. That this should be the case ought not to surprise us, bearing in mind that narrative is a human construct and that every use of human language is going to be imperfect in its attempt to express the entire truth. But we may indeed hope that further refinements of the narrative may reach further degrees of perfection as the Rawlsian tradition continues.

What we see reflected here is something that we see in all narratives: no narrative is ever constructed ex nihilo. Rawls draws on those who have come before him, just as those who come after him will draw on Rawls himself. But more than this, we see that Rawls's narrative is constructed in the light of an ethical insight: this – the inviolability of persons – is the 'raw material' that is shaped into the narrative, or the speck of dust which eventually leads to the pearl of the Original Position. Thus the Original Position is an attempt to express the in some ways inexpressible: its failure to do so fully should not blind us to its great achievement of expressing so much. And it does so in a way that opens up questions about the way that narrative works: for here is a narrative of universal application (or nearly so) that does not depend on any one culture or community for its justification, which raises the question: what other such narrative might there be?

Rawls as Narrative and as Anti-Narrative

Let us now attempt to sum up once again what we have learned through looking at the work of John Rawls.

---

[30] Sandel, Michael, *Liberalism and the Limits of Justice* (Cambridge: Cambridge University Press, 1987), pp. 122–32.

[31] Sandel, p. 132.

It is the contention of MacIntyre, Hauerwas and Engelhardt that all thinking is necessarily narrative thinking, even when it claims to be otherwise. Moreover, they aver, every philosopher is working in a tradition, even when they claim that what he advances is somehow free-standing. We have seen that this is true of Rawls: his work forms part of a long tradition of contractarian thinking, and is rooted in the American experience. But these considerations, which as we have seen Rawls more or less admits, do not mean that his work should be dismissed as just yet another view from somewhere. For while emerging from a particular culture, the Rawlsian narrative does to a large extent hold good for situations far removed from that culture.

It is Rawls's contention that the doctrine of Justice as Fairness and the expository device of the Original Position holds good for all situations. However, as he is forced to admit, it does not, for there are places where his work fails to arrive. The Original Position cannot help us in the case of the Famous Violinist, or of Kitty Genovese, or of the man who receives the charity of the Good Samaritan. Neither can we use the Original Position in order to distribute rights and duties in the family. However, we can and ought to use the Original Position in a wide variety of cases where distributive justice is in question. What these obvious limitations show, as we have argued earlier, is that the fundamental insight that fires Rawls – the inviolability of the person – does not find perfect expression in the Original Position narrative. But it does find a near perfect expression. The Original Position may not 'work' in all cases, but it will work in the vast majority of cases. Nor should this surprise us: the coincidence between truth and narrative is never going to be perfect, the condition of language and thought being what it is. No story says it all, not even Rawls's. But it may, and in this case does, point to the all. What we see here, then, is the incompleteness of a narrative, indeed the incompleteness of all narratives. Rawls's narrative, like every other, has to be taken further; the conversation has to go on, over the generations, as MacIntyre would say. People like Macedo, Okin and Galston, along with many others, are indeed taking that conversation on. By bringing Rawls into conversation with Urmson and Thomson we ourselves have tried to take the conversation onwards.

But we have also done something else, namely looked at Rawls in the shadow cast by the three narrative thinkers discussed in the previous chapter. In so doing we have seen one of the key claims that Rawls has made, namely that there can be a narrative that is not shackled to a particular community and tradition, and that the Original Position is just such a narrative. Whereas there is an unbreakable link between the narratives of Homer and Homeric society, the values of Achilles and the comprehensive doctrine of the heroic code of existence, there is no unbreakable link between the Original Position and a specific comprehensive doctrine. This is because the Overlapping Consensus on which the Position rests is not illusory, not a pact of convenience, but a moral reality. In other words the Original Position is a type of narrative that rises above historical particularity: it makes sense in a variety of cultures, whereas Achilles only makes sense in one culture, the culture that produced him. The Original Position transcends its origins in Cambridge, Massachusetts. This being so, it follows that there is more than one type of narrative at stake here, and that MacIntyre and others are wrong to posit an unbreakable link between narrative, community and tradition.

One way of refuting this would be to maintain that the Original Position is not a narrative in any real sense. This is usually done by maintaining that Rawls's people are disembodied selves and thus incapable of true decision-making. But this is not true. Rawls's people are real people, and Rawls advances an ideal of character for them; furthermore, a degree of disembodiment (equivalent to purity of heart) is necessary for the decision-making process, just as being too much embedded in a culture can mean decision-making becomes impossible. Every human being is in a culture, certainly; but every human being, at the same time, can distance themselves in his mind from his surrounding culture. Human beings are cultural animals, but they are not purely cultural animals and cannot be reduced to purely cultural phenomena. Therefore, the decision-making process envisaged by the Position is not a chimera. One can and indeed must put certain things, such as one's own interests, beneath the Veil of Ignorance if one is to be fair in approaching decisions. The idea of distancing oneself in order to be impartial has a long history in moral writing.[32]

We have spoken of the Position being a different type of narrative. It might best be described as 'polyvalent', finding as it does a suitably concordant fit with other more comprehensive narratives. It can be understood by a variety of people in a variety of cultural situations. Its appeal spans religious allegiances, or at least most religious allegiances. Its polyvalent quality means that one can be a Catholic Rawlsian, that the Rawlsian narrative can coexist with Catholicism in a real and not just merely apparent symbiosis. This is in marked contrast with Engelhardt's permission principle which cannot coexist with Catholicism except at the most superficial level, as it does violence to all that a Catholic holds. The polyvalency of the Rawlsian narrative thus tells us something about the nature of narrative.

Finally, the narrative proposed by Rawls alerts us to another very important point. There are, it seems, universal moral norms, and to turn to narrative does not mean to abandon universal moral truths; rather here is a narrative that is capable of encapsulating universal truths. Again we see in embryo an important truth about narrative that will have to be developed. A narrative may – if it is the right sort of narrative – be a bridge between lived particularity and universal truth. It can connect us, here and now in this culture, with truths that hold good for all cultures. The Original Position shows us one example of how this can be done. But there may be other stories too that find a suitably concordant fit with a variety of situations and which are valid whatever the setting in which they find themselves.

It is worth for a moment pausing to consider that the Original Position is a good story, and this is in part, perhaps, cause of the wide acclaim that Rawls has won. The story is easily visualized and neatly conceptualized; it is easily communicated to others, and one could see it being explained even to young children. It provides an easy entry into the world of thinking about justice. Moreover, as a story that claims to hold good for all circumstances, it fascinates the one who hears it, and challenges

---

[32] One such writer on this theme is Meister Eckhart. For his 'Treatise on Detachment', see Meister Eckhart, *The Essential Sermons, Commentaries, Treatises and Defense*, translated and introduced by Edmund Colledge and Bernard McGinn (New York: Paulist Press, 1981), pp. 285–94. See also 'Sermon 52', same volume, pp. 199–203, which talks of the detached man who 'wants nothing, knows nothing and has nothing'.

him or her to work out for themselves if this is in fact the case. Above all, truth is made accessible through this story, for a story is capable of bursting the bounds of this community or that tradition and attaining universal significance. For there is something in the Position – though the Position expresses this imperfectly – that shows us that Kant was right in pointing to timeless moral truths: the Position is a device, as Rawls says, that enables us to adopt the perspective of eternity,[33] which lifts us by virtue of reason above the time-bound and tradition bound condition in which we as narrative creatures may find ourselves. Narrative may well be all we have: but narrative does not have to restrict its sights to the particular horizon.

---

[33] Rawls, *A Theory of Justice*, p. 587.

Chapter 7

The Augustinian Approach

So far in our investigation we have come across two opposing points of view that can be summarized thus: the first sees particularity as the hallmark of narrative, which necessarily entails an abandonment of universality; the second sees universality as the hallmark of truth. But we have also seen the emergence of 'a third way' in our examination of John Rawls, namely the idea of a narrative, rooted in a particular time and place, yet at the same time sufficiently detached, that tends to universal truth. It is this third way that we now wish to explore further, in order to discover whether there can be a bridge between the particular and the universal and how exactly such a bridge might work.

There are allied questions too that still need to be answered. Is the human person to be seen as 'embedded' or as a 'disencumbered self'? To what extent are we bearers of tradition, and to what extent can or do we stand outside tradition? Again, is there a third way here too? Are human beings, formed by tradition, story-telling animals in the sense intended by MacIntyre, Hauerwas and Engelhardt, also able to distance themselves sufficiently from their environment in order to reform their traditions and reshape their stories, as Rawls suggests they can?

Furthermore, as we have already encountered, there is a plurality of stories that may exist on different levels (in the Rawlsian scheme of things), or which may be flatly contradictory (or 'incommensurable' in the MacIntyrean phrase). As MacIntyre further admits, without ever investigating the implications of it,[1] we may find ourselves 'in' two conflicting narratives at the same time. How are we to handle narrative conflict? Which is the right story? Which is the true story? Are all stories equally true, or is there a rational way of differentiating between the true and false? What is the relationship of the narrative to reality?

Lastly, we must confront the question of how people 'enter' or find themselves 'in' a narrative or choose a narrative. This question has largely been ignored by our authors so far. How does one of Hauerwas's Christians enter the narrative of the Gospels? How do MacIntyre's Athenians identify with the works of Homer, and how do those works shape their lives and community? What is it that impels Rawls's people to enter the Original Position? What exactly is the relationship between the reader (or hearer) and the narrative? And how can we speak of a person as being part of a narrative?

Only when we have considered questions like these, and arrived at answers, will we be able to work out a developed theory of narrative theology. In order to do so we shall examine some of the works of St Augustine, who, as we shall see, encountered

---

[1] MacIntyre, *After Virtue*, p. 213.

these questions, and also found solutions to them. In so doing we shall examine at a deeper level what a narrative is and how it works.

Narrative as the Bridge between the Particular and the Universal

Augustine is the author of two works of narrative that are also works of theology: the *Confessions* and the *City of God*; the first tells the story of his early life; the second is the story of the Church interleaved with that of Rome. Both are supremely of their time, and at the same time, for all time. The story of a young man growing up in North Africa in the late fourth century sounds on the face of it of little interest to us, living many centuries later. Likewise, the old controversies that exercised his mind in the *City of God* are unquestionably out of date. And yet both these books are of great interest, and are still in print. Over the centuries Augustine still speaks to us, which is remarkable. He is the proof that a narrative rooted in time and place can have universal resonance and application.

The popularity of Augustine in our age and in every age, the fact that succeeding centuries have regarded him as relevant to their concerns, may be taken as read. What we need to do is to ask how this phenomenon is possible. What is it in the *Confessions*[2] in particular that provides the bridge of understanding between his age and ours? What is it in this narrative that makes it rooted in a particular tradition and yet at the same time of so much wider import? How can something so narrow in scope be so vast in application?

Let us look first at the narrowness of Augustine: his narrative is a human creation, which starts with a first person experience. This first person experience is transformed through the act of narration to an every person experience, as we shall see. But how exactly does Augustine turn experience, the raw material of life, into a highly finished and indeed artificial, in the true sense, narrative? For a narrative is crafted in some way; the more natural it seems, the more crafted it usually is.

Until recently scholars have been divided over the question of Augustine's authorship of the *Confessions*: some saw the book as an autobiography, that is, a historically accurate and factual account of Augustine's life, but others saw it as primarily a theological book that adapted historical fact (or even made it up) to fit in with a theological schema.[3] What interests us here is the question of authorship, and the question of the author's relation to his material. Behind the question lies the notion that autobiography and theology are opposite poles and that the reconciliation of divine truth with a personal story is a hard task. Pierre Courcelle's project to establish the 'true story' that lies behind the overtly autobiographical passages

---

[2] Of the numerous translations of the *Confessions*, I have chosen to follow that of Maria Boulding, vol. 1 of *The Works of St Augustine, a Translation for the Twenty–First Century* (New York: New City Press, 1997). I have chosen to follow the original Latin text in the edition of James J. O'Donnell (Oxford, Clarendon Press, 1992).

[3] For a summary of the controversy see Pierre Courcelle, *Recherches sur les Confessions de St Augustin* (Paris: Editions E. de Boccard, 1968), pp. 7–12, 242–3.

assumes or at least confronts the contention that the subjective truth of autobiography is not the 'real' truth.[4]

So it seems there are two 'truths': the 'truth' of real events, and the 'truth' as Augustine tells it, which might not be the real truth, but rather fiction, namely that which is made, or even just made up. Narrative theology claims that we are story-telling animals, and the truth is contained in and expressed by the stories about themselves that people tell; moreover this is the only truth (for all is narrative) and the impersonal truth of history understood as the view from nowhere simply does not exist. Every view, including history, will be a view from somewhere. Thus the personal account of himself that Augustine gives is the truth about himself, and not to be put aside in favour of an impersonal truth that is to be mined from his writings. In fact to look for some other 'truth' that lies behind the truth of the narrative is to enter a hall of receding mirrors.

The *Confessions* are deeply personal, 'a unique history of the heart':[5] they are the history not of Augustine's life, but of his feelings, and not a history of his opinions or his intellect, except in passing.[6] This history of the heart is told from a particular standpoint, that of a middle aged man writing some thirteen years after the last events described in the book. But subjective and personal as the book is, it is also theological: it is cast from its very first lines as a conversation with God. Repeatedly the author turns to address his Creator, and every other relationship he has is seen in the context of this one overarching relationship.

But this is not to say that the book is a theological tract that makes use of a fictionalized past. The past was real to Augustine; he was writing for people who knew him; many factual details could be assumed;[7] one can also assume that the readers would have detected things that were blatantly fictional. The pear-tree incident[8] was a real one, Courcelle maintains, while noting that the incident is described in eight lines followed by seven pages of commentary on its significance.[9] This is symptomatic of Augustine's approach to his past history: the events are there, real enough, but his real interest is in his reaction to those events, both then and now. Events are not seen as existing in themselves, but as lived realities; the object makes sense and is important, because it has been experienced in some way, it has meaning for Augustine. It has become part of his personal narrative. And yet that object does have an independent existence of its own.

---

[4] Hence the debate, for example, about whether the fig and pear trees that play such interesting roles in the book are in fact 'real' or merely 'symbolic' trees. On this controversy see Leo C. Ferrari, 'The Pear-Theft in Augustine's Confessions', *Revue des Etudes Augustiniennes* XVI (1970): 240–47, and Pierre Courcelle, 'Le Jeune Augustin, second Catalina', in *Opuscula Selecta* (Paris: Etudes Augustiniennes, 1984), pp. 319–28, which is Courcelle's reply to Ferrari.

[5] Peter Brown, *Augustine of Hippo, A Biography* (London: Faber, 1967), pp. 169–72.

[6] John J. O'Meara, *The Young Augustine, The Growth of Saint Augustine's Mind up to his Conversion* (London: Longmans, Green and Co., 1954), seems to suggest otherwise in his telling subtitle.

[7] O'Meara, p. 5.

[8] *Confessions*, 2.9.

[9] Courcelle, *Recherches*, p. 51.

It is this double perspective that Peter Brown identifies as marking the *Confessions* as 'a very modern book'. Whereas previous works of literature portray heroes as ideal types, more symbols than characters, who have no memory except in the most conventional sense of the term, Augustine emerges as a man who is a creature of memory, formed by his past.[10] The real subject of the *Confessions* is introspection and the whole book is an exercise in remembering. This emerges very clearly in Book X where Augustine himself settles once and for all the controversy about whether the biographical passages are historical or not. Memory, he tells us, is selective:

> Now I arrive in the fields and vast mansions of memory, where there are treasured innumerable images brought in there from objects of every conceivable kind perceived by the senses. There too are hidden away the modified images we produce when by our thinking we magnify or diminish or in any other way alter the information our senses have reported. There too is everything else that has been consigned and stowed away, and not yet engulfed and buried in oblivion. Sojourning there I command something I want to present to myself, and immediately certain things emerge, while others have to be pursued for some time and dug out from remote crannies. Others again come tumbling out in disorderly profusion, and leap into prominence as though asking, 'Are we what you want?' when it is something different that I am asking for and trying to recall. With my mental hand I push them out of the way of my effort to remember, until what I want becomes clear and breaks from cover...[11]

As this passage makes clear, memory is both selective and active: we choose what we remember, we select the memories we wish to use, like someone rummaging through a storeroom. In addition, it is important to note that many of the images in the memory are not 'raw': they have been modified in the process of remembering, they have been interpreted – magnified, diminished or otherwise altered. This key passage sheds light on the way Augustine wrote the *Confessions*, and indeed on the way any author creates a narrative. Certain things over the passage of time become more important, others less so. Memory shapes sense perception and gives it new significance. Memory is the process that creates narrative out of perceptions. What was once thought worth remembering is discarded, and perhaps what was once considered of minor importance becomes of greater value. The author selects and evaluates: certain elements are used in the creation of the narrative and others not; certain things are given prominence and others less so. The criteria for selection will depend on the author's point of view and his purpose.

Indeed, Augustine picks and chooses which memories to use to illustrate the point he is making; memories become retrospectively important.[12] But if this is true, and it cannot be otherwise, for what narrative could possibly contain all memories, all possible elements, we are left with the idea that narrative is bound to be both subjective and selective, indeed partial in both senses of the word. Narrative by nature represents a narrowing or sharpening of reality – a reduction of reality to

---

[10] Brown, p. 173.
[11] *Confessions*, 10.8.12.
[12] O'Meara, p. 6. A similar point is made by Brian Stock, *Augustine the Reader* (Cambridge, Mass.: The Belknap Press of Harvard University Press, 1996), pp. 34–5.

manageable proportions through memory. At the same time the partial vision may indeed be magnificent, but it will still not be the whole picture. As such it can be dismissed as not having universal value; but it is the contention of Augustine the author and narrative theologian that this very selectivity and partiality are of universal significance. For the act of authorship and the creation of a theological narrative are one and the same. Narrative creation is bridge building between the particular and the universal, the creation of another double perspective, that of the here and now and that of the eternal. This double perspective is created through the act of authorship.

The author is the one who finds meaning in experience, and draws experiences together, forming them into a coherent whole. This act of authorship is thus an assertion of personal identity, for in the act of remembering, rearranging and forming the store of memories into a coherent narrative, the author claims those past memories for themselves. Identity and the continuity of the self are rooted in memory, and memory serves to unite the experiences of the past.[13] The author is not simply creating a story, they are also creating themselves.

> This I do [the act of remembering] within myself in the immense court of my memory; for there sky and earth and sea are readily available to me, together with everything that I have ever been able to perceive in them, apart from what I have forgotten. And there I come to meet myself. I recall myself, what I did, when and where I acted in a certain way, and how I felt about so acting. Everything is there which I so remember having experienced for myself or believed on the assertion of others. Moreover, I can draw upon this abundant store to form imaginary pictures which resemble the things I have myself experienced, or believed because my own experience confirmed them, and weave these together [*contexo*] with images from the past, and so evoke future actions, occurrences or hopes; and on all these as well I can meditate as though they were present to me.[14]

Once again we note the active nature of memory that weaves together the present and the past to form a unified whole, in other words to form a narrative. It is memory that guarantees our continuing identity, because memory is the place in which we exercise authorship and create the narrative that is personal to us, the narrative of our own lives. But memory is not something that is locked away in the past, it is active now, in the present, and can evoke future actions. Augustine the schoolboy and Augustine the Bishop are a continuous reality united by the remembrance of things past; thus that past is not dead, but alive in him now, looking to the future. Without this idea of continuity, no narrative is possible.

In the act of authorship, memory is ever present, the stuff of his existence and his identity. It is for this reason that the *Confessions* are so interesting to modern readers, being the first truly modern history of consciousness. They are also a history of much else, but that is by the way. Augustine's first concern is with the heart, his own heart; frustratingly for some, he never tells us clearly, for example, about his knowledge of

---

[13] Henry Chadwick, *Augustine* (Oxford: Oxford University Press, 1986), p. 70.
[14] *Confessions*, 10.8.14.

Greek;[15] nor does he tell us the name of the mother of his son. For a modern reader, brought up on the novel that reveals all, and its all-knowing consciousness, these are grave omissions. But Augustine is writing an interior history of the self. Much is in fact revealed about the exterior self – Augustine is the most knowable man of the ancient world[16] – but this is incidental to the real, interior, story. Other people, even Monica his mother, only enter the *Confessions* because of the contribution they make to that inner story.

This cursory glance at the *Confessions* tells us two things about narrative and narrative theology. First, Augustine shows us how narrative is created by an author. But this in turn is only possible because we think narratively, because experience, in so far as it is remembered by us, is remembered in a narrative fashion. We do not think raw thoughts, or raw images, but in the act of remembering we form a picture of ourselves that expresses 'what I did, when and where I acted in a certain way, how I felt about so acting.' This picture, created by the memory, is, through the very act of creation, an interpretation of reality, as opposed to a 'pure' representation of fact. The words 'in a certain way' and 'how I felt' suggest as much. Not only then is reality best perceived as narrative, it seems that there is no other way to perceive reality except as narrative. For the very act of mental creation (or authorship) is an exercise in narrative. This would suggest that there is no such thing as bare unadorned facts, but all is narrative.

Secondly, better than anyone else before him, and perhaps since too, Augustine establishes that the centre of truth and meaning is the individual consciousness. The act of writing the book is an act of faith in this proposition: for in discovering himself through the exploration of memory and consciousness he can come to truth, even to God himself. The authorship of the autobiography is also the authorship of the story of God as experienced by himself, for there is no human story that is not also a divine story, for the human heart is the place of encounter with the divine. But this proposition also underlies narrative theology itself. Human beings are centres of meaning and truth, therefore the stories they tell are expressive of meaning and truth. Truth is that which is to be found in the heart of mankind.

Because authorship – the creation of self through memory, and the recognition of the narrative nature of experience as crafted by memory – is common to all human beings, it is possible then that Augustine in writing his own story shows us how we too can write our own stories: in other words he discovers (in the sense of uncovers) for us a structure to existence that we all share. Thus the narrowness of Augustine's story serves to show us how we too may be centres of meaning and truth. The fact that we share a common nub of experience with him, different as we are, means that his story has a universal resonance.

The *Confessions* are presented not only as a deeply personal story, but also as a story of universal significance. They show that fiction and truth are not mutually exclusive terms, once we understand fiction in the right sense. Truth comes to us

---

[15] For a summary of this question, which has exercised so many, see Henri-Irenée Marrou, *Saint Augustin et la Fin de la Culture Antique*, fourth edition (Paris: Editions E. de Boccard, 1958), p. 28 and following.

[16] Marrou, p. x.

unadorned, perhaps, but the truth about ourselves is something that we create from the raw material of experience, through the memory which selects, transforms, and evaluates such raw material: thus truth is a narrative, rooted in reality, yet a human creation too, with a human author. Narrative theology thus becomes possible.

The Self as Embedded or Disembodied

From our observations on the *Confessions* in the preceding section we have examined the way that authorship works, and how the memory imposes structure on experience in order to create narrative. This authored narrative, a structured, necessarily selective and partial account, then reflects the truth about the person, their environment and their values; this truth in turn is the truth about all people, for there is something common to all experiences. Thus narrative, which is fiction in the best sense of the word, namely that which is made, is a reflection of the truth as we experience it.

What we now need to do is examine further the authorial 'I' that creates this narrative. How does the authorial 'I' relate to the world: put in the terms of narrative theology, is the author constituted by environment, embedded in a particular community? Or is the author a freestanding phenomenon, a disencumbered self? The first would be the view of MacIntyre, Hauerwas and Engelhardt; the second would be the position of Rawls. But Augustine points out a third way.

The 'I' is the person telling the story; but more than this, the 'I' is the person who writes or tells themselves into existence through the story, which creates their identity. The author is not a mere mouthpiece. The author exists, not simply in the present, in the act of telling, but also formed by the past and the act of remembering, as well as looking to the future in the act of anticipation and longing. This three-dimensional structure is essential to the constitution of the 'I'. Moreover, this authorial self that is narrating the *Confessions* is speaking to God[17] and perhaps also to himself, but also to an audience of fellow pilgrims:

> I confess not only before you in secret exultation tinged with fear and secret sorrow infused with hope, but also in the ears of believing men and women, the companions of my joy and sharers in my mortality, my fellow citizens still on pilgrimage with me, and those who have gone before and those who will follow, and all who bear me company in my life. They are your servants and my brethren...[18]

Once again we encounter three dimensions: the self, the fellow pilgrims and God, a triple audience; and the fellow pilgrims are also triply divided: his contemporaries, those who have gone before and those who will come after. Augustine the author addresses future generations (an important point to which we will return), but at the same time he speaks as one who is embedded in the present generation, one of a number of 'fellow citizens'. That Augustine is a typical man of late antiquity is the judgement of Marrou,[19] and his magisterial study on Augustine's cultural setting and

---

[17] *Confessions*, 1.1–6.
[18] *Confessions*, 10.4.6.
[19] Marrou, p. 543.

his education must be regarded as proving this point. It is not necessary to summarize the evidence that Marrou marshals to make his case, one hopes; but one can consider a few points that make Augustine so typical of his age. As Marrou points out, the young Augustine was steeped in two authors in particular, Virgil and Cicero, in poetry and prose respectively.[20] Augustine himself tells of his love for Virgil but with a qualifying note about the frivolity of Dido and Aeneas.[21] Despite this caution, when it comes to describing his traumatic desertion of Monica in Carthage while he sails off to Italy, this is done in clearly Virgilian terms.[22] This shows just how deeply Augustine was embedded in the culture of Virgil. He himself remarks in the *City of God*, that Virgil, best of poets, learned in childhood, is not easily forgotten,[23] and the departure from Africa passage in the *Confessions* proves his point: when Augustine the author wishes to describe a real experience, he expresses himself through the medium of a famous literary paradigm. His imagination is bounded by his reading. Similarly with the pear tree theft. It is hard to read this without being aware of other literary prototypes in mind – though which prototype is questionable. Courcelle sees it as a recreation of the Catalina story;[24] Chadwick sees it as a Garden of Eden story and adds interestingly that Augustine sees himself as Everyman in this scene;[25] in other words the story is an archetypal story – a concept to which we will return in due course. But whatever way we look at the pear tree, or the scene of Monica's abandonment, though there may be disagreement on which literary paradigm lies behind them, there can be general agreement that Augustine's imagination was formed by the books he read as a boy. His authorship fits into a literary tradition, though which precise tradition remains open to discussion.

So, Augustine the author's 'I' is a narrative reality, and a narrative reality that is culturally expressed, using the language of the culture into which he was born. However, though the foregoing are important examples of Augustine's embedded selfhood (as the MacIntyrean phrase would have it) and the fact that he is what he has read, at the same time (and this is important) his consciousnesses has transformed what he has read too. Augustine is not a mere purveyor of pastiche: he is both highly traditional and highly original. Through the shaping spirit of the imagination he transmogrifies his reading, producing something new. He is within a tradition, yet he also creates a new tradition. He is, as we shall try to show, an embedded self, but also a self that stands at some distance from what he has inherited. He is culturally informed but he is not culture bound in a restrictive sense.

Thus Augustine is not simply a MacIntyrean man: he is an embedded self, but much more than that – he was one who created a new tradition from the ruins of the old, and who was thus sufficiently disencumbered to do so. He was a typical man of late antiquity but also the first man of the modern era. He stands between two

---

[20] Marrou, p. 18 and *passim*.
[21] *Confessions* 1.13.20.
[22] *Confessions* 5.8.15. See also the note on this, by O'Donnell, pp. 307–08.
[23] *City of God*, I.3.
[24] Pierre Courcelle, 'Le Jeune Augustin, second Catalina', *Opuscula Selecta*, pp. 319–28.
[25] Chadwick, p. 68.

ages, one dying, the other about to be born. Yet such a point can be made with too much facility. Even though Augustine lived to see the sack of Rome by the Goths in 410, he still claims in the *City of God* that though Rome is in difficulty, she is not lost: 'However, the Roman empire has been violently buffeted by storms, but not shattered. It experienced violent storms too, before Christ's name was heard, but it weathered them all. Hence there is no reason to despair in our own times.'[26]

This must count as one of the least perspicacious comments ever made! Augustine was clearly not aware that the world in which he lived, the Latin Empire of the West, was in its death throes. The *Confessions* betray no awareness whatsoever of a world about to end in chaos.[27] Thus we see Augustine as an embedded self – one unable to imagine a world without the Roman Empire which was, after all the only world he had ever known.

At the same time this embedded self who is too embedded to see the approaching end of the Western Empire is one that criticizes the Roman Empire that has nurtured him. As Peter Brown points out, the *City of God* shows an intense ambivalence about the Empire; on the one hand Augustine is debunking the myth of Rome, claiming it is a *latrocinium* (thieves' conspiracy), based on the naked pursuit of power, and yet he praises it for being virtuous and successful; he contrasts 'your Virgil' with 'our scriptures' and the past has now become 'your literature'.[28] Here we see him once again inside the tradition and yet outside it as a vehement critic at the same time; an embedded self and a detached self too. This duality runs through the entire length of the immense book as even a superficial reading will show. In contrast with the Roman Empire, where true justice was never practised, as even Cicero admits, true justice is only found in the City of God, whose founder and ruler is Jesus Christ;[29] Cicero, quoted a few chapters previously with approbation, is 'a man of importance

---

[26] *City of God*, IV.7.

[27] When Augustine delivers his oration in front of the Emperor Valentinian II and the Consul Bauto (*Confessions*, 6.6.9), there is no hint of the decadence of the situation: Bauto is a Frankish barbarian, and the miserable boy Emperor is a puppet who will very shortly have his strings cut. As Claude Lepelley has convincingly shown, Augustine harboured great ambitions at this time, perhaps to be a provincial governor, quite unaware that soon there would be no provinces left to govern (Claude Lepelley, 'Un aspect de la Conversion de St Augustin: La rupture avec ses ambitions socials et politiques', *Bulletin de Literature Ecclesiastique*, 88 (1987): 229–46. Also, same author, 'Spes Saeculi: le Milieu social de St Augustin et ses ambitions séculiers avant sa conversion', in *Congresso Internazionale su S. Agostino nel XVI centenario della sua conversione, Roma, 15–20 sett. 1986, Atti*', vol. 1 (Rome: Institutum Patristicum Augustinianum, 1987), pp. 99–117. While he and Monica are caught up in ecstasy at Ostia (*Confessions* 9.10.23 et seq), they seem happily unaware of the usurper Maximin blockading the port and keeping them from travelling home. Naturally, Augustine was not writing a political history of his time, but this blithe confidence in the enduring nature of the Roman world seems astonishing. One only has to compare it with some of the apocalyptic comments about the barbarian incursions made by his contemporary Jerome in his letters 60 and 123.

[28] Brown, pp. 306–10; *City of God*, V.9 and V.12.

[29] *City of God*, II.21.

but a poor philosopher';[30] but Virgil, the best of poets[31] though a pagan, can be mined for quotations with which to garland the martyrs[32] even though he is the ideologue of Rome's divine vocation.[33] Yet Virgil the pagan even prophesies the coming of Christ.[34] The Roman Empire was not a true commonwealth, being devoid of justice,[35] but we are told more than once that it existed by divine providence:

> To be brief, Rome was founded – a second, and a daughter of the first, Babylon, as it were. It was God's good pleasure, by means of this city, to subdue the whole world, to bring it into a single society of a republic under law, and to bestow upon it a widespread and enduring peace. But this was to be accomplished only at the expense of titanic hazards, hair-raising exertions, and much mutual devastation…[36]

In the very phrasing of this passage we see Augustine's ambivalence to Rome, a sort of horrified fascination with its greatness. And one notices a contradiction: Rome was not a commonwealth, was devoid of justice, and yet was a 'republic under law'. At both one and the same time Augustine is determined to draw on his Roman culture and also to criticize it, to praise it and to damn it. He is within the tradition and capable of distancing himself from it at the same time. He is a divided self.

This concept of the divided self will, one hopes, illuminate our understanding of Augustine's authorship, and by extension, of the way other selves author their own existences as well.

We have already encountered discussion of the need for impartiality, as mentioned by both MacIntyre and Rawls, but the Augustinian vision goes much further. William Galston writes in a different context:

> Rawls's argument manifestly depends on a specific affirmative conception of individuality. Persons must be emotionally, intellectually, and ontologically capable of drawing an effective line between their public and non-public identities and of setting aside their particular commitments, at least to the extent needed to enter the original position and to reason in a manner consistent with its constraints.
>
> A number of contemporary liberals, in fact, have been drawn to such a conception of individuality: not the unencumbered self (which Sandel rightly criticizes) but, rather, the *divided* self. On the one side stands the individual's personal and social history, with all the aims and attachments they may imply. On the other side stands the possibility of reflection on – even revolt against – these very commitments. The self most at home in liberal society, so understood, contains the potentiality for such critical distance from one's inheritance and accepts the possibility that the exercise of critical faculties may in important respects modify that inheritance.
>
> This is in many ways an attractive view, with links to both the Socratic ideal of the examined life and the Enlightenment ideal of the rational society. Moreover, it draws

---

[30] *City of God*, II.27.
[31] *City of God*, I.3.
[32] *City of God*, II.29.
[33] *City of God*, V.12.
[34] *City of God*, X.27.
[35] *City of God*, XIX.21.
[36] *City of God*, XVIII.22. A similar point is made at V.21.

support from the liberal conviction that individuality is not only shaped but also threatened by community... [37]

As we have tried to argue, this is exactly the sort of self Augustine is: part of a tradition, as everyone has to be, but at the same time able to reflect on his tradition and keep his critical distance from it.

This certainly is the view of Courcelle, who goes into minute detail to prove his case that certain passages in the *Confessions* replicate almost word for word passages in Seneca:

> Augustine reproduces virtually word for word the expressions of Seneca... I do not make any claim at all that some of these passages may be the direct source of the corresponding passages in Augustine. But the Stoic origin of this body of doctrine seems beyond doubt... [However] correctly understood Augustine turns the doctrine into a Christian direction: he is careful not to mention our personal demon, in the same way as Epictetus does... [38]

What does this tell us? Augustine uses the tradition, but stands at a sufficient distance from it to be able to use it in a new and Christian sense. He does exactly the same with neo-Platonism. Porphyry is attacked on numerous occasions in the *City of God*[39] and yet in an explicitly Christian setting, Augustine can freely draw on ideas that Porphyry would have been familiar with, such as the ascent to the supreme good:

> Now as I said all this you cried out in longing for a beauty not seen as yet. Let your heart stretch beyond all familiar things, let its gaze go beyond all the things you are accustomed to think about which are derived from the flesh, all the thoughts drawn out from the fleshly senses and any kinds of fantasies. Drive the whole lot out of your mind; whatever presents itself to your thoughts, turn it down. Recognise the weakness of your heart, and whatever occurs to you, say of it, 'This is not the real thing, for if it had been, I could not even have imagined it.' In this way you will be desiring something good. What sort of good? The Good of all good, from which all good derives, the Good to which nothing can be added to explain what goodness is... simple good, sheer Goodness-Itself, in virtue of which all things are good...[40]

---

[37] Galston, *Liberal Purposes*, p. 153.

[38] '*Augustin reproduit presque mot à mot les expressions de Sénèque... Je ne prétends nullement qu'aucun de ces passages soit la source directe des passages correspondants d'Augustin. Mais l'origine stoïcienne de ce corps de doctrine ne paraît pas douteuse...* [However] *Bien entendu, Augustin infléchit la doctrine en un sens chrétien: il se garde de mentionnner notre démon personnel, comme faisait Epictete...*' Courcelle, *Connais-tu tois-même de Socrate à St Bernard* (Paris: Etudes Augustiniennes, 1974), p. 142. English translation by the author.

[39] *City of God*, X.11, 24 and 29 for just three examples.

[40] *Ennarationes*, 26/2.8 (*Works*, vol. 15, p. 279). For a similar example, this time using Platonic language to describe the universal desire for happiness, see *Ennarationes* 32/3 15–16 (*Works*, vol. 15, p. 415). The English translation of the *Ennarationes* that I have chosen to follow is that found in *The Works of Saint Augustine, A translation for the Twenty-First Century*, vols 15–18 inclusive. The translator is once again Maria Boulding. For the Latin original I have drawn on *Corpus Christianorum, Series Latina* (Turnholti: Typographi Brepols

There is nothing remarkable about this passage *per se*. It is standard Platonism for the masses – but what is remarkable is the context of the words: they form part of a sermon preached in church, indeed preached one Wednesday at Saint Cyprian's shrine. They thus form a clear example of the way Augustine is able to use what he inherited from Porphyry and others. As with Stoicism, so with neo-Platonism: Augustine is more than a mere eclectic, he is one who belongs to the tradition and at the same time stands outside it.

At this point we can make a connection with what we have discovered in earlier chapters and come to an important conclusion. We have already seen the cleavage between those who speak of embedded selves and those who allegedly speak of 'atomist' or disencumbered selves. But a divided self is one that is both encumbered and embedded (as MacIntyre would have it) and at the same time capable of disencumbering itself and entering the Original Position, as Rawls would have it. Or we can cast the insight in specifically Augustinian terms. The human being is capable of 'turning' (*conversio*), capable, rooted as they are and difficult though it may be, of refashioning their spirit through a change of their old life: *mutatione veteris vitae resculpimus spiritum nostrum.*[41] Again, they are capable of turning to something that is not themselves, that lies beyond the things that constitute themselves: *convertisti te ad aliud quod tu non eras.*[42]

The human being has a story and is constituted by the past, but can at the same time stand at a distance from this past through reflection. There is no necessary contradiction between the two. Put another way, Augustine is both a man of the late Roman world with all that entails, and also Everyman, who speaks to and for those who are strangers to his world. It is at this point then that we can understand the words of Augustine quoted earlier. He speaks to his fellow pilgrims, his fellow citizens, but also addresses himself to future generations: this is only possible because he is embedded in his own generation, yet at the same time sufficiently disencumbered to be able to speak to those who do not share all the preconceptions of his generation. If he were utterly embedded in his own time, he would make no sense to people who were not similarly embedded. Our conclusion must be, then, that the human being who authors their own existence is best understood not as an embedded self, or a disencumbered self, but a divided self. This will of course have very important ramifications for narrative theology and moral theology in particular, for we are now beginning to see how the rooted and personal can also have universal significance.

How to Decide Between the Conflicting Narratives of the Divided Self?

Internal division, so necessary to authorship, is also the subject of the drama about which Augustine the author writes. The divided self lives with (or sometimes between) two narratives, two ways of explaining the world. We have indeed already encountered this idea: MacIntyre mentions people who are torn between two

---

Editores Pontificii, 1956), vols XXXIX and XL. For the sake of convenience I shall give page references to the English translation.

[41] *Ennarationes* 6.5, (*Works*, vol. 15, p. 106).
[42] *Ennarationes* 25(2).11, (*Works*, vol. 15, p. 264).

narratives, and Rawls also speaks of those who hold two narratives, though at two different and non-contradicting levels. All the authors also speak of pluralism in society at large.

Augustine finds himself internally divided, but he also writes about a world that is divided: in the *City of God* the division spans the whole of history, which is the narrative of the struggle between the City of God and Babylon. The divided self finds itself called in different directions by the competing narratives in the world. The divisions in the microcosm of the human heart are reflected by the divisions in the macrocosm, the society in which humans find themselves. There is not one narrative, then, but many, both in society and indeed in the individual person.[43]

Charles Taylor has claimed that questions of selfhood and the good are intertwined.[44] My identity is related to my orientation in moral space,[45] my 'original situation' which has reference to my stand on moral questions.[46] The trouble with this is that I may not have a unified picture of the good; and I may thus be a disintegrated, or at the very least, confused character. But Taylor is surely right when he speaks of Augustine's *Confessions* as 'recasting our lives in a new narrative'.[47] This new narrative will also necessarily involve a new identity and a new understanding of social relations.[48] What is useful to note here is the fact that narrative comes with the question of identity and the question of sociality. The divided self is the person who is trying to discover both their own identity and their own relationship to the world: this is the story of the *Confessions*: the history of a divided self seeking integration, and its interior struggle between sin and the acceptance of the call of God, conceived as the search for a true and lasting narrative.

This struggle reaches its climax in the garden scene at Milan;[49] after this sin is defeated, though, as Book X shows, some of its effects live on. This is a particular story, that of one man in a particular place, but O'Meara insists: 'Augustine believes all men have similar experiences in their search for truth'[50] and that Augustine's conversion represents that of Everyman.[51]

The division within Augustine is internal and spiritual. James J. O'Donnell has written:

> If the *Confessions* are indeed 'the first modern biography' in any useful sense, it is because they assume that the soul is the scene of narrative, and that the narrative of the soul is the deepest and truest story of the person... But that form of story-telling depends on a

---

[43] The first point, about a divided society, is the basis of the first chapter of *After Virtue*; however, MacIntyre also admits that one person may have several narratives, as we have seen, without ever exploring the significance of this. See *After Virtue*, p. 213.
[44] Charles Taylor, *Sources of the Self, the Making of Modern Identity* (Cambridge, Mass.: Harvard University Press, 1989), p.3.
[45] Taylor, p. 28.
[46] Taylor, p. 36.
[47] Taylor, p. 97.
[48] Taylor, p. 105.
[49] *Confessions*, 8.29.
[50] O'Meara, p. 18.
[51] O'Meara, p. 13. See also Chadwick, p. 68 for a similar point re Everyman.

particular configuration of 'soul'. The soul must be a unity that has lost its coherence and seeks in life to regain it: whether the interpretative structure is Augustinian or Freudian, the fundamental assumption is the same.[52]

Indeed the Augustinian narrative is not about seeking therapy (which might have been provided by a dualistic creed like Manicheanism) but grace. The doctrine of Mani establishes the duality of the flesh and the spirit, good and evil: it is a convenient doctrine for those who find integration impossible; it systematizes the disintegration, just as does Engelhardt's permission principle; it does violence to the human soul's desire for integration. But the human person is a unity, for Augustine, of thought, memory and will,[53] just as it is a unity embodying past, present and future; in its disintegrated state it longs for unity. This longing can only be realized in God who has already accomplished it in the incarnation of Christ, the mediator who reconciles all differences.[54] This is the thought behind the famous first paragraph of the *Confessions*:

> Great are you, O Lord, and exceedingly worthy of praise; your power is immense, and your wisdom is beyond reckoning. And so we humans, who are a due part of your creation, long to praise you – we who carry our mortality about with us, carrying the evidence of our sin and with it the proof that you thwart the proud. Yet these humans, due part of your creation as they are, still do long to praise you. You arouse us that praising you may bring us joy, because you have made us and drawn us to yourself, and our heart is unquiet until it rests in you.[55]

This paragraph sums up the whole theme of the book. We are part of creation, but sin leads us astray, and only when we are re-integrated into the divine scheme of things will we find rest and joy.[56] This re-integration is effected by Christ, who is both God and Man.[57]

Augustine's disintegrated, divided self, brings with it a profound sense of alienation, which he seeks to overcome through a new and lasting narrative. This alienation is seen in his guilt over sin, which is strongly stressed throughout the *Confessions*. For example:

> Who will grant me to find peace in you? Who will grant me this grace, that you would come into my heart and inebriate it, enabling me to forget the evils that beset me and embrace you, my only good? What are you to me? Have mercy on me, that I may tell.

---

[52] James J O'Donnell. 'The Strangeness of Augustine', *Augustinian Studies*, 32, 2 (2001): 201–6, p. 205.

[53] David Peddle, 'Resourcing Charles Taylor's Augustine', in *Augustinian Studies*, 32:2 (2001):207–17, p. 210. See also *De Trinitate*, Chapter 20, part 26, for the Trinitarian nature of thought.

[54] Peddle, p. 212.

[55] *Confessions*, 1.1.1.

[56] *Confessions*, 10.27.38 for the climactic passage about integration, to be read in conjunction with the opening paragraph.

[57] *Confessions*, 7.18.24 and 10.43.68. For Augustine's thought on Christ the Mediator between [divine] Wisdom and [human] Knowledge, see *De Trinitate*, Book XIII, chapter 19. part 24.

> What indeed am I to you, that you should command me to love you, and grow angry with me if I do not, and threaten me with enormous woes? Is not the failure to love you woe enough in itself? Alas for me! Through your own merciful dealings with me, O Lord my God, tell me what you are to me. Say to my soul, I am your salvation. Say it so I can hear it.[58]

Here, as in so many other passages, he longs to be integrated and reconciled to God, from whom he feels alienated. But this sense of alienation is not just the alienation of the restless soul separated from God, but also the longing of one who longs for the coherence of a narrative and finds himself without one. It is seen in two other striking ways as well. The first of these is language, on which narrative itself depends.

Alienation and Language

As one who is *infans* (an infant, but literally, one unable to speak) as a child, he feels frustrated at being unable to speak:

> Little by little I began to notice where I was, and I would try to make my wishes known to those who might satisfy them; but I was frustrated in this, because my ideas were inside me, while other people were outside and could by no effort of understanding enter my mind. So I tossed about and screamed, sending signals meant to indicate what I wanted, those few signs were the best I could manage, though they did not really express my desires.[59]

He desires to speak but is reduced to a scream of frustrated rage and inarticulacy because there are no words, no bridge of communication, that can span the gap between different minds. One notices the dichotomy between 'inside' and 'outside', which no effort of understanding can bridge – a powerful symbol of alienation. The child may well have a story, represented by his desires, but he has no means to express this story. He is a narrative creature deprived of narrative.

Augustine discusses speech and language as the power to express meaning, but seems to deny the possibility of ambiguity: people make what they mean clear through words and gestures and facial expressions, which are unmistakeable and common to all races.[60] But this rather optimistic vision of language as a transparent medium of meaning receives a corrective when he speaks of his early love of Virgil: words, especially fine ones, lead him astray, for he can weep for Dido but not for himself and he pointedly remarks on the insanity of regarding these studies as more civilized and rewarding than the elementary tasks of learning to read and write.[61] In other words, literature can use words to pervert meaning, in contrast to the plainness of ordinary writing. He goes on to remark that poetry is untrue, frivolous,[62] a verdict that reminds us of Plato's: words can enlighten but also do the opposite. His speech

---

[58] *Confessions*, 1.5.5.
[59] *Confessions*, 1.6.8.
[60] *Confessions*, 1.8.13.
[61] *Confessions*, 1.13.21.
[62] *Confessions*, 1.13.22.

about Juno is all 'smoke and wind'.[63] And he makes the extraordinary statement that 'knowledge of letters lies less deep than the law written in our conscience'.[64] In other words, human letters, human language, are something superficial, which skates over truth and does not broach it; it is not at the same level as the infused truth of God's law.

These pointers alert us to a division between words and meaning, between the desire to speak truth (if words are meant to convey truth) and the inability to express truth in words. Thus a speaker is divided from himself: he wishes in his heart to communicate truth, but he finds himself mouthing vacuities. So while infants are in the unenviable position of having no language at all with which to express themselves, adults are in a position perhaps no less unhappy: they have a narrative, but they have only imperfect means in language with which to express it. Their narrative will thus be imperfect.

This theme is taken up again with greater intensity when he comes to speak of the Manichees. They are *delirantes*, *loquaces*, but essentially perverters of language, twisting syllables. Their speech is mere noise.[65] Likewise, rhetoric, his chosen profession, is subjected to criticism. It is empty talk and smoke.[66] Speech like all earthly things is transient.[67] The ear of the heart is deafened by vanity.[68] We perceive parts, but we long for the whole.

> Were your carnal perception able to grasp the whole, were it not, for your punishment, confined to its due part of the whole, you would long for whatever exists only in the present to pass away, so that you might find greater joy in the totality. When with this same carnal perception you listen to human speech, you do not want to halt the succession of syllables: you want them to fly on their way and make room for others, so that you may hear the whole.[69]

This is a Platonic truism, but it fits the speech-theme well: how can any finite words sum up or contain an eternal truth? We perceive parts, but we long to know the whole, and, alas, we cannot, defeated as we are by the contingency of language, which is contrasted with the absoluteness of truth. This would thus seem to lead to the conclusion that narrative, being a human and linguistic construct, is bound to failure if it attempts to express absolute truths; thus we may be left only with partial, and thus partially deceptive, narratives and have to live without one absolute narrative that justifies all.

Thus we may come to conclusion that because some narratives are false, all narratives are necessarily false. The Manichee Faustus is portrayed as 'a lethal trap set by the devil. Many people were ensnared by the persuasive sweetness of his

---

[63] *Confessions*, 1.17.27.
[64] *Confessions*, 1.18.29.
[65] *Confessions*, 3.6.10.
[66] *Confessions*, 4.2.2.
[67] *Confessions*, 4.10.15.
[68] *Confessions*, 4.11.16.
[69] *Confessions*, 4.17.

eloquence'.[70] But Faustus's pleasant style not only disguises his essential lack of content: all he has to offer are *longis fabulis*, longwinded tales. Augustine concludes that literary style and presentation, the two things he had spent his youth studying, have nothing to do with truth.[71] Language, meant to convey truth, can also be a trap for the unwary.

By contrast, Ambrose is not like Faustus:

> And so I came to Milan and to bishop Ambrose, who was known throughout the world as one of the best of men. He was a devout worshipper of you, Lord, and at that time his energetic preaching provided your people with choicest wheat and the joy of oil and the sober intoxication of wine.[72]

The opening phrase, *et veni Mediolanum*, recalls the earlier *veni Carthaginem* at the opening of Book III, and deliberately so: Milan is the city in which he is destined to be saved, whereas Carthage was the city in which he was lost; Milan's bishop is to be contrasted with Faustus, whom he met in Carthage; Ambrose's sermons are nourishing fodder, unlike the *fabulae* of Faustus. But conversion is still a long way off, as Augustine laments that he is still unable to distinguish style from content:

> I was taking no trouble to learn from what Ambrose was saying, but interested only in listening to how he said it, for that futile concern had remained with me, despairing as I did that any way to you could be open to humankind. Nonetheless as his words, which I enjoyed, penetrated my mind, the substance, which I overlooked, seeped in with them, for I could not separate the two.[73]

Once again we see the distinction made between style and content, outward form and inner substance, and the strong hint that there can be no true bridge of meaning between the two: even God is powerless to make himself understood as there is no way to him open to humankind – for language is a broken reed. But in a key passage, Augustine distinguishes human chatter from the eternal word of God: Victorinus, we are told, abandons 'his school of talkativeness', that is rhetoric, (*loquacem scholam*, the same adjective used of the Manichees) rather than 'forsake your word, through which you impart eloquence to the tongues of speechless babes'.[74] This brief passage provides a strong hint that the empty rhetoric of the Manichees and indeed of Augustine himself, is not the only language. There is another, and it can communicate truth. There is a way between humankind and God after all. In other words, in the world of false narratives, true narrative is possible. Something similar is said at an earlier point in the *Confessions*: the Manichees, again characterized as talkative, are also called dumb because God's word does not speak in them – *loquaces mutos, quoniam non ex eis sonabat verbum tuum*.[75] This pithy phrase and its oxymoron sum them up

---

[70] *Confessions*, 5.3.3.
[71] *Confessions*, 5.6.10.
[72] *Confessions*, 5.13.23.
[73] *Confessions*, 5.14.24.
[74] *Confessions*, 8.5.10.
[75] *Confessions*, 7.2.3.

well; it also points to the key to understanding Augustine's concern with language: our many words can only make sense if the One Word is heard in them.

In Book VIII, human discourse is to be overtaken by this other sort of discourse, and as the book progresses towards its climax Augustine encounters a series of books, which unlike the *Hortensius* and the *libri platonici* before them successfully bring him to God. This latter reading had brought about an intellectual conversion,[76] but now other books, culminating with that of St Paul's letters, are to bring about a spiritual conversion. Books of one sort or another are mentioned at 8.6.14 – the *Letters of St Paul*, 8.15 – the *Life of Anthony* and 8.17 – a reference to the abortive conversion effected by the *Hortensius*. And finally the voice from the neighbouring house invites him to take up a book and read – 8.12.29 – and it is through reading a book that Augustine is converted – just as the good bishop at the end of the third book had said he would be! 'He will find out for himself through his reading how wrong these beliefs are, and how profoundly irreverent,' the unnamed bishop had told Monica.[77]

Thus one can be led astray by the vacuities of language, but one can also be cured by the Word of God. The *tolle lege* is an invitation to conversion through reading; and it is also possibly addressed to the reader as well: they are invited to take up and read – the Scriptures or perhaps even the *Confessions* themselves – and be converted too.[78] Language, which once divided us from ourselves, can now heal our inner division. Narrative that once led us astray can be replaced by a narrative, indeed, the narrative, that leads us to truth.

Why is this important? It is not our intention to construct an Augustinian philosophy of language. Rather, what is of interest to us here is the following: we have seen language as an instrument of division. It divides us from ourselves in its inability to express what we know to be true. It is an instrument of oppression in that it allows us to bamboozle ourselves and other people. Language traps us in our own restricted world of stunted meaning. But it is equally true that one can find a new language that can give us access to wider truths, indeed truth itself. One can move from the (false) myth of Manicheanism to the (true) myth of Platonism and from there to the eternal truth of the Scriptures.[79] Each step represents a moral advance; the advance is effected by the divine word shattering our deafness.[80] The initiative is God's, one notes – the doctor of grace is hardly likely to maintain otherwise. In fact Platonism is never enough alone to cure man of sin.[81]

---

[76] *Confessions*, 8.2.3.

[77] *Confessions*, 3.12.21.

[78] Note also the introduction of Ambrose into the story, at 6.3.3, reading a book to himself, which is surely significant.

[79] *Confessions*, 7.20.26–21.27 describe how Augustine moves from Platonic reading to the reading of Saint Paul.

[80] As in the justly famous passage 10.27.38. The word *surdus* (deaf) is used at 9.4.11 and 10.6.8; *surditas* (deafness) is used as above and also at 13.13.44. This sparseness in the use of the word thus adds dramatic force to this climactic passage about God shattering his deafness.

[81] *Confessions*, 7.21.27.

Let us attempt a conclusion to our remarks on Augustine's divided self as seen through the perspective of language: the self can be healed through the invention (in the strict sense of the term – the discovery) of a new sort of language. But the new sort of language will only be discovered when the old sort has been proved to have failed. One discourse breaks down, and a newer and truer one takes it place. One narrative is replaced by another. A religious conversion, a moral conversion, involves a linguistic conversion. And any sort of conversion presupposes a disenchantment too, which may be just as important.[82] It seems then likely that a human being may have many stories over one life, and be even 'one of the most converted of men'.[83] But how do these changes take place over the course of a life? And to what extent can we talk of human beings being narrative creatures when narrative is rendered so difficult by language? These are topics to which we shall return.

Alienation and Sexual Desire

The second area in which Augustine feels himself divided from himself is in the field of sexual desire. His emphasis on sexual sin[84] is rather odd to modern readers. But again, this has to be carefully understood. Sexual sin in Augustine is never a purely physical phenomenon. The sinfulness is not in the body but in the will. In fact Augustine distances himself from the Platonic hatred of the body.[85] He stresses the necessity of the right ordering of the affections, not their being put to death, against the Stoics.[86] However the sexual passions are by their very nature unruly:

> It [sexual desire] practically paralyses all power of deliberate thought. This is so true that it creates a problem for every lover of wisdom and holy joys... Any such person would prefer, if this were possible, to beget his children without suffering this passion. He could wish that, just as all his other members obey his reason in the performance of their appointed tasks, so the organs of parenthood too, might function in obedience to the orders of will and not be excited by the ardors of lust. Curiously enough, not even those who love this pleasure most – whether legitimately or illegitimately indulged – can control their own indulgences. Sometimes their lust is most importunate when they least desire it; at other times the feelings fail them when they crave them most, their bodies remaining frigid when lust is blazing in their souls. Thus, lust itself, lascivious and legitimate, refuses to obey, and the very passion that so often joins forces to resist the soul *is sometimes so divided against itself* [*adversus se ipsa dividitur*; emphasis added], that after it has roused the soul to passion, it refuses to awaken the feelings of the flesh.[87]

One notes the specific reference to internal division. Because the passions are unruly, and unable to be subjected, hence his concept of sexual shame: something we feel

---

[82] R.A. Markus, *Conversion and Disenchantment in Augustine's Spiritual Career*, St Augustine Lecture, 1984 (Villanova: Villanova University Press, 1984), p. 2.
[83] As above.
[84] As at *Confessions*, 2.1.1.
[85] *City of God*, XIII.16.
[86] *City of God*, XIV.9.
[87] *City of God*, XIV. 16.

because sexual desire is not amenable to control of the will.[88] Before the Fall the sexual passions were amenable to control by the will;[89] but now the flesh, at least in this department, refuses to obey.[90] Hence the need for spiritual warfare against the passions,[91] something which adolescents find very hard.[92]

This last point is clearly drawing on his own experience. In his sixteenth year, he tells us, he wandered the streets of Babylon – an arresting image.[93] Babylon is the earthly city, the city of worldliness and sin, contrasted with the City of God throughout the book of that title. The point here is that Augustine is not a willing member of the city of Babylon; he has been 'seduced', as he puts it; his mother gives him sound advice, but he is unable to follow it;[94] he is divided from himself, a disintegrated person;[95] his sexual desires run counter to his 'real' desires; thus in sexual activity he finds that he encounters a divided self, a self that is not truly his own, because sexual desire is involuntary.

This explains several things in our reading of the *Confessions*. While Patricius is pleased to discover that his son is growing up, Augustine describes his sexual maturity in language that gives us pause:

> The thorn bushes of lust shot up higher than my head, and no hand was there to root them out. Least of all my father's: for when at the baths one day he saw me with unquiet adolescence my only covering [*inquieta indutum adulescentia*], and noted my ripening sexuality, he began at once to look forward eagerly to grandchildren, and gleefully announced the discovery to my mother.[96]

The child's adolescence is disturbed, unquiet – a symptom of the rebellion of the flesh against the will. Likewise the name Adeodatus speaks volumes: we are told that the child is born 'against the parents' wishes – though once they are born one cannot help loving them'.[97] The child is given by God, but not wanted by his father, though he is later loved for himself. The essential point is that Adeodatus's conception is the result of an action that takes place despite the will of his father – he is a gift of God, not something freely chosen by Augustine, because in matters of sex one cannot choose freely. Even the parting from Adeodatus's mother is a terrible wrench: 'So deeply was she engrafted onto my heart that it was left torn and wounded and trailing blood';[98] he wishes to part from her but this means doing violence to his desires. Indeed, he soon takes up with another, explaining that he is a 'slave of lust' and at the same time in 'cold despair'.[99] One can but note the contrast.

---

[88] *City of God*, XIV. 17, 18, 19, 20.
[89] *City of God*, XIV. 21–22 and 24.
[90] *City of God*, XIV.24.
[91] *City of God*, XXI.15.
[92] *City of God*, XXI.16.
[93] *Confessions*, 2.3.8.
[94] *Confessions*, 2.3.7.
[95] *Confessions*, 2.1.1.
[96] *Confessions*, 2.3.6.
[97] *Confessions*, 4.2.2.
[98] *Confessions*, 6.15.25.
[99] As above.

Integration comes, of course, through conversion to continence,[100] for it is only in continence that Augustine is able to integrate all the desires of his heart and thus undo the damage that humankind sustained thanks to the Fall. Thus once again we see another discourse take the place of a former discourse: the disordered unruly passions are replaced by the vision of Lady Continence; and the unnamed 'second' concubine is mentioned no more. Once again we have a narrative (contemporary sexual mores) being replaced by another (the vision of Continence). But more than this is taking place: in order for the change to be effected, an area of human experience (in this case sexual desire) from being intractable becomes tractable. While before Augustine finds sexual desire as something that resists inclusion into a narrative, because it is unruly and impervious to reason (unless that narrative is the dualism of the Manichees), by discovering the vision of Lady Continence he also discovers that sexual desire can be integrated into a narrative. The important point here seems to be this: the intractable can become tractable, it can be integrated into a coherent and inclusive narrative.

What does all this tell us? It tells us that one who is embedded in the mores of the Roman Empire is not as deeply embedded as we might suppose, as we have mentioned in the previous section above; he is capable of disembedding himself; it tells us too that someone who is subjected to desires that refuse to obey the will can bring those desires to heel through the integration of the human heart. Desire, in this case for God, is the key to the integration of the human heart, as Robert Innes maintains in an interesting and valuable article.[101] Desire for God is the basic drive that brings us to wholeness, an idea that has its background in neo-Platonic philosophy.[102] Desire can of course and often does subject us to restlessness, but it can also bring us to happiness when we desire the truly right thing.[103] 'God himself supplies the power to draw together the different strands of selfhood into a coherent whole.'[104] In other words, this desire for God can help us to arrive at a coherent narrative.

Now let us look at these ideas in a somewhat wider context. The self in both language and sexual desire finds itself divided from itself: it wants to and does not want to at the same time – wants to control its urges and finds itself unable to do so; wants to express truth and finds language an inadequate instrument for the task. If we accept that language and sexual desire are given to all human beings, then this predicament is universal one, in so far as it is perceived. A degree of reflection, or some personal crisis, may well lead to these predicaments making themselves felt. The peaceful soul's tranquillity may be disturbed by unrequited love, or sudden infatuation, or the inability to express clearly what one wishes to say, or the inability to formulate deeply held truths in words. The phrase 'I do not know what to say' is a common one; so too is the intuition that there are certain truths that cannot be

---

[100] *Confessions*, 8.11.27.
[101] Robert Innes, 'Integrating the Self through the desire of God', *Augustinian Studies* 28:1 (1997): 67–109.
[102] Innes, p. 71.
[103] Innes, p. 96.
[104] Innes, p. 109.

put into words, but can only be expressed in poetry and music or indeed silence. Language is a very blunt instrument and one that often refuses to obey our will; so is sexual desire.

Thus Augustine the protagonist in the drama of human internal division alerts us to the centrality of conflict in human experience but also to the possibility of the resolution of such conflict. He shows us that a single narrative, or what MacIntyre calls the narrative unity of a life, is not something that is given to us automatically, but is rather the gift of grace.[105] Augustine's story is the story of a person coming to just such a point, that is the discovery of the narrative unity of his life; in his case the transition is one from restlessness and alienation to peace. MacIntyre's people, one feels, are people who have already made this transition: they have escaped the world of division and philosophical conflict and found a refuge in the calm waters of Thomism. Engelhardt himself has turned his back on the secular and found a refuge in the language and liturgical practices of Orthodoxy. But how are these changes effected, and is it possible that there is a universal narrative that can provide safe shelter for all? These are the questions to which we shall now turn, and once again Augustine shall be our guide.

But a conclusion is possible even at this juncture. It seems that the narrative nature of human existence, of which MacIntyre, Hauerwas and Engelhardt speak, should not be understood in a monolithic sense. People may well rely on narrative in their self-understanding, but they may feel the pull of conflicting narratives. In addition, the narrative that constitutes their self-understanding may be, in important aspects, incoherent, a narrative that is in process of becoming rather than one that is fully formed. This is the state in which we find ourselves – people with conflicting and sometimes contradictory narratives inside us; it is not simply society that is divided in itself, people are divided too. But this interior division, according to Augustine, is susceptible to integration; that which seems to be beyond human control can through grace be brought into a coherent narrative. This in turn suggests that though we are embedded selves – how could we be otherwise? – we are also people capable of perceptions that go beyond our embedded nature. We are aware of our culture and at the same time its restrictions, aware of something that is beyond culture and which informs culture – a basic grounding to experience that, if we could but grasp it, would enable us to discover the true narrative grounding of our lives.

---

[105] In complete contrast, one can but note, Rawls's people seem to be unaware of the reality of conflict in this sense. Yet attempts to think in the Original Position may be hampered by inarticulacy or conflicting desires. But Rawls does not deal with sin which is a theological concept or that of alienation (see John Macquarrie, *Existentialism* (London: Hutchinson, 1972), pp. 158–60, for a discussion of the theme of alienation in existential philosophy). His people are not people who find that their wills do not obey them, or that their expectations of their own selves constantly disappoint them. Rawls presupposes an integrated self with the capacity to make decisions; that the person or persons thinking in the Original Position are able to think, that is, that they have a language that is capable of making their thoughts transparent to themselves and others.

Alienation from Others

So far we have considered Augustine the protagonist and the author as a divided self and hinted that he may be taken as our Everyman. The author and the protagonist stand inside culture, but can also abstract themselves from one culture and embrace another culture. They are embedded but also detached, able to contemplate themselves and their allegiances. The protagonist seeks the serenity to make moral decisions through the integration of the self.

But before we go any further there is another aspect of Augustine that we must consider: his treatment of others. The *Confessions* are largely about himself; but they are addressed to an audience, and a most unusual one too. We have already mentioned our suspicion that the famous words '*tolle lege*', clearly the climax to the book, are addressed to the readers of the book. Pick up and read so that you too may be converted and live. The occasion of the writing of the *Confessions* may have been a request from Paulinus of Nola;[106] but this would only have been the occasion: the real audience is much wider than any individual; it is the whole human race, says Augustine:

> But to whom am I telling this story? Not to you, my God; rather in your presence I am relating these event to my own kin, the human race, however few of them may chance on these writings of mine. And why? So that whoever reads them may reflect with me on the depths from which we must cry to you.[107]

This sense of the book being addressed to all (as opposed to a specific patron or dedicatee) is one of the points that underlines the *Confessions* as the story of Everyman. Again, in a passage we have already touched upon,[108] Augustine proposes a dialogue between himself and his readers; indeed a three-way dialogue between himself, his readers and God. He calls his readers, even future ones, 'my fellow pilgrims, your servants and my brethren'.[109] Thus Augustine's introspection is not something that is done in isolation – it is done with an audience in mind, it is addressed to others, as every narrative must be.

It has been observed by Brown that Augustine was hardly ever alone in his life and was highly dependent on his friends[110] and indeed on his family members.[111] Introspection did not mean solitude. Being for Augustine means being-with-others.[112] His story is also his mother's[113] and that of the other characters, both named and not, who appear in the *Confessions*. He himself speaks of the importance of friendship[114]

---

[106] For a discussion of this question, see O'Donnell, vol. 2, pp. 360–62.
[107] *Confessions*, 2.5.
[108] *Confessions*, 10.4.5.
[109] *Confessions*, 10.4.6.
[110] Brown, pp. 61, 63, 180, 200–01, 411.
[111] Brown, pp. 32, 199, 227, 411.
[112] C.J.N. Paulo, *Being and Conversion*, doctoral dissertation at the Gregorian University, 1995, pp. 65–6.
[113] Serge Lancel, *Saint Augustin* (Paris: Fayard, 1999), p. 30.
[114] *Confessions*, 4.4.7. Though it is important to notice that true friendship is a gift of Divine Grace: 'Friendship is genuine only when you bind fast together people who cleave to

and gives huge emphasis to his grief at the loss of an unnamed friend of his youth.[115] Even his conversion is a moment shared with Alypius and of course Monica.[116] Monica gets special treatment, and her short biography is a parallel to Augustine's own, with her own particular conversion scene.[117]

All these others are clearly important, but the main other to whom the *Confessions* are addressed, as the title suggests, is God. The book is cast as a conversation with the Almighty, right from its opening paragraph; it is the story of man who is coming at last to communion with God; the story of one who is deaf, gradually learning to hear, until the moment God shatters his deafness. The Augustinian self is conceived, therefore, as an interlocutor with other people, but above all as an interlocutor with God Almighty: a dialogical being.

But his path to realizing that one is a dialogical being is fraught with difficulties, on both the human and the divine plane. Even as a tiny child he supposes – based on later observation of other babies – that his relationship with his wet nurse was one blighted by egotism:

> I have watched and experienced for myself the jealousy of a small child: he could not even speak, but he glared with livid fury at his fellow nursling... Is this to be regarded as innocence, this refusal to tolerate a rival for a richly abundant fountain of milk, at a time when the other child stands in greatest need of it and depends for its very life on this food alone?[118]

While the child's smile is a sign of contentment and satisfaction, this is not the whole picture; the child is trapped, as we have seen, in his own world, unable to communicate with others, thanks to his lack of language.[119] Being at school means getting beaten, despite his intelligence, and his prayer to escape beatings cannot be counted as disinterested: indeed, he pictures God in 'the guise of some great personage' able to bestow favours.[120] There is no meeting of minds with his schoolmasters, and no meeting of minds with God. His beloved mother speaks to him repeatedly – and he does not listen to her: in rejecting her, he also rejects God.[121] Fond as he is of her, in his early years he listens to her hardly at all, and in the end flees her without the courage to tell her that he is leaving.[122] This last scene is eloquent of a total failure of communication: Monica loves him, but he does not – at least in his actions – love her.[123] Again his grief for his beloved friend is characterized as selfish indulgence

---

you through the charity poured abroad in our hearts by the Holy Spirit who is given to us.' This point is made as it were in passing, but, as we shall see, is of great importance.

[115] *Confessions*, 4.7.12.
[116] *Confessions*, 8. 29–30.
[117] *Confessions*, 9.17 et seq.
[118] *Confessions*, 1.7.11.
[119] *Confessions*, 1.6.8.
[120] *Confessions*, 1.9.14.
[121] *Confessions*, 2.3.7.
[122] *Confessions*, 5.8.15.
[123] *Confessions*, 5.9.16.

of feeling,[124] strongly contrasted with his later restraint when Monica dies.[125] All these are vivid illustrations of his failure to relate to other people thanks to his basic egotism. He is a prisoner of his own selfishness. 'I had roamed away from myself and could not even find myself, let alone you':[126] unaware of himself, he is unaware of others and unaware of God. The picture that emerges of Augustine, in other words, is of a thoroughly selfish young man, trapped in his own egotism, out of which he can find no opening. For him, at this stage of his life, others have no real existence.

While we have a cast of people to whom Augustine did not listen, with whom he failed to engage truly, we also have those with whom he experienced a true meeting of mind, heart and soul. Once again Monica takes pride of place. The so-called ecstasy of Ostia is a communion with God and a communion between mother and son: one notes the repeated use of the first person plural. From an 'I' narrative Augustine has moved to a 'we' narrative, and this is significant, particularly given the wide use of the first person singular that precedes it throughout the book: *staremus... instaurabamus... conloquebamur quaerebamus... inhiabamus... cogitaremus... perambulavimus... ascendebamus... venimus... transcendimus... attingeremus* and so on. Also to be noted is the presence of '*tu*': the second person is mentioned seven times in two brief paragraphs.[127] Also crucial here is the perfect unity between the horizontal and the vertical planes. He experiences communion with God because he can now experience communion with his mother, a fellow human being – or is it the other way round? This is the climax of the book in many ways, representing the final breakdown in the barriers that had separated him from God and from others, and which even the previous platonic ecstasies[128] had been unable to breach.

One detects the beginnings of this new way of relating in his account of Ambrose, even though his dealings with Ambrose were slight. Ambrose is an angel of God in Monica's eyes,[129] but Augustine himself has a more arresting phrase to use: he speaks of Ambrose's heart as God's holy oracle.[130] For Monica, Ambrose is God's messenger, but for Augustine it is the heart of Ambrose that speaks. Augustine witnesses the bishop's unusual habit of reading silently to himself; he comments: 'What exquisite delights he savoured in his secret mouth, the mouth of his heart, as he chewed the bread of your Word'.[131] This highly unusual phrase alerts us to a concept rich in meaning. Ambrose's heart is an oracle – it speaks clearly the words of God, unlike pagan oracles which Augustine has previously dismissed, and unlike Faustus:[132] but it is the secret mouth of the heart rather than the usual physical mouth that is spoken of here. This is the real difference between Ambrose and the smooth-tongued Faustus. We can contrast this with what Augustine says later in the same

---

[124] *Confessions*, 4.7.12.
[125] *Confessions*, 9.13.34.
[126] *Confessions*, 5.2.2.
[127] *Confessions*, 9.10.23–24.
[128] *Confessions*, 7.10.16.
[129] *Confessions*, 6.1.1.
[130] *Confessions*, 6.3.4.
[131] *Confessions*, 6.3.3.
[132] *Confessions*, 5.13.23.

book about his divided heart being tossed hither and thither,[133] a marked contrast to the stillness and recollection of Ambrose, who though silent, is the great orator. It seems clear that it is the integrity of his heart, which in its turn is derived from his reading the word of God, that makes Ambrose's heart truly eloquent. Hearts can only speak to other hearts, and listen to other hearts, when they are healed of their internal disintegration. True dialogue is always going to escape us until this happens; until it does we are condemned to relationships which do not give an opportunity for true dialogue; we will use other people, like the baby at the breast, but we will never truly know them as people, only as things. Just as the integration of the heart can only be brought about in Augustine's eyes by God, so too authentic relations with others depend on an authentic relationship with God. Hence the duality – Augustine speaking to others, Augustine speaking to the Other – is not a duality at all. The two go together.

One can read these relationships using some of the language of Emmanuel Levinas. Augustine at the breast does not encounter an Other,[134] but rather reduces that Other to the same, an extension of himself as it were. Likewise as a Manichee he conceives God as a thing being on the same level as evil[135] and having extension.[136] In other words, God, the wholly Other, is conceived as part of a totalizing system and his infinity is denied: God is *finitum*, limited; *grandius*, larger than evil, but not infinite.[137] God in the Manichee scheme of things is reified in order to suit a scheme that helps to justify the division of Augustine's own heart: God at the service of man and not the other way around. Augustine cannot conceive God as a person, hence his difficulty with the divinity of Christ and the Incarnation.[138] God is part of the system, reduced to the same, tamed and domesticated, belittled, never the Other. When God becomes the Other,[139] he does so after a series of relationships in which Augustine

---

[133] *Confessions*, 6.11.20.

[134] Levinas's major work, *Totality and Infinity*, translated by Alphonso Lingis, (Pittsburg: Dusquesne University Press, 2000), originally published in French as *Totalité et Infinité* (The Hague: Martinus Nijhoff, 1961), contests totalizing systems such as Hegel's with the insight that the Other represents a reality that defies insertion into a totalizing system. In encountering an Other, I am faced with an irreducible reality who cannot be reduced to a component part of any system and who must call me into question. (*Totality and Infinity*, p. 197).

[135] *Confessions*, 5.10.20.

[136] *Confessions*, 7.1.1.

[137] *Confessions*, 5.10.20.

[138] *Confessions*, 7.19.25.

[139] Augustine's conversion can be expressed in Levinasian terms. For example: 'The idea of Infinity is *revealed*' (*Totality and Infinity*, p. 62); it is revealed in the Face which is an epiphany (*Totality and Infinity*, p. 196). In meeting an Other, in this case God, I encounter someone who is other than myself, who is not an object but a subject, who cannot be reduced to an object. 'The invoked is not what I comprehend: *he is not under a category*. He is the one to whom I speak – he has reference only to himself; he has no quiddity' (*Totality and Infinity*, p. 69). Moreover: 'To recognise the Other is to recognise a hunger. To recognise the Other is to give. But it is to give to the master, to the lord, to him who approaches as 'You' [Vous] in a dimension of height' (*Totality and Infinity*, p. 75). Furthermore: 'To welcome the Other is to put in question my freedom' (*Totality and Infinity*, p. 85). And: 'The Other imposes himself as an exigency that dominates this freedom… If I can no longer have power over him it is

becomes aware of the Other: with Ambrose, with Simplicianus,[140] but above all through retirement to a small garden (which may be of symbolic significance) and *secretum meum*, my innermost self.[141] Indeed the conversion takes place when Augustine retires into 'the secret profundity of my being'[142] though the final catalyst, the child's voice from the next house, is something external to himself.[143] Self-knowledge that comes through knowledge of others, leads to knowledge of God, with the help of an external catalyst.

At the same time, one can never truly know oneself: 'No one knows what he himself is made of, except his own spirit within him, and yet there is still some part of him which remains hidden even from his own spirit.'[144] In addition, one can never truly know another person: 'The first constraint that hems in the human race, and a harsh one it is, is our ignorance of anyone else's heart',[145] a constraint from which only God can liberate us.[146] One wants to know and be known[147] but I remain a question to myself and an abyss.[148] Once again we see the need for grace in Augustine's scheme of things. Like oneself, God always eludes our grasp in the end. If he were graspable, he would be reducible to the same, not an Other. But God is infinite, as is Augustine's own character: by looking within we see an image of the infinity of God.

In the Augustinian scheme of things we see the essential place that difference, alterity, the Other and infinity play. Gradually a human being can come out of their shell, imposed by egotism and selfishness and disordered desire, and come to a realization of the Other before them. The protagonist becomes aware that they are not alone, and that there are two possible ways of dealing with the Other before me: to treat that Other as Other, not reducible to the same, or to try and 'murder' the other, as Levinas puts it, by denying that Other's nature as not reducible to an extension of myself.

It is only in relationship with others and the Other that Augustine comes to discover the mystery of his own being. Hence Book X comes after the conversion scene not before it. His journey of discovery is of others, his own self and God. If the self is to be understood as a narrative reality, and if the self changes as it discovers others and itself, then we can conclude that the self, in its voyage of discovery, changes narratives.

---

because he overflows absolutely every idea I can have of him' (*Totality and Infinity*, p. 87). One can see here the contrast between the Levinasian idea of the Other and the Manichean idea of God as a limited thing.

[140] *Confessions*, 8.1.1.
[141] *Confessions*, 8.8.19.
[142] *Confessions*, 8.12.28.
[143] *Confessions*, 8.12.29.
[144] *Confessions*, 10.5.7. Levinas would agree; his insight into the epiphany of the Face says the same thing. See *Totality and Infinity*, p. 196.
[145] *Ennarationes*, 30/2.13 (*Works*, vol. 15, p. 332).
[146] *Ennarationes*, 30/2.15 (*Works*, vol. 15, p. 333).
[147] *Soliloquies*, 2.1.1 and *Confessions*, 10.27.38.
[148] *Ennarationes*, 41.13 (*Works*, vol.16, p. 251).

What we have discovered so far may be summed up thus: every narrative, and Augustine's is no exception, is a narrative addressed to an audience. Narrative is necessarily a social phenomenon, and never takes place in a vacuum. Similarly, the casting of one's life into a new narrative, which is the theme of the *Confessions*, means casting one's mode of relating to others in a new way. The identity of the self cannot be conceived without reference to the way the self relates to others. Narrative, the narrative unity of a life, or the narrative unity-in-becoming of a life, involves some engagement with others, with a community of others, just as Hauerwas, MacIntyre and even Engelhardt, all in their different ways, maintain. Thus Augustine acts once again as an exemplar of one of the chief claims of narrative theology, and indeed moral theology. Furthermore, narrative has to be understood as in some way being open to infinity: the infinity that is the self and the infinity that is others, as opposed to some sort of system that reduces the infinite to an object (or reification as it is called). A narrative is not that which reduces human beings and human experience to something that can be contained in a system: rather it opens our understanding towards an infinite horizon – but what this means in practice we need to examine further.

Augustine's Changing Narratives

What has emerged from our examination of Augustine so far is that there is a difference in quality between various narratives.

In his youth Augustine believed in the narrative of the Roman people and Empire, summed up in Virgil's *Aeneid*.[149] However, Augustine's attitude to Roman power changed over his lifetime. If we take the work of Lepelley as definitive, the young Augustine was a typical man of the late Empire, an ambitious provincial on the make, a true believer in the *cursus honorum*, seeking a role for himself in the Empire, presumably one who, though never a pagan, believed in the mission of Rome as summed up by Vergil. But the Augustine of the *City of God* is very different: he regards himself as a citizen of the heavenly city that is above, and not the Babylon that is below. Roman history is now seen as one typifying strife, discord and instability.[150]

---

[149] He himself tells us that Virgil is the greatest and best of poets, who, once read, is never easily forgotten (*City of God*, I.3). His own work bears testimony to this – Virgil is cited by him numerous times and the *Confessions* are conceived as a spiritual *Aeneid*, according to many (for an overview, see Sabine MacCormack, 'Vergil', *Augustine through the Ages* (Grand Rapids, Michigan/Cambridge, UK: William B. Eerdmans Publishing Company, 1999). He would have imbibed the famous line *imperium sine fine dedi* [I give a limitless empire] (*Aeneid*, I: 279, quoted in *City of God*, II.29), and there is evidence to suggest that even after the fateful year 410, the year of the sack of Rome by Alaric and the Goths, he still believed to some extent in the eternal mission of the Roman Empire *parcere subiectis et debellare superbos* [to spare the vanquished and conquer the proud] (*Aeneid*, VI: 853; see *City of God*, II.29 and IV.7).

[150] *City of God*, III.24, 25, 26.

What we see here is a clear change of narrative. The Roman youngster – born in Africa, and of Berber blood at least on his mother's side[151] but thoroughly imbued with Roman culture and of a family that saw itself as Roman through and through – one who bore an imperial name and was probably connected to the family of Romanianus, the local bigwig – has now adopted another story, that of the Christian faith. The Christian and the secular stories intertwine in the course of the *City of God*, but it is clear which is the better one, which is the true one. There has been a radical shift in Augustine's self-understanding. This is the fruit of his conversion: as Lepelley has pointed out, that involved the renunciation of the '*spes saeculi*': his conversion was a profound rupture with the mentality of the times, his social milieu and a long held family strategy of social advancement.[152] In other words his conversion also was a change in narrative, self-understanding and identity.

Augustine's experience mirrors that of the two '*agentes in rebus*' whose story is told in the eighth book of the *Confessions* and which has such a profound effect on him.[153] Again, as Lepelley points out, while Monica might have had no difficulty in reconciling a glittering career with religious belief, the story of the two *agentes in rebus* paints a rather different picture: for them, important as they are, the favours of princes are very uncertain and the Tarpeian rock uncomfortably close to the Capitol. They reflect on the vanity of earthly things and become monks.[154] Interestingly, they do so because of a story they have read, that of Saint Anthony; Saint Anthony himself, as readers of the *Confessions* would have known, was converted by a story too – that of the Rich Young Man. So here we encounter not one story but a succession of stories: the story of the Rich Young Man; the story of Anthony; the story of the *agentes in rebus*; the story of Augustine: each one mirrors the story that goes before; we perceive a sort of domino effect. Finally, and most important perhaps of all, we have the story of the reader themselves, who, taking up and reading (*tolle lege*) adds him or herself to the continuing tradition.

So, conversion is a matter of one story being replaced by another. But this of course begs many questions. For a start, it takes for granted all those assumptions that underpin narrative theology, and which we have discussed in these pages; in addition, it simplifies, indeed oversimplifies, the Augustinian experience. For Augustine was 'one of the most converted of men', as R.A. Markus remarks and his disenchantments are perhaps as important as his conversions.[155] Why, then, was his conversion to Manicheanism not lasting? Why did he become disenchanted? Was this purely an intellectual process, as O'Meara seems to suggest in the subtitle to his book, something to do with the growth of Saint Augustine's mind? Marrou mentions something that goes much further, namely the examples of men who break with their milieu to become philosophers and reorganize their culture around philosophy. This is not a mere intellectual change, but also a moral and social one; indeed a radical

---

[151] O'Meara, p. 28.
[152] Lepelley, 'Spes saeculi', p. 116.
[153] *Confessions*, 8.6.
[154] Lepelley, 'Spes saeculi', pp. 111–14.
[155] R.A. Markus, *Conversion and Disenchantment in Augustine's Spiritual Career*, St Augustine Lecture 1984 (Villanova: Villanova University Press, 1984).

change in their conception of life.[156] This sounds much closer to what one feels is happening with Augustine, whose conversions consists not so much of a change of opinion but a change of vision. A pity, though, that the examples of this that Marrou gives are Seneca, Marcus Aurelius, and Apuleius.[157] None of these strike one as highly inspiring.

At the same time one cannot discount the intellectual voyage that is a major component of the existential journey that is the *Confessions*. Augustine adopted the doctrine of Mani because it seemed to solve an intellectual problem, namely the existence of evil,[158] and he abandoned it when he saw that there was another, better solution to the problem, namely that evil was a privation,[159] as opposed to a physical substance. Likewise with the 'problem' of the inconsistencies in the Old Testament.[160] As Henry Chadwick points out, it was Platonism that provided Augustine with the key to his intellectual struggles and the solution to the problem of the relation of the one to the many through emanation.[161] But Augustine's story is more than the story of a man who discovers neo-Platonism. The real story is about the human heart and the integration thereof: neo-Platonism merely provides the type of language necessary to put certain important ideas into words. Neo-Platonism facilitates the conversion but does not cause it. The *Confessions* cannot be reduced to the story of a man who discovers a new narrative and that narrative neo-Platonism. The key moment in the *Confessions*, the garden scene, alerts us to the possibility, which we would dearly like to prove, that conversion is something more than just changing narratives: Augustine's acceptance of Christ is qualitatively different to his acceptance, as a disillusioned Manichee, of the doctrines of the neo-Platonists. In this qualitative difference is to be found the difference between mere narrative thinking and narrative theology as such.

The qualitative difference emerges when we compare Augustine's description of himself reading the *Hortensius* and his conversion in the garden: the latter is described in more vividly emotional terms: in other words, the level of his involvement seems more profound. The *Hortensius* episode[162] represents a conversion of his mind (which was not lasting), the garden scene a conversion at a deeper level of his entire self, followed by an enduring and complete change of life. The first, intellectual, 'conversion' means moving from one closed horizon of meaning to another; the new horizon may be wider, it may be better, but it is essentially still closed. We are citizens of this city or that city, which is a bigger and more important city, but they are both cities bound by a wall. But the conversion in the garden means moving to a city that has no wall, a city which is a different type of city. Augustine's allegiance to the Roman Empire, and his allegiance to the doctrine of the Manichees, even his espousal of Platonism, represent shifts in the horizon of meaning, but all are closed

---

[156] Marrou, p. 172.
[157] As above.
[158] *Confessions*, 6.20.
[159] *Confessions*, 7.5.7 and 7.12.18–13.19.
[160] *Confessions*, 3.13–17.
[161] Chadwick, p. 19.
[162] *Confessions*, 3.4.7.

worlds. Christianity, however, represents a different type of shift, an upwards one, which relativizes his allegiance to Rome, and makes his allegiance to the Manichees impossible. Citizenship of the City of God is not the same as earthly citizenship, but represents a new identity, a new mode of being and relating. He does more than just change narratives: the two narratives are qualitatively different. The first has a closed horizon of meaning, the second has a horizon of meaning that is open to infinity. Or in Levinasian terms: the first represents a totalizing system, the second recognizes that the Other cannot be reduced to the same, and represents the breaking in of infinity. The first may be characterized as intellectual, the second must be described as existential.

That said, we are still left with questions that must be answered. What do we mean by a 'horizon of meaning'? Are we claiming that there is a qualitative difference in the types of narrative that can claim human allegiance? The answer to this last question must be positive, but we will leave our answer to it until we come to examine the question of genre in narrative in more detail. For the moment though we wish to examine just how Augustine envisages the way human beings accept the narrative of Christ. This will entail examining the way he reads the Scriptures, the very activity that converted him in the garden.

How to Enter a Narrative

We have already touched upon the fact that a narrative is addressed to someone which means more than that every story is told with some audience in mind; it means that even if only one person is writing or speaking, the narrative is to some extent a dialogue. The narrative does not simply exist as words on a page, but also as words that assume a meaning in the mind of the reader. These words, in the mind of the reader, assume the form of a collaboration between the writer and the reader. No reader understands a text in exactly the same way as another; each generation has its own reading of a classic work: this is not necessarily to deform the text or to abuse it, but rather to arrive at a personal understanding of it.

Thus, if a narrative is addressed to us, we too address ourselves to the narrative. Reading is an active process. The activity of teasing out meaning necessarily involves the person who reads or listens. Our reaction to the narrative will tell us something about ourselves: reading a book – as for Augustine – is a voyage of self-discovery. We remember his words about the *Hortensius*: *mutavit affectum meum*,[163] it changed my way of feeling. The book speaks to us, and we speak to the book, and in this conversation we change. Human life is dialogical. The narrative nature of human existence is dynamic: we have stories, but they are always changing, perhaps growing, and never in isolation, for they are constantly challenged by what we read. Hence the whole point of the Confessions, as we have said: they invite us to take up and read (*tolle lege*), so that we too, like the author who is also the protagonist, may attain salvation. What we wish to examine now is how we read a text, and in particular, how we are to read the Scriptures, the text that saved Augustine.

---

[163] *Confessions*, 3.4.7.

154 Narrative Theology and Moral Theology

Commenting on a verse of Psalm 8, Augustine has this to say:

Because I will see the heavens, the work of your fingers, the moons and the stars which you have established. The moon and the stars are set in heaven, because both the Church universal which is often represented by the moon, and the individual churches in specific places are, I think, adumbrated by the word, 'stars', are placed together in the same scriptures; and these scriptures, as we believe, are referred to by the term, 'heavens'. Why the term 'moon' is rightly interpreted to mean 'Church' will be considered more appropriately in another psalm...[164]

This is one way of reading, but this allegorical interpretation of Scripture is deeply unsatisfactory to the modern mind. It is telling us, in effect, that behind the words lie another set of words, and that this second set of words is the true reading. But why stop there? Why not continue until we regress to infinity? In this sense it is surely right to insist that there is no '*hors-texte*' and that the text must mean what it means. Allegory does violence to the integrity of the text, the nature of the story, unless that story is intended to be an allegory.

Indeed the most feeble of Augustine's expositions of the psalms are those where the traces of an allegorical reading are not far to seek. If we take *Ennaratio* 17: 17–20 we find a rather perfunctory description of God rescuing humankind: the text of the psalm provides a parallel text to God's intervention on humanity's behalf.[165] What is missing here is human participation in the drama of salvation. It is almost as if God saves us *ab extra*, from without, by a special intervention that is in no way willed by ourselves. The human being in this passage is passive. There is no nexus between us and him.

Again, we have in certain *Ennarationes* the idea that Christ has saved us almost by example: 'The Lord himself, who is judge of the living and the dead, stood before a human judge, to give us a lesson in humility and endurance. He was not defeated, but was providing every soldier with a model of how to fight... Take Job too.'[166] There follows some rather obvious moralizing on the patience of Job. The suggestion is that we make Christ and Job models for our own life: that is to say we reduce them to allegorical figures who stand in for ourselves. What we have read of Gustafson[167] should warn us off this. Augustine is using Job and Christ to exhort his audience: 'Well then, brothers and sisters, what are we to make of the fact that enemies have done such terrible things to Christians, and have rejoiced in it and gloated over them? When will it be clear that their rejoicing was hollow?'[168]

And so on. The role of Christ and Job is to appear as exemplars, people we read about who encourage us to stand firm (through our own efforts?) in time of trial. But where is the living link between the people we read about and we who read about them? Why should the story of Job mean anything to me? What is he to me or I to him? He is just a figure in a book. Are the Scriptures then just to be mined for such

---

[164] *Ennarationes*, 8.9, (*Works*, vol. 15, p. 134).
[165] *Ennarationes*, 17.17–20, (*Works*, vol.15, pp. 192–3).
[166] *Ennarationes*, 29/2. 7 (*Works*, vol. 15, p. 306).
[167] Gustafson, p. 180.
[168] *Ennarationes*, 29/2. 7, (*Works*, vol. 15, p. 307).

texts that can be used to encourage the faithful? Are we to read about Job in the same way as we are to read about Aeneas, as someone who will, through reading, provide us with a moral lesson?

There is also another type of exhortation in the *Ennarationes* which is perhaps more to our taste, more in keeping with a Christian tradition that has lasted to our own day, namely that of the use of the imagination in the meditation on the Scriptures. Here Augustine encourages us to make an imaginative leap into the story. In order to exhort his hearers to be humble he tells them to 'make the words of the psalm your own' and 'be the Lord's beast; be gentle, I mean'. The hearers are to imagine that they are the donkey which bears Christ into Jerusalem on Palm Sunday.[169] But the fact remains, no matter how great the imaginative effort made, a congregation will remain a congregation, no matter how much they think themselves into the role of a donkey, though this is not to deny the usefulness of the imagination as a tool for entering the story. Again, in the succeeding paragraph, the saint urges his congregation *excitate ergo in vobis amorem, fratres*: 'Stir up this love in yourselves, my bothers and sisters', giving them the example of the enthusiasm of the crowds who watch charioteers and *venatores*.[170] No doubt this is a helpful way of whipping up their enthusiasm, but the fact remains that the congregation is a congregation not a mob at the circus. There seems to be an unbridgeable chasm between the readers and what they read.

While the use of exemplars will always have a place in Christian preaching, qualitatively different is another approach of Augustine's. We will quote this passage[171] at length and comment on it as we proceed.

> Who are the upright? Those who direct their hearts in accordance with the will of God. If human frailty unsettles them, divine tranquillity consoles them; for though they may privately [*privatim*] in their mortal hearts want something that serves their present purpose, or promotes their business, or meets their immediate need, once they have understood and recognised that God wants something different, they prefer the will of One better than themselves to their own, the will of the Almighty to that of a weakling, the will of God to that of a human being. As God is infinitely above his human creatures, so is God's will far above the will of men and women.

We note the natural ease with which Augustine discusses Christian existence in neo-Platonic terms. Morality is a question of preferring the good and the higher to the less good and the lower. But what we also notice is the emphasis on will. Indeed, morality is seen as centred on the will[172] – indeed centred on the perfect alignment of our will to that of God. But these two wills, though very different, live in a sort of symbiotic union. God's will is infinitely 'above' the human will – there can be

---

[169] *Ennarationes*, 33/2.5 (*Works*, vol. 16, p. 26).

[170] *Ennarationes*, 33/2.6 (*Works*, vol. 16, p. 28).

[171] *Ennarationes*, 33/2.2 (*Works*, vol. 15, p. 393).

[172] 'The conception of the will was Augustine's – invention? Or discovery? In his own eyes at least it was a discovery, but a discovery of what had always been the case', MacIntyre, *Whose Justice? Which Rationality?*, p. 156. and pp. 146–56 of the same for MacIntyre's commentary on Augustine's moral theory and the centrality of will in it.

no doubt about that – but this makes it all the more amazing that human beings can make the will of God their own. They can will what God wants; they can direct their hearts in accordance with the divine will. It is at this point that a Platonist would have to break with Augustine, on the grounds that such a thing is simply impossible: the human and the divine are too far apart, too qualitatively different ever to be in union. We remember that Plotinus had to invent the Demiurge to get round this problem of the abyss between God and the world. So how is this symbiosis, this meeting of wills, possible? The next paragraph tells us.

> That is why Christ took the mantle of humanity [*gerens hominem*], set us an example [*regulam nobis proponens*], taught us how to live and gave us the grace to live as he taught. To this end he let his human will be seen. In his human will he embodied ours in advance [*in qua sua figuravit et nostram*], since he is our head and we all belong to him as his members, as you know well. Father, he said, if it is possible, let this cup pass from me. It was his human will speaking here, wanting something individual and private as it were [*tamquam privatum*]. But he wanted the rest of us to be right of heart, and whatever might be even slightly warped in us to be aligned with him who is always straight, and therefore he added, Yet not what I will, but what you will be done, Father (Mt 26:39). But was Christ capable of wanting anything bad? Could he, in the end, will anything other than what his Father willed?

The answer to our question is problematic, at least at first sight. For a start, Augustine uses a rather weak phrase to describe the reality of the Incarnation. *Gerens hominem* – acting the man, perhaps – 'putting on the mantle of humanity' could be interpreted in an almost monophysite key: Christ not really taking up the flesh but merely adopting the disguise of the flesh in order to give us a lesson, *regulam nobis proponens*. One notes too that Augustine proposes an exact parallel between Christ in the garden of Gethsemane and the townspeople of Carthage to whom this sermon was preached: both suffer a conflict between private business and the will of God: the word *privatim* is used of one, and *tamquam privatum* of Christ. It is only that *tamquam* that stands between Christ in the garden and the merchant of Carthage in his counting house. In other words we could be led to think that Christ is an all too human exemplar and no more.

However, this would not be the entire picture. We must pay attention to the important phrase 'in his human will he embodied ours in advance' which translates the rather difficult *in qua suam figuravit et nostram*. As we shall see this verb *(trans)figuravit* has huge significance for Augustinian theology, and narrative theology too. It is true to say that only a *tamquam* stands between the garden of Gethsemane and the counting houses of Carthage because the hearers of Augustine are being told that their own wills existed in the will of Christ. In other words that we, the people of Carthage, or whoever listens to the sermon or reads the scriptural passage, were present in the Garden and that the struggle of Christ, between the two wills, the human and the divine, embodied, before our births, the struggle that we feel now. In other words, the story of Christ in the garden of which we read is our story too, and for two reasons: Christ became incarnate, he took on the mantle of humanity, and *gerens hominem* he stood for all men and women; secondly: 'He is our head and we all belong to him as his members, as you know well.' Why add that *sicut nostis*, 'as you know well'? It is perhaps Augustine's way of drawing attention to how we became members of Christ – though baptism. And it was through baptism that we put on Christ, but what is more important here, he put on us (*transfiguravit in se* is the usual phrase), bringing us into his story. Thus in reading of Christ we read of ourselves. And in identifying our own will with God's we adopt a new narrative – made possible by the action of Christ who identified himself with us.

Let us now see what direction Augustine will take this in. He continues:

> They are one in godhead, so there can be no disparity of will. But in his manhood, he identified his members with himself [*transfigurans in se suos*], just as he did when he said, I was hungry and you fed me (Mt 25:35), and as he identified us with himself [*quos in se transfiguravit*] when he called from heaven to the rampaging Saul who was persecuting God's holy people, Saul, Saul, why are you persecuting me? (Acts 9:4), though no one was laying a finger on Christ himself. So too in displaying the will proper to a human being he displayed your nature, and straightened you out [*ostendit te, correxit te*]. 'See yourself reflected in me [*ecce vide te in me*],' Christ says, 'because you have the capacity to want something of your own account that is at variance with God's will. This is natural to human frailty, characteristic of human weakness, and difficult for you to avoid. But when it happens, think immediately about who is above you. Think of God above you, and yourself below him [*illum supra te, te infra illum*], of him as your creator and yourself as his creature [*illum creatorem, te creaturam*], of him as Lord and yourself as servant [*illum dominum, te servum*], of him as almighty and yourself as weak [*illum omnipotentem, te infirmum*]. Correct yourself, subject yourself to his will and say, Not what I will, but your will be done, Father. How can you then be separated from God, when you now will what God wills? You will be straight and upright, and praise will be your fitting occupation, for praise befits the upright.'

We see at once that the former rhetor of Milan has lost none of his old skills! We notice the hammered home repetition that underlines again and again the parallelism between *illum* and *te*. But parallelism is not the right word: it is identity. The hearer of the sermon or the reader of the scriptural text stands in a relationship to Christ that is one of complete identity, because Christ has identified his members with himself. 'How can you then be separated from God?' when the prayer you make has already been made by Christ, when Christ has already prayed on our behalf: indeed we were praying in Christ in the garden. The garden story is my story. Notice too the use of the preterite tense: *ostendit te, correxit te*: these things have already happened. Thus we can conclude that Christ in the garden of Gethsemane does not merely provide an example for struggling humans, but rather he has already fought their battle for them, and won it, for he has identified us with himself.

This doctrine of transfiguration is the key to understanding Augustine's narrative theology. Michael Cameron sums up Augustine's theological achievement in the *Ennarationes* thus:

> For Augustine the voice of the *totus Christus* is the radiating hermeneutical centre of the Psalms. This *una vox* opened the way for incorporating the soteriological principle of 'exchange' into the bishop's hermeneutic of the Psalms by uncovering an ecclesial sense as part of the traditional christological interpretation. In this exchange the church, already present in the flesh of Jesus, receives the grace and beauty of divine life, while Christ

takes on flesh, sin, corruption and death. This occurs by a dynamic of the incarnation that Augustine, borrowing Paul's language in I Corinthians 4:6 and Philippians 3:21, called 'transfiguration' (30[2].1.3; 43.2; 60.3; 87.3; 101.1.2). Christ represented and transformed all humanity by 'carrying the person' of the old sinful humanity. Besides the cry from the cross, Christ signalled this assumption especially clearly in his desperate prayer in Gethsemane ('Let this cup pass from me,' Matt. 26:38). Here, says Augustine, we see the passage (*transitus*) from the head to the body (142.9). The next sentence, 'Not my will but yours be done,' shows the Lord 'bending' our crooked nature to be flush with the straightedge of God's will (32[2].1.2).

The *totus Christus* refers not just to objective content as thought the Psalms merely taught *about* Christ and the church; rather, because Christians say with their head, 'We are Christ' (26[2].2; 100.3), they are its living subjects and *de facto* participants in the voice speaking there. In psalm after psalm 'we discover our own voice' (40.6; 45.1). 'Who is singing? The body of Christ. Who is this? You are, if you will it – we all are, if we will it' (83.5). Since our voice is in the psalms we cannot pray them 'without deep feeling' (*sine affectu*) because we sense ourselves to live 'in the same place' (*indidem*; 59.1). For Augustine, therefore, the Psalter is not only informative but also performative... Augustine thus awakened his hearers to themselves as subjects of the paschal mystery and participants in its dynamic of charity. Unwittingly, he also gave an intriguing reply to the hermeneutical conundrum created by the modern division between participant and observer, subject and object, positing their conjunction not by mere fiat but by uncovering the engine of participation in the structure of redemption itself.[173]

This is exactly the same conclusion that we have reached, though in different language. But what Cameron does not go on to say is how this way of thinking has important implications for narrative theology. A story can remain external to the hearer/reader. They may choose to enter into the world of the story by *fiat*, or not, as the case may be. But the story of Christ is not this type of story: it is performative not merely informative: we enter it through the incarnation of Christ, who taking up the flesh took up our flesh as well. And thus emerges what we have already said about the qualitative difference in types of narrative: the narrative of Christ is of a higher quality than a mere human narrative. For in the narrative of Christ we read of ourselves: we are in the story through the grace of Christ who *transfiguravit se in nos*, and not through any imaginative leap or act of the human will alone. This is the key to reading the Scriptures that Augustine the reader gives us.

Transfiguravit Se in Nos as a Key to Reading

The word *transfiguravit*, or its cognates, appears seventeen times in the *Ennarationes* which is some indication of how widespread the use of the theme is in the work as a whole; there are other occasions too, when the word is not itself used, but the theme is invoked. For example, in *Ennaratio* 3, Augustine says that in this psalm the whole Christ is speaking: *Potest et ipse psalmus accipi ad personam Christi alio modo, ut totus loquatur. Totus, dico, cum corpore suo cui caput est...* He goes on to say that

---

[173] Michael Cameron, 'Ennarationes in Psalmos', in *Augustine through the Ages*, p. 293.

'in the human Christ Jesus, the church has been taken up [*suscepta est*] by the Word, who was made flesh and dwelt among us, because God has made us sit together with him even in the heavenly places.'[174] Here we see underlined the key point: through the incarnation we participate in the story of Christ, and through his headship of the body, we, his members, take part in his story. The union is real, as opposed to purely sentimental or imaginary. Thus throughout the *Ennarationes* we see two interweaving strands of narrative: the story of Christ and the stories of the believer. The psalms are interpreted in Christological key, and Christology is personal to the believer. We see a constant interweaving of pronouns. Augustine turns a theology of 'he' and 'they' into a theology of 'you' and 'me'. 'Because I am among them, you will fill me can be the words I use.'[175] The gap between 'them' and 'me' has been filled by the incarnation of Christ.

It is for this reason that time too is a barrier that has been overcome. The Christ-story is not a past event, forever inaccessible. Preaching on a Good Friday,[176] Augustine makes it clear that though Christ died but once and his passion only happened once, we re-enact the passion every year: does this mean that Christ dies many times? 'No, yet [*tamen*] the yearly remembrance in a sense makes present [*quasi repraesentat*] what took place in time past, and in this way it moves us as if [*tamquam*] we were actually watching our Lord hanging on the cross, but watching as believers, not mockers.' Let us note the use of *tamen... tamquam*; the condition of our being present is faith – we have to be there as believers, not mockers, unlike the Donatists. Here we see in embryo at least the doctrine of anamnesis: the actual making present of a past event through *memoria*. The re-enactment, though, comes through the action of Christ, not the will of human beings. This takes care of the objection to *imitatio Christi* theology that worries Gustafson. Further on in the *Ennaratio*[177] he underlines the idea of the common lot shared by Christ and the Christian: this is further evinced in the fact that the assembly for which Christ suffered is 'this assembly, this Church'. In other words the present congregation is intimately connected with the sufferings of Christ on Good Friday. The usual barrier presented by historical time has been dissolved. All of us are a single person in Christ, he says elsewhere,[178] meaning that we are not separated either by space or time. The story is universal: a historical event, taking place in time and place, yet not bound by time and space. Indeed, further on in the same *Ennaratio*[179] he says that the crucified Christ 'is both there and here, there in himself, here in us' [*et ibi est, et hic: ibi in se, hic in nobis*] – a pithy summary of the situation. Indeed Christ speaks in our words so that we might speak in his, because he has transfigured us into himself: *qui non est dedignatus assumere nos in se, non est dedignatus transfigurare nos in se, et loqui verbis nostris, ut et nos loqueremur*

---

[174] *Ennarationes*, 3.9 (*Works*, vol. 15, p. 81).
[175] *Ennarationes*, 15.10 (*Works*, vol. 15, p. 184). For similar interweaving, this time of 'he' and 'we', see *Ennarationes*, 34/2.1 (*Works*, vol. 16, p. 59).
[176] *Ennarationes*, 21/2.1 (*Works*, vol. 15, p. 227).
[177] *Ennarationes*, 21/2.23 (*Works*, vol. 15, p. 236).
[178] *Ennarationes*, 29/2.5 (*Works*, vol. 15, p. 305).
[179] *Ennarationes*, 29/2.22 (*Works*, vol. 15, p. 314).

verbis ipsius.[180] He speaks with our words and we speak in his: the two discourses interpenetrate. For this reason 'we recognise ourselves [*et nos ipsos agnoscamus*] in the words of the prophet',[181] that is in the words of the psalmist. Thus, the words of Christ ought to be our words too.[182] Indeed head and body speak with one single voice and 'we are within his body, provided that we have sincere faith in him, and unshakeable hope, and burning charity'.[183] These three, it seems are the *sine qua non* of being able to enter the story of Christ.

One might expect this last point to be made with greater insistence by Augustine: in other words for him to answer with greater emphasis the question 'What must I do to enter into the story, to find myself transfigured into Christ?' But this is not a question in which the saint is much interested. Like Gustafson, he concentrates on what Christ has done, not what we must do. Hence there is no danger in reading Augustine of getting the wrong impression that salvation is an egotistical enterprise. But, briefly we might pick out a few features that recur in the *Ennarationes*. One is the prayer of unceasing desire, *clamor cordis*.[184] In addition to this, and linked with it, as we see in the *Confessions*, is the theme of confession itself, which leads to redemption.[185] Indeed the theme of confession is mentioned several times in the *Ennarationes*, as is that of conversion or 'turning'.[186] But on the whole this is a minor theme, partly, one suspects, because Augustine is preaching to the already converted; partly, and perhaps more importantly, because his main emphasis in the *Ennarationes* is on the action of Christ, and the story of Christ, as opposed to the personal story of the believer, except as read through that of Christ. It is this emphasis that leads us away from any interpretation of Augustine's theology in egotistical key, such as that which Gustafson applies to Thomas à Kempis.[187] The *Ennarationes* are not 'about' us, they are 'about' us-in-Christ, who *transfiguravit nos in se*. The protagonist of the story is Christ, just as the chief protagonist of the *Confessions* is God. The believer's narrative has God for its centre, not themselves.

Indeed, the *Ennarationes* are proposing a sort of Christian existentialism. If we examine what Augustine has to say about time in *Ennaratio* 38,[188] we see that his existence has two strands to it: on the one hand there is the time of human existence which is sliding towards extinction, something that makes him say 'I am so nearly non-existent'; contrasted with this is the time of the God who describes himself as 'I am who am'. The human being who believes exists between the two dimensions:

> As we regard our sin, our mortality, our fleeting seasons, our groaning toil and sweat, the stages of our life that succeed one other and will not stand still, but slip imperceptibly from infancy to old age as we regard all these, let us see in them the old self, the old day,

---

[180] *Ennarationes*, 30/2.3 (*Works*, vol. 15, pp. 322–3).
[181] *Ennarationes*, 30/3.1 (*Works*, vol. 15, p. 334).
[182] *Ennarationes*, 33/2.3 (*Works*, vol. 16, p. 25).
[183] *Ennarationes*, 37.6 (*Works*, vol. 16, p. 150).
[184] *Ennarationes*, 37.14 (*Works*, vol.16, p. 158).
[185] *Ennarationes*, 37.15 (*Works*, vol.16, p. 158).
[186] *Ennarationes*, 25/2.11 (*Works*, vol. 15, pp. 265–6).
[187] Gustafson, p. 180.
[188] *Ennarationes*, 38.7–9 (*Works*, vol. 16, pp. 176–9).

> the old song, the Old Covenant. But when we turn to our inner being, to all that is destined to be renewed in us and replace the things subject to change, let us find there the new self, the new day, the new song, the New Covenant, and let us love this newness so dearly that the oldness we meet there does not frighten us. As we run our race we are passing from the old to the new. This transition is effected as the old things decay and the inner are made new, until our outer decaying self pays its debt to nature and meets its death, though it too will be renewed at the resurrection. Then all things which for the present are new only in hope will be made new in the very truth. You further the process now as you strip yourself of the old and run toward the new.[189]

It is clear from this and the whole tenor of the sermons that make up the *Ennarationes* (as well as from the *Confessions*) that the human being experiences the old and the new at one and the same time. The process is a continuing one that takes a lifetime. This may seem a rather obvious point, but it is worth stressing that Augustine sees the conversion process as historical and incarnational, across a lifetime; and the conversion process gives what MacIntyre would doubtless call the narrative unity of a life. In other words, accepting the story of Christ, entering that story, and being conformed to it (all thanks to the doctrine of what Christ has done through transfiguration), one accepts a narrative, rather than merely consenting to a set of propositions. This narrative embraces past, present and future, and at the same time relativizes the concept of time, placing it in the shadow of eternity, the time of God. However, at the same time, this narrative is not the only narrative present in the believer's life: the old still persists, and will do so until death: the two move in parallel, in dialectic almost, with the new overcoming the old. Augustine's people stand between two worlds; they are always divided selves, divided between decay and renewal. It is this reality that MacIntyre fails to stress; likewise, the historical emphasis of MacIntyre and Hauerwas (not to mention Engelhardt) does not stress the double nature of time, as outlined above, and the co-existence of the eternal with the temporal.

> He has some stake in this world under the sun and some stake in the world beyond it. Here under the sun he has the business of waking and sleeping, eating and drinking, feeling thirst and hunger, thriving and being tired, growing from a child into a youth, and then into an old man, being unsure what to hope and what to fear. All these even Iduthun experiences under the sun, even though he is one who leaps beyond. Where does he get the impetus for his leaping? From his desire: Make known to me my end, O Lord. The desire is something beyond this sunny world; it does not arise from the world under the sun. All things we can see are under the sun, but whatever is invisible is not under the sun. Faith is not visible, charity is not visible, kindliness is not visible, neither is that chaste fear that abides forever. In all these Iduthun finds sweetness and consolation; he lives beyond this sun because he is a citizen of heaven.[190]

Iduthun here stands for the Christian, one who lives between two worlds. But does this passage reflect Augustine's Platonism for the masses? Is it vulnerable to two terrible objections? First, the world is all that is the case; and secondly, of that which

---

[189] *Ennarationes*, 38.9 (*Works*, vol. 16, p. 179).
[190] *Ennarationes*, 38.10 (*Works*, vol. 16, p. 180).

we cannot speak – what lies beyond the world – must be passed over in silence?[191] But Augustine's Platonism must be understood in a Christian sense: the human being in themselves is a single entity living in two dimensions. There are not two worlds, this one and one beyond our experience. Rather time is always experienced against the backdrop of eternity. Without that backdrop, time makes no sense at all. Indeed it would be impossible to understand time without the sense of eternity; motion only makes sense because we have an idea of stillness. This idea of stillness or eternity may well be *a priori*, for we do not find it in the world, where everything is in motion, but we can deduce it from what we see around us.

Where is this leading us? We are divided selves, selves capable of stepping back from our experiences and looking at them *sub specie aeternitatis*. That is to say that we are capable of entering something like an Original Position. We never see perfect fairness in the world, but we can picture a situation in which perfect fairness and equality are at least thinkable. The Original Position of John Rawls never existed in reality – but it exists in our minds as a measure of reality, a means by which we can examine that which is and ask ourselves what ought to be.

It is this double nature of human beings, their already and not yet dimension, that is responsible for the chief feature in Christian life for Augustine, namely the life of desire.[192] We desire what we know but that which we do not yet possess absolutely. Indeed, how is desire possible in any other terms? How can one desire what is utterly unknown? Hence we move by gradual stages from the known to the less known, in a platonic ladder of perfection reminiscent of Saint Bonaventure's *Itinerarium*, an inward and upward journey.[193]

We have on several occasions referred to Augustine's debt to Plato and Plotinus; but far more important is the debt he owes to the Christian story. For this is the source of the narrative that enables us to live between two worlds, that enables us to search for the Good in Platonic terms. As he says, commenting on Psalm 42, 'Let us each of us be within Christ's body, and we shall be the speaker here' – *sit uniusque in Christi corporis, et loquetur hic*. It is being in Christ that gives us the language with which to speak, gives us the story to tell.

Conclusion: Augustine as Narrative Theologian

What has this examination of Augustine told us about narrative theology? It is our contention that Augustine's approaches examined here illustrate in a precise way both the presuppositions of any narrative method in theology, and the challenges that a narrative approach will encounter.

Augustine's approach presupposes the primacy of the first person as opposed to the third. The person, either telling the story, or hearing the story and interiorizing it, either as author or as reader of the narration, the one who responds to the invitation *tolle lege*, is the one who, in the experience of being in a story as protagonist,

---

[191] The objections are of course those of Wittgenstein. See *Tractatus Logicus-Philosophicus*, theses 1 and 7.
[192] *Ennarationes*, 41.2 (*Works*, vol.16, pp. 240–41).
[193] *Ennarationes*, 41.7 (*Works*, vol. 16, pp. 244–5).

experiences truth. Augustine creates a story about himself out of the raw material of his life and his cultural setting, and in this story, in this act of authorial creation, he discovers God, for in the story he discovers himself. One goes into oneself to discover God; but one goes into oneself through coming to know the narrative of one's life through the act of authorship. This narrative of one's life, which though rooted in particularity, clearly has universal import, may only emerge after several false starts and false narratives have been overcome.

Augustine writes the *Confessions* in order to know himself. A narrative is a way of piecing together the seemingly random events of the past, seeing the pattern in them, and discovering one's identity. Knowing himself then enables him to know others, for knowledge of his own identity is the necessary precondition of knowing anything at all; but once he knows himself he can then know others, know the world in which he finds himself, and above all know the ultimate reality, God. There is a Platonic scale of progression at work here: one's own being, other beings, the world's being, Ultimate Being. Of course Platonism is a story, for Augustine the story, that explains the world, but there may be other such stories available.

From Augustine we learn that narrative puts the self as central. Narratives tell us who we are and tell us of our relation to the world. The way of relating to the world will be moral or otherwise, depending on the truth of the narrative we create for ourselves.

But while we have spoken of the narrative we create for ourselves, in reading Augustine, in taking up the *tolle lege* invitation, we are also aware that there is a pre-existing narrative. Augustine did not invent Platonism, but found it ready made for him: he tried it on and it fitted. The only thing that Augustine invents, and even then not from scratch, but taking up the numerous materials he found around him, is the character of Augustine and the story of his life. This, as we have said, was the necessary step that had to be taken before he could try on the garments of Platonism. But more important than the *libri platonici* are the Scriptures, the narrative par excellence, that Augustine discovers as opposed to invents. We make up our own story and this story then encounters other stories that we did not invent. The story of the Paschal Mystery has its own objective existence that does not depend on us. This then is the great challenge of all narrative theology: how does my story relate to that of Christ?

As we have seen from our readings of the *Ennarationes*, there are several possible answers, of which only one is right. The first is to see one's life as a parallel to the life of Christ; the second it to try and recreate one's life through the imagination using Christ as one's pattern; both are doomed to failure, for the parallel is too distant, the effort of imaginative recreation too hard. The third and correct approach is to see that in the incarnation Christ has transfigured us into himself: in other words, the work has been done for us in an act of grace. Only in this way can we see the essential connection between the doctrine of grace which is central to Christianity and narrative. This too is the conclusion of the *Confessions*: we make our lives, but in the end discover that the final conversion is a gift given to us in Christ. We create various narratives for ourselves until we final arrive at that narrative which enables us to accept the narrative created for us by Christ.

Having thus examined the Augustinian contribution to the question of narrative, we can now turn to a detailed examination of the workings of a truly narrative theology.

Chapter 8

Three Models of Narrative Theology

In this chapter we shall attempt to identify three models of narrative which can be the basis of a narrative moral theology. So far we have encountered several contrasting models of narrative which give rise to different forms of narrative theology. The first is that which sees narrative firmly rooted in community and tradition, and unable to exist independently of them: but even in this model we see important differences, and not merely differences of emphasis, in the relationship between narrative and reason. The second model, that of John Rawls, advances a narrative that embodies a way of reasoning, which is universally (or almost universally) applicable, and which can exist in a variety of settings. Finally, we have seen the way Saint Augustine uses narrative, and how a man who is rooted and embedded in a particular history, culture and time, is able to provide us with a model of narrative that transcends its origins. It is this third approach which holds out the promise of a narrative which can arrive at universal moral norms.

We now propose to examine these three models in some detail, so that we can come to an exact understanding about the way narrative works in moral theology and provides an ethical language for moral theology.[1]

---

[1] The bibliography on the subject of narrative and story, and their impact in theology, is vast indeed. Here we can only refer to some of the books which have been found useful in writing this chapter, and which are as follows:

Robert Alter, *The Pleasures of Reading in an Ideological Age* (New York: Simon and Schuster, 1989); Wayne C. Booth, *The Company We Keep, an Ethics of Fiction* (Berkeley: University of California Press, 1988); David Carr, 'Narrative and the Real World: An Argument for Continuity', *History and Theory*, 25 (1986): 117–31. Stephen Crites, 'The Narrative Quality of Experience', *The Journal of the American Academy of Religion*, 39, 3 (1971): 291–311; John Dominic Crossan, *The Dark Interval, towards a Theology of Story* (second edition, Sonora, California: Eagle Books, 1988); Robert Detweiler, *Breaking the Fall, religious readings in contemporary fiction* (San Francisco: Harper and Row, 1989); John S. Dunne, *Time and Myth, a Meditation on Storytelling as an exploration of Life and Death* (Notre Dame: University of Notre Dame Press, 1973); Paul S. Fiddes (ed.), *The Novel, Spirituality and Modern Culture* (Cardiff: University of Wales Press, 2000); Michael Goldberg, *Theology and Narrative, a critical introduction* (Nashville: Abingdon Press, 1982); Philip S. Keane, *Christian Ethics and Imagination* (New York: Paulist Press, 1984); Wesley A. Kort, *Narrative Elements and Religious Meanings* (Philadelphia: Fortress Press, 1975); Mark Leadbetter, *Virtuous Intentions, The Religious Dimensions of Narrative* (Atlanta, Scholars Press, 1989); Gerald Loughlin, *Telling God's Story, Bible, Church and Narrative Theology* (Cambridge: Cambridge University Press, 1996); W.J.T. Mitchell (ed.), *On Narrative* (Chicago: University of Chicago Press, 1981); John Navone, *Seeking God in Story* (Collegeville, Minnesota: Liturgical Press, 1990); Paul Nolan, *Narrative and Morality, a Theological Enquiry* (University

The First Model: The 'Closed' Narrative

The first model presents us with a story that is rooted in a community, in a tradition and in a place. This story isolates certain features of existence inside a structured narrative, presenting us with a picture of life that is accessible, and essentially limited: it is the imposition of limit that makes the truth the story contains accessible to human understanding. This structured and limited picture of life reflects our own experience as lived in our histories and at the same time exhorts the reader or hearer to approximate their behaviour to that which is modelled by the story.

A 'closed' narrative has a beginning, a middle and an end. It makes sense of life: events are seen as essentially connected and coherent. The narrative purports to explain certain aspects of human behaviour; it tells us why some things are as they are; it puts events, that otherwise might seem random, into perspective. While the raw experience of life may often seem incoherent, the narrative imposes form on this incoherence and reduces it to that which can be understood.[2] Life may seem to be all middle – we are *in medias res* – but the narrative gives us the sense of a beginning and a sense of an ending, by telling us how we got here, and where we are going. These stories serve to tame the threatening and unknowable and enable their hearers to believe that what they see around them has purpose, meaning, and is essentially beneficent. They persuade us that all is not without purpose, and that there is, after all, despite evidence to the contrary, a special providence even in the fall of a sparrow.

Into this category fall (or at least seem to fall) several of the narratives that we have encountered so far: the liturgy in the Antiochene church, as envisaged by Engelhardt; the stories that are told in the church as envisaged by Hauerwas; the Homeric poems and the role they played in ancient Athens, as described by MacIntyre.

How does the story that purports to be such a vehicle of meaning work? These stories have plot; they rely on some sort of time scheme; and they all have some sort of setting; they contain characters.

Plot is the imposition of order and form on what may seem to lack both. The artist – and indeed the person in the world – may find that events and experiences come to him or her in no particular order and without connection. They make the connections and establishes order and form. Whatever our personal epistemology, we perceive things that are bundles of sense perceptions, but our minds make connections between these things perceived and makes them into wholes, into unities.[3] Human

---

Park: The Pennsylvania State University Press, 1987); David Tracy, 'Theological Classics in Contemporary Theology', *Theology Digest* 24, 5 (Winter, 1977): 347–57.

[2] Literature, says John Navone, isolates experience, captures it and makes it accessible, Navone, p. 54.

[3] Iris Murdoch makes this essential point at the start of her book *Metaphysics as a Guide to Morals*. She writes: 'The idea of a self-contained unity or limited whole is a fundamental instinctive concept. We see parts of things, we intuit whole things. We seem to know a great deal on the basis of very little. Oblivious of philosophical problems and paucity of evidence we grasp ourselves as unities, continuous bodies and continuous minds. We assume the continuity of space and time… The urge to prove that where we intuit unity there really is unity is a deep emotional motive to philosophy, to art, to thinking itself. Intellect is naturally

activity considered in its bareness seems fundamentally meaningless: we see a man digging in the garden.[4] It is very clear from a physical point of view what he is doing. We see the motions, we see the results – but sense perception – our eyes – do not tell us why he is digging in the garden. We have the facts – the man digging – but we do not have the 'story' – why the man is digging. Is he digging in order to cultivate the ground? If so, why? Because his wife has asked him to? Because he wishes to plant vegetables as it is spring? Because he believes in the therapeutic value of gardening? Mere single actions cannot convey story on their own. We need to know more. Hence, story is a human invention: the projection of meaning onto events that we perceive or imagine. This is what we call plot.

The realistic novel or play which so often exemplifies this type of narrative invites us to enjoy a representation of life that is under control, that has been fitted into a form that we find manageable and digestible. In this recognizable genre, so beloved of the past, no end is left loose at the conclusion, all is tied up, all is explained and put in its proper place. In the detective novel all those clues that were passed before our uncomprehending eyes are now shown to have played a vital role in the denouement. Indeed the word 'denouement' tells us that there is a truth that can be revealed to us in the closing pages. Everything connects. The puzzle is not really a puzzle after all, for there is a solution, ingenious, perhaps a little far fetched, but a solution all the same. The plot works: it satisfies our longing for order, and assuages our anxiety that in this world there is only chaos and that the murderer usually gets away with it. The plot could be seen as a form of escapism – the temptation to believe that the world is really as it is in books and not in life – in other words, a world that is susceptible to order.

However, very few people actually believe (though many may want to secretly) that the world is as it appears to be in detective novels. But the detective novel is only an extreme form of a much wider phenomenon. Other novels that do not work within the confines of this highly unusual genre, whose appeal we have outlined above, nevertheless do conform to the same basic pattern. The good are rewarded, the wicked are punished. Our mistakes are rectified by a combination of common sense and good luck and kindly fate (as in comedy); or else, (as is the case with tragedy) our mistakes come back to haunt us, but nevertheless, we are brave enough to bear our punishment, though often undeserved, and we rise above our miserable fate, showing the nobility and dignity that is inherent in our characters. In both comedy and tragedy, humankind triumphs, though in radically diverse ways. In comedy, we see our resourcefulness and guile rewarded; in tragedy we show that our best side is often seen in adversity.[5] Both tragedy and comedy make sense of life.

---

one-making. To evaluate, understand, classify, place in order of merit, implies a wider unified system, the questing mind abhors vacuums' (p. 1).

4   The example is Alasdair MacIntyre's. See *After Virtue*, p. 206 et seq.

5   There are numerous examples one could cite to support this view. Consider how Hamlet, Lear and Othello achieve an intense nobility in adversity. Likewise, Shakespeare's comic heroines show us their innate resourcefulness and their capacity to forgive people and reconcile opposites, all the qualities we associate with greatness of heart. In both genres events, though seemingly random, contribute to these outcomes.

Both forms, indeed all forms, show events as connected. In Shakespeare's *King Lear* we are told that 'the dark and vicious place where thee he got cost him his eyes'.[6] In other words, the Earl of Gloster, fathering an illegitimate son, brought down upon himself the punishment of being blinded. This is, at first sight, hard to fathom. But several things are happening here. First there is a casual connection: Gloster conceives the wicked Edmund, and Edmund later is at least partially responsible for his father's being blinded. On another level: Gloster's wicked sin, in begetting the child, and bringing him up in the way he does, has blighted his moral sense and this leads to the situation in which he is blinded by Regan and the Duke of Cornwall. On yet another level: Gloster is morally blind, and on losing his sight, as a result of his sins, regains the ability to see morally.

The story works then on a series of levels, and causation can be physical as well as moral, but the important point is that within the confines of story we accept causation without difficulty. To be told that a man is punished twenty or thirty years after the event for the sin of fornication or adultery by being blinded, is, on the face of it, both outrageous and preposterous. We know that life is not like that – but within the context of plot, we have no difficulty in seeing that the two events are connected on a variety of levels. One has caused the other. The wheel has come full circle.

This sort of causation is not found in nature: it is not the physical causation of science, not the sort of causation which we associate with economics or history. It goes beyond all of these, though it may contain elements of some of them. The causation of literature, narrative and story is essentially a human construction, something imposed upon the data of life which makes sense of such data. For while they may be accidents in daily experience, a convincing and well-structured narrative convinces us that accidents do not happen. The world of narrative is different from the world as we experience it in its rawness: it is a world in which events have meaning and are governed by unseen powers that we can call fate or the gods. There is a wheel, turning, reaching full circle, and we are on it. There is a purpose to history, and to our histories.

Allied to the idea of plot is the idea of authorship. The events which unfold – as opposed to merely happen in a random way – do so under the presidency of an author who hovers over the story as a benign (or malign) presence. In some stories this authorship is in the hands of the gods and the person telling the story is in fact just the teller of the tale, not the author. Homer's people live in a world dominated by the gods – the poet recounts the way the gods intervene, but it is the gods and the heroes themselves who make the story. In modern literature this idea is not entirely absent: events can happen because the gods are the ones who bring them about, though not through crude direct intervention. But more often in the modern novel or play, events unfold under the presidency of the author, who stands for God: all seeing, all-knowing, they have access to the secrets of all human hearts, and it is the author who introduces the stroke of good or bad luck, malign or benign fate; it is the author who decides on the outcome of events, who moulds them into the form we call plot. The author plays God with the characters, bringing them to life and killing them off or rewarding them as they see fit. In other words, in the world

---

[6] *King Lear*, Act V, Scene iii, line 172.

of story, there is always a presiding intelligence, either explicitly or implicitly. And yet, through observation of the world, one can perhaps detect no such presiding intelligence guiding the universe. In this way too, narrative and story represent the imposition of meaning onto what seems essentially formless.

Yet we must question the word 'essentially'. If the world were essentially formless it would not be amenable to subjection to the forms of plot. Seemingly realistic events can be fitted into plot structures without being forced because there is in real events an affinity with order. It is perfectly true that certain plots do not work, and that we throw certain books aside in exasperation, saying that such things could never happen. But it is also true that knowing the world as we do, we also believe in plots: in other words, we see that the world, events, life, are amenable to being ordered. This suggests in turn that the raw data of experience can of its very nature be ordered: it contains within it the seeds of its ordering. For plot, in so far as it is convincing, is not extraneous to life: plot-based story and life find a fit between them, and this shows us that the world is not utterly without meaning.

This point can be expanded through analogy. We hear in the world a variety of noises; we can make noises by blowing through pipes, by rubbing strings together, by striking various surfaces. These noises often seem cacophonous and downright ugly. One noise seems to clash with another. The aural universe can seem like an unordered chaos – and often it is. But if various notes and instruments making those notes are harmonized the result is music. Music is after all only ordered noise, but music proves that sounds are amenable to order and harmony if these are imposed on them by human agency. This proves that sounds are not inherently inharmonious, but contain within themselves the potential to be made into music. The same is true of words. There is music in words – in poetry for example. While words can be brutal and ugly, they are also amenable to being arranged in such a way that they become harmonious, have rhythm and meaning. This ordering is imposed by the poet, but the poet would be powerless to do so unless words were themselves intrinsically capable of being harmonious and poetic.

What we see here is the emergence of one of the foundation stones of a narrative theology: we can make sense of the world because the world, as we discover through making stories, is intrinsically meaningful. While events may in real life come raining down on our heads without any obvious rhyme or reason, we can, nevertheless, make sense of such events through our ability to construct plots.

Just as plot represents the ordering of the universe into a manageable whole, so too does the 'closed' narrative tame time. Everything that happens to us, happens to us in time; there is nothing that we experience which is not temporal. If we recount an event, our interlocutor can always ask with reason 'When did this happen?' and even if we are unable to answer, the question always makes sense.

Every 'closed' narrative compresses time. The action of a play, or a book, may cover several years, but these years are compressed into the space in which we read the book or watch the play. The story of a life may be squeezed without difficulty into three hundred pages. Not only is time concertinaed in narrative, allowing us to view a considerable length of time at a sitting – something that would otherwise be impossible – time is also rendered tractable in another way. In narrative, time past, time present and time future are seen as essentially one through character and plot.

This is one of the great discoveries and achievements of narrative: it shows us that time is not simply a succession of disjointed moments, but a continuum. I am who I am now because I was the person I was then, and I will be in the future as I am now, at least to some extent. Characters grow and develop over time, certainly, but this growth is rooted in a substratum of character that stays the same. Time's never ending stream does not carry away with it our identity: we remain the same people over a lifetime. If this were not so there could be no story, no narrative – but narrative maintains that there is continuity in life.

Finding ourselves in time, we are also aware that time is of two different sorts. There is time measured by the clock, the revolution of the heavens, which is impersonal, and there is also the time that is personal to me. Impersonal time is all of equal value. One minute is exactly like another; each contains sixty seconds. Personal time is somewhat different: there are privileged moments in every life, as we have said, moments of insight which count more than other less important times for the individual. For us some minutes may feel very long indeed, others may flash by with our hardly noticing them. And thus it is in narrative too: a story-teller may jump forward, compressing times in which little happens, and then dwell with care on other short moments that are full of import. For in every life, as in every narrative, it is these 'spots of time' that really count: they are the moments of revelation.[7] They are the moments in which we are able to gain insights that make sense of the past or reassure us about the possible course of the future.

Time is a frightening concept. We are faced with deserts of vast eternity – time stretches away in every direction, it seems, reducing us to insignificance. 'Man that is born of woman hath but a short time to live.' But narrative takes the sting out of time, by showing us that time can have meaning: it is not simply an endless duration. Narrative gives meaning to time, which threatens us with meaninglessness.

Much of what we have said above about the concept of time in narrative must apply to the concept of character as well. The people who appear in narrative do so as 'characters' not as entities hidden behind comic or tragic masks, nor as ideal types or symbols. A character is a centre of unity and meaning, the place where disparate experiences over time are solidified. A character is one who knows and feels and understands, one who has a continuing identity over time. Moreover a character is a dynamic reality, changing yet the same, whose character makes sense of experience, whose character sums up the totality of personal experience.

It is a literary truism to claim that character is fate. Things do not simply happen to us out of the blue – our destiny, our fate, is shaped by our character. Misfortune may make us brave, resourceful and in the end triumphant: events mould us in accordance with our capacity, as characters, to be moulded. We are as we are, not because fate has made us this way, but because we have made our fate. We are

---

[7] Goldberg (pp. 98–9) makes the interesting point that the autobiographer is one who turns *chronos* into *kairos*, that is impersonal time into personal time, depending on and reflecting the author's present standpoint. 'The standpoint, the determination of what will be recalled and how, gives a life its unity, its coherence, its shape – in short, its story.' Following Crites, Goldberg refers to Augustine. For our own discussion of how Augustine manipulates his material, see the previous chapter.

authors of our own existences, or better co-authors of our own existences: clearly we have no control over many aspects of our environment, but we can shape ourselves in accordance with the circumstances in which we find ourselves. We are and remain morally free: disaster and even death can be shaped by our wills, for we can choose how to react to these things, and in this way, in a sense, overcome them. We are faced with restricted choices, but within these restricted choices we have a multiplicity of options. A person may face certain death, but within that certainty they have a choice of how they face death – and it is in this choice that the person authors their own existence, even overcoming death in a sense.

But is this merely a matter of will? The character faces a certain plight in narrative – how to react to the circumstances that hem him or her in, but the will never faces destiny simply and solely. Decision is of course the task of the will, but it is much more than merely the task of the will. The will could simply try and impose itself on the world it meets, but this would in the end change very little about the world. The will always has some object in view, and the character can decide to choose Good: the will makes no sense if it does not choose some object; on its own the will is senseless. The idea of an object of choice means of course that the will, in choosing, also thinks, using the reason, and also the reasoning of the heart. The act of the will is thus the act not just of part of a person, but the whole person, the whole character.

What the will chooses, narrative teaches us, will depend, to a large extent, on what it has chosen in the past. For the will, the expression at that moment of the character, the manifestation of the character, is formed like the character itself by the accretion of past choices and experiences. The selfish character will, on the whole, carry on being selfish, for each decision simply confirms that character in the selfish choice of acting they have always had. The generous person likewise will continue being generous. Hence the concern in narrative for the themes of childhood and education: early choices form later ones: the child is father of the man. But if this is all that is the case, this would mean that characters go forward like trains on fixed rails, turning neither to right or left, that character is fixed. But it is not so. Change, as opposed to mere development, is possible – even dramatic change. Hence the idea, also so common in narrative, of crisis and change of heart. But often the crisis will merely serve to bring the character to an awareness of what they knew already and suppressed. And here we see another important facet of character. We tend to live life on the surface, but characters have depths of which we may not be aware. Conversion, or revelation of what was known but hidden, is always possible.

Finally, what we have said rests on the idea that character is an not an illusion, that individuals are individual and do have a continuing personal history, an identity, which is immune to total disintegration despite the centripetal forces to which it may be subject. But it is precisely this that narrative proves, if the narrative makes sense, and is coherent: it tells us that human life is capable of meaning something and human experience is capable of coherence.

Just as we are immersed in time, we find ourselves too in space: this place, as opposed to that, here rather than there. Narrative is in this world, and aware of diverse places in this world. Often characters, being in one place, wish they were elsewhere: they feel a sense of exile and alienation from place. But place and setting are undeniable realities for all of us, and in this too narrative reflects life. As with time and plot, narrative reduces place to a manageable 'setting': a country, a town, a village, an island, even a ship at sea. Narratives of the closed sort never deal with the whole world directly but only with part of the world.

Narratives often treat our relationship to our environment, our setting. The human and animal and natural beings that surround us have an effect on us. It is assumed that setting forms our characters, our way of acting. Our relationship with our setting may be one of harmony or it may be one of alienation, or some point between the two. Characters may seek peace within their setting, or they may face a challenge to their settled sense of belonging. Reconciliation or dis-ease and disillusionment leading to change may be the conclusion of the narrative. This shows that our relationship with those who surround us is of vital importance to us. Narrative treats of the full range of sorts of environment that we can encounter: natural, animal, the built environment, the family. The closed narrative brings each of these into our personal world. Narrative is about characters coming into contact with a world not their own and being changed by the encounter, but at the same time mastering that which was previously alien. It is about the conquest of space, and its reduction to setting.

Setting establishes a world which is bound by a horizon. What lies beyond the horizon is not in our world. But what lies within the horizon is in our world, and is susceptible, by the very fact that it forms part of the narrative, to being meaningful for us. The story, by establishing this horizon, convinces us that what lies within the horizon is not the world, alien and other, but our world, knowable and ownable. Sometimes this may be a cruel illusion, and within the confines of the story there may lurk monsters of the like of which we have not dreamed. What may seem to be a safe, comfortable and closed world may turn out to be no such thing: but the story, as it unfolds, may teach us or show us how to tame these intrusive and alien elements.

So the device of setting, without which no story can function, or so it seems, enables us to impose meaning, or rather to find meaning in the world that surrounds us.

In everything we have discussed so far we have come across the idea of limit. To sum up: narrative is that which imposes a limit on the world of experience. In narrative we confront this person in this place at this time, doing this action for this reason. Narrative deals with the particular, the this, as opposed to the universal: all people, in all places at all times, doing all the things they might do. The human mind cannot comprehend the all, the infinite possibility: narrative tames the infinite, imposing limit, making it particular and comprehensible.

It is because the type of narrative we have been outlining here imposes limit that we have dubbed it the 'closed' model of narrative. We shall now look at its implications for theology, its advantages and drawbacks, as well as its presuppositions.

The First Model: Theology

This first model of narrative provides us with some important mental categories which are essential for moral theology, and underlying them, an equally essential epistemology.

This first 'closed' model assumes a continuity between the narrative and life. In other words, the narrative faithfully reflects lived reality, or at least faithfully reflects the readers' (or hearers') experience of reality. In hearing or reading the story, they recognize themselves in the story. Thus they judge the narrative to be true to life, and in that sense true, a true representation of life. The story has common elements (continuous elements) with their perceptions of life.

This basic perception, which makes the story interesting – in reading the story we are reading about ourselves – can be countered by a simple contrary argument which maintains that the story is in fact sheer make believe which bears no resemblance to reality at all. In other words, the narrative and the reality of the world are radically discontinuous.

Against this, we have argued so far that the closed narrative strongly suggests that the events that surround us are amenable to being ordered, that phenomena contain within them the seeds of their ordering; that this model of narrative shows us that time too is amenable to ordering and human understanding, that it is a continuum, not a mere jumble of moments; that this model of narrative presents us with lives that form a unity, and that it reduces the limitless to something that can be comprehended. All of these conclusions are broadly in agreement with those of David Carr. In an interesting article,[8] he discusses two opposing views about narrative. The first sees narrative as continuous with real life, as portraying reality, telling us about what did happen or what could have happened; the second, though, sees a radical discontinuity, maintaining that 'Real events simply do not hang together in a narrative way', which means that 'every narrative will present us with a distorted picture of the events it relates'.[9] One such exponent of the latter view is Louis Mink who claims that 'narrative structure, particularly the closure and configuration given to the sequence of events by a story's beginning, middle and end, is a structure derived from the act of telling the story, not from the events themselves.'[10] Likewise, Roland Barthes claims that art cannot represent life. Paul Ricoeur, meanwhile says that narrative synthesizes the heterogeneous,[11] which begs the question, one might think, as to how it does this, and surely suggests, as we have argued above, that the heterogeneous is amenable to being synthesized. But Carr maintains that this discontinuity theory is wrong and that life is not a mere sequence of unconnected events.[12] He says that 'The structure of action, small-scale and large, is common to art and life'. This in its turn disproves the thesis that 'ordinary life is a chaos of unrelated items'.[13] He goes on to say that a good story is selective, while real life is not. The story-teller knows the story, possesses the knowledge of what will happen and has an *ex post* standpoint that enables him or her to see the whole.[14] Thus the difference between

---

[8] David Carr, 'Narrative and the Real World: An Argument for Continuity', *History and Theory*, 25 (1986): 117–31.
[9] Carr, p. 117.
[10] Carr, p. 118.
[11] Carr, p. 119.
[12] Carr, p. 121.
[13] Carr, p. 122.
[14] Carr, p. 123.

story and life is a question of the point of view.[15] We all try to be the story-teller in our own lives, and thus to adopt a point of view that makes sense of the whole.[16] Carr concludes with the by now familiar points about the social nature of narrative and how narrative constitutes community.[17] But the main thrust of Carr's work is quite clear: there is continuity between narrative and real life; as we have already argued, narrative makes sense, and real life is at the very least amenable to being ordered. There is sense in events, and human beings can impose sense on events, because such sense is intrinsic to events. Our emphasis has been rather different to Carr's, but the conclusion is the same. Narrative and the real world, art and life, are continuous. This means that narrative is a way of discovering meaning in reality: it provides both story-teller and listener with a basic shared epistemology.

Thus, first and foremost, a narrative of the first model establishes meaning through the credibility of the story as continuous with life. In so far as this story is shared by the community, it establishes a group epistemology. The story held by the community acts as a shared basis for belief.

Beyond this important foundation, the narrative also provides us with important categories. The first of these is identity, emerging in time, yet impervious to it. This makes human responsibility possible: the things I did twenty or thirty years ago are my actions still: I cannot disown my past self or deny responsibility for my past self; and that past self informs my present and hints at my future to come. The idea that all times are eternally present in personal identity is a *sine qua non* of moral reasoning: by constructing narratives of our own lives and the lives of others, we are able to reflect on our experience and evaluate it. If the past were irredeemably lost, or the present an ungraspable split second, this would not be possible. So the structure of narrative provides an important tool for moral theology.

The phenomenon of narrative, through the concept of character, helps us think in terms of a moral theology of the first person, rather than the third. It brings us to an understanding of human beings. Moral norms are abstract but humanity is concrete and dynamic: narrative, through asking us to consider the figure of the protagonist, invites us to question the validity and appropriateness of abstract moral norms and to come to a deeper understanding of them through the stories we read and tell. Thus narrative invites a new approach to moral problems, not starting from the point of view of norms and their application, but from the actual vital situation of the human being who faces a moral dilemma.

Moral theology has traditionally been concerned with circumstance: the narrative asks us to consider characters in their setting and as springing from their setting and upbringing. Thus we are enabled to see moral dilemmas in their true context, without which their meaning may be deformed. The narrative isolates what is important, what is to be considered relevant to the case that is each character.

But 'dilemma' is not quite the right term in this context. A dilemma suggests the clash between two seemingly conflicting norms or calls of duty. This in itself suggests an already high degree of abstraction: the mental category of dilemma has

---

[15] Carr, p. 124.
[16] Carr, p. 125.
[17] Carr, pp. 127–8.

been imposed on the situation – it is a kind of narrative. But the truth of the matter may be that the person feels a pervasive unease about their life without any clear idea of why this should be the case. The categories of narrative may well help to tease the hidden significance out of this situation of angst. Indeed it is hard to see how any moral situation can be approached without some idea of the category of character.

From the above we see that the practice of story-telling in a community gives that community the ethical language that it needs in order to confront the world of ethics: the terms cause and effect, setting and circumstance, motive and character, are all narrative terms. In addition, a closed narrative performs the useful task of making a subject approachable by reducing it to manageable dimensions, by closing it off from other situations. In that the narrative excludes so much, it makes what it includes easily accessible. In so doing, the narrative presents an essential truth to the community that believes it, the belief that marks out the community's identity, its essential difference from those outside the community. The narrative, a closed reality, marks out the community as a closed space, a moral exclave. In a world where community identity is often threatened by centripetal forces, the narrative acts as a focus for unity.

The usefulness of this is not to be discounted in an ecclesial context. The narrative acts as a marker of Church membership and identity, against those forces which threaten such an identity. It acts in each retelling as a reinforcement of the Church's tradition as distinctive, even counter-cultural. It is an emblem of what makes the Church herself.

This strength, however, can also be a drawback, in that the narrative, particularist and closed as it is, making sense only to those who live it out in this particular community, nourished by this particular tradition, may also act as a barrier to those outside the exclave, shutting them out of the charmed circle of the story-telling and story-listening church. The outsider, though acknowledging the narrative to be continuous with reality, may not see it as necessarily so, and may choose not to accept the narrative, and thus to remain outside: for there is nothing in the narrative that compels acceptance. As the narrative dramatizes one piece of reality, one can legitimately ask: why this piece of reality? Why not some other piece? Why not all reality? The narrative of course presents all its hearers or readers with a choice – that of acceptance or not – but the choice is not necessarily compelling. Some may find the narrative fits with their experience of reality, and thus enter the Church, others may find the fit less than compelling, and decline the invitation. It depends on the consent of the individual hearer, whether they opt for Antioch, for example, or Rome. If the narrative's appeal is aesthetic, then it may well appeal to many, but it may equally repel others.

Here we see another drawback of the closed narrative: it depends on the willed consent of the hearers, those who may choose it – or not. As such it bears a resemblance with the improving literature of yesteryear. The narrative presents us, in moral terms, with a model of behaviour. We assent to the narrative when we find this behaviour admirable; and we make a further assent when we try to imitate this behaviour ourselves, adapting it to the circumstances of our own lives. Thus the will becomes central in our moral lives.

Wayne Booth writes of the idea, once very common, and still with us, that literature can improve one's character, just as bad literature can have a deleterious effect: his examples include *Northanger Abbey* and *Sanditon*. Catherine Morland can be 'saved' by judicious reading which will undo the damage done to her by the *Mysteries of Udolpho*. Literary figures are types who are advanced as models to be imitated, and this point was considered obvious to Jane Austen and her contemporaries.[18] Every reader can draw up their own list of characters from fiction-as-propaganda. One of the most famous examples in the English speaking world is *The Coral Island* by J. M. Ballantyne. Generations of boys when confronted with tricky situations doubtless asked themselves 'What would Jack, Ralph or Peterkin have done?' – until, of course, William Golding came and put paid to this dream of imperialist self-sufficiency in *Lord of the Flies*.

This model of reader reaction seems to accord with stories of the first type: they invite us to enter the closed world of the story and to identify with the characters therein. And here we see a serious theological problem, if we equate the story of Christ with the stories of heroes like Jack, Ralph and Peterkin.

The First Model: Reading the Narrative

The assent of the will to the story of Christ, such as that contained in numerous lives of Christ once so popular, is fraught with difficulty. James Gustafson sees the idea of the Christian conforming their life to the pattern of Christ's life as suggesting that the believer is trying to attain salvation, in this case conformity to Christ, through their own efforts.

> From Thomas à Kempis and William Law one gains the overwhelming impression that at the fundamental source of the Christian life, though not the exclusive source, is human striving towards the source of perfection… God's work in the cross is an 'assistance' and makes our achievement possible, for the work of the cross could not be more complete, and we are to rely on the 'subduing power of Christ'. But the seriousness with which the implications of this acknowledgement are taken is not great. Our own striving comes prior to the assistance from God; he helps those who work hard to earn his help. Thus the Christian life takes on a grim determination to achieve peace and happiness through self-mortification.[19]

Clearly Gustafson, working in the Protestant tradition, has difficulty with this, as it smacks of justification by works; but equally Catholics should feel uncomfortable with an idea that does not provide much room for grace. The story of God, in this scheme of things, becomes an adjunct, or even a postscript to the story of my own efforts to conform my life to Christ's. The personal narrative becomes the main focus. As Gustafson concludes: 'The goal becomes egocentric.'[20]

---

[18] Booth, pp. 227–35.
[19] Gustafson, p. 180.
[20] As above.

The objection outlined above will be applicable to what Hauerwas advances as 'the divine vocation to imitate God'[21] unless we intend the idea of *imitatio Christi* in the right way. It seems that our imitation must not be intended in the sense that Gustafson warns against. Quite apart from this theological objection, any sort of Pelagianism in this field will surely lead to eventual failure. One simply cannot become like Christ through a sheer effort of the will.

Again Gustafson warns us of making Christ 'primarily a pattern for a universally valid moral way of life', which distorts the meaning of Christ.[22] Not only are the gospels not primarily moral tracts, as Gustafson rightly says; in addition, the gospels are not reducible to 'closed' stories: they do not propose a system, but rather challenge the very idea of systemization. The Gospels offer a new type of relationship with God, in Jesus, as opposed to a new set of rules: 'The Christian life has its integrity in relation to God, and its moral concerns are grounded in that relation'.[23] To reduce Christ to a moral ideal is to miss much of his significance. Again, if we are to take the life of Christ as our paradigm, which Christ of the many are we to choose? What picture or story of Christ is appropriate, Gustafson asks?[24] In short, Gustafson's cautions remind us that when we propose the story of Jesus as *the* story (and we might add, any other story as *the* story) we do not mean to propose a story like any other story: Christ is not a figure from the past who is of foundational significance, and *imitatio Christi* is not to be seen in the guise of some sort of hero worship or cult of personality. Christ is not some admirable character from fiction like Jack, Ralph or Peterkin.

So, when we talk of conforming our own narratives to the narrative of Christ, we cannot mean, for want of a better term, a physical or actual conformation, one that is brought about through a naked act of the will. The morality of 'What would Jesus have done?' is a mistaken morality. Naturally, one reads the Bible in the hope it will have some improving moral effect on one, and this is a deeply rooted idea, but the story of Christ as contained in the Gospels is not to be confused with pious 'improving' literature, the various lives of Christ in particular, that have often taken its place. To do so would be to reduce Christ to the level of an instrument of moral coercion. It is for all these reasons that one must disagree with Navone when he speaks of the re-enactment of the Jesus-story by successive approximations.[25] Quite simply, the Jesus-story cannot be re-enacted by mere human beings: that is to ask the impossible.

---

[21] *The Hauerwas Reader*, p. 123.
[22] Gustafson, p. 182.
[23] Gustafson, p. 183. One notes however, the opposite view from James McClendon in his book *Biography as Theology: How Life Stories can remake Today's Theology* (New York: Abingdon Press, 1974): 'Whatever difficulties scholars may find in the re–creation of the chronological biography of Jesus, his character is a touchstone of Christian life.' He refers to Paul's letter to the Philippians to back this up (Phil 2: 5 et seq.) (p. 33). But this misses the point, namely that the Jesus of the Bible is not a character like any other and he does not have a biography in the same way as other historical characters, simply because he is not a 'historical character', though in history, for he transcends history.
[24] Gustafson, p. 181.
[25] Navone, pp. 89–90.

How then are we to understand the concept of *imitatio Christi* in the context of stories of this first type? Clearly reading about Christ, reading the Christ-story, is not a bad thing in itself. It is good for us to be engaged by the story of Christ. The re-telling of the story of Jesus in a way that is accessible and interesting is a task of major importance for the Church.

Every narrative to be a success must win the interest of the reader: if we are bored by the story, we put down the book, and that story never gets told. Wesley A. Kort writes that we must be receptive to the work in order 'fully to enter it'.[26] The reader is engaged by a text: the text is addressed to them, they address themselves to the text: the text is the place where a meeting of minds takes place. The young Augustine had little in common with Aeneas, but he loved to hear of his adventures; we all (or nearly all) love adventures, for however sedentary our occupations, there is something of the adventuring spirit left in us all. The heroic character speaks to the hero that lurks within us all. In other words, in a successful story, the reader identifies[27] themselves with a character: that character's trials and tribulations become, for the space of the book, his own. This is how we 'enter' the world of the book, through the power of the imagination. In one lifetime we lead many lives[28] through the power of the shaping spirit of the imagination, and we build for ourselves many worlds, for 'narratives create their own power and meaning'.[29] This world of meaning becomes our own and we lead (hopefully) vivid interior lives. Thus reading the story of Christ, or any other hero, helps us to understand the life of Christ at the level of the imagination, and this is not be dismissed. The facts of the life of Christ may have a profound effect on the reader if they are appropriated imaginatively in this way. Because of this the Church has traditionally acknowledged the importance of art as a means of evangelization: the picture, the poem, and nowadays the film, can speak of Christ in a profound and moving way.

Through their imaginations, believers enter the world of the Gospels. In prayer and attentive reading, they absorb their atmosphere. But the truth of the matter is, as much as they pray and read, they will never be able to travel back in time to first century Galilee. They live in their own time, and live their own lives. Thus 'identification with Christ' is a phrase always to be treated with caution.

The imaginative appropriation of the Gospel world is in fact a symbiosis which is feasible with any historical or literary figure; it is a constant part of the Christian life, but it is not all the Christian life has to offer. Entering the story must mean far more than this; though the imagination will be part of it, it will not be its essential part. Thus while we can acknowledge that the closed story that asks for assent does have a useful function to play in a community, and even in the community of the Church, we also see the limits of this model of narrative. It is ultimately Pelagian in tendency,

---

[26] Kort, p. 12.

[27] Realistic fiction entices the reader into role playing; through identification we forget our selves and identify with other selves. It is thus we involve ourselves in the plot. Thus Detweiler, p. 8.

[28] Detweiler, p. 7. These many roles that we play prove that the self is not monolithic, an important point.

[29] Kort, p. 18.

as well as being particularist. We now wish to examine a second model, which builds on the first, but goes much further.

The Second Model: The Narrative with a Permeable Limit

In considering the first model, we have noticed the idea of limit. In the second model we shall now consider that the idea of limit remains, but it becomes permeable, that is to say, the narrative is no longer to be understood as absolutely or entirely limited. What exactly do we mean by this? What is the structure of a story of this second type?

First of all, as we have seen, a character in narrative finds themselves bound by time, place and setting. We are this person, not all the persons in the world. We live in a concrete situation: our possibilities are limited, and yet within the limit imposed by the story, our possibilities are infinite. This is not a contradiction. The lack of physical freedom does not impede our moral freedom. We remain free to choose how to respond to the situation in which we find ourselves. In other words the world that bounds us in does not take away our ability to make of that world the world of our choosing. Circumstances do affect us, but despite this we are not determined in a moral sense, but free.

Likewise the character is in one place, but this one place, howsoever restricted, may well stand for the whole. My village, ship, island or town may in fact be a microcosm of the world. This suggests strongly that my experience as a character in this place will have parallels amongst other characters in other places. The particular can be general. Indeed, it would be hard to see the appeal of narrative unless this were so. Few would want to read about particular experience in particular closed spaces unless this had some application to us as well. Thus the closed space can sometimes be taken as a sort of laboratory, a place in which results are obtained that may hold good for other cases as well.[30]

Moreover, being aware of limit, we are also aware that limit is limit, and that beyond it lies the unlimited. That which is defined is defined against a background of the infinite. Nothing comes to us as purely limited: everything comes to us carrying with it the hint of eternity. A single thing, a single word, may define something, but coupled with that definition, it may carry with it the hint of what lies beyond what is defined. Likewise, a work of art, a narrative, may have a particular meaning, in time and place, but this meaning is not confined to time and place, but goes beyond them, having a universal validity, for all times and places. Some works of art, some

---

[30] It is not hard to think of some very clear examples. Jane Austen's novels are mainly restricted to closed communities but this does not mean that they are without general interest: indeed, the closed community forms a world that reflects the wider world. Two famous novels take an island and treat it as a microcosm of the world – R.M. Ballantyne's *The Coral Island* and William Golding's *Lord of the Flies* – with startlingly different results. Both are trying to say something about human nature which transcends mere place and circumstance.

stories, may be 'classics' and their meaning may overflow their particular setting in which they were first told.[31]

Narrative, as we have said, gives accessible form to human experience. It tells us what oft was thought but ne'er so well expressed: but beyond the form of narrative lies that from which narrative was hewn in the first place, namely the vast unlimited mass of human perception. It is against this background that every narrative is to be understood.

Our discussion so far has fixed on certain common features in narratives of the closed variety. We have spoken of 'well-made' books and plays, and mentioned in passing the concept of 'realistic' literature. But these are broad-brush terms that are of limited use, and there are many types of narrative to which they do not apply. While some narratives, the closed types, may suggest that all ends may be tied up, others suggest that beyond the limits of the narrative, there lie things that cannot be systematized into any narrative, things that go beyond our ability to understand: these things cast their shadow on the content of the narrative and call it into question. The narrative, that of the second type that we are discussing here, assumes its meaning not only from what it says about reality, but also from what is passed over in silence as lying beyond the narrative's limits but which can nevertheless not be ignored.

To help us understand this, we must invoke the concept of a horizon of meaning. Every story, however complex or simple, involves the idea of limit, as we have said, and this in turn depends on a horizon of meaning, that is to say a set of concepts without which the story is incomprehensible. The tale of Cinderella makes no sense unless first we accept the basic *données* of the situation: the existence of weak fathers, ugly sisters and fairy godmothers, not to mention princes who give balls and fall so easily in love. To question the plausibility of any of these elements is to destroy the story. To ask why Cinderella did not leave home and become a stenographer is to destroy the story. Such a question makes no sense within the horizon of meaning of the tale. Thus to enter into the world of the story we need to grasp first a set of concepts which go to make up the world of the story. We need to suspend our disbelief as Aristotle would put it; in other words to abandon, albeit for a short time, our own world, and enter into another world, that of the tale. Clearly, to enjoy *Cinderella*, we have to put to one side many of our preconceptions about social life. The story is not 'realistic' in the normal sense of the word. It employs a different horizon of meaning.

At the same time, Cinderella's audience are aware that beyond the horizon of meaning they have imposed on themselves for the duration of the story lies another world, the world in which, in fact, girls do leave home to become stenographers. Beyond the horizon of meaning of the particular story is a wider horizon of meaning that is personal to the audience. Thus the audience may well have a particular idea of justice, and hearing the story of Cinderella they may well seethe with anger at

---

[31] David Tracy is one writer who has developed this idea through what he calls the idea of a classic. See his 'Theological Classics in Contemporary Theology', pp. 347–57. A classic has a particular origin, but it discloses meaning and truth in a way that is accessible, in principle to all human beings; it is public and never private, he says (p. 349). An example of this is the work of Dante which transcends its origins in fourteenth-century Florence (p. 350). A classic challenges our horizons, confronting them and transforming them (p. 352).

the unjust way she is treated by her ugly sisters; they may even think that the happy ending is not so happy after all, and that Cinderella sells herself short by settling for Prince Charming. They may further be saddened by the knowledge that the world does not contain fairy godmothers, ever ready to intervene in the name of justice. The resonance of the story for its audience depends on the echo created by the gap between the story's horizon of meaning and their own horizon of meaning. This explains why the story will have a different impact according to the culture and preconceptions of its audience. For not only is there Cinderella *tout court* as enjoyed by children, there is also the Marxist Cinderella, the story of the oppressed; the feminist Cinderella, which may sympathize with the ugly sisters who are victims of 'lookism'; the Catholic Cinderella, a story of redemption, and many others besides.[32]

The existence of a horizon of meaning peculiar to the audience also explains why some stories may arouse bafflement and incomprehension, because the horizon of meaning on which they depend has been lost. Everyone loves Shakespeare's *Romeo and Juliet*: that world, the world of teenage love, is still a real world, its horizon of meaning is still with us. The story has been successfully transposed to Belfast and New York. But hardly anyone outside a university has any time for *Titus Andronicus*: the tragedy of blood and the honour code of revenge simply have no meaning in our society today, though one can but note that cannibalism has a perennial fascination.

Every narrative that we have examined so far depends on a horizon of meaning: a set of preconditions and suppositions without which the story has no meaning. The narrative implicit in the Aristotelian city state includes gentlemen who are given to *theoria*, but it excludes women, idiots and slaves. It makes no provision for universal human rights – that lies outside the horizon of meaning. The religious narrative of Engelhardt relies on the insights of the Greek Fathers, but leaves Augustine to one side. A horizon of meaning includes certain things and excludes others. Even Rawls, who tends to universalism, must exclude those who do not accept his difference principle, those whose religious or other beliefs involve the violation of human rights: certain creeds will wither away, or at least not flourish, in a Rawlsian society. Thus a horizon of meaning can be defined two ways: in accordance with what is included, and in accordance with what is excluded, by what lies within the horizon, and by what lies beyond it.

What emerges here is a prejudice, if we can call it that, for the widest possible horizon of meaning. A narrative may have a particular restricted horizon of meaning, but the audience has a double horizon of meaning: that of the particular narrative, and that which they use to evaluate the particular narrative. A story makes sense internally, and we make sense of it externally when we judge it according to our own horizon of meaning. An example: Aristotle's world makes perfect sense for Aristotle, but it makes only limited sense for Susan Moller Okin,[33] who points out that this world makes no provision for women and children. Ms Okin, with her views

---

[32] For a discussion of the huge variety of retellings of the tale see Barbara Herrnstein Smith, 'Narrative versions, Narrative Theories', in *On Narrative*, edited by W.J.T. Mitchell (Chicago and London: University of Chicago Press, 1981), pp. 209–32, especially p. 211.

[33] Okin, p. 55 et seq.

on the rights of women and children, has a wider horizon of meaning (at least on this question) than Aristotle, to whom the question of female emancipation would have made no sense at all, lying as it did beyond his horizon of meaning. But we stand with Okin and not with Aristotle; we read Aristotle's narrative with twenty-first century eyes, and we see its limits. Thus between Aristotle and Okin we see a widening of the horizon, by bringing women and children into the city state and the question of justice. This is not to say, however, that the perspective of Okin is *the* perspective, and that she has the last word on the matter. There remains more to be said. A city state that makes provision for the rights of women and children is a better city state than Aristotle's but it is not the perfect city state: all city states are in process of becoming. For beyond Okin's perspective lies the infinite horizon, and the suspicion, surely well grounded, that there is always more to be said about justice.

In fact we have already 'proved' this point, in our earlier discussion of supererogatory acts that are defined as beyond justice. The Good Samaritan, indeed the Splendid Samaritan, goes beyond what anyone could reasonably expect, beyond the prescriptions of law. Thus we have a triple perspective in this case which can be pictured thus: the limited horizon of the particular narrative which says help those who form part of your family or tribe; the wider perspective that urges us to universal justice on the Rawlsian model; and finally the infinite perspective that urges us to go beyond justice. Just as the justice of the city state is put into perspective by the wider call of Rawlsian justice, so Rawlsian justice too is rendered relative by the infinite call of supererogatory acts. As we practice Rawlsian Justice (as envisaged by Judith Jarvis Thomson) we become aware that even this is not enough.

Are we then in a hall of mirrors, the reflections of which regress to infinity? In a sense, yes. Every act of knowing is made against the infinite horizon, which is the precondition of all knowledge.[34] Every limit imposed by a story's structure is to some extent permeable, at least in stories of the second model.

Now we are in a position to clarify and distinguish between narratives of the second and first model. Narratives of the first model propose a closed horizon of meaning; it is possible that a person may hold several such narratives at one time, without experiencing contradictions between them. Each narrative will exist in a watertight compartment of its own. However, at some point the watertight or sealed narrative may be challenged in some way, and the holder of the narrative may become aware that the previously impenetrable barrier has become permeable: one may become aware of something that lies beyond the horizon, and challenges the previous limit.

Augustine's allegiance to the Roman Empire and his allegiance to the doctrine of the Manichees represent narratives of the first model, for both are closed worlds. His espousal of Platonism, however, represents a narrative of the second model, which challenges and modifies his allegiance to Rome, and overthrows his allegiance to the Manichees. For Platonism is not a closed narrative; even less so is citizenship of the City of God, which represents a new identity, a new mode of being and relating. He does more than just change from one closed narrative to another: the two narratives

---

[34] A point we shall develop later with the help of Karl Rahner.

are qualitatively different. The first has a closed horizon of meaning, the second has a horizon of meaning that is permeable.

We now wish to look at the structure of these stories of the second type in some detail, distinguishing them from stories of the first type.

Discussing the role of narrative in *After Virtue*, MacIntyre has the following to say:

> It is through hearing stories about wicked stepmothers, lost children, good but misguided kings, wolves that suckle twin boys, youngest sons who receive no inheritance but must make their own way in the world and eldest sons who waste their inheritance on riotous living and who go into exile to live with the swine, that children learn or mislearn both what a child and what a parent is, what the cast of characters may be in the drama into which they have been born and what the ways of the world are… Mythology, in its original sense, is at the heart of things.[35]

These tales, generally called fables or fairy stories, or what MacIntyre calls 'mythology in its original sense', are not, to use a broad-brush term, 'realistic': that is to say, they do not use plot, time, character and setting in the same way as narratives of the first model.

These stories are not of this earth in the first place: fairy tales exist in a parallel universe, a landscape that is both like but not like our own. Yet, despite this, or perhaps because of it, for MacIntyre's point is surely a valid one, we learn about our own world through reading tales about a world quite different to our own. These tales exist within a horizon of meaning quite alien to our own, and yet they still speak to us. Such themes as love and duty and heroism and sacrifice resonate with us, despite (or perhaps because of) the magical setting. The fairy tale is not of our world, and yet its very appeal rests on the fact that it speaks to us, from an infinitely remote place, about our world.

Just as the fairy tale is set in a remote place, and through the telling of the story makes that place accessible to us, it is set too in a time that is not ours, the time of 'once upon a time'. It makes no sense to try and place Snow White or Cinderella in their historical context. They are outside time in so far as anyone can be outside time – which is to say that their stories are for all time, just as they are for all places. These stories speak to us of timeless truths, things that recur throughout human experience. The figure of the wicked stepmother is hardly a historical phenomenon, but she speaks to us of a human truth (the possibility of unkindness) that is a constant in human history.

So fairy tales, as narratives of the second model, challenge the idea of limit, while engaging our interest. They speak to us, yet they are not of our world. We have to ask just how this is possible. What is the bridge of understanding that links us, rooted as we are in time and place, characters that we are, with people who are unlike ourselves and beyond any time and place that could possibly be familiar to us? How can what is so unlike speak to us in this way and seem like? This question, which seems so sharply thrown into relief through the examination of fairy stories, is also valid for other types of story too, which are half way between the realistic

---

[35] MacIntyre, *After Virtue*, p. 216.

and the unrealistic. Why are we interested in hearing about Hamlet or Romeo and Juliet when their worlds are remote from our own, when we ourselves will never find ourselves in situations similar to theirs? Why should the story of a prince deprived of his inheritance who meets the ghost of his father urging him to revenge resonate with us, who are not princes and who are far from the conventions of the revenge code? Why should we be interested in a couple of teenage lovers who live in a world where a friar dispenses almost magical potions? One possible answer is because these stories encapsulate values that endure: Hamlet is every confused young man trying to come to terms with an environment that he did not choose, Romeo and Juliet stand for everyone who has ever been in love. But this answer only takes us so far. We need to work out a proper theory of Everyman if we are to try and understand the appeal of narrative.

Does Everyman exist? The narrative of Rawls assumes that he does, and that there are stories that fit not just a certain set of individuals at a certain time, but which fit the whole of humanity, and which are universally true. But is this figure of Everyman a useless concept, an illusion? Or does the idea of Everyman constitute a useful idea in moral theology? Again much depends on this, simply because if the concept of Everyman is an empty one, then there can be no concepts of universal validity in moral theology, or indeed in any type of theology. That universalism is a chimera is of course the view of Engelhardt and Hauerwas, but we see in Rawls the Kantian prejudice that what is true must be universally true if it is to be true at all.

Once again we see a bifurcation in the way: some of the authors we have looked at see narrative as rooted, historical and particular, rather than universalist in import. These are narratives of the first type. The story is this story, our story, rather than the story of Everyman. But at the same time even a passing acquaintance with the world of narrative alerts us to another phenomenon, narrative of the second type, which suggests something altogether different and more interesting, namely the way narratives can cross boundaries. Great stories are timeless and universal. That some things never go out of fashion is a sign that there are universal truths.[36] But at the same time universal truths are discerned through history; in other words, experience is always historical but it is not just historical.[37] The truths gleaned through experience can permeate the limit imposed by time and place and history itself. The self, the 'I' stands rooted in their living environment, but is at the same time open to what lies beyond it and 'above' it. Like a character in a novel, they are aware that this is the story, but at the same time this is not the only story.

Narratives of the second model traverse boundaries and point not to a closed horizon of meaning, but a permeable one. Though they may start with a character whose story seems to be earthbound, rooted in time and place, they also point to universal truths, things that are valid for all times and all places. We have already dealt with examples of such stories. Augustine's *Confessions* are set in time and place, and the social setting can be deduced from what we read; but Thagaste, Carthage, Rome and Milan, though real places, are not the primary focus of the story, and the story is not a novel. The real locus of the action is the heart of Augustine

---

[36] Just this is what Stephen Crites suggests. Form is not accidental, he says (p. 291).
[37] Goldberg, p. 60, for a brief discussion of this problem, but in a different key.

and it is this that makes the story the story of Everyman, because what holds true for the man of Thagaste holds true for all people everywhere. Augustine's biography is the occasion for the story, but it is not the story itself. The real story rises above the particular, and reaches for the universal.

The Second Model: Theology

Just as closed narratives of the first model perform a useful function in theology, indeed an essential one, pointing to the innate rationality of the world, narratives of the second type, which build on and expand what narratives of the first model achieve, also play a useful role.

First of all, because theology and moral theology in particular is in a state of becoming, the concept of a horizon of meaning, which is essential to understanding narrative, can also enlighten our understanding of theology. For this concept makes us aware of the continuing challenge that the call to do good presents to us; and it also makes clear to us the necessity of progress in moral theology.

Ethical questions can (and sometimes must) be understood within a closed horizon of meaning. When confronted with a case like that of Judith Jarvis Thompson's Famous Violinist, we can ask what are the demands of justice in the case, understanding the rights and duties involved in a sense limited by the closed narrative of the Famous Violinist. Our obligation to do something is bound, perhaps, by the circumstances in which we find ourselves, by the nature of the act we are contemplating, by our understanding of the consequences of that act – the so called *fontes moralitatis*. Furthermore, our duty to act may be circumscribed by our physical capacity to do so, and by the urgency of other duties that present themselves to us at that moment. Thus the right thing to do may be the result of a balancing of possible resultant goods from rival courses of action. But this is only possible if we see the 'story' before us as something limited by a closed horizon of meaning. If we perceive that horizon as permeable we may find that our initial response is inadequate. The morality of the situation changes radically in accordance with the horizon we impose on the situation. Once we introduce into the story the concept that justice is not to be confused with the rules of justice alone, then the story presents us with a challenge that cannot be answered within the confines of the story. This is an example of a closed story breaking down: in other words a story of the first model becoming one of the second.

Stories of the second type and those of the first frequently co-exist side by side; a story of the first type can develop into one of the second type, and one of the second type can degenerate into one of the first. A historical example of this can be seen in the developing attitudes to slavery and the morality of slave-holding. St Paul, a citizen of the Roman Empire, saw nothing wrong with the institution of slavery; indeed he accepted it; this should not surprise us, for within the closed narrative of the Roman Empire, slavery made perfect sense. It is only when this narrative's limits become permeable, and the rival narrative of universal human rights breaks in (which was a remarkably late development) that slavery *per se* (as opposed to the question of the treatment of slaves) is open to question and eventually becomes unsustainable.

The existence of narratives of the second model must convince us then of the fact that every position we hold is a position capable of development; the story marks a conclusion that is provisional, but as its limit is permeable, this provisional conclusion is always open to further development.

This points to a different type of ecclesiology to that outlined when talking of closed stories. While the latter serve to reinforce group identity and apartness, open stories serve to remind the Church of the wider picture and the necessity of dialogue with the world and all people of good will. Our story exists alongside other stories which are also coherent, and must take account of them, even if it is only to reject them in the end. Dialogue, then, is not simply a favour one does to those outside the exclave: it is vital for the moral health of those inside the exclave. Indeed the exclave should be understood not as a closed city, but as an open one, constantly open to fertilization by outside influences: though those wedded to the first model of closed stories will often see those outside influences as infections that threaten the body of the Church.

Also of note for a narrative theology that bases itself on the second model of narrative is that the second model requires a different type of rationality to the first. The first model asks for the consent of the will, which may be arbitrary or not. The more arbitrary the consent, the less likely it is to be durable. But the second model asks for an altogether more sophisticated response.

The second model asks us to consider two things at once: first, it asks us to consider the people in the story, their particular characteristics; and secondly, it asks us to make a bridge between the particular, as exposed in the story, and the universal, that which exists beyond the story's limit, and which is hinted at by the permeable nature of that limit. In *Hamlet*, Shakespeare asks us to consider the particular world of Elsinore and that there is something rotten in the state of Denmark, while at the same time inviting us to consider the wider world, and the universality of human experience that the Prince epitomizes. Likewise a religious narrative may ask us to consider the nature of the Church and the nature of the world which 'lies beyond' the frontier of the ecclesial narrative; this frontier being permeable, the narrative asks us to consider the Church in the light of the world's experience, and, vice versa, the Church as light of the world. This involves a form of reasoning that is more complicated than the mere consent involved in the first model.

Such reasoning will progress in particular and concrete terms, but it will also have to think in universal terms as well;[38] such reasoning will start with the particular and concrete, but it will not end there. Essential to the reasoning process will be the ability to make connections between the two and to give reasons for the connections one makes, to be able to justify oneself, to make oneself accountable to oneself and others, for one will be engaged in a dialogue not just with those who are within

---

[38] For the universal nature of thought, see Immanuel Kant, *Foundations of the Metaphysics of Morals*, translated by Lewis White Beck (New York: Bobbs-Merrill, 1959), p. 53.

one's narrative, but also with those outside it. This reasoning process will be the foundation of dialogue and indeed friendship.

Reason weighs beliefs in the balance and evaluates them, and is prepared to discard that which seems untenable. It does so by seeing connections and grasping relationships.[39] If X is true, then Y must follow. Thus reason is able to grasp matters such as cause and effect, condition and what is conditioned. It can also see how the relative depends on the absolute, the caused on the uncaused, and the conditioned on the unconditioned. In other words, reason is the capacity to relate objects to the absolute, to judge contingent things against norms that are absolute, necessary and universal. Narrow-mindedness and bias will militate against reason, for reason deals with that which is universal. In the terms of this discussion: reason is the ability to see how what is inside the story is related to what lies beyond the story's limit. To insist on a closed story in the face of overwhelming evidence that the story is indeed not closed after all, is to deny the reality of reason.

In other words, reason is the ability to do two things: to see how things connect, to explain their 'why', to show how one thing has led to another, how one state of affairs has entailed another state of affairs. But it is also the ability to see things against their background, which is another way of forming connections, to see how the particular is a manifestation of the general, to see how the concrete example is connected to the absolute. To do this, of course, it is necessary to do two other things as well: first of all, one must be aware that one's own narrative is not the only narrative, but exists in a world of narratives and against the background of a universal absolute narrative; and secondly, one must adopt a certain critical distance from one's own narrative (this second condition will depend to some extent on the first), ridding oneself of bias and partiality, in so far as this is possible.

Thus we see that reasoning using the second model of narrative involves closeness and distance at the same time. This is something that MacIntyre sees as desirable, and so does Rawls: the moral person is one who acts in purity of heart, in the Rawlsian phrase, and it is the story itself that helps us to achieve purity of heart. It does this by objectifying our circumstances and then inviting us to look at those circumstances in the light of the truths that lie beyond the limit of the story, so that we may re-evaluate them.

The story is a distancing device: asking us to listen to a story, the author asks us to enter a world that is familiar, perhaps, but not our own world; in other words to think about things at one remove. The story also introduces us to the fact that there are many stories and that my own story is only one among the many. Perhaps most importantly, what opens up for me amidst the multiple vistas of narrative, is the idea of absolute value, for the particular points to the general, and the many to the one. I am thus able to see how I, in my here and now state, relate to that which is universal, necessary and true. In other words, the story presents me with the challenge presented by universal values, and asks me how my own story typifies those universal values.

Clearly a story of the second model will require an act of the imagination so that one can enter its world, and an act of the will, but these of themselves are not

---

[39] In this paragraph we follow some of the points made by Joseph de Finance, *An Ethical Enquiry* (Rome: Editrice Pontificia Universitas Gregoriana, 1991), pp. 186–8.

sufficient. A story of the second type also requires some sort of moral commitment, and such a commitment does not come about through the imagination alone, though the imagination will certainly nurture and encourage our commitment. To enter the world of Cinderella, we have to blame the Ugly Sisters and her weak father; to enter the story of the Original Position we have to accept the principle of an overriding human dignity and worth. We cannot will morality into being, as we have said before, still less imagine it into being. If this were true, then it would simply be a question of making up the story that best fits us and sticking with that, until such a time as we change our minds, and one story really would be as good as another.

What rescues us from this tail-chasing is the fact that the story is prior to us and to other stories. We did not make it up, it makes us up. Again Kort says that the creative act implies a judgement on the situation prior to the act:[40] from which we can deduce that the creative act – such as reading[41] – is not a creation *ex nihilo*. The form of the story is prior to us, as Crites maintains.[42] The story of the second model at least hints that in the story we find something that is prior to ourselves, something that we do not make up, but rather discover. As we have already seen, this was our conclusion with Rawls, whose Original Position exemplifies a story of the second model.

The Third Model: The Open Narrative

Having seen how the first two models work, and how the second model moves beyond the restrictions imposed by limit in the first model, we now wish to go further and examine a third model, one which we will characterize as the narrative that is open not just to other narratives, but to infinity itself.

The Bible presents us with stories of this kind. It is a mistake to try and read the Bible as if it were a novel, a closed narrative. Adam and Eve are types, not characters, Eden is a situation rather than a place. Likewise, though Galilee is a real place, and Jerusalem too, Jesus is not a character like any other, and his inner life remains stubbornly beyond us: it is hinted at but never revealed. The figure of the Lord is of universal, cosmic significance, his suffering and death are events that transcend time and place but embrace the whole of human history. They happen in history, but go beyond it. They represent the irruption into history of something that is before all history and beyond it too. Any attempt to read the Gospels as a 'realistic' novel kill their meaning. One can speculate about the exact relationship Jesus had with Mary Magdalene or with Judas but in so doing one misses the point of the Gospel narrative. It is for this reason that Gerard Loughlin talks of the story of Jesus as being 'absolutely prior'.[43] It is not a story, it is *the* story.

But what we have outlined above may seem to be the product of wishful thinking. One can easily argue that the Biblical stories are closed narratives, products of their time and place, and only to be understood by entering the mindset that created them, which may be very hard to do: for how is a twenty-first century reader to enter the

---

[40] Kort, p. 5.
[41] Kort, p. 12.
[42] Crites, p. 291.
[43] Loughlin, p. x.

world of the writer of the Psalter? Or else one can argue that the stories of the Bible are of the second type, stories with a permeable limit: time and place bound, yet capable of relating to us now in a very different world, capable of being transposed thanks to 'lines of persistence'. However, even purity of heart may well not be enough to discover such lines. But if we are to argue further to these positions that the stories in the Bible are revelatory of infinity, we shall have to advance a particular theory as to how this is done.

Karl Rahner claims that there are great scenes in literature which burst the confines of the story, pointing to truths that go beyond time and place which cannot be reduced to mere words or a structured story, a didactic passage in a novel as such. We have in scenes of this quality what Rahner calls 'the silent mystic presence of the nameless'. He writes:

> Now, strictly speaking, every word that is really a word, and strictly speaking, only the word has the power of naming the nameless. No doubt, the word expresses, designates and distinguishes, demarcates, defines, compares, determines and arranges. But as it does this, he who has ears, he who can see (here all the senses of the spirit are one) experiences something totally different: the silent, mystic presence of the nameless. For that which is named is conjured up by the word. And so it advances from the encompassing, quiet and silent source from which it arises and where it remains secure; that which is described and distinguished by the word, by the distinctive name, combines with the other as it is distinguished from it, in the unity which comprises the comparable and akin, and so points silently back to the one origin, loftier than both, which can indeed preserve both unity and distinction in one. The word puts individual things in order, and so always points to a fundamental background order which cannot itself be ordered but remains the perpetual *a priori* antecedent to all order. One can miss all this when one hears words. One can be deaf to the fact that the clear spiritual sound can only be heard when one has first listened to the silence beyond each distinct sound...[44]

This passage of Rahner is certainly dense! But there is much that is at stake here. As far as Rahner is concerned, and we would have to agree, no word stands alone; each word resonates against a horizon of meaning that is infinite, and that lies beyond culture. Each word summons up a mystery, something greater than itself, and it is only against this greater thing, that the particular word has meaning. So, any tragic scene only makes sense, only has meaning against a cosmic pathos: the particular only resonates because we are aware at the same time of the general and the universal. The essence of pathos transcends the particular example, and the particular example alerts us to the existence of the transcendent reality: we move beyond the horizon of the particular to perceive a wider horizon that embraces all humanity. The essence of the scene, as in all true literature, is more than the sum of its parts.

There is always something 'more' in literature,[45] something that goes beyond the bare meaning of the words of the story as such. Rahner speaks of the use of *Urworte* in poetry, but this may be applied to prose as well.

---

[44] Karl Rahner, 'Poetry and the Christian', in *Theological Investigations*, vol. 4 (London: Darton, Longman and Todd, 1966), pp. 358–9.

[45] Keane, p. 15.

> In every primordial word [*Urwort*] there is signified a piece of reality in which a door is mysteriously opened for us into the unfathomable depths of true reality in general. The transition from the individual to the infinite in infinite movement, which is called by thinkers the transcendence of the spirit, itself belongs to the content of the primordial word: it is the soft music of the infinite movement of the spirit and the love of God, which begins with some small thing of this earth, which is seemingly only the thing that is meant by this word. Primordial words (as one might explain it to the theologian) have always a literal meaning and an intellectual-spiritual meaning, and without the latter the verbal sense itself is no longer what is really meant. They are words of an endless crossing of borders, therefore words on which in some way our salvation depends.[46]

Thus any genre opens up more than can be comfortably delineated in a neat definition. Tragedy, to put it bluntly, is more than a story with an unhappy ending, or a tale with a moral. The story's moral goes beyond the actual situation it describes, opening up a door to transcendence: the words start with the particular, but point to the infinite; they cross borders.

Rahner has something of interest to say to us about the seemingly atheistic literature of the twentieth century.

> Even in cases where Christianity is explicitly or implicitly denied, or seems to be so in the course of pursuing this aim to express existence as a totality, caution is required in coming to a judgement on this. A statement such as this which sounds like a denial and perhaps actually is one, can nevertheless be an expression of a new situation for the Christian and for Christendom as a whole which is unfamiliar and which has not yet been brought under control. Such a statement can be the false or inadequate explanation and interpretation of a quest for the fullness of life which is, nevertheless, under God's blessing, Christian.[47]

What Rahner is *not* saying is that a seemingly atheist author asserts what they attempt to deny. The key concept here is 'totality': every piece of literature, every story tries, *qua* work of art, to give a picture of totality. Every story has a beginning, a middle an end, in short a structure, and a certain unity of tone, if it is to be a success. Some works of art may give a picture of a world which is totally deprived of good, and which bears not a shred of comfort, a world which can only be escaped via death (what we have called a closed story of the first type). This sort of world is all too familiar to us, alas, in the totalitarian horrors of the twentieth century. But is such totality – which may be unfamiliar, and truly not yet under control – yet so total? For we may encounter in such a scene words which blow apart the nihilistic totality of the scene. These are akin to Rahner's *Urworte*, 'the primordial words that reveal the mystery'.[48] What this brings us back to is the central datum of transcendental philosophy, expressed thus:

---

[46] Karl Rahner, 'Priest and Poet', in *Theological Investigations*, vol. 8 (London: Darton, Longman and Todd, 1967), pp. 294–317, p. 298.
[47] Karl Rahner, 'The Task of the Writer in Relation to Christian Living', in *Theological Investigations*, vol 8 (London: Darton, Longman and Todd, 1971), pp. 112–29, p. 118.
[48] Rahner, 'Priest and Poet', p. 296.

The simple fact that we affirm in every act of knowledge, namely, that every individual act of knowledge is possible only within an infinite process which will never be ended from our side; this simple fact tells us again and again that what we know lives by what lies beyond our knowledge, that our comprehension lives by the power of what is incomprehensible.[49]

In other words the incomprehensibility of tragedy has as its necessary background all that is good, beautiful and comforting. Furthermore, there are simple human facts that blow apart the totalizing system which is the enemy of alterity and morality in the philosophy of Emmanuel Levinas, the reminder that the human person, always other, transcends all totalization.

The remarks of Rahner, briefly reviewed here, make the important point that, though coherent, narrative can move beyond mere coherence to point to something that transcends it. Or to put it into Levinasian terms, the story is cultural, but it points to some truth beyond itself that is before all culture.[50] There is a story to be told about people, but they deny us the possibility of putting them in a totalizing system. Or as Augustine says, man is an abyss,[51] a question to himself. The story, well told, makes us aware of the abyss, aware of the question. This is a useful corrective to the view that one might deduce from a superficial reading of Hauerwas and MacIntyre, namely that the story says it all. It does not. There is always more; behind the story looms the infinite background. Every story of the type we are discussing here provides us with a bridge of meaning that connects the particular with the universal, the individual with the infinite; against every act of knowledge lies the infinite horizon, the presence of which makes knowledge possible. Each and every story of this type, by presenting us with a horizon of meaning, asks us to go beyond that horizon, until we encounter infinity. But we never encounter infinity in the world: we encounter finite situations that are informed by infinity. Our culture, whatever it may be, bears the imprint of that which is precultural, the sensation that that which is is discerned against an infinite horizon.[52] Indeed the finite is only perceived as finite because we have a sense of infinity. The closed horizon only makes sense because we are, at some level, aware of an infinite and open horizon.

What this brief examination of Rahner has shown us is one possible approach that enables us to show how narrative builds a bridge between the particular and the universal. The Rahnerian approach thus breaks open the self-contained nature of narrative and makes it a vehicle of universal meaning. In other words, it pushes out the frontiers of narrative. Whereas the first model gives us stories that are closed, and the second stories that are closed with a permeable limit, Rahner's insight points to a third type of story that is open to infinity.

---

[49] Karl Rahner, 'Theology and the Arts', *Thought*, 57 (1982): 17–29: p. 21.

[50] An article by Peter C. Blum makes this point forcibly: Peter C. Blum, 'Overcoming Relativism? Levinas's return to Platonism', *Journal of Religious Ethics*, 28 (2000): 91–117.

[51] *Ennarationes* 41.13.

[52] This is one of the insights of Emerich Coreth, *Metaphysics* (New York: The Seabury Press, 1973), English translation by Joseph Donceel. See for example, pp. 64–5; also pp. 108–9.

The Third Model: A Story Open to Infinity

Having established this very important idea of infinity that is signalled in tales of this sort, now let us ask what these sorts of stories of the third type are like, bearing in mind what we have already said about stories of the second type, and seeing how they go beyond, for example, fairy tales.

The first characteristic that strikes us about these tales is their setting. Even if the places that are mentioned are real, little detail is provided, and the significance of the place transcends mere geography. The Galilee of Jesus is the setting for the drama of salvation, rather than a politically constituted place: St Matthew's custom's house doubtless 'existed' but it is not the political frontier it marks that counts, but rather the frontier between two different calls in the soul of Matthew. The Sea of Galilee, scene of Christ's preaching, and of his later post-Resurrection appearances is much more than a mere lake, and place for catching fish: it is the place for catching souls.

Secondly, a similar point can be made about time. The time of 'once upon a time' of the fairy story is not the time that we know.[53] This phrase alerts us to a new type of time, a time beyond time. But stories of the third type go beyond this: St Luke places Christ's birth in time, in the days of King Herod (Luke 1:5) and of Augustus and Quirinius (Luke 2:1–3) but these seemingly historical details merely serve to underline the rolling away of real history, and the coming of a new type of history, sacred history, the culmination of prophecy as represented by Zechariah, Elizabeth, Simeon and Anna, and Mary herself. The angels who appear 'suddenly' (Luke 2:13) announce the irruption of a different type of history, just as do the canticles. Again, the arrival of Christ in Galilee inaugurates the fulfilment of prophecy (Luke 4:22), the close of the old age and the inauguration of Messianic time. 'It dates from the day of his going in Galilee.'[54] With this in mind, we can understand the vagueness of 'real time' in the Gospel stories. We do not know whether Christ's ministry lasted three years or just one, but this is an irrelevant question. Real history has been overtaken by sacred history. Indeed time is a category that is stretched, remade, in the Christ-story. It is overtaken by infinity.

---

[53] 'The formula "once upon a time" suggests a narrative in which time, place and other conditions are minimal considerations,' unlike modern fiction where setting, and the way characters come to terms with it, is of great significance, says Kort, p. 20. This point seems to have a superficial validity, but it is misleading as it obscures the significance of the formula. Fairy tales are not stories in which time and place count for little, but rather where they count for much – the time involved is, in a sense, eternity, and the place, everywhere: in other words, the events related have a universal significance. Thus the formula alerts us to the special importance – the time involved is not just a time, it is *the* time. Kort also maintains that the Bible minimizes setting but affirms the religious significance of time, place and circumstances (p. 21). One can but agree, and note how the minimalist setting underlines the universalist import of the story.

[54] Gerard Manley Hopkins, *The Wreck of the Deutschland*. See *Oxford Book of English Verse*, edited by Dame Helen Gardner (Oxford: Oxford University Press, 1972), p. 778.

As Father de Caussade writes:

> From the origin of the world Jesus Christ lives in us, he works in us at every moment of our life. He who will run until the end of the world is a single day. Jesus has lived and he lives still, he has begun in himself and he continues in his saints a life which will never end. O life of Jesus which includes and overflows all epochs![55]

It seems clear then that the life of Christ is understood by Father de Caussade as being a life unlike any other: it embraces, indeed exceeds, all time. The same is true, but in a more limited sense, of Augustine, who plays fast and loose with time in his *Confessions*: but his is not a linear history, but a history of the heart, true for all centuries. However, the story of Augustine is not of the same infinite importance as that of Christ. The permeable nature of the limit imposed by time is present in the gospels, but it is overtaken by the way time is, in the Pauline phrase, 'rolled up'.[56]

Thirdly, we see in these stories a marked reticence with descriptions of character. Jesus is not a character in the sense of a character in a novel. In these stories, there is no sense that character is fate. Jesus in the pages of the Gospels lives in an eternal present, unshackled by psychological realism. We may feel we know him, but we do not know him in the same way as we know Tolstoy's Anna Karenin. None of the characters in the Biblical stories have background, they are extraordinary; if they do have background, they do not conform to it (Luke 4:23) which causes alarm and dismay.

Finally, the events that are described are not ordinary historical events, but rather events of cosmic significance which invite us to question the very significance of history itself. The Passion of Christ is to be seen in this light. It marks the threshold of a new era, symbolized by the ripping of the Temple veil. The old dispensation has passed away and the new one has come, as the Letter to the Hebrews (Hebrews 1:1–2) makes clear. Likewise, the scene in the synagogue at Nazareth (Luke 4:16–30) has some of the characteristics of a normal Sabbath day, but these merely serve to underline the novelty of the situation. The Scripture is rolled up, handed back to its keepers, consigned to the archives, because it has now been fulfilled in your hearing. A new type of time has come, a new age has dawned, something the populace finds deeply threatening and unsettling, as well they might.

Time, setting, plot and character are the four staples of narrative in the usual sense of the word. But there are narratives, which we have called the third model of narrative, that make do without any of them in the usual and accepted senses of the words. Indeed, they challenge the very preconceptions of time, plot, character and setting. People in the Bible are constantly doing things that contradict what we

---

[55] '*Dès l'origine du monde Jésus-Christ vit en nous, il opère en nous tout le temps de notre vie. Celui qui s'écoulera jusqu'à la fin du monde est un jour. Jésus a vécu et il vit encore, il a commencé en soi-même et il continue dans ses saints une vie qui ne finira jamais. O vie de Jésus qui comprend et excède tous les siècles!*', Jean-Pierre de Caussade, *L'Abandon à la Providence Divine* (Paris: Desclée de Brouwer, 1966), p. 139. English translation by the author.

[56] 'Brothers, this is what I mean: our time is growing short' (I Corinthians, 7:29). The Greek is συνεσταλμενος which can have the sense of 'wrapped or rolled up'.

would think of as normal literary behaviour. Those who complain that the Gospels are full of lacunae miss the point: the Gospel writers were not writing history, still less novels.

We are now in a position to see the gradation between stories of the first, second and third models. The first model relies on a closed limit; the second has a permeable limit, the third does without a limit at all, being open to infinity. A narrative can move from being understood as the first, to the second and even to the third. To understand how this is done, the reader may like to consider a narrative: Plato's myth of the Cave.[57] In it the reader is invited to leave behind dim reflections and to consider things in the light of the fire; then invited to the upper air and to see things in the light of the sun. The dim reflections and the fire represent two different horizons of meaning; the sun represents the infinite horizon and to those who are used only to the light of the fire, the light of the sun is blindingly incomprehensible. But what Plato does not say is how one moves from the cave to the upper air, at least not in the context of this story. *The Republic* as a whole does give an answer – through the study of philosophy one comes to see things in the light of the sun, but this begs too many questions.

The Third Model: Theology

The existence of this third type of narrative helps us expand the reach of a narrative moral theology. The first model helps people understand themselves, their reasons for acting and their membership of the group; the second model helps people to do this in a more profound way, and helps them to attain purity of heart, and to understand others, and the way their group relates to other groups and the world at large. The third model, however, points to those aspects that burst beyond the confines of the story as such. It thus provides a solution to the problem posed in the first chapter: if a story is a human thing, are stories about God human as well? The answer is that there are stories that may be human in origin but which are informed by infinity.

Paul Fiddes gives us a typical definition of the phenomenon of narrative theology while at the same time alerting us to the fact that there is more to it than that:

> Theological reflection on the nature of the spiritual life has also been preoccupied in recent years with the idea of story. A religious tradition is understood to be less – in the first place – a collection of doctrines, than a collection of stories by which a community lives. A formative story, say the encounter of God with Abraham, or the life death and resurrection of Jesus Christ, *moulds the beliefs and the practices of the group that owns it and repeats it in its worship* [emphases added]. This kind of insight connects with a good deal of modern critical theory which has exposed the way that *language itself creates a culture*, rather than being the mere tool of cultural beings as we like to suppose: rather the word can make the world. A 'narrative' approach to the text of the Holy Scriptures, reading them for story rather than for dogma, can also help to overcome what has become *an artificial distinction between 'historical fact' and the interpretation of the event through the imagination of faith*. Some spiritual traditions have given a central place to

---

[57] Plato, *The Republic*, 509E. English Translation by Benjamin Jowett, pp. 303–7, (Danbury, CT: The World's Great Classics, Grolier Enterprises Corp., no date given).

story as a vehicle for the contemplation of God. In the Ignatian Exercises, for instance, the participant is urged to enter imaginatively into the Gospel story of Jesus. In the tradition deriving from Denys the Areopagite, the believer is encouraged to re-enact the story of the ascent of Sinai by Moses, to 'approach the dark cloud where God was'.[58]

There are two very important points touched upon here, albeit glancingly. The first is that language creates a culture, and that the story moulds the community that repeats it in liturgy. Fiddes thus assumes the logical priority of the story: it is the story that creates the culture and not vice versa. While one can imagine a person or a people 'picking' the story they wish to own (the first model), in order to illustrate their self-understanding, at the same time Fiddes points out, stories do not simply illustrate understanding, they create it too: if we mould the story, the story also moulds us. This is true of the stories of the first and second models, but even more so of the stories of the third model: they are prior to us in every sense, for infinity is not something we invent, it is something we discover.

The second point made by Fiddes is that the imaginative process of composition forms a bridge between the facts of history and the events as interpreted by us, using the imagination of faith. This can, however, be intended in two ways: one can see fact as collapsing into 'mere' interpretation, or else one can see the interpretation having the authority of fact. What we wish to stress here is the latter: a story of the third model points to an origin to the tale that lies beyond ourselves: the interpretation we give to a story of the third model is inspired by objective facts that have been discovered and not invented by ourselves.

History, then, is a lived experience – though this must not be allowed to discount the phenomenon of group or personal self-delusion. Some interpretations of history can lose sight of the facts and be plain wrong. At the same time, no interpretation can ever be utterly exhaustive. No story can ever tell the whole truth about the person, because persons remain a mystery to themselves and each other; or as some prefer to express it, subjective self-knowledge is athematic and defies conceptualization.[59] Thus the story points to the infinite horizon which informs our meanings but also transcends them at the same time. Every story gives only part of the picture, while hinting at a bigger picture; it is a partial history; there is no story that is complete. To turn to Fiddes again:

> At the same time, we might see a similar blend of openness and closure in the endings of all narratives. While a story achieves resolution, it has been a mark of so-called postmodern literary criticism to point out that the end always 'bursts open'; elements that have been suppressed in the story reassert themselves, easily won polarities are blurred and the constructed end 'deconstructs' itself for a continual harvest of further meaning.[60]

There is no such thing then as a perfect ending in stories of the third model: in other words, despite the appearance of architectonic neatness, every story leaves unfinished, or perhaps better, continuing business. Fiddes mentions the problematic

---

[58] Fiddes, p. 2.
[59] Abignente, p. 55.
[60] Fiddes, p. 6.

endings of many of Shakespeare's comedies. We might mention the open-endedness of each of the four Gospels. St Mark does not conclude, he breaks off. St Matthew and St Luke emphasize the continuing mission of the Church which is just beginning; St John places the ball firmly in his reader's court, inviting him or her to faith in Christ. Each of the Gospel writers passes the baton: the end of the Gospel signifies the beginning of something else, the story of the reader's faith. The story 'overflows': as Father de Caussade points out, the Gospel is a book that continues to be written on human hearts.

> The soul receives orders from Jesus Christ at each moment and carries them on beyond this; the Gospel makes us see the continuation of these truths in the life of Jesus Christ and that the same Jesus who is still living and always working, still lives and produces new things in holy souls. If you wish to live according to the Gospel, live in pure and complete abandonment to the action of God. Jesus Christ is the source of this; he is yesterday, he is still today constantly continuing his life and not starting it afresh; that which he has done is done, that which remains to do, he does at each moment. Each holy person receives a share of this divine life; Jesus Christ is different in all, yet always the same; the life of each holy person is the life of Jesus Christ, is a new Gospel.[61]

Both Fiddes and Caussade point to something that has also been raised by Rahner. The story is not a closed reality, but something that bursts open, something that takes us beyond the starting point of the story itself towards an infinite horizon. Again, we should examine the very phrasing of the passage we have just quoted from Caussade. Every Christian life is the writing of a new Gospel page, because Christ is for all time: the story of Christ cannot be contained in one epoch, but overflows to embrace all time. The story starts with a particular time and place, starts with the individual, but flows over into the infinite, for the individual contains within it the imprint of the infinite. Thus we see the way a story makes a bridge between ourselves, rooted and particular as we are, and the infinite; between the closed historical event, in Fiddes's phrase, and the interpretation of religious meaning.

This then must be our first conclusion with regard to stories of the third type: they are able to contain, or better, point to, that which cannot be contained, and thus become vehicles of religious meaning. This means that when we speak of narrative theology we need not restrict ourselves to the closed first model, that which makes sense in a given place, time and culture; or even the second model, that which makes sense in a given time, place and culture, but with reference to a much wider field; we can, through the third model, talk about that which is valid through all times and cultures, and which may be truly categorized as religious.

---

[61] '*L'âme de Jésus-Christ reçoit les ordres a chaque moment et les produit au dehors; l'Evangile fait voir la suite de ces vérités dans la vie de Jésus-Christ et le même Jésus qui est toujours vivant et toujours opérant, vit et opère encore des nouvelles choses dans les âmes saintes. Voulez–vous vivre évangéliquement, vivez en plein et pur abandon à l'action de Dieu. Jésus-Christ en est la source; il était hier, il est encore aujourd'hui pour continuer encore sa vie et non pour la recommencer; ce qu'il a fait est fait, ce qui reste a faire se fait a tout moment. Chaque saint reçoit une partie de cette vie divine, Jésus-Christ est différent en tous, quoiqu'il soit le même; la vie de chaque saint est la vie de Jésus-Christ, c'est un évangile nouveau*', de Caussade, p. 138. English translation by the author.

Stories of the third model are to be approached in a way that does not encounter the difficulties experienced by other models. Whereas the first model asks for the consent of the will (which may in certain circumstances be in conflict with the reason) and the second model asks for what we have called purity of heart, the third model asks for a response that is quite different still.

We have already seen the difficulties with the morality of 'What would Jesus have done?' Imitation of Christ is an impossibility if we take the story of Christ to be one of the first or even second models. But if we see the story of Christ as one of the third model and ask 'What would Jesus do?' the result is somewhat different. The use of the present tense alone is enough to alert us to one of the chief characteristics of the Jesus story as a third model story. It is not time bound: while it dates from the day of his going in Galilee, it has no end point. Christ, in the phrase of Caussade,[62] fills and overflows all epochs. He is not a character bound by time; he is present tense. The person who asks 'What would Jesus do?' assumes, as part of their horizon of meaning, that Jesus is here and now making the decision through and with the deciding person, not that the deciding person is trying to make a decision for themselves based on the teachings of a Jewish Socrates. The 'What would Jesus do?' question presupposes a symbiosis between the person asking the question and Jesus himself, in other words, Caussade again, that Christ is living in the believer.[63] What does this mean, though, from the point of view of narrative and from the point of view of narrative theology?

That Christ lives in the believer means more than the sort of symbiosis that comes about from imaginative leap required to enter a story of the first type, or even the discovery of a moral commitment to purity of heart involved in entering a story of the second type. A story of the third type involves a symbiosis with the figure of Christ of the sort outlined earlier in our examination of the *Ennarationes in Psalmos* of St Augustine. In the third model we discover not that we identify ourselves with people in the story (as in the first and second models) but rather that Christ has identified himself with us; in other words, entering the story does not depend on the reader's initiative, but is an act of grace on the part of Christ. Thus the third model presents us with a narrative theology which is also a theology of grace. We shall now examine this proposition by looking at some examples from the scriptures, one from the Old and one from the New Testament.

---

[62] Caussade, p. 139.
[63] As above.

Chapter 9

A Narrative Moral Theology in Practice

Now that we have examined the way that a narrative moral theology works, and the varying models that such a narrative moral theology can rely on, we wish to turn to some concrete examples, and to examine the way such stories work. The two examples that follow are both taken from the Bible, one from the New Testament and one from the Old. Both are justly famous stories.

The story of David and Bathsheba has attracted a lot of critical attention.[1] One reason for this is because it is an engaging story: it interests the reader, and this is the *sine qua non* of good narrative theology.

The story is told in 2 Samuel 11:1–12: 25, though its exact limits are open to discussion. Perhaps we should bear in mind the Ammonite war of Chapter 10 as a necessary preamble; and the later career of Bathsheba in the closing moments of David's reign are certainly of interest (1 Kings 1 et seq.). Indeed the story we are considering can be taken as the first episode in what has been called 'The Succession Narrative': the story of the origins of King Solomon, David's eventual and in many ways unlikely successor.[2] We have termed this episode, that of David's adultery, a 'story'. Many Biblical critics prefer the term 'novella',[3] but the episode seems

---

[1] In this chapter I have drawn on the work of the following authors: James Ackerman, 'Knowing Good and Evil', *JBL*, 109,1 (1990): 41–64; Randall C. Bailey, *David in Love and War, the Pursuit of Power in Samuel 10–12* (Sheffield: JSOT, 1990); Sergio Bastianel, *Teologia Morale Fondamentale* (third edition, Rome: Editrice PUG, 2001); Adele Berlin, 'The Characterisation of David's Wives', *JSOT*, 23 (1982): 69–85; Athalya Brenner, *The Israelite Woman, Social Role and Literary Type in Biblical narrative* (Sheffield: JSOT, 1985); David Daube, 'Nathan's Parable', *Novum Testamentum*, xxiv, 3 (1982): 275–88; Moshe Garsiel, 'The Story of David and Bathsheba, a different approach', *CBQ* 55, 2 (1993): 244–61; Hugo Gressmann and other scholars, *Narrative and Novella in Samuel*, translated by David E. Orton and David M. Gunn (Sheffield: The Almond Press, 1991); D.M. Gunn, *The Story of King David*, JSOT Supplement Series 6 (Sheffield: JSOT, 1978); Eugene H. Maly, *The World of David and Solomon*, (Eaglewood Cliffs: Prentice-Hall, 1965); Martin Noth, *The History of Israel* (second edition, London: A &C Black, 1960); Regina H. Schwarz, 'Adultery in the House of David', *Semeia*, 54 (1991): 35–55; Meir Sternberg, *The Poetics of Biblical Narrative* (Bloomington: Indiana University Press, 1987).

[2] For a discussion of the so-called 'Throne Succession Narrative', see Gressmann and others, especially p. 9 et seq. and also Bailey, p. 7 et seq for a useful summary of all the views expressed.

[3] See Gressmann, p. 71. and p. 97.

to have more in common with the standard English short story, a sort of novel in miniature.[4]

How are we to read this story? We have already touched upon one interpretation – the opening scene of the succession narrative – if indeed there is such a thing as a succession narrative. Other interpretations are more far fetched, going further than the text can allow, indeed, involving a rewriting of the text itself into a 'real' text that somehow lies beyond it.[5] But we must take the text as we find it, not as we would rather have it be. The text is prior to us the reader: we cannot recreate the text in our own image, tempting as this might be.

Bailey's attempt is one such, involving the shifting of the time perspective (putting the story after Absalom's rebellion) and giving Bathsheba a new identity unsupported by the text, that of Ahitophel's granddaughter. Or else we can, being more faithful to the text, suggest that Bathsheba is an archetypal female victim of male intrigue: Adele Berlin tends to this feminist reading.[6]

However, while we must not recreate the text and substitute the original for a text we would prefer, the text certainly has to be interpreted; indeed it invites interpretation on every line – and it is this that makes the story so interesting. Why are these people acting the way they are? This is an open question, for at no point in 2 Samuel 11 are we given any hint as to their motivation.

Consider the following. Why is Bathsheba bathing naked on her roof? Does she realize she can be seen? Is she doing it deliberately, setting her cap at the king? Does she come to the palace and sleep with him willingly? How does she feel when she finds she is pregnant? What does she expect the King to do? Does she know that her husband is murdered? Does she collude in his murder as an accessory after the fact? Is her elevation to the King's household purely accident, or the result of her feminine wiles?[7]

In fact careful attention to the text would seem to indicate the Bathsheba is a passive character throughout, an instrument in the hands of others, and not her own woman, certainly not controlling the flow of events. She is described as 'Eliam's daughter, the wife of Uriah the Hittite' (11:3): her identity is defined in relation to the men in her life; even her name, Bathsheba, means 'daughter of Sheba'. Later on, to confirm this, we see that she is not a particularly successful intriguer nor adept at exercising influence when she takes up the cause of Adonijah (1 Kings 2:12 et seq.) and she ends up effectively sidelined by her own son. Even in the intrigues before David's death she seems no more than a tool in the hands of the men around

---

[4] All these terms are archaic, but this does not stop critics using them. Note too the archaic use of the term 'harem' by many of our authors (e.g. Maly, p. 80). In fact David had no harem in the modern sense of the word (Gressmann and others, p. 31). This illustrates neatly the way an ancient story such as 2 Samuel is read through the prism of succeeding narratives. The term harem belongs to the Arabian nights.

[5] Thus Bailey, especially pp. 87–98, also pp. 100, 120.

[6] Berlin, pp. 72–3, on how Bathsheba is merely part of the mechanics of the plot and not a character, even a minor one, in her own right.

[7] We simply do not know what Bathsheba is feeling at any point in the story, but as Bailey points out (pp. 42–3) these emotions are felt by the reader – another way of our taking an active part in the story. Garsiel makes the same point, p. 245. Likewise, Sternberg, p. 191.

her (1 Kings 1:11 et seq.). This Bathsheba is no Jezebel:[8] but this is a conclusion the reader has to work out for themselves, through careful interpretation of the text. We collaborate with the anonymous author in teasing out the meaning of the story. Nothing is cut and dried – the story has to be excavated from the text and the facts it presents.

What does this tell us? It tells us that reading is an active as well as passive process. The text requires a response from us, and though the text delineates what that response will be – for some interpretations cannot be sustained – nevertheless the text leaves us free within certain parameters to interpret the story. Clearly our picture of Bathsheba will depend on who we, the readers, are: some may see her as a sultry and manipulative temptress,[9] others as a hapless victim of her circumstances. We know she mourns for her husband (11:27): was this purely conventional? Or did she love him? Or was it the deepest hypocrisy? The text leaves us free to choose. Its *a priori* nature binds us, but within those bounds leaves us with a wide choice.

The behaviour of King David too presents a puzzle. We are told that 'the woman was very beautiful' (11:2) and this no doubt explains why he decides to sleep with her. Lust plays its part. But his behaviour is not purely lustful. Why does he try to cover up the fact that he is responsible for her pregnancy? Is it to save her from the penalty of being caught in adultery, namely death by stoning? Does he love her?[10] Or does he merely feel a sense of guilt and responsibility? Or are his machinations purely to save own reputation? The stupidity of Uriah and his impeccable behaviour, in marked and ironic contrast to his King and his general Joab, drive David to compass his murder, and here we see that the King is not in control of events.[11] Joab carries out orders with no questions asked, but Uriah will not do as he is told. The King's power is not absolute: like many other human beings he is faced with a situation of his own making that is spinning out of control. Again, we are reminded that we are not necessarily masters in our own households, even if we are kings. Here we see again the essential point about the intractability of experience: David tries to construct a story that will get him off the hook, but this does not work until he breaks God's law by having an innocent man killed. Sin is the desire to construct a story that flies in the face of the facts that are established by the ultimate master, God.

---

[8] Brenner (pp. 17–18) points out that unlike Jezebel, Bathsheba does not enjoy the title of Queen or Queen Mother, nor does she seem to have any of the power of the later Queen (pp. 20–21) who acts as a deputy for her husband.

[9] Brenner provides us with a catalogue of such characters in the Bible, but does not place Bathsheba among them, pp. 106–14.

[10] Maly (p. 81) describes Bathsheba as 'a clear example of the King's favourite', but there is no textual evidence for this at all. Nor is there any evidence for what he calls 'an overpowering personal attachment' on David's part equal to his former love for Jonathan (p. 105). These judgements are wishful thinking. Far closer to the truth is Garsiel (p. 261) who points out, surely correctly, that the characterization of David and Bathsheba's feelings is deliberately sketchy, for a discussion of their motives would generate sympathy for the sinful pair and thus spoil the point of the story. The author does not want us to identify overmuch with David, as this would blunt our response to the moral point the story is making.

[11] Thus Ackerman, p. 48. The idea of the King losing control of events is closely paralleled in the plot of Shakespeare's *Macbeth*.

Again, the Bathsheba episode must be seen in the wider context of the story of David and indeed the history of Israel. David has been chosen to be shepherd of the people of Israel in place of Saul, the same Saul who took David's wife Michal away from him and gave her to another. Now David is doing the same thing. Likewise, the Israelites, once slaves in Egypt making bricks, are now reducing the Ammonites to the status of brick making slaves (12:31). David the just king now seems indistinguishable from Pharaoh. David's sexual sin, in wanting Bathsheba, is seen as not isolated. His 'real' sin is the sin of all tyrants – the disregard for the claims of others, and his sexual sin is just the manifestation of that essential sin. Clearly this sin of tyranny is long established by the time the Bathsheba episode takes place, for Joab does not question his master's orders: the structure of tyranny is well in place.

What emerges so far is that this is a story of the second model: we are aware of the story, and we become aware of the other stories pressing against the thin barrier of its limit; the events on the inside of the story are seen in the light of events and narratives that lie beyond it. David's behaviour and that of Bathsheba cannot be judged by criteria that are purely internal to the story.

Now let us consider the parable the prophet Nathan tells David. Nathan chooses to confront David with his sin in an oblique manner, via a parable. This is important and gives us pause. It shows that narrative may well be the only way in which tyranny can be confronted; its oblique nature can be tolerated, whereas a more direct approach would not be allowed; it illustrates too the way art can be subversive of the established order. Nathan the parable teller prefigures Jesus the teller of tales.

Nathan's story is not an allegory,[12] and it is useless to try and fit all the elements of his tale into an allegorical scheme. The parable has one point: the rich man has been selfish and unfeeling (not, one notes, lustful *per se*.) David's reaction is what one would expect: he condemns such behaviour, and seemingly quite sincerely. Then comes the punch line: 'You are the man', says the prophet (12:7). By condemning the man in the story, David has thus condemned himself. The moment of moral enlightenment consists in the following: through the story David has seen the injustice for what it is, and through the words of the prophet – 'You are the man!' – he has come to identify himself with the man in the story. Nathan's tale is a distancing device (the story of another man in another city) the distance of which is suddenly brought close with devastating effect, which David cannot escape. The story is in fact his story. He recognizes himself in the story: and it is this moment of recognition that is the key to narrative theology. It is at this moment that the story becomes impossible to ignore and has to be acted upon. It is at this point that infinity breaks in.

The change in David's outlook is evinced by his behaviour over the dying child (12:15 et seq.), which even his attendants find hard to interpret. The child in question has no name, being less that a week old and thus as yet unnamed, and yet this totally insignificant human being is the object of David's concern. This is in marked contrast to the rest of the Old Testament, where the death of children is not seen as a matter

---

[12] Daube, pp. 275–6, calls Nathan's story inept, quite missing this point.

of great import.[13] But the David who intercedes for the nameless infant is a different David to the one who had so coldly sent Uriah to his death.[14]

In conclusion, what this passage shows us is that it is the story within the story, Nathan's parable, that is the turning point for both the King and the reader too. The story opens up continual vistas of exploration for us; the parable allows us to see the situation from another point of view, that of infinity. It is through the parable that the divine logic breaks into the human situation. This divine logic overtakes human logic, rendering it redundant. And the divine logic is contained in the power of the parable. For the parable changes our perception of the situation, opening our eyes to the truth. Nathan's parable invites us to look at a situation (in this case the David and Bathsheba episode) in a new way, before which all human excuses, all human stories, collapse. What makes Nathan's parable compelling is the way that David (and by extension all people) can identify with it. Once this identification is admitted, the divine logic becomes irresistible; and we note that David not only acknowledges his guilt, but accepts what he had previously rejected, namely the infinite worth of all human beings. Uriah was expendable, but the tiny child who counts for nothing in the human scale of things, is not.

An Example from the New Testament: The Story of the Good Samaritan

The parable of the Good Samaritan (Luke 10:29–37) ends with a question: 'Which of the three, do you think, proved himself a neighbour to the man who fell into the brigands' hands?' (10:36). If this were not enough, we also have the concluding words: 'Go, and do the same yourself.' (10:37). Here we have spelled out for us what is only implied in the Bathsheba story, namely that the story involves us in a judgement or decision, and that the story will, or ought to, change our behaviour. The story makes, then, a double claim. It is improving literature, albeit of a special type; and it makes a special claim on the reader's attention, by demanding that they judge the characters in the story. But neither of these claims are altogether new to us: as we have seen, all literature entices us into the drama and invites us to take sides; much literature also tries to be improving, drawing a sharp contrast between behaviour that is to be imitated, and that which is not to be imitated. If we were to find in this parable the same qualities that we find in, for example, the improving literature of the nineteenth century, and nothing more, that would be something of a disappointment.

The parable ends with a question, because it is provoked by a question: 'Who is my neighbour?' (v. 29). The question is put by a lawyer who is anxious to justify himself. The parable is an unexpected way of answering this question. Instead of attempting a definition of 'neighbour', which is what the lawyer asks for, after all,

---

[13] True, we have the Niobe like figure of Rachel weeping for her children, Jeremiah 31:15, but this is purely conventional. The Rachel of Genesis does not weep over any dead children. For the more hardhearted and typical approach we have the two women who come to Solomon for judgement (1 Kings 3:16 et seq.), which hardly betrays a sentimental attitude to babies.

[14] A point also made by Garsiel, p. 244.

Jesus immediately launches into a story. Nor does the story provide an illustration of the definition of a neighbour, or a direct answer to the question: for the story tells us what a good neighbour is; it does not tell us what a neighbour is *per se*. In other words, there is something rather strange going on here: Jesus is not proceeding from definition to precept, defining what a neighbour is, and then laying down his obligations; rather he is showing us a refulgent example of good neighbourliness that relativizes all other moral concerns. The Good Samaritan is the ideal neighbour, the perfect form of charity in action: his example invites us to revisit all our previous assumptions and thoughts on the subject of charity and neighbourliness. It also asks us to re-evaluate, to place in a new order, the urgency or otherwise of our other moral concerns.

What we see here straightaway is a parallel movement: the lawyer asks 'Who is my neighbour?' but he receives an answer that is much wider in scope than his rather narrow question might be thought to warrant; likewise, the people listening to the story have their horizons widened and their preconceptions challenged. The story represents the bouleversement of their dearly held beliefs.

As we attempt a reading, let us remember that the story is full of stock figures, even though its setting is specific.[15] The man who falls among thieves is just 'a man' (v. 30). The other characters are types: a Priest, a Levite and a Samaritan. The Priest and the Levite 'pass by on the other side' (vv. 31 and 32); this suggests that they are on their way *up* to Jerusalem, as opposed to the man who has fallen among thieves and who was on his way *down* from Jerusalem.[16] Because the Priest and the Levite are on their way up (even though we are told that the Priest is going 'down the same road' (v. 31)), in other words making the ascent to the Temple and the Holy City where they are presumably to perform their liturgical functions, they are careful not to touch the man who has fallen among thieves and been left for dead. For neither of them can risk the ritual contamination that would come from touching a corpse. In other words the fulfilment of the Law and the fulfilment of the worship of the Temple is more urgent, more important to them, than the possible help they might be able to give to someone who is quite possibly dead. In this, of course, they are quite correct: for what could be more pleasing to God than the worship offered him in his Temple?

However the Samaritan, standing as he does outside the law, and therefore beyond the pale of ritual purity, cannot be moved by such considerations. Indeed, the Samaritan does not hold Jerusalem to be the exclusive site of divine worship, preferring another mountain to Mount Zion;[17] but this (from the Jewish perspective) impiety frees him to act charitably towards the man fallen amongst thieves. So what

---

[15] For a description of this setting, see H.V. Morton, *In the Steps of the Master*: (London: Methuen, 1934/1984), pp. 91–4.

[16] The up/down distinction is to be taken literally, as Morton, see above, points out. There is roughly 3000 feet in difference between Jerusalem's elevation and that of Jericho. But also the up/down distinction must also be taken in the English idiomatic sense, 'up' meaning towards the capital, 'down' meaning away from it. Note the Old Testament idea of going up to Jerusalem as 'ascent'.

[17] See John 4:20.

we have here is a reversal of expectations: the pious men act badly, the impious man acts in an exemplary fashion; it is the very fact of their piety that prevents the pious from acting well, and it is his lack of it that allows the exemplary Samaritan to act as he does. This must therefore lead us either to question the usefulness and value of the Samaritan's actions (which would be very hard to do), or else to question the Laws and regulations that govern the Temple cult. Essentially the parable is telling us that what God wants is not sacrifice (in the Temple) but love (of neighbour). This in turn must cast light on the immediately preceding passage, Luke 10:25–28. Which comes first then, love of God, or love of neighbour? Can the two contradict each other? If so, which must be given priority? Or is it that the love of God is revealed in the love of our neighbour and that there is no contradiction, but rather identity between them? In other words, is the Samaritan, in his charitable action, offering a more perfect sacrifice to God, than either the Priest or the Levite will do in the Temple?

What we have outlined above may be termed the subversive nature of the parable. It is after all a parable as opposed to a story pure and simple: it lulls us into a false sense of security and then it overturns our expectations. The good people are not good after all, and the traditional stage villain turns out to be the hero. We think we know the terrain, but it turns out that we do not. Parables are meant to challenge us, not reassure us.[18]

Crossan sees myth as the sort of tale that aims to mediate irreducible opposites, whereas parable creates division:[19] in other words the parable can destroy what the myth builds up. And the myth destroyed here is that what God wants is the worship in the Temple above all other things.

But even if this the correct interpretation, we immediately find ourselves confronted with a further problem. If the parable is about the Law and the Temple cult, given that both Law and Temple cult are of purely historic interest to most readers of the parable, then what is the significance of the parable today? For if this story is about, among other things, a Temple that no longer exists, then the only way that it can be understood is if we enter into the tradition of the Law and the Temple, which are not our own, even in a cursory manner, in order to try and understand the story from the inside. The alternative would be to take the story and forget its background and supply a new one in its place. This in fact has often been done, when the story has been read not as a parable, but as an allegory. But the effect of this is often to change the entire focus of the story: the story becomes a story about something else, for example, about man's fallen state in the world, and incidental details assume a disproportionate importance. The very idea of allegory thus can be a hall of distorting mirrors: which is the true story? Whatever we want it to be? The story eventually melts away into pure subjectivity and every age and tradition is free to make of it what it will.

The antidote to this tendency must be to keep our minds focussed on the self-declared subject matter of the story contained in the two key sentences 'Who is my neighbour?' and 'Go and do likewise.' These provide the frame to the narrative and the key to its interpretation. They point to the idea that the narrative is to do

---

[18] Crossan, p. 39.
[19] Crossan, pp. 33–4, 38.

with the concept of what constitutes a neighbour and the duty to live out the call to be a neighbour to others. Looked at from this angle we can see that the story, so particular in its setting, is about the universal nature of the call to be a good neighbour to strangers, irrespective of the ties of nationality and religion. Indeed one could interpret it in this universalist key: the parable takes a known category – that of the duty of good neighbourliness – and then reinterprets it, declaring the duty to be not just to fellow clan members, but to all humanity. This surely correct interpretation would accord with what we have already said. The parable overturns our own deeply held concepts and widens our horizons.

What the parable shows us then is the way a closed narrative, that of the Temple cult, is overtaken by an open narrative, that of the call to charity to one's neighbour, which effectively calls the first narrative into question: indeed the first closed narrative collapses under the pressure of the second narrative, and we now see that the worship God wants is rather different to the one presented by the closed narrative. The Priest and the Levite deny reality by passing by on the other side: that is their condemnation.

Also of note is that the charity exercised by the Samaritan has no upper limit, as Judith Jarvis Thompson[20] so rightly recognizes: he is not a minimally decent Samaritan, or even just a good one, he is a splendid Samaritan. He is not obliged to act the way he does, and he does so at a considerable risk, for the thieves who left the man for dead might still be lurking nearby. There are no rules that can impose this type of response, as we have seen. Indeed the point of the parable is that love goes beyond law and takes precedence over it, even the Law of the Temple cult. Just so that we are in no doubt about charity's upper limit, St Luke makes it clear to us: 'Next day, he took out two denarii and handed them to the innkeeper. "Look after him," he said, "and on my way back I will make good any extra expense you may have"' (v. 35). Not only is the Samaritan giving away a considerable sum, equivalent to two days' wages, with no hope of ever getting it back (after all the man has been robbed, and has no money), he is also contracting, for his word is his bond, to pay any other expenses, with no upper limit fixed. This is generosity to the point of folly. It shows us that the Samaritan's charity is infinite: once again worldly considerations and narratives give way before the irruption of infinity, in this case, the infinite love of God.

Interpreting the Examples

We now wish to look at both these stories together to see how they exemplify (if indeed they do) what we have said about narrative theology, bearing in mind the distinctions we have made about the three models.

First of all, both stories are rooted in a particular culture and a particular epoch. Moreover, both stories form part of what one might call a narrative tradition: they are embedded in a raft of preconceptions without which they may appear to make little sense. For example the Bathsheba story is one of a cycle of stories about King

---

[20] See p. 112 above.

David, called by Biblical scholars the 'Succession Narrative'; it relies on certain concepts being clear to its hearers – concepts about kingship, the Law of God, the Covenant. (This would point to a first model interpretation.) But at the same time it goes beyond all these things. King David is presumably, as is the audience, familiar with the sixth commandment; but the story contains a deeper and more profound appreciation of what that commandment entails and how the commandment against adultery is linked to the precepts of justice and the idea of the Covenant. This story assumes we know about the sixth commandment, but its overall purpose is to widen our horizons about just what keeping that commandment entails. Hence, Nathan's story is not a story about adultery, but rather about justice.

Likewise we have seen that the Samaritan story is embedded in the preconceptions of the time. It is a story about the Temple and about ritual purity, but its concerns go far beyond these matters. Indeed, the story 'sets up' these concerns only to burst them apart, and to present us with the call of universal charity. Just as the Bathsheba story tells us that there is no understanding of either kingship or adultery outside the wider concept of universal justice, so the Samaritan story tells us that there is no understanding worship outside the context of universal charity. So, though both stories start in an embedded manner, both move towards the unveiling of a universal moral value, without which there can in fact be no particular or embedded moral value. There is no Davidic kingship without justice, just as there is no true Temple worship without charity. Thus we see that both stories take conceptions and then transform them through the revelation of a new horizon of meaning. They start with the particular and end with the universal. They begin as first model stories, reinforcing the beliefs of the tribe, continue as second model stories, showing how the values of the tribe are to be understood against a wider horizon, and end as third model stories, unveiling universal and infinite values.

This movement can also be seen in the way the stories treat time, place and character. Both start in distinct places which nevertheless become symbolic landscapes which stand for the world, our world, and for situations that all of us can experience. The characters involved can stand for either you or me, in other words, they are Everyman: King David is every man who encounters an object of desire; the Samaritan is every man who encounters a person who asks, even mutely, for compassion and help. Further to this, the values of charity to strangers (the man who falls among thieves, the child of less than a week old) stretch forth towards an infinite horizon.

The way both stories 'work' is also similar. They invite us into their world, challenging us to ask ourselves how we ourselves would have acted in similar circumstances. In other words, the circumstances of David and the Samaritan become our circumstances. A response, a moral judgement, is required from us: even if we refused to reply to the story, that is an illusion, for the refusal to reply is in itself a response. Above all, the stories are a gift of grace, a divine revelation, literally, because they form part of the canon of the inspired Scriptures, but also in a wider sense, in that they stand before us showing us a way of acting that is not something that we have constructed for ourselves. These stories are not the result of human ingenuity or cleverness, but rather they overtake all human ingenuity and cleverness, showing us a way that transcends the purely human, while never abandoning human language. In this sense, every story is a revelation – showing us something that we had not suspected to be there. Like the people in the Original Position, like Augustine in the gardens of Milan and Ostia, we are aware that we are before something that we did not create and did not choose, a mystery that asks us for acknowledgement and consent. These two stories ask us to take on the role of the Good Samaritan, the role of the repentant David, but these are roles that the stories themselves have prepared for us. We are free to consent; we are not free to deny that these roles exist. In a sense the grace-filled nature of these stories makes redundant all talk of their justification, for grace goes beyond mere argument and reasoning.

At the same time these are human stories as well, representative of the way we receive experience, as opposed to mere sense perceptions, and our innate ability to make sense of life through language and through our ability to make connections. But language, our existence, our ability to construct stories, the fact that the world can make sense – are not willed into existence by us. They are prior to us. It makes sense to talk of them as *a priori*. Thus, though story and narrative are human inventions, they are not human inventions purely and simply – they are founded in reality. The reason that underpins narrative is found in the reason that underpins the universe.

The *a priori* nature of these things does not detract from human freedom. Life is a datum, but we are free to mould it. In this sense though subject to our universe, we are also masters of it. We have a choice as to the type of story we construct – the story can approximate to the truth to a greater or lesser degree, depending on how much we wish to live in the truth or deceive ourselves or others. We have seen this in the stories themselves, where characters construct 'stories' to justify themselves, stories that prove to be unable to resist the one true story that is the story itself, before which all excuses give way.

We have seen this in the examples we have considered: David tries to construct an excuse – the story as a way out – and no doubt the Priest and the Levite have their excuses too – the urgency of going up to the Temple – but each of these has to give way before the calls of charity (as exemplified by the Good Samaritan) and justice (as exemplified in Nathan's parable). Thus we see once again the way that stories of the first and second models are overtaken by the story of the third model.

How the Three Models Relate to Each Other

In the course of this book we have met a variety of stories: they vary not just in content but in the model they use, which determines their content and meaning. Some can find a suitably concordant fit with each other; others will be flatly contradictory. You can be a Catholic and a boy scout; you cannot be a Catholic and a member of the Komosol. If a human being tries to unite in one life two conflicting stories, either one of these stories will break down, or they will. As we have tried to show, you can be a Catholic Rawlsian; but to be an Engelhardtian Rawlsian would be impossible, as there is a flat contradiction between Rawls and Engelhardt over the use of reason.

Without prejudice to the above, it is also true that various narratives may be held to be true at various levels, depending on the various levels of concreteness associated with the narrative. Some narratives are highly concrete, time and place bound; others are less place and time bound but at the same time no less concrete, though their concrete character is of a different type. It is now impossible to live as a Roman gentleman of the fourth century, for the Roman Empire has passed away; but it is still possible to live as a Christian, even though the world of primitive Christianity is equally lost. Christianity and *romanitas* are both narratives, but of a different sort. One is tied to time and place, the other not. One is particular, the other universal. One is a narrative of the first type, another of the third. They are not inherently contradictory (provided that *romanitas* is purged of its more bloodthirsty elements, such as a love of gladiatorial combat), because they both rely on different models of understanding. Because this is so the Christian narrative can find a suitably concordant fit with a range of more closed narratives, either of the second or the first models. Likewise Rawls has argued that his narrative can find a suitably concordant fit with a variety of other narratives of a more embedded (that is first model) nature.

The third model narrative means that we take sides in the great debate on ethics that has been with us since the beginning. Yes, there are universal moral values that transcend time, place and culture (though their application will always reflect time, place and culture.) Mankind is not the measure of all things, for we find ourselves in a world we did not create, faced with moral exigencies that are *a priori* to us. Holding this view, we can now see in its true light the further problem that dogs narrative theology: the question of justification. If all is narrative, which narrative do we choose? The one that suits us best? Is it all down to personal choice in the end, or rather the choice dictated by our culture and our history?[21]

The answer to this must be no. Personal choice in narrative has to take account of the objective nature of the world. Narrative is subjective, but this is not to say that subjectivity is not the locus in which we come to understand objectivity.[22] A narrative that denies the objective truth of the world, as appreciated subjectively, is to be rejected. Narratives can be correct and can be false; their correctness or falsity is to be judged by the way they fit with the facts we know about the world. To say that Temple worship takes priority over charity, or that a King can arrange things in such a way as to escape his responsibility, is simply not true; one can delude oneself

---

[21] Goldberg tackles this question at the conclusion of his book: 'Surely, the *mere narration* of a story is not enough to justify its position as the basis of one's moral behaviour. One must make some attempt to give reasons why that story ought to hold that position in one's own life – or in anybody else's. Otherwise, there is only the kind of relativism that makes moral argument across 'story-lines' altogether impossible. Unless there are some criteria for judging the adequacy of various storied claims which are not themselves dependant on any one story alone, then all we are left with is the rather dismal prospect of saying to one another (or *shouting* at one another?) 'I've got my story; you've got yours. That's all there is to it!' If a narrative theology cannot adequately address this kind of problem, then whatever suspicion there may be surrounding the legitimacy of the use of narrative for theology will have been well founded' (p. 192). Quite so, as we have found repeatedly in this investigation so far. However, Goldberg's attempt to find such criteria in his concluding chapter (pp. 194–240) is deeply disappointing, though we should be grateful that he has raised the question.

[22] A point made by Josef Fuchs. See, for example, *Christian Ethics in a Secular Arena* (Washington, DC: Georgetown University Press, 1982), p. 29.

that it is, or one can delude oneself that it is not important, but in the end these delusions must collapse under the weight of the truth we live every day.

But as we have said already, a narrative can make a more modest claim, not to the whole truth, but perhaps to one aspect of it. But even here the task of verification is urgent. Here we are helped by the interaction of various narratives: for, however strong the sense of tribal togetherness that our closed narrative of the first type may offer, this barrier will not be able to ignore the rest of the world forever. First model narratives have to develop to remain living and they may well develop into second model narratives. The Antiochenes may have to acknowledge the existence of other approaches. Again, hearing the story of the Good Samaritan, we can maintain that Temple worship is important, but we cannot deny the urgency of charity. Because narratives live side by side in the world, they learn from each other in a continuous interaction, a dialectic. We come to see that the urgency of the Temple cult must give way to another more important urgency. No narrative is completely 'sealed' or airtight, much as it may wish to be; each narrative must thus breathe and thus adapt itself. The idea of separation from the world of the larger narrative is not possible or desirable. Sectarianism has a poor track record in keeping its powder dry.

But what about the larger second model or even universal third model narrative, which is the ultimate verification of all other narratives? How is that to be verified? Rawls has argued that the Original Position is its own verification – one could not reasonably choose anything else. The Original Position makes best sense of the facts of social interaction. I choose it because the Original Position advances the best approximation of the citizen I wish to be, and the other citizens I wish to live among. Thus one can verify the Original Position against the facts as I perceive them; likewise, as the Original Position verifies my personal narrative, this works in the opposite direction as well. It is the universality of the Position that is its ultimate verification: the fact that is finds a suitably concordant fit with a wide variety of narratives. But as we have shown, through examination of Judith Jarvis Thompson's parable, the Rawlsian narrative is not universal; it is vulnerable to the call of universal charity as expressed in the question of acts of supererogation. It is a second model narrative that may well develop into, or point the way towards, a third model narrative and the existence of the infinite horizon.

So, a third model narrative can justify itself by claiming universal import. Yet there exist or have existed several narratives that have made this claim: how do we justify our own theological narrative as the universal narrative? What reasons do we advance for holding the narrative of Jesus Christ as foundational and of universal import – in other words that all other narratives must accord with it or at least not contradict it? We cannot invoke the inspired nature of the scriptural text here, but rather we wish to find that which is intrinsic to the narrative itself. Why this narrative and not some other? Why do we choose the narrative of the Good Samaritan as foundational?

One answer advanced is that this is the one that appeals, this is the one that makes sense. Most believers would advance an argument along these lines. The world of the Good Samaritan, the world of boundless charity is the world in which we choose to live. In practical terms this almost aesthetic argument may in fact be the most compelling. As we have touched on earlier, this is the type of answer given when justifying a closed first model narrative, though this is not to say that the same argument cannot be advanced in the cases of second and third model narratives too. But it is not the only argument. The Christ story is the story *par excellence* because it is the best story for making sense of the human condition, certainly. It is also the best story in the sense that it is the most universal story: it is not time and place bound, yet at the same time it does not have the amorphous quality of myth. It combines the concrete nature of narrative with the timelessness of eternal truths. That too is a compelling argument.

More than this, the Christ story draws in the reader and makes him or her a character in the action. Of course every story must do this in some way or another if it is to attract an audience, but the Jesus story and many of the stories of the Bible do this in a way that is unique and profound. As we have shown in our discussion of the phenomenon of identification, we identify ourselves with characters in stories;[23] those characters stand for us; we choose to make them stand for us, for we recognize that their dilemmas and situations resemble our own; we have a kinship with them. But this kinship is something that we ourselves establish; we can decide conversely that we have nothing in common with Jane Eyre and opt for the novels of Gissing instead; or we can abandon fiction as a hopeless enterprise, though this would be the action of one who essentially places themselves beyond the human family.

But in the Christ story the question of kinship is raised in another manner. While we may decide that we have a kinship with Christ, this is quite overshadowed with something that is logically and historically prior: Christ has established his kinship with us – *transfiguravit nos in se*. As we read the story we can of course choose to reject the proffered kinship and identification. We are free to do so, but the offer is there.

It seems therefore that there is an essential connexion between narrative theology, and narrative moral theology, and the doctrine of grace, and this is seen in stories of the third model. This is what is distinctive about the Christ story: it is the offer of grace, quite prior to any human merit, that is contained in the narrative. Christ has already identified himself with us. It is up to the reader to accept or reject this identification – to enter the narrative and become part of it, or not. Faith is an offer of grace; and it is through faith that we enter the narrative of Christ.

It may seem that no book on ethics can change the world, but this is not true for the Jesus story, as the Jesus story is not simply descriptive or even prescriptive, but performative. The doctrine of Christ's identification with us of which St Augustine makes so much builds the bridge between us and the story, making that story our own. Thus when Hopkins says that 'It dates from the day of his going in Galilee',[24] he is talking as much about his own story as that of Jesus.

Thus, in the ascent from first to second to third model of narrative, we see a progressive widening of horizon, from closed to permeable to open; but we also

---

[23] 'Very few people will take the trouble to read a novel or story unless they can somehow "identify" with the characters, live with them inwardly as though they were real at least for the duration of the reading', says Alter, p. 49.

[24] Gerard Manley Hopkins, 'The Wreck of the Deutschland'. See the *New Oxford Book of English Verse*, pp. 777–85.

see a progressive development of the type of response that the stories ask of us: the consent of the will (sometimes without that of the reason), the consent of the reason and the will with the moral commitment that involves; and finally the offer of grace and the free consent thereto.

Furthermore, of interest here is the fact that one story can be believed by differing people in different ways: some may see the story of Christ as a closed first model story; others may treat it as that of the second model, still others as one of the third. This explains how Christian belief develops, not just in its content, but also in depth, which in turn must affect its content. Whether we see Christianity as a first, second or third model narrative will determine whether we have a vision of a fortress Church, or one of the Church in the world, or one of the Church as Kingdom of God.

How Narrative Theology may be Part of Moral Theology

Moral theology ought not simply to concern itself with moral norms, even though moral norms are of great importance. Single actions cannot be seen in isolation from other actions of the person. Indeed all actions, though they can be considered in isolation (which may be misleading), are actions of people, and as such part of the narrative of a continuing life. Every action has to be considered in the context of the life of the agent: as a fruit of previous actions and convictions, as a manifestation of character, which is in turn formed by social setting and culture. A moral norm, therefore, ought not to be understood as a bare thing, but as an expression of a certain type of character and a certain type of culture. Examining a moral norm, in order to understand it, we need to ask of what narrative is it a part. A narrative theology gives moral norms their context, outside of which they make only limited sense.

However, narrative is not subordinate to moral theology. Moral theology should not be seen as essentially norm-based, with the narrative element added on to help explicate the meaning and the application of the norms, which will be the fruit of abstract reasoning, perhaps from the nature of the act they are either recommending or proscribing. Thus the narrative element is reduced to the role of exemplifying the norm. But this is not a true narrative theology, which starts instead with a consideration of human existence and works from there, basing itself on the conviction that there is no essence that is independent of existence, placing existence prior to essence.

One should favour existence as a starting point rather than essence, because existence is what we experience at first hand, and that essence is temporally posterior, being an abstraction from existence. Narrative deals with individual existents, not with essences, people who find themselves in a community, living a tradition and a culture, expressing this in stories or liturgy. But if we deal with individual existents, how can we ever hope to arrive at general and universalizable moral principles? This is indeed the fundamental question that we have tried to answer in the present volume, and we have answered it by sketching a bridge of understanding between the particular and the universal contained in narratives of the second and third models, but not the first.

To restrict ourselves to a norm-based moral theology is to restrict ourselves to a narrow picture of human reasoning; but human reasoning is a wider phenomenon as narrative makes clear. Human reasoning, before arriving at the non-contradictory moral norm, is not only discursive but also imaginative: it deals not only with that which is before us, but also takes into account the 'What if...?' factor. As moral theology has to deal with human beings, considered in its totality, it is an art rather than an exact science, as there is much that is unpredictable in human behaviour.[25] Thus it makes more sense, given the way human existents are, to ask not: 'What norm or system of norms are you proposing?', but rather: 'What is your narrative?' Thus, the morality of a people will be better expressed by its narrative, rather than its bare moral norms.

We have examined the way that narrative and life are continuous. This seems to be the basis of all narrative-based theology, and not just narratives of the first model: there is a basic alignment, a continuity, between narrative and life, moral insight and narrative; there is, in other words, a narrative structure to reality. Because of this the language of narrative provide us with the language of ethics.

Narrative structure (of all models, but especially the second and third ones) is transcultural, insofar as it finds expression in every culture, and that all people tell stories, and that it is through stories that they come to understand themselves and tell others who they are.[26] This means that reality may seem to be unstructured, but it is susceptible to being structured by narrative without doing violence to the nature of reality. In sum: narrative meaning is not grafted onto experience but is inherent in it; of course, we give meaning to our surroundings, but our surroundings are structured in such a way as to make this possible. The impact for moral theology should be clear: if what we have said above is true, and if there can be established a strong parallel between narrative and moral theology, then it follows that moral theology, or ethics, is not a projection, the fruit of wishful human thinking, but is in fact inherent in reality itself. In other words, narrative theology gives an ontological basis to ethics.

But these assertions will fall apart if we make the counter-assertion: 'Why this particular story? Why not some other story?' Likewise the normative nature of the story will be destroyed if we refuse to believe that there is a real coincidence between the story and living reality. If we see the story as mere projection or wishful thinking, then its normative impact collapses. So for a narrative theology to work one has to accept as its basis that life is of its very nature narrative. And one has to find some way in which to justify this narrative as opposed to that narrative which goes beyond mere personal and irrational whim.

Our answer to this question will depend on what has been said above. If a closed first model narrative is divorced from reasoning, but seen as an alternative to reason, then it cannot give reasons for itself. But if we believe there is such a thing as reason, then every narrative must be held accountable at the bar of reason for its claims. Thus we can rightly talk (as Hauerwas seems to do) about narratives finding a fit with experience, of them making sense, and that this justifies them. This would then justify the choice of a first model narrative.

---

[25] Thus Keane, p. 16 et seq.
[26] Thus Crites, p. 291.

But we can go further than this: in dealing with second model narratives or even first model narratives that make wide or even universalist claims, we can reject all narratives that do not make sense of the entirety of human experience; that is to say we can put aside (or at least view as of secondary importance) narratives that seem to describe only a part rather than a whole, bearing in mind that no narrative of this type will ever describe the whole in its entirety, as infinity overflows the capacity for human expression. But the basis of justification will be the following: 'To what extent does this narrative do justice to all the facts of the case that we are able to perceive?' Naturally this means that every narrative is a contingent one, awaiting further explication. Totalitarian narratives are *per se* false.

Bearing this in mind, when we come to the key point of how narratives are to be justified, and how one narrative is to be justified against another, we have seen a fundamental bifurcation in those who claim the mantle of narrative theologians.

On the one side there are those who suggest or who seem to suggest that choosing a narrative has little to do with rational choice; indeed, Engelhardt seems to say that it is the decision that gives force to the morality of the choice, and that no narrative can really be justified from a purely rational perspective; one perspective is very much like another: so the choice is ours as to which narrative we choose. Hauerwas, unlike Engelhardt, tries to sidestep the issue, claiming that we start inside a narrative, that all is narrative, therefore the idea of justification of that narrative is a sort of non-question. Both authors, one feels, are taking MacIntyre's point about incommensurability very seriously. If incommensurability is in fact the case, then all justification of narratives in terms foreign to the narrative are completely futile. Thus the inescapable conclusion is that narrative is what you take refuge in once rationality has failed.

This conclusion is mistaken, however. In the first place, narrative, if it is to be narrative at all, is a rationality: it can be justified by internal criteria: the story makes sense in its own terms. But more than this, narrative can be justified by external criteria as well. All narrative, if it is to command an audience, will do so because it bears resemblance to the reality we call 'life'. There is a connexion between narrative and reality; and as long as we admit that reality is susceptible to some sort of rational analysis, then we must also accept that narrative too is rational. The mistake of Engelhardt is to divorce narrative from life: once so divorced, narrative loses its purpose,[27] for there is such a thing as historical rationality.

In fact it is our conclusion that narrative is a way of speaking about the reality that makes it more accessible to human understanding. And this has been illustrated in our discussion of John Rawls: he presents us with a narrative that acts as a way in to moral reasoning. When we ask: 'Why are we doing this?' the answer will be: 'Because it is what we would have chosen in the Original Position.' The narrative

---

[27] Engelhardt would, of course, point out that his narrative is closely related to life, or at least one form of life, the community and liturgical life of the Antiochene Church. But this sort of 'life' is too narrow a conception to win general support; the beliefs and practices of the Antiochenes may be coherent, but they are not reasonable as far as the wider community is concerned. Thus Engelhardt's narrative, as contained for example in *Christian Bioethics*, will not speak to a wider public.

of the Original Position discloses the rationality of the choice we have made. In addition, and this is one of the attractions of Rawls's work, the narrative of the Original Position, which is so simple that even young children could grasp it, acts as a form of moral shorthand (as opposed to short cut): this one narrative opens up to us a world in which moral choice and the conditions of moral choice are important. It enables us to move towards Kantian universalism without having to be Kantian metaphysicians first. But the justification of the story rests in the fact that it 'works' in the vast majority of cases. And this working is checkable against daily experience: at the end of the process one arrives at a moral judgement in the sense of the categorical imperative.

What we hope to have shown, therefore, is that incommensurability is more apparent than real. This must hold good for narratives of the first and second model – but what about the narrative of the third model, which claims to be the measure of all things? This, of its nature, cannot be checked against another narrative, for it claims to be the narrative *par excellence*.

But at this point we must sound a note of caution: narratives are in a state of becoming rather than finished products. The third model narrative is open to an infinite horizon and is not to be confused with a moral system which represents a finished product, that is to say the distillation of moral insight into coherent and rational form. It is easy to see in the works of Saint Augustine that he is advancing a moral theological system that we could call Christian Platonism: this system is susceptible to pithy and concise expression.[28] But this system, valuable as it is particularly in preaching, represents the end point of a moral process, not its beginning. The splendour of the finished product may however distract us from the question of its origins. To those origins we now briefly turn.

We are recipients of moral insight which carries with it an urgent sense of obligation: we see what we have to do, and we feel we have to do it, whatever the consequences.[29] We find ourselves faced with the necessity of moral judgement. There are several elements here that need to be isolated. For a start, we are capable of receiving such an insight, having what can be termed a conscience. Secondly, this insight comes to us distinct from the laws of the state, sometimes opposed to them; it is not of human origin, in other words. Thirdly, this insight is obligating, whatever the consequences; in other words we do what we have to do because it is perceived as intrinsically right, and not because of its good consequences. Finally, and perhaps most importantly, in experiencing this phenomenon of morality we are aware of something that transcends our earthly situation and something that we ourselves did not create. Morality is that into which we find ourselves 'thrown'.[30]

---

[28] A good example is *Ennarationes* 30:8, (*Works*, vol. 15, p. 180). But see *Ennarationes*, 26/2.8 (*Works*, vol. 15, p. 279) and *Ennarationes* 32/3.15–16 (*Works*, vol. 15, p. 415).

[29] This is in fact what happens to Antigone: she realizes she has to bury her brother, in defiance of Creon and the laws of the land, at whatever cost to herself. She bears witness to the fact that there is a higher law than Creon's, a law worth dying for. The burial of her brother *per se* does not seem to be of overwhelming importance: the real point is being true to the insights of conscience.

[30] For the concept of 'throwness' (*Geworfenheit*) see Macquarrie, p. 149. Antigone's predicament is a good example of this *Geworfenheit*, as indeed is the predicament of any

This sense of obligation,[31] which we can attempt to flee from, but can never truly escape, and which has to be faced in the end, is however, as it first comes to us, 'raw' and unformed. We are 'thrown' into morality, but at the same time it throws us, we are thrown by it, in the sense of confused, disorientated, unable to respond, unable to make sense of the phenomenon. We need time to work out what exactly it is that the call of doing right is asking us in this case to do. In other words we need to translate the unformed raw sense of obligation into something concrete;[32] we need to shape it, give it form, and make it graspable. In short, we need to find the story that fits with our sense of moral obligation. Once we have found that story, then we will be able to quieten our consciences and live with the sense of obligation that we have. If this sense of obligation should at some future time no longer be able to keep our consciences settled, then this may well mean that the story is not fulfilling its function and needs to be amended, or even abandoned and replaced by something new.

What we are proposing is a relationship between morality and narrative that is revealed in moral judgement. Morality is unformed yet palpable; inescapable, yet difficult to put into words, because transcendent; constantly pushing us to go beyond ourselves; story is that which gives shape and manageable content to morality. The narrative provides the language with which to express moral concepts and to talk about them. The narrative gives us something to point to when we wish to express what we mean by good.[33] The narrative brings the question of the good and moral obligation 'down' into the realms of that which can be discussed. The concept of narrative provides us with an ethical language, against those who maintain that no ethical language can make sense.

But the concept of narrative can indeed do more: by giving us the story that enables us to clothe moral insight in words, it can also, through the very structure of narrative, give us a model of ethical reasoning. Narrative categories can provide us with a way of discussing moral arguments and reasoning about morality; in other words, the internal dynamics of the story that is morality will enable us to put moral discourse on a sound and rational basis. So, we may find that the story of Antigone enables us to discuss the question of the priority of individual conscience over the will of the state as expressed in its laws – the right of conscientious objection – in a way that escapes from mere emotivism or clash of wills between those who say yea and those who say nay. But at the same time we may find that there are other stories

---

tragic hero: they did not choose the difficult situation in which they find themselves – it chose them.

[31] See de Finance, pp. 88–102 for a discussion of the phenomenon of obligation.

[32] For Antigone, the call of the divine higher law is made concrete in the task of burying her brother; it is by carrying out this very specific action that she fulfils her sense of obligation to the higher powers.

[33] A good example of this is the use of the Gospels in moral discourse. The Gospels are not moral tracts, they contain no system of morality; however, when faced with the somewhat amorphous sense that we should love our neighbour, the best way to understand what this means is through reading the Gospels, all of which make incarnate the meaning of the obligation to love. This is not to say that the Gospels are purely texts that act as exemplars, but rather that they express the inexpressible and give us a language to do the same ourselves.

that merely serve to underline the ambiguities of a moral situation and point to certain issues as being beyond resolution. Again, we may come across two rival stories, both advancing subtly different positions: how could we determine which was the right one? How can one decide between stories? We have already said that these stories must be checked against objective reality: but the fact will always remain that every narrative will be an invitation to take things further, an invitation to enter into a tradition. It invites us to probe, to think and to feel, and to make the story our own, and thus subtly to change it, thus moving the narrative tradition forward. Thus narrative, by its very nature, breaks the deadlock that marks the stand-off between those who espouse radically diverse traditions.

Thus narrative gives us a handle on experience, but at the same time it can never utterly tame that experience.[34] There will always be something that remains beyond. The ending may seem like a conclusion, but will often contain something that disturbs us and reminds us that all endings are in fact just truces rather than lasting peaces.[35] Indeed, Rawls himself admits that there are places where his narrative fails to arrive, and we have shown that one cannot really employ the reasoning of the Original Position when trying to confront the question of supererogatory acts.

It is important, therefore, not to assume that narrative is to be understood in one particular way: narrative should not be a straightjacket. Narrative can liberate our thoughts rather than enclose them. Narrative should not be seen to make thought impossible. We are people embedded in a tradition, but capable of adopting other perspectives. Narrative makes our identities;[36] but identity may be a fluid concept. We can see ourselves as trying on stories as we try on clothes, looking for a suitable fit to our pre-existing beliefs. While some may fervently embrace a particular exclusive identity, this should not blind us to the fact that for many more people, identity is not something fixed and pre-existing, but something that is dynamic and changing. The person who says 'I am an Ultra-Orthodox Jew' seemingly has no doubts and a very clear idea about their identity; but for most people, identity is something in becoming as opposed to already in being. This is not to undervalue the influence of culture entirely: it is, though, to emphasize that though culture binds us, we still to a large extent are free to choose our identities. We are unable to choose our first language and nationality of our birth, or our parents, but within these bounds, our choices are almost infinite.[37] So it is misleading to characterize identity as a straightjacket: it is a far looser and more adaptable garment. And indeed it has been

---

[34] For a start, the material of the story is not exclusively ours: we received the material of the story, we did not create it *ex nihilo* (Navone, p. xvi). Likewise, it is unlikely that the form the author gives to his material will ever create the perfect work of art – the material of the story will always be intractable to some extent. Art shows our dominance over our environment but may also show at the same time that this dominance is limited. Sometimes we may find ourselves using mythological language that transcends complete comprehension, Navone p. 75. Or in Crossan's terms, we may have to resort to parable, p. 105.

[35] Crossan, p. 37. But remember *Twelfth Night*, which ends without a perfect reconciliation. How wrong Leadbetter, p. 6, in his assertion: 'The very structure of narrative suggests completion, fullness and wholeness.' It may in fact suggest the opposite.

[36] Kort, p. 128, p. 183.

[37] MacIntyre, *After Virtue*, p. 216, says the same thing.

our contention in this final chapter that people can ascend from one narrative model to another, until they touch the outer edge of infinity, at each stage deepening their sense of personal identity and kinship with others.

This debate between the embedded and the disencumbered self has far reaching consequences, for with it come two conflicting models of moral choice. The embedded school claims that the person who decides cannot do so in a vacuum; the decision is not simply about what is being decided but also about the self who decides: the decision marks the latest step in the narrative unity of a life. The disencumbered school would reply that every decision has to be taken with a degree of impartiality that involves stepping back from one's own personal history and placing one's prejudices under some sort of veil of ignorance. One invites us to think in particular and historical terms, the other in universal and abstract terms.

This dichotomy goes to the heart of moral theology. But in recent years there have been two trends in moral theology: the first is to see decisions as decisions of persons, in particular circumstances, with all the attendant histories that persons bring with them to decision-making, in opposition to the rather disembodied theology of the manuals. The second has been to stress conflict situations. What no one has pointed out, though, is that these two tendencies are in opposition to each other. If one is a situated person, one will feel very few conflicts, or at least those conflicts one does face will be easily resolvable. If one is constantly torn by conflicts, it is a sign that one is 'twisting in the wind', that is, not sufficiently situated, for otherwise your situatedness would have given you the answer.

The concept of the divided self helps us overcome this false dichotomy for it explains to us that while we are situated to a degree, we are still capable of independent thought; that while we are rooted, we are still capable of changing our minds and our ways of life; while we are committed to one way of life, we are still capable of being distracted and tempted away from it. It also explains to us that we are people of divided loyalties, often, and people capable of growth in so far as we are capable of coming to an increasingly deeper awareness of what our situation requires of us.

This realization that we are divided selves should give us a deeper appreciation too of the import of narrative for moral theology. Moral theology does not just employ narrative, it is narrative, in the sense that moral theology covers the same ground as narrative, namely the territory in which human beings make decisions. These decisions are the stuff of both morals and narrative; and these decisions assume that we are divided selves, struggling and sometimes failing to do the right thing, to make the decision that will lead to enlightenment. In other words, the divided self is the locus where the dialectic between good and evil is played out and the categories of narrative are necessary if we are to understand how moral decisions are made. Furthermore, the concept of the divided self brings us to a true realization of what is meant by the narrative unity of a life: this unity is not to be understood in a monolithic sense, but in a dynamic sense. The unity of a life emerges through the decisions that the person makes. Hence we are truly co-authors of our own existences. Our life is not simply the reproduction of a tradition, but the reforging of a tradition, for which process some critical distance from the tradition is necessary.

Judgement and narrative are activities that are carried out in traditions and communities moulded by these traditions, but they are also transcendental activities, that is to say, activities that are open to an infinite horizon. The concrete is where we start, but what is concrete is shaped by the infinite horizon of meaning that lies beyond it. Thus certain types of narrative are open to the communication of universal moral values, valid for all times and places, and it is wrong to assume that by turning to the concrete and to narrative in particular that we must renounce the search for universal truths. In fact we have argued the very opposite: it is by turning to the concrete and narrative that we discover universal moral truths that we did not create and which call our very existence into question.

Bibliography

Abignente, Donatella, *Decisione Morale del Credente, il Pensiero di Josef Fuchs* (Casale Monferrato: Piemme, 1987).
Allen, A., 'MacIntyre's Traditionalism', *Journal of Value Enquiry*, 31 (1997): 511–25.
Allen, Richard C., 'When Narrative Fails', *Journal of Religious Ethics*, 21 (Spring 1993): 27–67.
Alter, Robert, *The Pleasures of Reading in an Ideological Age*, (New York: Simon and Schuster, 1989).
Annas, Julia, 'MacIntyre on Traditions', *Philosophy and Public Affairs*, 18 (1989): 388–404.
Aquinas, St Thomas, *Summa Theologiae* (London: Blackfriars, 1964–81).
Aristotle, *Ethics*, translated by J.A.K. Thomson (London: Penguin,1953).
Augustine, *The City of God*, translated by Demetrius Zema and Gerald Walsh (Washington: Catholic University of America Press, 1977–81).
———, *The Works of Saint Augustine, a Translation for the Twenty-First Century*, (New York: New City Press, 1997–).
Ballard, Bruce W., *Understanding MacIntyre* (Lanham, Maryland: University Press of America, 2000).
Barry, Brian, *Justice as Impartiality*, (Oxford: Clarendon Press, 1995).
Baum, Gregory, *Journeys* (New York: Paulist Press,1973).
Bell, Daniel, *Communitarianism and its Critics* (Oxford: Oxford University Press, 1993).
Berkman, John and Cartwright, Michael (editors), *The Hauerwas Reader* (Durham, NC and London: Duke University Press, 2001).
Berthoff, Warner, *Literature and the Continuances of Virtue* (Princeton, NJ: Princeton University Press, 1986).
Blum, Peter C., 'Overcoming Relativism? Levinas's return to Platonism', *Journal of Religious Ethics*, 28 (2000): 91–117.
Bonaventure, *The Soul's Journey into God, The Tree of Life, The Life of Saint Francis*, translated and introduced by Ewert Cousins (New York: Paulist Press, 1978).
Bond, E.J., 'Could there be a Rationally Grounded Universal Morality? (Ethical Relativism in Williams and MacIntyre)', *Journal of Philosophical Research*, 15 (1989–90): 15–45.
Booth, Wayne C., *The Company We Keep, an Ethics of Fiction* (Berkeley: University of California Press, 1988).
Bouchard, Larry D., *Tragic Method and Tragic Theology*, (University Park: Pennsylvania State University Press, 1989).
Brooks, Cleanth, *The Hidden God* (New Haven: Yale University Press, 1966).
Brown, Peter, *Augustine of Hippo, a biography* (London: Faber, 1967).
———, *The World of Late Antiquity* (London: Thames and Hudson, 1971).

Buber, Martin, *The Eclipse of God* (New York: Harper and Row, 1952).
———, *Good and Evil*, (New York: Charles Scribner's Sons, 1952).
———, *Between Man and God*, translated by Ronald Gregor Smith (Boston: Beacon Press, 1955).
———, *Selected Writings*, introduced by Will Herberg (New York: Meridian Books, 1956).
———, *I and Thou*, translated by Walter Kaufman (New York: Scribner, 1970).
Caney, Simon, 'Liberalism and Communitarianism, a Misconceived Debate', *Political Studies*, 40 (1992): 273–89.
Carr, David, 'Narrative and the Real World: An Argument for Continuity', *History and Theory*, 25 (1986): 117–31.
Chadwick, Henry, *Augustine* (Oxford: Oxford University Press, 1986).
Chapman, Mark D., 'Why the Enlightenment Project Doesn't have to Fail', *Heythrop Journal*, 39 (1998): 379–93.
Cochrane, C.N., *Christianity and Classical Culture, a Study of Thought from Augustus to Augustine* (London, New York and Toronto: Oxford University Press, 1957).
Colby, Mark, 'Narrativity and Ethical Relativism', *European Journal of Philosophy*, 3 (1995): 132–56.
Coles, Robert, *The Call of Stories* (Boston: Houghton Mifflin Co., 1989).
Connolly, William E., *The Augustinian Imperative: A Reflection on the Politics of Morality* (Newbury Park: Sage Publications, 1993).
Courcelle, Pierre, *Les Confessions de St Augustin dans la Tradition Littéraire* (Paris, Etudes Augustiniennes, 1963).
———, *Recherches sur les Confessions de St Augustin* (Paris: Editions E. de Boccard, 1968).
———, *Connais-toi toi-même de Socrate à Saint Bernard* (Paris: Etudes Augustiniennes, 1974).
———, *Opuscula Selecta* (Paris: Etudes Augustiniennes, 1984).
Crites, Stephen, 'The Narrative Quality of Experience', *The Journal of the American Academy of Religion*, 39, 3 (1971): 291–311.
Crossan, John Dominic, *The Dark Interval, Towards a Theology of Story* (second edition, Sonora, California: Eagle Books, 1988).
Dagens, Claude, 'L'Interiorité de L'Homme selon Saint Augustin: Philosophie, Theologie, et Vie Spirituelle', *Bulletin de Littérature Ecclésiastique*, 88 (1987): 249–72.
Daly, L., 'Psychohistory and St Augustine's Conversion Process', *Augustiniana*, 28 (1978): 231–54.
D'Arcy, Martin et al, *A Monument to Saint Augustine* (London: Sheed and Ward, 1930).
Demmer, Klaus, *Shaping the Moral Life* (Washington, DC: Georgetown University Press, 2000).
Detweiler, Robert, *Art/Literature/Religion* (Chico, California: Scholars Press, 1983).
———, *Breaking the Fall, Religious Readings in Contemporary Fiction* (San Francisco: Harper and Row, 1989).

Douglass, R. Bruce and Hollenbach, David (editors), *Catholicism and Liberalism, Contributions to American Public Philosophy* (Cambridge: Cambridge University Press, 1994).
Dunn, Allen, 'The Ethics of Mansfield Park: MacIntyre, Said and Social Context', *Soundings*, 78 (1995): 483–500.
Dunne, John S., *Time and Myth, a Meditation on Storytelling as an Exploration of Life and Death* (Notre Dame and London: University of Notre Dame Press, 1973).
Engelhardt, Hugo Tristan, Junior, *Bioethics and Secular Humanism* (London: SCM, 1991).
———, *The Foundations of Bioethics* (second edition, Oxford: Oxford University Press, 1996).
———, *The Foundations of Christian Bioethics* (Lisse: Swets and Zeitlinger, 2000).
Engelhardt, Hugo Tristan, Junior, and Cherry, Mark (editors), *Allocating Scarce Medical Resources, Roman Catholic Perspectives* (Washington, DC: Georgetown University Press, 2002).
Fackre, Gabriel, *The Christian Story, a narrative interpretation of basic Christian doctrine* (Grand Rapids, Michigan: W.B. Eerdmans, 1978).
———, *The Doctrine of Revelation, a narrative interpretation* (Edinburgh: Edinburgh University Press, 1997).
Fiddes, Paul S. (editor), *The Novel, Spirituality and Modern Culture*, Cardiff: University of Wales Press, 2000.
Ferrari, Leo C., 'The Pear Theft in Augustine's Confessions', *Revue des Etudes Augustiniennes*, XVI (1970): 240–47.
———, *The Conversions of Saint Augustine (The St Augustine Lecture 1982)* (Villanova: Villanova University Press, 1982).
Finance, Joseph de, *An Ethical Enquiry* (Rome: Editrice Pontificia Universitas Gregoriana, 1991).
Fontaine, Jacques, 'Une Révolution Littéraire dans L'Occident Latin: Les Confessions de Saint Augustin.', *Bulletin de Littérature Ecclésiastique*, 88 (1987): 173–93.
Fowl, Stephen E., 'Could Horace Talk with the Hebrews? Translatability and Moral Disagreement in MacIntyre and Stout', *Journal of Religious Ethics*, 19 (1991): 1–20.
Frankena, William, 'MacIntyre and Modern Morality', *Ethics*, 93 (1983): 579–87.
Frend, W.H.C., 'The Family of Augustine: A Microcosm of Religious Change in North Africa', in *Congresso su S. Agostino nel XVI centenario della conversione, Roma, 15–20 settembre 1986, Atti*, vol. 1 (Rome: Institutum Patristicum Augustinianum, 1987): 135–51.
Fuller, Michael, *Making Sense of MacIntyre* (Aldershot: Ashgate, 1998).
Galston, William A., *Liberal Purposes: Goods, Virtues and Diversity in the Liberal State* (Cambridge: Cambridge University Press, 1991).
Gamwell, Franklin I., *The Divine Good* (San Francisco: Harper, 1990).
———, *Democracy on Purpose: Justice and the Reality of God* (Washington, DC: Georgetown University Press, 2000).
Gardner, John, *On Moral Fiction* (New York: Basic Books, 1978).

Gauthier, David, *Morals by Agreement* (Oxford: Clarendon Press, 1986).
George, Robert P., 'Moral Particularism, Thomism, and Traditions', *Review of Metaphysics*, 42 (1989): 593–605.
Glicksberg, Charles I., *The Self in Modern Literature* (University Park: Pennsylvania State University Press, 1963).
Goldberg, Michael, *Theology and Narrative, a Critical Introduction* (Nashville: Abingdon, 1982).
Gunn, Giles B., *Literature and Religion* (New York: Harper and Row, 1971).
Guroian, Vigen, 'Tradition and Ethics: Prospects in a Liberal Society', *Modern Theology*, 7 (1991): 205–24.
Gustafson, James M., *Christ and the Moral Life* (New York: Harper and Row, 1968).
Gutmann, Amy, *Liberal Equality* (Cambridge: Cambridge University Press, 1980).
Hankey, Wayne J., 'Between and Beyond Augustine and Descartes: More than a Source of the Self', *Augustinian Studies*, 32 (2001): 65–88.
Hardy, Barbara, 'Towards a Poetics of Fiction: An approach through Narrative', *Novel*, 2 (1968): 5–14.
Harrison, Carol, *Augustine: Christian Truth and Fractured Humanity* (Oxford: Oxford University Press, 2000).
Harper, Ralph, *The Existential Experience* (Baltimore: Johns Hopkins University Press, 1972).
Hattingh, Herselman and van Veuren, Pieter, 'Identity and the Narrative Structure of Life', *South African Journal of Philosophy*, 14 (1995): 60–71.
Hauerwas, Stanley, *Vision and Virtue* (Notre Dame: Fides, 1974).
———, *Character and the Christian Life* (San Antonio: Trinity University Press, 1975).
———, *Truthfulness and Tragedy* (Notre Dame: Notre Dame University Press, 1977).
———, *A Community of Character* (Notre Dame: Notre Dame University Press, 1981).
———, *The Peaceable Kingdom* (Notre Dame: University of Notre Dame Press, 1983).
———, *Against the Nations* (Minneapolis: Winston Press, 1985).
———, *Christian Existence Today* (Durham, NC: Labyrinth Press, 1988).
———, *After Christendom* (Nashville: Abingdon Press, 1991).
———, *In Good Company: The Church as Polis* (Notre Dame: Notre Dame University Press, 1995).
———, *With the Grain of the Universe: the Gifford Lectures for 2001* (Grand Rapids, Michigan: Brazos Press, 2001).
Hauerwas, Stanley, and Waddell, Paul, Review of *After Virtue*, *The Thomist*, 46 (1982): 313–22.
Hauerwas, Stanley, and Jones, L. Gregory (editors), *Why Narrative? Readings in Narrative Theology* (Grand Rapids, Michigan: William B. Eerdmans Publishing Co.,1989).
Heeley, Gerard F., *The Ethical Methodology of Stanley Hauerwas: An Examination of Christian Character Ethics*, doctoral thesis, (Rome: Angelicum, 1987).

Hibbs, Thomas S., 'MacIntyre's Postmodern Thomism: Reflections on *Three Rival Versions of Moral Enquiry*', *The Thomist*, 57 (1993): 277–97.

Hollenbach, David, *Justice, Peace and Human Rights, American Catholic Social Ethics in a Pluralist World* (New York: Crossroad, 1988).

Holmes, Stephen, *Passions and Constraints: On the theory of Liberal Democracy* (Chicago: University of Chicago Press, 1995).

———, *The Anatomy of Antiliberalism* (Cambridge, Mass.: Harvard University Press, 1999).

Horton, John and Mendus, Susan (editors), *After MacIntyre: Critical Perspectives on the Work of Alasdair MacIntyre* (Notre Dame: Notre Dame University Press, 1994).

Innes, Robert, 'Integrating the Self through the Desire of God', *Augustinian Studies*, 28:1 (1997): 67–109.

Jacobs, Alan, 'What Narrative Theology Forgot', *First Things*, 135 (Sept./Aug. 2003): 31–36.

Jones, L. Gregory, 'Alasdair MacIntyre on Narrative, Community and the Moral Life', *Modern Theology*, 4 (1987): 43–59.

Jonsen, Albert R. and Toulmin, Stephen, *The Abuse of Casuistry* (Berkeley: University of California Press, 1988).

Kant, Immanuel, *Foundations of the Metaphysics of Morals* (New York: Bobbs-Merrill, 1958). (Original title: *Grundlegung der Metaphysik der Sitten*, 1785.)

Keane, Philip S., *Christian Ethics and Imagination* (New York: Paulist Press, 1984).

Keenan, J. and Shannon, T. (editors), *The Context of Casuistry* (Washington, DC: Georgetown University Press, 1995).

Kennedy, Terence, 'The Intelligibility of Moral Tradition in the Thought of Alasdair MacIntyre', *Studia Moralia*, 29 (1991): 305–21.

Kenney, John Peter, 'Augustine's Inner Self', *Augustinian Studies*, 31,1 (2002): 79–90.

Kingwell, Mark, *A Civil Tongue: Justice, Dialogue and the Politics of Pluralism* (University Park: The Pennsylvania State University Press, 1995).

Knight, Kevin (editor), *The MacIntyre Reader* (Cambridge: Polity Press, 1998).

Kort, Wesley A., *Narrative Elements and Religious Meanings* (Philadelphia: Fortress Press, 1975).

Lancel, Serge, *Saint Augustin* (Paris: Fayard, 1999).

Lebacqz, Karen, *Six Theories of Justice* (Minneapolis: Augsburg, 1986).

———, *Justice in an Unjust World* (Minneapolis: Augsburg, 1987).

Ledbetter, Mark, *Virtuous Intentions, the Religious Dimension of Narrative* (Atlanta: Scholars Press, 1989).

Leppelley, Claude, 'Spes Saeculi: Le Milieu Social d'Augustin et ses Ambitions séculiers avant sa conversion.', in *Congresso su S. Agostino nel XVI centenario della conversione, Roma, 15–20 settembre 1986, Atti*, vol. 1, (Rome: Institutum Patristicum Augustinianum, 1987): 99–117.

———, 'Un aspect de la conversion d'Augustin: La Rupture avec ses ambitions socials et politiques', *Bulletin de Literature Ecclesiastique*, 88 (1987): 229–46.

Levinas, Emmanuel, *Autrement qu'être ou au delà de l'essence* (The Hague: Martinus Nijhoff, 1974).

———, *Totality and Infinity,* translated by Alphonso Lingis (Pittsburg: Dusquesne University Press, 2000).

Loughlin, Gerard, *Telling God's Story: Bible, Church and Narrative Theology* (Cambridge: Cambridge University Press, 1999).

Lynch, William F., *Christ and Apollo* (New York: Sheed and Ward, 1960).

Macedo, Stephen, *Liberal Virtues* (Oxford: Clarendon Press, 1990).

MacIntyre, Alasdair, *Secularisation and Moral Change* (Oxford: Oxford University Press, 1967).

———, *After Virtue* (London: Duckworth, 1981).

———, *Whose Justice? Which Rationality?* (London: Duckworth, 1989).

———, *Three Rival Versions of Moral Enquiry* (London: Duckworth, 1990).

———, 'How can we learn what *Veritatis Splendor* has to teach?', *The Thomist*, 58 (1994): 171–95.

———, *Dependent Rational Animals, why human beings need the virtues* (Chicago and La Salle, Illinois: Open Court, 1999).

Macquarrie, John, *Existentialism* (London: Hutchinson, 1972).

Markus, Robert A., *Conversion and Disenchantment in Augustine's Spiritual Career* (the Saint Augustine Lecture 1984) (Villanova: Villanova University Press, 1984).

———, *The End of Ancient Christianity* (Cambridge: Cambridge University Press, 1990).

Marrou, Henri-Irenée, *Saint Augustin et la Fin de la Culture Antique*, fourth edition (Paris: Editions E. de Boccard, 1958).

Matthews, Gareth B., (editor), *The Augustinian Tradition* (Berkeley: University of California Press, 1999).

McClendon, James William, Junior, *Biography as Theology, How Life Stories can remake Today's Theology* (New York: Abingdon Press, 1974).

McMylor, Peter, *Alasdair MacIntyre: Critic of Modernity* (London: Routledge, 1994).

Milhall, Stephen, and Swift, Adam, *Liberals and Communitarians* (Oxford: Blackwell, 1992).

Miranda, Ashley, *An Assessment of Alasdair MacIntyre's Theory of Virtue,* doctoral thesis (Rome: Salesian Pontifical University, 1999).

Mitchell, W.J.T. (editor), *On Narrative* (Chicago and London: University of Chicago Press, 1981).

Murdoch, Iris, *Metaphysics as a Guide to Morals* (London: Penguin, 1993).

Murphy, N., Kallenberg, B. and Nation, M.T. (editors), *Virtues and Practices in the Christian Tradition: Christian Ethics after MacIntyre* (Harrisburg: Trinity Press International, 1997).

Murray, John Courtney, *We Hold These Truths* (New York: Sheed and Ward, 1960).

Melina, Livio, *Sharing in Christ's Virtues* (Washington, DC: Catholic University of America Press, 2001).

Navone, John, *The Dynamic of the Question in Narrative Theology* (Rome: Gregorian University Press, 1986).

———, *Seeking God in Story* (Collegeville, Minnesota: Liturgical Press, 1990).
Nelson, Paul, *Narrative and Morality: A Theological Enquiry* (University Park: Pennsylvania University Press, 1987).
Neuhaus, Richard John, 'The Hauerwas Enterprise', *Commonweal*, 109 (1982): 269–72.
Nisbet, Robert A., *The Quest for Community* (second edition, Oxford: Oxford University Press, 1969).
Nolan, Paul, *Narrative and Morality, a Theological Enquiry* (University Park and London: The Pennsylvania State University Press, 1987).
Novak, Michael, *Freedom with Justice, Catholic Social Thought and liberal institutions* (San Francisco: Harper and Row, 1984).
Nussbaum, Martha, *Love's Knowledge* (New York: Oxford University Press, 1992).
Oakes, Edward T., 'The Achievement of Alasdair MacIntyre', *First Things*, 65 (Aug.–Sept., 1996): 22–6.
O'Donnell, James J., 'The Strangeness of Augustine', *Augustinian Studies*, 32, 2 (2001): 201–6.
Okin, Susan Moller, *Justice, Gender and the Family* (New York: Basic Books, 1989).
O'Meara, John J., *The Young Augustine, The Growth of Augustine's Mind up to his Conversion* (London: Longmans, Green and Co., 1954).
Outka, Gene, 'Character, Vision and Narrative', *Religious Studies Review*, 6 (1980): 110–18.
Paffenroth, Kim, 'Tears of Grief and Joy', *Augustinian Studies*, 28, 1 (1997): 141–54.
Peddle, David, 'Resourcing Charles Taylor's Augustine', *Augustinian Studies*, 32, 2 (2001): 207–17.
Polinska, Wioleta, 'Alasdair MacIntyre on Traditions and Rationality', *Koinonia: Princeton Theological Seminary Graduate Forum*, 6 (1994): 228–63.
Porter, Jean, 'Openness and Constraint: Moral Reflection as Tradition-Guided Enquiry in Alasdair MacIntyre's Recent Works', *Journal of Religion*, 73 (1993): 514–36.
———, *Natural and Divine Law, Reclaiming the Tradition for Christian Ethics* (Grand Rapids, Michigan: Novalis, 1999).
Rahner, Karl, 'Priest and Poet', *Theological Investigations*, volume 3 (London: Darton, Longman and Todd, 1967): 294–317.
———, 'Poetry and the Christian', *Theological Investigations*, volume 4, (London: Darton, Longman and Todd, 1967): 357–67.
———, 'The Task of the Writer in Relation to Christian Living', *Theological Investigations*, volume 8 (London: Darton, Longman and Todd, 1971): 112–29.
———, 'Theology and the Arts', *Thought*, 57 (1982): 17–29.
Ramsey, Paul, 'Liturgy and Ethics', *The Journal of Religious Ethics*, 7 (1979): 139–71.
Rawls, John, *A Theory of Justice* (Cambridge, Mass.: The Belknap Press of Harvard University Press, 1971).
———, *Political Liberalism* (New York: Columbia University Press, 1993).

———, *Collected Papers*, edited by Samuel Freeman (Cambridge, Mass.: Harvard University Press, 1999).

———, *The Law of Peoples, with The Idea of Public Reason Revisited* (Cambridge, Mass.: Harvard University Press, 1999).

———, *Lectures on the History of Moral Philosophy* (Cambridge, Mass.: Harvard University Press, 2000).

Reynolds, Terence P., 'A Conversation Worth Having: Hauerwas and Gustafson on Substance in Theological Ethics', *Journal of Religious Ethics*, 28 (2000): 395–421.

Rosenblum, Nancy (editor), *Liberalism and the Moral Life* (Cambridge, Mass.: Harvard University Press, 1989).

Rosmini, Antonio, *Principles of Ethics*, (Leominster: Fowler Wright Books, 1988).

Ross, Steven L., 'Practice (+ Narrative Unity + Moral Tradition) Makes Perfect: Alasdair MacIntyre's After Virtue', *Journal of Value Enquiry*, 19 (1985): 13–26.

Rossi, Philip, 'Narrative, Worship and Ethics', *Journal of Religious Ethics*, 7 (1979): 239–48.

Sandel, Michael, *Liberalism and the Limits of Justice* (Cambridge: Cambridge University Press, 1987).

Santilli, Paul, 'MacIntyre on Rationality and Tradition', *Lyceum*, 1 (1989): 12–24.

Schneewind, Jerome B., 'Virtue, Narrative and Community: MacIntyre and Morality', *Journal of Philosophy*, 79 (1982): 653–63.

Siebers, Tobin, *Morals and Stories* (New York: Columbia University Press, 1992).

Smith, James K.A., '*Confessions* of an Existentialist: Reading Augustine after Heidegger', *New Blackfriars*, 82 (2001): 273–82 and 335–47.

Sparrow Simpson, W.J., *St Augustine's Conversion* (London: SPCK, 1930).

Stroup, George, *The Promise of Narrative Theology* (Atlanta: John Knox Press, 1981).

Swindler, J.K., 'MacIntyre's Republic', *The Thomist*, 54 (1990): 343–54.

Taylor, Charles, *Sources of the Self, the Making of Modern Identity* (Cambridge, Mass.: Harvard University Press, 1989).

———, *The Ethics of Authenticity* (Cambridge, Mass.: Harvard University Press, 1991).

TeSelle, Eugene, *Living in Two Cities, Augustinian Trajectories in Political Thought* (Scranton: University of Scranton Press, 1998).

TeSelle, Sallie, *Literature and the Christian Life* (New Haven: Yale University Press, 1966).

Thompson, C.J., 'The Character of MacIntyre's Narrative', *The Thomist*, 59 (1995): 379–407.

Thomson, Judith Jarvis, 'A Defense of Abortion', *Philosophy and Public Affairs*, 1 (1971): 47–66.

Tracy, David, 'Theological Classics in Contemporary Theology', *Theology Digest* 24,5 (Winter 1977): 347–57.

———, *The Analogical Imagination* (New York: Crossroad Publishing Co., 1981).

Urmson, James O., 'Saints and Heroes', *Essays in Moral Philosophy*, edited by I.A. Melden, (Seattle: University of Washington Press, 1958).

Vokey, Daniel, 'MacIntyre and Rawls: Two Complementary Communitarians?', *Philosophy of Education: Proceedings*, 48 (1992): 336–41.

Walzer, Michael, *Spheres of Justice, A Defence of Pluralism and Equality* (New York: Basic Books, 1983).

Weaver, Mary Jo (editor), *What's Left? American Liberal Catholics* (Indianapolis: Bloomington, 1999).

Wicker, Brian, *The Story Shaped World*, (London: The Athlone Press, 1975).

Williams, Bernard, *Shame and Necessity* (Berkeley: University of California Press, 1993).

Wolf, Susan, 'Moral Saints', *The Journal of Philosophy*, 79 (1982): 419–39.

Index

Abignente, Donatella 69, 195
Ackerman, James 199, 201
Alter, Robert 165, 211
Aquinas, Saint Thomas 48, 51
    on faith and reason 58
    on human acts and law 68–9, 113
    on theological method 1–3
Aristotle 22, 23, 25, 26, 30, 68, 107
Augustine, Saint 4, 15, 50, 57–9, 123, 165
    on alienation
        and language 137–41
        and sexual desire 141–4
        from others 145–50
    as narrator 124–9
        changing narratives 150–53
        providing a hermeneutic key to narrative 153–62
        as a narrative theologian 162–4, 182–3
    on the self 129–37
    as related to MacIntyre, Engelhardt, Hauerwas and Rawls 132, 134–5, 144, 150, 162
    works
        The City of God 15, 16, 58–9, 64, 130–33, 141–2, 150–51
        Confessions 4, 15, 39, 124–31, 135–41, 142–3, 145–50, 151–3, 163
        Ennarationes in Psalmos 133–4, 149, 154–63, 191, 215
        Soliloquies 149
Austen, Jane 176, 179

Bailey, Randall C. 199, 200
Ballantyne, R. M. 176, 177, 179
Barry, Brian 102
Bastianel, Sergio 199
Berlin, Adele 199, 200
Blum, Peter C. 191
Booth, Wayne C. 165, 176
Brenner, Athalya 199, 201

Brown, Peter 124, 126, 131, 145

Cameron, Michael 157–8
Carr, David 165, 173–4
Caussade, Jean-Pierre de 193, 196–7
Chadwick, Henry 127, 130, 152
Cicero 4, 131–2
Coreth, Emerich 191
Courcelle, Pierre 124, 125, 130, 133
Crites, Stephen 10, 12, 18, 74, 165, 170, 184, 188, 213
Crossan, John Dominic 8–9, 47, 165, 205, 217

Dante 23, 64
Daube, David 199, 202
Demmer, Klaus 90
Detweiler, Robert 165, 178
Douglass, R. Bruce 106
Dunne, John S. 165

Eckhart, Meister 120
Eliot, T.S. 64
Engelhardt, Hugo Tristan, Junior
    on experience as narrative 49–4
    on moral pluralism 47–9
    on the narrative nature of belief 1
    on tradition as ecclesially embodied narrative 54–61
    on tradition as irrational 61–72
    on Rawls 60–61, 81, 103–4, 119
    related to Hauerwas and MacIntyre 47, 49, 54, 68, 71–2, 73–5, 123
    works
        Allocating Scarce Medical Resources 56–7
        Bioethics and Secular Humanism 50, 52–3, 57–8, 59, 60, 64, 66, 70
        The Foundations of Bioethics 47–9, 51–2, 53, 60, 61, 62–6, 71, 116

The Foundations of Christian Bioethics 49, 50, 51, 55, 57, 59, 70–71, 102, 104, 214

Ferrari, Leo C. 125
Fiddes, Paul S. 165, 194–6
Finance, Joseph de 187, 216
Fuchs, Josef 43, 209

Galston, William 62, 96, 98–9, 104, 119, 132–3
Garsiel, Moshe 199, 201, 203
Goldberg, Michael 165, 170, 184, 209
Golding, William 176, 179
Gressmann, Hugo 199, 200
Gunn, D.M. 199
Gustafson, James M. 35, 44–5, 154, 176–7

Hauerwas, Stanley 33–4, 177
    compared and contrasted to Engelhardt 73–5, 123
    on Kant 42–3
    on the rationality of religious tradition 39–46
    on Rawls 81, 82, 100, 114, 119
    relationship to MacIntyre 33, 37, 38, 41, 42, 73–5, 123
    on religious experience as narrative 34–6
    on tradition as Ecclesially embodied 36–9
    works
        A Community of Character 36, 37–8, 41, 100, 114
        The Peaceable Kingdom 34–6, 39, 41, 42–4
        Truthfulness and Tragedy 36, 37, 39–40
Hollenbach, David 105–6, 117
Holmes, Stephen 96
Homer 20–21, 41
Hoose, Bernard 27
Hopkins, Gerard Manley 192, 211

Innes, Robert 143

Kant, Immanuel 1, 6, 42–3, 52, 75, 86, 116, 186
Keane, Philip S.165, 189, 213

Kempis, Thomas à, 35
Kort, Wesley A. 165, 178, 188, 217

Lancel, Serge 145
Leadbetter, Mark 165, 217
Lebacqz, Karen 116
Lepelley, Claude 131, 151
Levinas, Emmanuel 148, 191
Loughlin, Gerald 165, 188

McClendon, James 177
Macedo, Stephen 87–9, 119
MacIntyre, Alasdair 13, 91, 187
    compared and contrasted to Engelhardt and Hauerwas 73–5, 123
    on faith and reason 42
    on the inescapability of narrative 14–18
    on Kant 42
    on narrative quality of experience 18–20
    on Rawls 81, 119
    on tradition 20–31
    tradition as rational 26–31
    tradition as socially embodied 20–25
    works
        After Virtue 14, 15, 16, 17, 18, 19, 20, 21, 25, 26, 27, 28, 29, 30, 31, 47, 54, 68, 72, 79, 81, 89, 90, 123, 167, 183, 217
        Dependant Rational Animals 24, 25, 30, 54, 82, 115
        Three Rival Versions of Moral Enquiry 15, 17, 23, 25, 26, 29, 51, 54
        Whose Justice? Which Rationality? 14, 16, 20–22, 23–4, 25, 26, 27, 28, 30, 106, 155
Macquarrie, John 144, 215
Maly, Eugene H. 199, 200, 201
Markus, R.A. 141, 151
Marrou, Henri–Irenée 128, 129–30, 152
Mitchell, W.J.T. 165, 181
morality
    as matter of lived tradition 3
    as particular or universal 6
    as narrative 6–8
Morton, H.V. 204
Murdoch, Iris 96, 166–7
Murray, John Courtney 90, 104

narrative
    definition 1
    intelligibility 10–11
    particularity 6
    universality 8–9
narrative structure
    as 'closed' structure 166–72
    reading 176–9
    theology 172–6
    'open' narrative 188–94
    theology 194–7
    as structure with permeable limit 179–85
    theology 185–8
narrative theology in practice 206–19
    New Testament 203–6
    Old Testament 199–203
Navone, John 165, 166, 177, 217
Nietzsche 15, 25, 26, 54, 66, 68, 71
Nisbet, Robert A. 79, 85, 96,
Nolan, Paul 165
Noth, Martin 199

O'Donnell, James J. 136
Okin, Susan Moller 103, 119, 181–2
O'Meara, John J. 125, 126, 135

Paulo, C.J.N. 145
Peddle, David 136
Plato 194
Porphyry 4, 133
Porter, Jean 91

Rahner, Karl 182, 189–91
Rawls, John 37, 60–61, 67, 76, 165, 187
    on finding consensus 89–99
    on justice 99–104
    as narrative 118–21, 184, 210, 217
    Original Position 76–80, 81–9, 117–18
    works

A Theory of Justice 77, 83, 84, 85, 86, 91, 94–5, 98, 99–102, 106–7, 109, 114–16, 117, 121
Political Liberalism 77, 82, 84, 86, 87, 89, 91–4, 96–7, 102–3
Collected Papers 77n., 83, 85, 90, 99, 103, 104, 116, 117
The Law of Peoples, with the Idea of Public Reason Revisited 77, 79
    on works of supererogation 109–12, 114, 116
Reynolds, Terence P. 45

Sandel, Michael 82, 118
Schwarz, Regina H. 199
Seneca 133
Shakespeare, William 167, 168, 181, 186, 195–6, 201, 217
Smith, Barbara Herrnstein 181
Sterberg, Meir 199, 200
Stock, Brain 126

Taylor, Charles 79
Thompson, C.J.N 27, 28, 29
Thomson, Judith Jarvis 111–15, 119, 182, 185, 206
tradition
    as related to narrative and community 3–5
Tracy, David 166, 180

Urmson, James O. 109, 110, 112, 119

Virgil 4, 130–32, 137, 150

Walzer, Michael 115, 117
Williams, Charles 135
Wolf, Susan 110, 112

Yoder, John Howard 36